Ruellia peninsularis

Fremontodendron 'California Glory'

Romneya coulteri

Caesalpinia pulcherrima

SHADE AND COLOR

with
Water-Conserving Plants

by
James E. Walters
and
Balbir Backhaus

TIMBER PRESS
Portland, Oregon

Information herein, to the best of our knowledge, is accurate and complete. It is based on years of observation, study and hands-on experience by the authors, and was checked by others knowledgeable on the subject. However, no guarantees are made or implied, and the authors and publisher disclaim any liability arising from the use of this book.

Mention of trademark, proprietary product, or vendor does not constitute a guarantee or warranty of the product by the publisher or the authors and does not imply its approval to the exclusion of other products or vendors.

Line drawings by Ralph A. Backhaus. Photographs, except where noted, by Balbir Backhaus.

ISBN 0-88192-214-5
Printed in Hong Kong

TIMBER PRESS, INC.
9999 S.W. Wilshire, Suite 124
Portland, Oregon 97225, U.S.A.

Library of Congress Cataloging-in-Publication Data

Walters, James E.
    Shade and color with water-conserving plants / by James E. Walters
and Balbir Backhaus.
        p.   cm.
    Includes bibliographical references and index.
    ISBN 0-88192-214-5
    1. Drought-tolerant plants--Southwest, New. 2. Landscape
gardening--Southwest, New--Water conservation. 3. Xeriscaping-
-Southwest, New. 4. Color in gardening--Southwest, New. 5. Shade
trees--Southwest, New.   I. Backhaus, Balbir. II. Title.
SB439.8.W35 1992
712--dc20   91-26607
                                                   CIP

Contents

viii

Contents

Landscape photographs follow page 22; color plates 1–219 follow page 54.

To Balbir's children, Jaclyn and Benjamin Backhaus, who were born as work progressed on this book, and to Jim's bride of nearly 50 years, Virginia Frances Walters. Their combined patience, goodwill and support made it possible. Also, with deep appreciation to Richard Abel, retired editor and publisher of Timber Press, for his vision, encouragement and guidance in this project.

Foreword

Over the past two or three decades a nationwide trend has slowly gained momentum, the trend toward informal landscapes featuring native and naturalized plants. There are several reasons for this movement, not the least of which is a greater appreciation of the beauty of natural landscapes—those landscapes we see from the interstates as we travel from city to city.

I believe this appreciation is, to some degree, a legacy from the ecology movement of the late '60s and early '70s. If this is true and if the forecasters who predict the '90s will be the "environment decade" are accurate, then we may see an even greater appreciation in the near future. Certainly the public perception of native plants as weeds is diminishing, thanks in large part to their use in public plantings such as street medians and right-of-ways.

Another reason for informal, natural landscapes is the perception of reduced maintenance. Maintaining a formal landscape of trimmed hedges, extensive lawn and ill-adapted plants consumes valuable leisure time which many Americans would prefer to spend in other pursuits.

Proponents of native plants argue that the plants have adapted to the insects, diseases, climatic extremes and other problems of a given area and so should require less care. Unfortunately, this is not always the case. We imported many of the insects and diseases which afflict our urban landscapes, and native plants are just as susceptible to these as the exotics which they replace. Other problems, such as soil compaction, are a direct consequence of our activities.

We are also very generous with the term "native." A Chihuahuan Desert plant from west Texas can hardly be called native when grown in the Sonoran Desert city of Tucson. As a later chapter explains, the two deserts are very different climatically. A major difference, and probably a principal reason for bringing the plant to Tucson, is that the Chihuahuan Desert is colder and the plant will be better able to survive an extreme Tucson winter.

Although I used the term "naturalized" earlier, it has bad connotations in that a naturalized plant is one that has escaped cultivation and become established in the wild population, a true weed such as tumbleweed or Russian thistle. A better term is "adapted," for a plant conditioned to perform well in a particular environment without excessive care. A landscape composed of adapted plants should require less maintenance but will not be maintenance-free.

In the arid Southwest we have an additional incentive to consider a natural landscape: water. Our water sources are tentative at best. Many communities depend entirely upon limited groundwater supplies. Others are adjacent to rivers or import water from rivers that ultimately depend upon the amount of snowfall at the river's source. Successive years of drought or poor snowfall can result in water restrictions.

While there are many ways we can conserve water, changing our landscape tradition is perhaps the least painful and most rewarding. It is least painful because it has a relatively minor impact on our lifestyle, and most rewarding because water used for landscape maintenance—unlike most water we use—cannot be recovered, treated and reused. It is lost either to the atmosphere or to ground percolation. By carefully selecting and properly maintaining plants native to or adapted to arid environments, we can restrict this one-time use of a precious resource and retain a pleasant landscape to enhance our lives.

Please note that both selection and maintenance are important. Proper selection depends, to some extent, on understanding the plant. Desert plants have adapted, not necessarily to use water efficiently, but to survive drought. Many annuals escape drought by completing their life cycle during wet seasons and survive dry seasons as seed. Most trees, shrubs, succulents and semisucculents must survive dry seasons in a relatively active state.

Succulents and semisucculents such as cactus, yucca, agave and sotol have adopted characteristics that enable them to restrict water loss. They conserve water during good times and bad and usually have a slow growth rate as a result.

Desert trees and shrubs also have water-conserving characteristics, but they are more committed to finding and using water with extensive root systems that explore a relatively large volume of soil. Some of their water-conserving characteristics are evident only during times of drought. An irrigation schedule that does not take this into account will not fully exploit the water-saving potential of these plants.

In this book, Balbir Backhaus and James E. Walters provide information that will help you select and maintain these plants in a pleasing, water-conserving landscape whether you live in California, west Texas or somewhere in between. It is one of the few books that truly addresses the entire Southwest, an ambitious project and an approach that is sorely needed. Although it will be tempting to skip to the plant descriptions, I urge you to read the opening chapters carefully. A water-conserving landscape is more than just desert-adapted trees and shrubs with a drip irrigation system. Soil is the foundation of a landscape, and much of what happens later depends upon what you do before you ever transplant a plant. Understanding the geography and climate of your area will help you appreciate your soil, select proper adapted plants and care for them.

In the plant section of this book you will find an extensive description of some 300 species and cultivars of commercially available, arid-adapted plants. Included in the description is a guide for pronouncing the scientific name (a tremendous benefit), a general characterization of the plant habit, landscape uses, climate adaption, cultural requirements and possible problems.

As noted, all these plants are commercially available, although perhaps not at your local nursery. While the selection of arid-adapted plants at most retail nurseries is increasing, their sources can be sporadic. If you are persistent and willing to travel, you can probably buy most of these plants somewhere. In addition, the authors include suggestions on propagation in the plant descriptions.

I commend Balbir and Jim for producing such an extensive and detailed work. I am sure it will become a valuable resource to homeowners, hobbyists, nursery professionals and landscape architects alike. I am also convinced that readers will find this book most useful in planning, developing and maintaining a pleasing, water-conserving landscape.

Jimmy L. Tipton, Ph.D.
Arid Ornamentals Specialist
Department of Plant Sciences
University of Arizona, Tucson

Acknowledgments

We would like to thank the following people for their help in preparing this book:

John Augustine, owner, Desert Tree Farms nursery, Phoenix, Arizona.

Dr. Ralph A. Backhaus, professor, Arizona State University, Tempe, Arizona.

Jeff Bohn, co-owner, Tree of Life Nursery, San Juan Capistrano, California.

Chris Clarke, Skylark Nursery, Santa Rosa, California.

Dr. Mark Dimmitt, curator of plants, Arizona–Sonora Desert Museum, Tucson, Arizona.

Mike Evans, co-owner, Tree of Life Nursery, San Juan Capistrano, California.

Ron Gass, owner, Mountain States Wholesale Nursery, Glendale, Arizona.

Dr. Howard Scott Gentry, research director emeritus, Desert Botanical Garden, Phoenix, Arizona.

Alan George, Coates Irrigation Consultants, Phoenix, Arizona.

Don Hodel, horticulture agent, University of California Extension, Los Angeles County, California.

Lisa Iwata, landscape architect, Land Interactive, San Clemente, California.

Steve Martino, landscape architect, Steve Martino & Associates, Tempe, Arizona.

Judy Mielke, senior horticulturist, Desert Botanical Garden, Phoenix, Arizona.

Bob Morris, University of Nevada–Reno Cooperative Extension Service, Clark County, Nevada.

Dr. Ed Mulrean, plant pathologist, Arid-Zone Trees nursery, Swan Hill Nurseries and White Tank Palms nursery, Phoenix, Arizona.

Warren G. Roberts, superintendent, University of California–Davis Arboretum, Davis, California.

Carol Shuler, landscape architect, C. F. Shuler, Inc., Scottsdale, Arizona.

Greg Starr, owner, Starr Nursery, Tucson, Arizona.

Dr. Jimmy L. Tipton, arid ornamentals specialist, University of Arizona, Tucson, Arizona.

Joe Tyler, superintendent of grounds, Arizona State University, Tempe, Arizona.

A special thanks also to Rena Hughes for her help in proofreading the manuscript.

CHAPTER 1

The
Water-Efficient
Landscape

Concern for the environment, saving money and reduced maintenance are typically listed as major reasons for using water-efficient plants in landscaping. These concerns are important, of course. But sheer beauty may actually provide a better explanation for the growing interest in switching to water-efficient landscapes.

While gardeners offer different reasons for living in harmony with nature, all the explanations come down to a single thing: common sense. Since humans can't exist without water, the limited supply of water needs protection. Any other course can only lead to disaster.

Future generations are likely to wonder why water-guzzling plants were ever regarded as desirable in the Southwest and similar near-desert environments, where water shortages have been and remain a potential or immediate threat to life.

By the early 1990s, a well-founded awareness had developed that water-conserving plants could provide not only shade, color, beauty and durability but also a distinct regional flavor and low-maintenance performance. Drought-imposed water rationing and soaring water costs drove the message home. Shade became increasingly important as air conditioning costs skyrocketed.

Before World War II, local vegetation had served the Southwest's relatively small and scattered population well. The war brought thousands of servicemen to the region's training camps, which led to the first postwar surge in population. High-tech industries provided a further spark for a gigantic postwar migration. The major factor in both cases was the lure of balmy winter temperatures. By 1990, studies indicated that as many as four out of five South-

1

west adult residents had moved in from other areas, most of which were characterized by much colder winters.

As has been the case in every human migration, nostalgia for the familiar played a major role in the newcomers' selection of the water-guzzling plants common in the more temperate North American landscape. Not the least of these landscape traditions was the installation of large lawns.

Since adequate water was still available, it was perhaps natural to give little regard to what was happening to supplies. In addition, little attention was paid to the extraordinary amount of time and money needed to keep ill-adapted plants presentable and to regularly replace them. These costs seemed an integral part of the new lifestyle.

But, in time, more and more gardeners began to question this premise. What began as a small ripple, pushed by environmental concerns and water costs, grew into a giant wave as many people took their first close look at climate-adapted landscapes. They were astonished and delighted to find attractive plants capable of providing shade and color without high levels of maintenance. They also found arid-adapted plants suitable for virtually every landscape use.

Unfortunately, many early efforts at arid landscaping projects focused only on cactus, agave, yucca and similar plants surrounded by gravel or decomposed granite. Such gardens did save water and maintenance time, but a little of the look went too far for most people. The resulting landscape baked under the sun instead of providing a cool, green haven. As a consequence, the first efforts to implement the water-saving concept fell short in public acceptance.

Other problems lay in the way of quick acceptance. Climate-adapted plants often looked unattractive in the container sizes sold at nurseries. In addition, many gardeners regarded them as weeds. And newcomers, even when intrigued, found it difficult or impossible to acquire reliable information on the drought-tolerant plant's growth habits, culture or availability. Another problem was the existing landscapes: retrofitting poorly chosen but long-established plants was at best a difficult undertaking.

Early protestors of excessive use of water in Southwest landscaping included Eric A. Johnson of Palm Springs, California; DeWitt Wheat and Ron Gass of Phoenix, Arizona, and Warren Jones and Rodney Engard of Tucson, Arizona. While later recognized as notable voices in an expanding trend, their early efforts were often ignored or resisted.

Jones, for example, a professor of landscape architecture at the University of Arizona, drew guffaws in the 1970s when he suggested limiting lawns to 10 ft. by 10 ft. (3×3 m), or 100 sq. ft. (9 sq. m). In time he was vindicated when removing most of the existing lawn became the first recommendation for homeowners switching from conventional to water-saving landscapes.

Most lawns, of course, exist for cosmetic reasons rather than purposes such as foot traffic, recreational pursuits or use by pets. A desirable cool, green look can be obtained using plants other than lawn grass.

Equally important as saving water are such precepts as using plants adapted to a local area and grouping them according to their moisture, light, climate and other needs. The result is that pruning, weeding, fertilizing, controlling pests and similar maintenance practices are greatly reduced. In short, keeping plantings simple and natural also means easy care.

Using indigenous plants, often called regional landscaping, creates landscapes that blend with the natural environment and reflect an area's distinct beauty and character. These provide a refreshing alternative to the repetitive landscapes travelers often see in going from place to place. In cases where large-scale destruction of vegetation accompanies urban development, regional landscaping becomes the means to revegetate native species.

An unexpected bonus for people with allergies to plant pollens is that low-water-use plants, in general, cause fewer allergic reactions.

By the 1980s, "xeriscape" had became a buzzword. Defined as water conservation through creative landscaping, using plants adapted to low-water conditions, "xeriscape" is generally credited to a 1981 promotion by the Denver, Colorado, Water Department. The department's demonstration garden, using drought-tolerant plants, won wide acclaim for color, design and texture. Subsequently a growing number of localities and organizations began promoting xeriscaping. The National Xeriscape Council, Inc., P.O. Box 163172, Austin, Texas 78716-3172, trademarked the term to prevent its use as a product or corporate name for private gain. Similar concepts appeared under a variety of names, such as Naturalscapes and Naturescapes.

Typical of the community response was the SAWARA (Southern Arizona Water Resources Association) Xeriscape and Solar Demonstration Garden that opened October 13, 1988, in the Tucson Botanical Gardens. A sharp contrast to water-intensive plantings, this garden "is dedicated to each of you who passes through and takes home an idea turned into action that will lead us all to a more beautiful, water-saving community."

"Conserv 90," a national conference on water supply issues, was held in Phoenix in mid-1990. Organizers polled the key executives of 22 cities in advance of the sessions and reported that 27 percent of the cities were experiencing current water shortages and 41 percent anticipated shortages within the next five years. Of those polled, 59 percent reported their city had an organized public awareness program to support water conservation. Many programs focused on water conservation through landscaping techniques but also included such items as fixing leaking toilets and adding surcharges for higher-than-average water usage.

The importance of landscaping was reflected in a report from authorities in Tucson crediting xeriscaping techniques with much of their success in reducing public water consumption by 30 percent.

How much water is used in a home landscape depends on many variables: the weather and climate in a given region, the kinds of plants used, soil type, planting density, irrigation methods and so on. But regardless of any variables, the situation, in a broad sense, is still like a bank account: disaster is inevitable if withdrawals, in this case, of water, exceed the amount available.

CHAPTER 2

Climate and Geography of the Warm-Arid Southwest

The warm-arid U.S. Southwest is a low-rainfall region with many days of sunshine, long growing seasons, often-marginal soils and frequently quite warm temperatures. Geographically, it runs through parts of California, Arizona, Nevada, New Mexico and Texas and includes three deserts: the subtropical Sonoran and the warm-temperate Mojave and Chihuahuan. Areas adjacent to the deserts are often transitional, sharing many similar features with the deserts.

Generally, the areas adjacent to the deserts are arid grassland or coastal sage-scrub communities. Rainfall in these transitional areas exceeds that in the adjacent deserts, and temperatures are more moderate. But evapotranspiration (loss of moisture) rates remain high.

Other Western regions, such as the San Francisco Bay Area and the Great Basin Desert, which is the classic high desert of northern Nevada and parts of Oregon, Idaho and Utah, are not included specifically in this book, as they do not fit the definition of a warm-arid climate. However, many plants we discuss can be grown successfully in these areas.

Annual minimum temperatures in the warm-arid region, on average, range from $10°F$ $(-12°C)$ to above $40°F$ $(4°C)$, and the region corresponds to USDA Plant Hardiness Zones 8, 9, 10 and 11 (see map, Figure 2-1). Plants that do best—the ones included in this book—fall into a general range of cold and heat hardiness: most are hardy to around $15–20°F$ $(-9$ to $-6.5°C)$ in winter and are tolerant of high summer temperatures. Some tolerate more cold but less heat.

Temperatures alone, however, do not tell the whole story of what plants grow where.

6

2

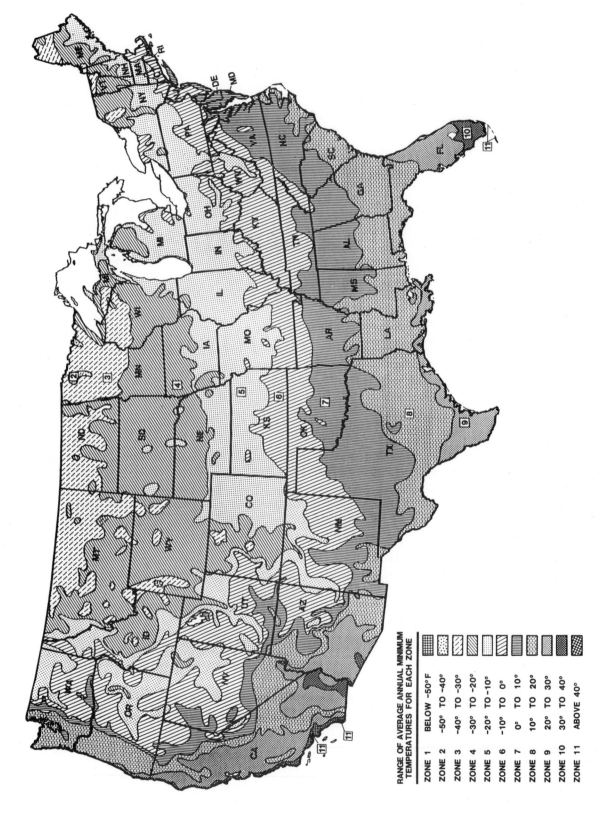

Figure 2-1. USDA Plant Hardiness Zone Map of the United States shows average annual minimum temperatures. Source: USDA, ARS Misc. Publ. 1475

Also important are the total annual rainfall, the varying times when it does rain and the humidity. For example, average temperatures are similar in Tucson and Sacramento, California. Texas sage (*Leucophyllum frutescens*) flourishes in the Tucson area, but has a tough time around Sacramento because lingering winter fogs promote root rot. Conversely, while a chaparral plant such as ceanothus or manzanita (*Arctostaphylos* spp.) grows successfully in a Sacramento landscape, it may not survive the frequent summer rainfall in Tucson, let alone the somewhat higher summer temperatures.

So, to avoid disappointment, gardeners must consider carefully the different plant-growing conditions of each locality. Mild and harsh conditions, while likely, may vary sharply from place to place. Hot, scorching summers and mild winters characterize a locality such as Phoenix. Southern California is relatively mild year-round, but searing winds from the desert can desiccate plants. Las Vegas, Nevada, El Paso, Texas, and Tucson have high summer temperatures and winters with some frosts and even snow.

Even the limited precipitation may not give the total picture. Desert rainfall patterns, in particular, can be erratic and undependable, leaving long periods of stressful conditions at a given location. Microclimates, which are discussed later in this chapter, also can have a great impact on how a plant performs at a given site.

Within USDA Hardiness Zones 8–11, the main growing areas of the warm-arid Southwest are the low deserts, the mid-elevation deserts, the colder and higher deserts, California's Central Valley, the inland valleys and foothills of southern California and coastal southern California.

While areas with similar growing conditions can be identified, keep in mind that these are general—based on conditions of temperature, humidity and so on. They are not meant to be an infallible guide to exactly what grows where, but indicate only basic patterns.

ZONE 8

Zone 8 includes the colder, higher desert areas that represent the upper elevation limits of the warm-arid Southwest. The average annual minimum temperatures for this zone are 10–20°F (−12 to −6.5°C). These areas should not be confused with the Great Basin Desert, which is colder and higher. Much of the Mojave Desert and the Chihuahuan Desert are in Zone 8. These two deserts are colder than the Sonoran, so even though Las Vegas in the Mojave Desert (at about 2,000 ft., or 670 m) is lower in elevation than the Sonoran's Tucson (2,200 ft. or 690 m), it is colder in winter. Other Zone 8 cities include Lancaster, California, El Paso, and Las Cruces, New Mexico. Winter low temperatures in Las Vegas go into the mid-teens and outlying areas can be in the single digits. Lancaster and Las Vegas have similar average winter lows, but Las Vegas is hotter in the summer.

Unlike the Sonoran Desert, much of the Mojave Desert receives no summer rainfall. Relative humidity remains lower than in the Sonoran Desert much of the year. Desiccating winds, especially in the Las Vegas area, are a problem for new plantings. With an average rainfall of under 4 in. (10 cm), Las Vegas is definitely a dry, cold and challenging environment for many plants.

Most of the Chihuahuan Desert is at elevations above 3,000 ft. (930 m), with the highest areas over 6,000 ft. (2,000 m). Creosote bush (*Larrea tridentata*), one of the most abundant species of the Mojave and Sonoran deserts, extends its range east to the plains and mesas of this desert. Rainfall is concentrated in the summer months. El Paso receives most of its average 8 in. (20 cm) between July and October. Summer highs average about 10–20 degrees (5–10°C) cooler than in the Sonoran Desert. In El Paso, summer high temperatures are often around 95°F (35°C), but sometimes hit 104°F (40°C) in June. Around July, cooling summer rains bring some relief to heat-weary plants. In winter, El Paso, at 3,900 ft. (1,200 m) elevation, is colder still than Las Vegas or Lancaster. The average low for January is around 30°F (−1°C), but temperatures of 10°F (−12°C) or even lower are possible. One or two light snows are also likely. The hybrid mesquites (*Prosopis*) are borderline hardy here, but the native honey mesquite (*P. glandulosa*) and desert willow (*Chilopsis linearis*) grow success-fully. Oleanders (*Nerium*) experience considerable freeze damage throughout this zone but recover in spring. Dwarfs are most affected.

ZONE 9

With average annual minimum temperatures from 20–30°F (−6.5 to −1°C), Zone 9 consists of the low- to mid-elevation deserts and California's Central Valley.

Mid-elevation Deserts

The mid-elevation deserts include parts of the Sonoran Desert lying between roughly 2,000 and 3,000 ft. (670–1,000 m) elevation and portions of the Mojave Desert. Tucson, Safford and Wickenburg are Arizona communities in this zone. In the Mojave Desert, Twentynine Palms, California, at roughly 2,000 ft. (670 m), is considered mid-elevation. Temperatures tend to be somewhat extreme, with hot summers and winters that are colder than in the low desert but not as cold as in the higher deserts. In a location such as Tucson, temperatures can vary greatly depending on topography. Tucson reports winter lows averaging in the upper 30s°F (2–4°C), although some parts of the city frequently get down into the 20s°F (−7 to −2°C). Citrus is grown in some locations, but only a short distance away, it can be too cold.

The cold-sensitive saguaros growing around Tucson provide a good example of how elevation affects temperature. They are concentrated on hillsides and gentle slopes where cold air drains away to basins below. Summers are not quite as hot as in the low deserts. Summer highs in Tucson can be 5–10°F (3–6°C) cooler than in the low-desert city Phoenix. Precipitation averages around 12 in. (30 cm) in Tucson. Summer and winter rainfall amounts run about equal. As in the lower Sonoran Desert, summer rains bring many of the desert plants out of dormancy into active growth, making the desert look nearly lush. In winter, a few inches of quickly melting snow are possible.

California's Central Valley

The Central Valley of California, comprising the Sacramento and San Joaquin valleys, lies on a north-south axis between the Coast Range on the west and the Sierra Nevada to the east. Long growing seasons and relatively mild winters have made the region well-known worldwide for agricultural production. This area of grasslands and oaks stretches for 500 miles (800 km) from north to south, but is only 50–100 miles (80–160 km) wide. Elevations range from about sea level to around 400 ft. (120 m) near Bakersfield. Climate is influenced mainly by the continental air mass rather than the ocean. Temperatures are therefore more extreme in this zone, with colder winters and hotter summers than near the coast. Winter is cold enough to provide the chilling hours needed by many deciduous fruit crops, but summer is hot enough for some desert-adapted landscape plants.

Like much of California, the Central Valley enjoys a Mediterranean-type climate, with cool, wet winters and dry summers. Most rainfall comes in November through February. The long, arid period reduces many crop-disease problems but is stressful for many landscape plants. Relative humidity is high during winter. The famous tule fogs, lasting up to three weeks, can engulf the area in winter and create an ideal environment for the growth of plant pathogens.

Just inland from the San Francisco Bay Area, marine air flows through a break in the Coast Range and moderates temperatures somewhat. In this area, in the vicinity of Sacramento and as far south as Modesto, summer temperatures are a bit cooler and the winter lows are warmer than either to the north or south. With refreshing breezes coming off the bay, plants in this transitional area emerge from summers looking a little more robust and perky; likewise, in winter, slightly milder temperatures here inflict less cold damage to plants.

Generally, precipitation decreases from the Sacramento Valley area south into the southern San Joaquin Valley. While Sacramento receives an average 17–18 in. (43–45 cm) of rainfall annually, Bakersfield gets only 5–6 in. (13–15 cm). Winters in the Central Valley also get milder at lower latitudes. The Sacramento area can expect an average of 17 days of winter minimums of 32°F (0°C) or below; in Bakersfield, only about 11 nights will get this cold.

The dry, north winds occurring in the spring quickly dessicate plants. They may require more frequent irrigation under these conditions.

The Low Deserts

The low desert areas of Zone 9 include areas of the Sonoran Desert under 2,000 ft. (670 m) and the lower elevations of the Mojave Desert. The Sonoran areas are perhaps the world's richest in native desert vegetation.

Major cities in the low Sonoran Desert include Phoenix and Palm Springs. This climate extends from southern Arizona west into southeastern California and south into the Mexican states of Sonora and Baja California. Citrus and bougainvilleas flourish. Very hot summers limit the use of other traditional plants but pose no problem for the many desert-adapted trees and shrubs that are popular, including palo verdes, desert willows, cassias and daleas.

Winter lows in urban areas average in the upper 30s°F (2–4°C), although temperatures in colder, outlying locations often are lower. Frosts tend to be infrequent, light and of short duration, only slightly damaging plants. Every 10 years or so heavier frosts cause greater damage and kill frost-sensitive plants. Summers bring desert heat and triple-digit temperatures. Readings of 110°F (43°C) are not uncommon. Summer temperatures peak in July. Many plants stop growing until moisture and/or more moderate temperatures return.

Rainfall amounts vary. Phoenix receives an average of about 7 in. (18 cm) a year, while Palm Springs gets less than half this, about 3 in. (8 cm) annually. Rainfall occurs in two distinct seasons in most of the Sonoran Desert, with about equal amounts in winter and summer. Summer precipitation is an important element of the climate: increased humidity alone visibly perks up plants. Storms are often short and intense, leaving swollen, rushing washes and flooded plains. In Palm Springs, most rain falls in winter. Rainfall tends to be erratic in the entire desert, and, at least as far as timing, can be an undependable source of moisture for gardeners. Wind is an additional stress for plants everywhere, but especially in the Palm Springs area, where it blows frequently.

ZONE 10

Milder Low Desert

While most of the low desert is in Zone 9, there are low desert areas in Zone 10 that are milder in winter than in Zone 9. They include parts of the Sonoran and Mojave deserts. They have average minimal lows from 30–40°F (−1 to 4°C) and mainly occur near the Colorado River in Arizona and California, and in Baja California. Yuma, Arizona, seldom freezes and is hotter than Phoenix in the summer. Precipitation is only about 3 in. (8 cm) annually.

Zone 10 also includes inland and coastal areas of California that have much less rainfall, fog and humidity than to the north. This decidedly more arid climate starts south of Point Conception near Santa Barbara.

Inland Southern California

Inland southern California includes the valleys and foothills where most of the population is concentrated. The foothills usually begin several miles inland from the coast and extend to the mountain ranges that create a barrier to interior climates. This inland zone is transitional between the coastal strip and the interior environment. An area such as Pasadena is borderline between the coastal and the inland climates. Pasadena receives some marine influence but is largely dominated by the continental air mass.

Traveling inland from the coast, humidity drops and temperatures become less moderate. Winter lows drop further in Pomona and the San Fernando Valley than in downtown Los Angeles. Alternately, San Bernardino experiences drier conditions and colder winter nighttime temperatures, making conditions somewhat more challenging for growing plants than in Pomona. Summer high temperatures average in the mid-90s°F (35°C) in the hottest areas such as the San Fernando Valley and Riverside. Coastal fogs become less important, even though they sometimes affect plant-growing conditions as far east as San Bernardino. Frosts are a possibility throughout this zone but are more common farther inland.

For example, in winter, Redlands averages about 39 nights registering 32°F (0°C) and 8 nights at 27°F (−3°C). Topography also affects temperatures. The lower, gently sloped foothills form thermal belts where temperatures are warmer than in the valleys below. Frost-susceptible plants are safer on such slopes. Above the foothill slopes, temperatures decrease markedly. In locations of rapid elevation changes, temperatures typically change demonstrably within a short distance. Periodic, dry, gusty winds blowing off the deserts, known as "Santa Anas," present a problem not only for plants but pose a fire danger as well. Parts of this zone occur within or adjacent to the natural range of the chaparral, so many of its plants such as ceanothus, toyon (*Heteromeles arbutifolia*) and sugar bush are well adapted. Some of the arid-adapted plants such as desert honeysuckle (*Justicia spicigera*) and the cassias also do well.

Coastal Southern California

Essentially dominated by the Pacific Ocean, the coastal areas of southern California enjoy much more moderate temperatures than the hot interiors. Also, the fogs inundating the northern California coast are not as intense in the south and rainfall also decreases. Subtropical and succulent plants thrive in the mild winters and summers of this region. The growing season is about 360 days a year, so the region is not entirely frost-free. Winter lows average in the low to mid-40s°F (4°C), while summer highs are generally in the comfortable 70s°F and 80s°F (21–27°C). Periodic short heat waves of 100-plus°F (38°C) days sometimes occur. Most of this region receives an average of 10–14 in. (25–35 cm) of rain annually, with almost all of it occurring between October and April. Many plants native to the coastal sage-scrub community make adaptable and attractive garden subjects in this zone. These include California buckwheat (*Eriogonum fasciculatum*), bush sunflower (*Encelia californica*), purple sage (*Salvia leucophylla*) and sugar bush. The larger trees and shrubs must be sufficiently sturdy to withstand the frequent onshore breezes.

ZONE 11

This zone includes the mildest coastal areas of southern California, such as occurs in the Los Angeles and San Diego areas. The climate is much like the rest of the coast but the average minimum temperatures are slightly milder, above 40°F (4°C), and there seldom are frosts.

MICROCLIMATES

In addition to the weather and climate of the general regions, the very localized conditions in each garden also must be taken into account. Conditions created by local microsite topography and architectural factors around trees and shrubs are referred to as microclimates. Microclimates are one reason gardening can never be an exact science but require the gardener to consider many variables simultaneously.

The microclimate plays a significant part in determining how well a plant actually does in a given location. For example, in winter the lantanas bordering the street may defoliate while those next to the house retain their leaves. Night temperatures next to the house are not only somewhat insulated from general conditions but also warmed by heat radiating from the home (see Figure 2-2). Such slight variations can make the difference between a plant that does fine through winter and one frozen back and killed.

Microclimates are created by a multitude of factors: sun, shade, north-facing versus south-facing exposures, overhangs, barriers, local topography and so on. All factors affect temperature and air patterns. A bougainvillea growing in Tucson benefits from planting on a south-facing wall to minimize cold damage. In Phoenix, tropical sage suffers when planted in the reflected sun and heat of a south-facing wall, but does fine if planted a few yards away in a location shaded in the afternoon. The gardener can create microclimates by controlling such simple things as planting trees for shade or screens for wind protection.

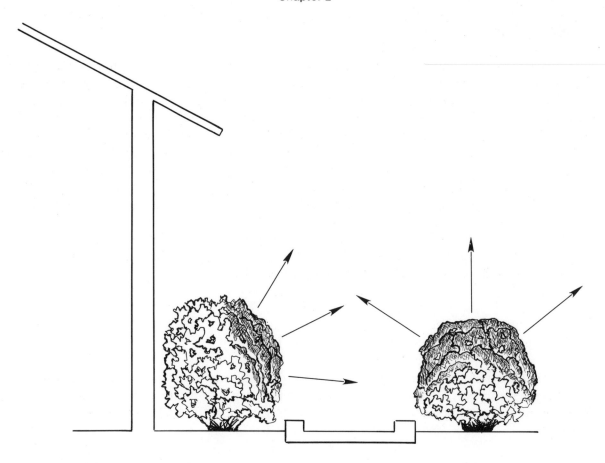

Figure 2-2. Due to microclimate effects, radiant heat from the home affords some protection for a cold-sensitive shrub. Unprotected portions of the shrub and the shrub planted in the open show damage from heat loss.

PLANT HARDINESS

Temperature readings are meaningless without some basic understanding of plant hardiness and of the hardening process itself. Hardiness generally is expressed by the degree of cold, heat and other stresses a plant is able to withstand without being killed. The physiological basis for surviving such stress is determined by the plant's genetic makeup, and different species differ in their ability to withstand all forms of stress. Most of the species described in this book are heat tolerant but vary in cold hardiness.

Plants (except for those growing in tropical regions) undergo a hardening process each year as temperatures and day length decrease in late summer and early fall. Reduced supplies of nitrogen and water also promote hardening. This hardening process enables plants to eventually tolerate the colder conditions of winter. Untimely frosts occurring before plants are fully hardened damage or even kill plants that would be perfectly hardy later in the season. Similarly, unseasonable warm spells in winter or early spring reverse plant dormancy. If this period is followed by a quick cold snap, plants are placed in jeopardy.

Two factors affecting hardiness must always be kept in mind: (1) the timing of low temperatures and (2) the duration of low temperatures. An hour or two at a critical low reading may only slightly damage a plant, while an entire night at this same temperature may prove lethal. Plant parts also vary in their degree of hardiness. Flower buds are less hardy than leaf buds. Early spring frosts are especially risky for fruit trees whose spring flower buds are susceptible to killing. Roots are not as hardy as tops, but are protected from fluctuating air temperatures by the soil. Young plants are often less hardy than older, established ones, and therefore require more protection in cold weather.

PLANT ADAPTATIONS TO DROUGHT

All drought-tolerant plants have developed adaptions or mechanisms which enable them to survive arid conditions. These mechanisms vary considerably. The desert ephemerals, such as many of the wildflowers, are annuals which complete their life cycle in only a few weeks while conditions are moist. They survive dry periods as seeds, thus escaping drought altogether.

Drought-avoiding species have developed efficient mechanisms to prevent the desiccation of their tissues. For example, desert trees such as mesquites have dual root systems: shallow roots that absorb water from light rainfall and deep roots that tap into water reserves deep in the soil. Succulents, such as cactuses and agave, avoid desiccation by limiting transpiration to nighttime and by storing large amounts of water in their tissues.

Some plants are drought-deciduous and shed their leaves and even branchlets when water stress becomes too great. The palo verdes may lose leaves during the growing season if drought-stressed but are able to carry on photosynthesis via the green bark.

Other plants, such as creosote bush, are truly drought resistant and are able to withstand desiccation of their tissues. These species can endure considerable drought stress and resume growth when moisture becomes abundant after irrigation or rainfall. The leaves of many drought-tolerant plants often exhibit features such as reduced size, gray coloring and hairy surfaces that absorb less heat, or a waxy coating that retards moisture loss from the leaf.

Plants from arid to semiarid, nondesert regions such as the chaparral and grasslands have similar, water-saving features. California's chaparral occurs in the foothills, low mountains and some valley areas where a Mediterranean-type climate exists. This means dry summers and cool, wet winters. Plants of the chaparral are characterized by their extensive root systems; dense, stiff, branching habits and small, evergreen leaves with thick cuticles. Most of their growth occurs in the spring, when soil moisture and air temperatures are optimal. During the dry summer, plants drop some of their leaves and go almost dormant. In the landscape, chaparral plants tend to resent summer watering and are very susceptible to soilborne diseases if overwatered at this time.

HEAT TOLERANCE VERSUS DROUGHT TOLERANCE

All of the plants in this book demonstrate some sort of drought tolerance; they are able to grow and perform well with relatively little water. However, the degree of water stress they tolerate can vary considerably. One misconception is that all drought-tolerant species also possess heat tolerance. Many chaparral plants, such as manzanitas and ceanothus, are extremely drought tolerant but only when temperatures are not too high. They do very well in landscapes in inland or coastal regions but perish in low-elevation-desert gardens. Conversely, many of the drought-tolerant desert species such as creosote bush and fern of the desert (*Lysiloma thornberi*) appear to require high summer temperatures for good growth. When these species are planted in cooler, inland or coastal gardens, they grow slowly, do not flower and appear ragged and often die.

Another misconception is that plants with high heat tolerance also exhibit drought tolerance. Examples of such plants include mulberries and cottonwoods, which grow well in hot but heavily irrigated, low-desert areas.

A final class of plants are those drought-tolerant species which grow well both in extremely hot and cooler climates. Examples of these are oleanders, *Myoporum parvifolium* and the *Washingtonia* palms. Robust specimens of these can be found from coastal to inland to desert regions.

Consider these possible differences when experimenting with plants new to your area.

CHAPTER 3

Soils

Soils of the arid Southwest vary widely—from coarse sands to loams to fine clays, and from shallow to deep. Though much of this land is sparsely vegetated and would be considered barren by many, its valleys have some of the world's most agriculturally productive soils, well-drained and high in nutrients. California's Central Valley is the foremost example of this. But even soils in most desert valleys become quite productive when nitrogen and water are provided for plant growth.

Gardeners should have some basic understanding of soils to achieve the best results with plants, which depend on their growing medium not only for an anchor but also water and nutrients. Obviously, soils—and growing conditions—differ from place to place. Fortunately, they can be modified somewhat.

The technical details fill countless books, but in brief, soils are composed of mineral particles, organic matter, liquids, gases and microbes. The solid portion of soils consists of mineral particles with varying amounts of organic matter. The space between particles, or pore space, holds water and gases such as oxygen and nitrogen.

Particular soils were formed by factors such as their original material, climate and vegetation. However, all soils have properties that influence how they behave, and they can be classified based on such properties. One of the most important is texture: the relative amounts of sand, silt and clay.

In the USDA soil classification system, sand particles are the largest (0.05–2.0 mm in diameter), silt is intermediate (0.05–0.002 mm), and clay is the smallest (less than 0.002 mm in diameter). The proportion of each in a given soil determines its texture. For example, a soil with 30 percent clay and 70 percent sand is considered a sandy clay loam (see Figure 3-1). Loam soils fall in the middle in terms of texture and properties, and thus are the most desirable for plant growth. Soil texture determines many of the soil's properties, including porosity and drainage.

Soil depth and structure also influence how soil behaves. Soil depth determines the amount of soil available to roots and the soil's capacity for drainage. Soil structure refers to

15

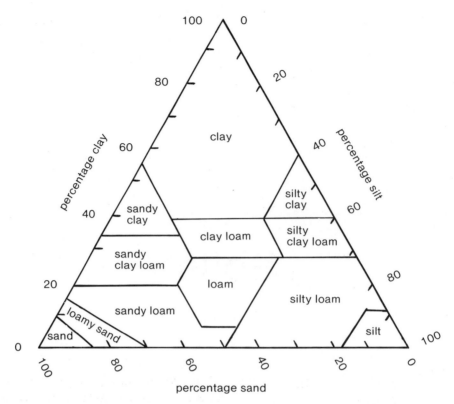

Figure 3-1. Soil textures are determined by analyzing the percentage of sand, silt and clay in the soil and locating the corresponding textural class on the triangle. For example, a soil which is 30 percent clay, 30 percent silt and 40 percent sand is a clay loam. Source: USDA

the way particles are distributed. Particles can occur individually or as aggregates, or clusters of particles that are "glued" together. Structure affects the amount of pore space available for water and oxygen as well as the soil's permeability to water.

Arid Southwest soils present some special problems and challenges in their management. They are often alkaline with a high pH. Alkaline soils result from the high levels of salt that accumulate in arid-region soils. The low amounts of rainfall prevent salts from being leached downward. And the high temperatures result in high evaporation rates from the soil, which move salts upward. Therefore, salts in the root zone can become concentrated at levels harmful to plants, particularly for those not adapted to such conditions.

Many non-native plants such as eucalyptus become afflicted with iron chlorosis after a few years in alkaline soils. Iron is one of several micronutrients that become insoluble—and thus unavailable to plants—in high pH soils. Others include manganese and zinc. Acidifying the soil with sulfur products brings the pH down and helps to solubilize these nutrients.

Those who previously gardened in the eastern United States will recall using lime as a rite of spring to raise the pH. Applying lime is counterproductive in much of the Southwest, since a higher pH is not desirable. Ashes from wood fires are in the same category. So using plants adapted to alkaline conditions is the only sensible way to avoid problems.

Calcareous soils, or those having high levels of calcium carbonate, are commonly found throughout the Southwest deserts. At the soil level where calcium accumulates, a layer of hardpan called caliche can form. This cementlike layer prevents water above it from draining, can impede root growth and creates shallow soil conditions. Caliche varies from an inch or so to many feet in depth. It can occur at or near the soil surface or many feet under.

Any gardener digging a planting hole and finding caliche at the bottom is justifiably discouraged. But the extra effort taken at that point, whether by pick or backhoe, to break through this layer will greatly reduce drainage problems later.

Surface compaction also slows down water penetration. Thus the operation of heavy equipment at construction sites, by breaking down the soil structure and leading to compaction, causes watering problems.

Poor water infiltration can occur in clay soils high in sodium because sodium causes clay particles to disperse, destroying soil structure. Any water applied to such dispersed clay soils may literally stand at the soil surface, ultimately being lost to evaporation. An application of gypsum, or calcium sulfate, usually remedies this situation. It removes soil sodium by "replacing" it with calcium ions, thus improving soil structure.

Good drainage is necessary for the optimum growth of many plants. Soils that drain well are better aerated, for they allow more oxygen to reach plant roots, and generally provide a greater soil volume for moisture and nutrient uptake. Many of the arid-adapted plants such as mesquites grow best in deep, well-drained soils where their roots are able to reach deep soil moisture reserves.

How well a soil drains depends on several factors, including soil texture, depth, topography and so on. Coarse-textured or sandy soils drain easily. But from a plant's standpoint, this can be as undesirable as a slow-draining soil since quick-draining soils have low moisture-holding capabilities and dry out quickly. By contrast, water upon entering a fine-textured soil drains more slowly. If precipitation or irrigation levels become too high, a fine clay soil can become waterlogged and literally drown out a plant's oxygen supply.

Stratified soils and those composed of layers having different textures also lead to drainage problems. Water does not generally drain easily from a layer of one texture to a layer of another. For example, if a soil has a coarse layer above a fine one, water accumulates above the fine-textured layer, and only drains slowly into it, so leaving the coarse layer saturated for an extended period of time. Conversely, a fine soil layer above a coarse one also leads to the saturation of the fine soil layer until the water moves into the coarse layer. This kind of layered saturation is called a perched water table. Clay or caliche hardpan layers as well as surface compaction can create perched water table drainage problems. Similarly, even an improperly prepared planting hole can lead to serious drainage problems. This happens when the backfill soil differs greatly in texture from the native soil, thus impairing drainage and allowing water to collect around the roots. Backfill should contain a good amount of native soil to help prevent this problem.

No matter what kind of soil is native to a planting site, save in the case of perfect loam, the garden will usually benefit from the addition of organic matter. Organic matter such as forest mulch, compost and so on, not only enriches sandy soils but augments their moisture-holding capacity. Conversely, tight clay soils are "opened up" and so drain better with the addition of organic matter. Supplying organic matter to soil which contains little naturally—as is the case in most desert soils—also adds to the population of useful microorganisms which can enhance plant growth.

But, as with most things, too much organic matter is definitely not better in the garden. When planting trees and shrubs, total organic matter content should not be more than about 25–33 percent of the total volume of the backfill mix. More only leads to drainage problems, for water simply sits in the planting hole because it drains too slowly into surrounding soil.

Indeed some experts on soil caution against the use of organic amendments altogether. Their studies have shown that plants planted in soil akin to their native soil not only grow better without organic material but also that disease is promoted with its use. Nonetheless, when landscaping in the desert or situations in which the topsoil has been removed, plants will usually benefit from the addition of small amounts of organic matter at planting time.

CHAPTER 4

Planning the Landscape

In planning a home landscape, think of the outdoor space as an extension of the indoors, reflecting those qualities or activities the occupants enjoy. The challenge in the arid Southwest is to meet such human desires while conserving water, thereby maintaining a proper relationship with the environment.

Some priority questions: Is entertaining outdoors important? Is an area for peaceful solitude essential? Will young children need play areas? Is minimal maintenance desirable? Be candid and pragmatic in listing dreams and expectations.

In the last decade of the twentieth century, space has become more important as living areas become more confined by downsized housing and leisure time becomes more limited. Carefully planning the outdoor area can add greatly to one's sense of space.

Typical outdoor needs, as always, include shade, greenery, screening for privacy, seasonal color and recreational areas. Water-thrifty, climate-adapted plants have increasingly become the answer in arid regions. The bonus: reduced maintenance costs.

The challenge to a landscape designer, whether a professional or a do-it-yourselfer, is to create something both pleasing to the eye and functional. A landscape is more than the haphazard arrangement of plants. Focus on the overall picture, not simply individual plants. Mere planting and growing do not make a pleasing landscape.

Though informal gardens lack the symmetry associated with traditional, formal landscapes, they must still create a coherent and balanced visual effect. Plants used in conjunction with structures and paving should provide an inviting feeling and visual interest. Variation, repetition and balance of plant groupings should provide unity to the design, with each plant fulfilling a particular role. Massed plantings of a few species normally are more appealing than one of this, one of that and a few of another.

Consider also the form, texture and color of plants. Southwest plants are rich and diverse in these qualities. But while contrasting textures and colors create a dynamic display, diversity is not to be overdone. Desert landscapes often abound with the striking forms of cactuses and succulents. They can be softened and unified through the use of soft-textured shrubs such as daleas, creosote bush and cassias, just as such mixtures occur in the true desert.

Another basic rule: landscaping should complement dwellings or other structures when viewed from outside and should provide an attractive view from inside. The goal is an entrancing look from every point where a person may stand or sit.

It is important to group plants according to their water needs. Plants that require more water are best placed near the house for convenience in watering and to provide a shady, oasis effect. Place the most drought-resistant plants in outer or transitional areas.

Different plants have different degrees of usefulness and adaptability, of course. So our recommendation is that gardeners study the individual plant descriptions in this book carefully before deciding which plants are best suited to a projected use.

When it is time to put thoughts on paper, begin with the typical landscape needs—privacy, shade, leisure, play and so on. Plot these out on a rough sketch of the yard. An example of a final plan is shown in Figure 4-1.

Be sure the plan considers:

- screening for privacy or as a noise buffer
- shade and energy conservation
- leisure use and personal space
- framing views
- color for accent or focal points
- erosion control.

For most people, screening for privacy is the most important consideration, especially on smaller lots. Screening also works to eliminate undesirable views, as a windbreak and as a noise buffer, as, for example, near roadways. In general, shrubs give the quickest effect at lowest cost. Many provide maximum impact within two growing seasons. Select plants that are 6 ft. (2 m) or more in eventual height and space them according to the needed density. Plants such as oleander, Arizona rosewood (*Vauquelinia californica*), and hopseed bush (*Dodonaea viscosa*) make attractive dense screens. Taller-growing trees can also be used. Plants suggested for screening are listed under "tall screening" and "plants for low screens" in the Appendix.

Achieving shade is likely to take more time since trees are slower to reach their eventual size than shrubs. If large trees already are present, do not automatically discard them because they use a lot of water. Consider carefully whether they can be retained until more water-efficient trees take hold. Many drought-resistant trees are very fast growing.

Some fairly simple ideas cut energy costs significantly. Think of the cooling comfort of a shady place on a hot day. Homes can be similarly cooled by planting trees strategically to shade the home in the direction of the most intense sunlight, usually the south and west sides. Deciduous trees are ideal for this purpose as they shade the home during the warmest months, but allow the sun to reach and warm the house in winter (Figure 4-2). Vines on walls shade and thus insulate them.

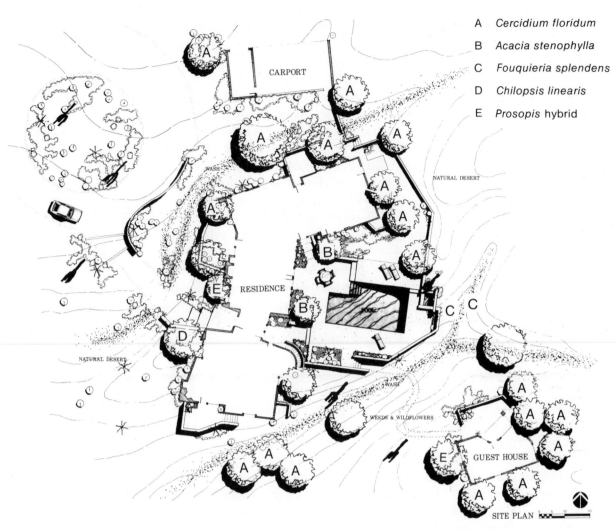

A *Cercidium floridum*
B *Acacia stenophylla*
C *Fouquieria splendens*
D *Chilopsis linearis*
E *Prosopis* hybrid

Figure 4-1. This award-winning landscape design creates comfort and beauty in harmony with the existing site. Desert plants provide shade and color in a landscape that is a tribute to the natural beauty of the surrounding desert. STEVE MARTINO & ASSOCIATES

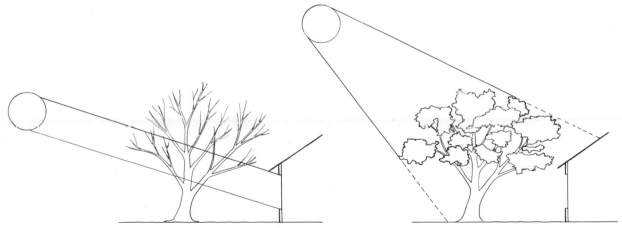

Figure 4-2. The bare branches of this deciduous tree allow warming rays of sunshine to pass through in winter. In summer, the tree shades and cools the home.

Directing the air flow around a home also contributes to energy conservation and comfort of living. Plant windbreaks perpendicular to the wind direction to reduce the wind's effect. Conversely, channel cooling breezes toward a house by creating an opening at appropriate places in the windbreak planting.

In planning for leisure use and personal space, consider patio areas for entertaining, small lawns for recreation and retreats such as an open spot under a grove of trees.

Any scenic views of mountains, valleys or bodies of water can be attractively accented by framing them with trees and shrubs. Be sure to select plants of the proper size at maturity so that the view does not eventually become obscured by overgrowth.

Concentrate small areas of color where they are likely to be most appreciated, such as next to patio areas. Color in entryways and along paths also draws the eye and creates a focal point. Use annual and perennial flowering plants or long-flowering shrubs.

Erosion control is a major concern on hillsides and small banks. Plants with spreading root systems help bind the soil.

Irrigation systems should be appropriate for the plant material and properly maintained to reduce plant losses and water waste through runoff and evaporation. Use water harvesting techniques to collect rainfall and divert it to plants. Simple watering basins built up from the soil around plants are effective. See Chapter 5 for more details on watering.

Converting an existing, water-guzzling landscape to a water-conserving one may seem daunting, but sweeping changes usually are not necessary. The first step is to sharply reduce lawn size.

Limit turf area to what is needed for active use. Lawns have traditionally been a major component of landscapes, even though lawn activities usually require only a small area. Place the small plot of turf where it is most likely to be effective, such as adjacent to a backyard patio area.

Lawn removal is best done when the lawn is in an active growth state—spring and summer for grass such as Bermuda. Water deeply to encourage active, green growth before applying a herbicide containing glyphosate (sold under trade names such as Roundup and Control). Follow label directions carefully. Do not allow the spray on any greenery not destined for elimination. Respray any regrowth. In the case of Bermuda grass, it often helps to remove the dead grass layer as completely as possible to discourage resprouting.

Rather than using a grass-killer, it is possible to remove Bermuda grass by digging a shovelful at a time and discarding the roots after knocking the soil from them. This can become a major project except in small areas. As with glyphosate, be prepared to eliminate any regrowth.

Desert plants create a lush backdrop to a patio setting.
STEVE MARTINO & ASSOCIATES

A front-yard alternative to a lawn combines attractive textures and colors.
LISA IWATA, LAND INTERACTIVE

Arid-adapted plants in an array of forms, colors and textures create a natural, yet dynamic display in the entryway. STEVE MARTINO & ASSOCIATES

Masses of flowers (*Verbena gooddingii, Penstemon parryi, Encelia farinosa*) herald springtime in this garden. Careful planning yields year-round color in the warm Southwest. STEVE MARTINO & ASSOCIATES

Plants soften the man-made elements in our world and provide a transition to the natural environment around us. STEVE MARTINO & ASSOCIATES

Wildflowers such as this *Machaeran-thera* add a natural look, vibrant color and a special charm . . .

Perennial planting—Southwest style—with *Melampodium leucanthum, Verbena gooddingii, Salvia farinacea* and the annual *Baileya multiradiata.*

Once covered with lawn, this back-yard now features an extended patio and low-maintenance, water-saving plants such as *Cercidium microphyllum* and *Leucophyllum frutescens* that blend well with the natural environment.
STEVE MARTINO & ASSOCIATES

This traditional, ordinary-looking landscape has undergone a remarkable transformation . . .

Drought-tolerant trees, shrubs and ground cover and the addition of low walls and a trellis replace the large front lawn. The result is a shady oasis that is more interesting and inviting. C.F. SHULER, INC.

CHAPTER 5

Culture

Plants adapted to low water consumption have a well-earned reputation for needing little care. But it does not follow that the gardener can simply bring such a species home from the nursery, dig a hole, put it in the ground and the gardener and plant live happily ever after.

Before purchasing, the gardener must determine if the plant is suited for the location being considered. Will it eventually become too large for available space? Will shedding leaves, seed pods and other litter be a problem, such as around a swimming pool, for example? Can it reasonably be expected to handle the environmental stresses—such as sun, wind, heat or cold—it must tolerate in the planned site?

Only plants which are near-perfect for low-water-use situations are included in this book. But, as in every other aspect of life, there are degrees of adaptability and usefulness. A species ideal in one landscape may prove a nightmare elsewhere. The reader must refer to the individual plant descriptions to confirm that a particular plant is suitable for the use projected. Our best advice to readers is to take their time, to first come to a full understanding of the site.

This chapter is devoted to the detailed mechanics of planting, fertilizing, watering, pruning and propagating. But before turning to these matters, some preliminary observations aimed at providing the reader with a well-rounded understanding of growing plants in a warm-arid environment seems to be in order.

Most of the plant species included here, once established, need little, if any fertilizer. "Once established" are the key words. If the plants are putting on the growth and providing the landscaping effect being sought, they probably don't need any.

A newly installed plant should be watered once or twice a week through the warmest months and about every other week in cooler weather for the first year or two. After this period, if it is making satisfactory growth and looks healthy, back off to determine whether supplemental watering is still required. If the plant seems to start suffering, apply an inch or two (3–5 cm) of water and see if this helps. If it does, wait about a month to see if more watering is needed. Filling a watering basin with an inch or two of water is an easy way to measure the amount applied.

In general, overwatering is a serious problem for the plants included in this book. They simply cannot handle constantly moist soil. But natural rainfall may not be sufficient in some years. Wilted foliage usually is a good indication of too little water. Sometimes the leaf color becomes dull. Some experience is required to come to understand such nuances. A good rule to remember: Established plants probably won't die from lack of irrigation, they just won't grow very fast or look as good.

PLANTING

Most plant problems arise from the care they receive after planting. So following a handful of guidelines at planting allows the gardener to adjust for certain conditions, getting plants off to a better start.

The timing of planting makes quite a difference. Commercial landscape operations tend to run year-round, but generally, the best season to plant in the warm-arid climates is fall. Fall planting allows for root growth, enabling plants to recover and better withstand the stressful heat of summer. This can be crucial not only in the deserts, but also in the more moderate climate zones of California, where spring-planted natives might succumb to fungal diseases from overwatering during the summer. Early spring is considered the next best time for planting, especially for cold-tender species. The most cold-hardy plants, which include deciduous and bare root trees, are best planted during the winter.

Almost every measure undertaken at planting is a reflection of existing soil conditions. Is the soil a tight clay or light sandy type? Are there underlying stratified layers that might interfere with drainage, a condition that may not be apparent until digging starts? How was the soil treated during construction? Was there significant compaction?

Amending the soil can alleviate many drainage problems. Most soil types benefit from adding an organic mulch or humus-type material. Manure is also useful to this end, but can be very high in salts. Mulch helps open up a tight soil, permitting it to drain more easily. Sandy soils are better able to retain moisture when organic matter is added.

Desert soils usually lack organic matter and adding it at planting time stimulates microbial activity and improves drainage. Mulching also improves soils stripped of their upper layers of topsoil during construction. Most nursery-produced plants are grown in a mix that is fairly high in organic matter. Adding additional organic matter to the backfill creates a better transition zone to the native soil. However, too much organic matter may create problems (see planting steps below).

The plants in this book are fairly well-adapted to their recommended growing areas. So making the correct choice coupled with the following steps should lead to successful planting (see Figure 5-1):

1. Dig a hole twice as wide and twice as deep as the container size. Fill with water. It should soak into the ground quickly. If it does, drainage is satisfactory and the moist environment will benefit the new plant. If the water remains in the hole for several hours, bail it out and dig deeper to locate the problem. If further excavation does not turn up a hardpan layer, abandon the hole and try elsewhere. Hardpan is common in the Southwest. This impervious layer of caliche (solidified calcium carbonate) must be broken with a pick or similar tool since roots are not able to penetrate it. Digging a "chimney" through this bottom layer is often all that is required to create an acceptable planting site.

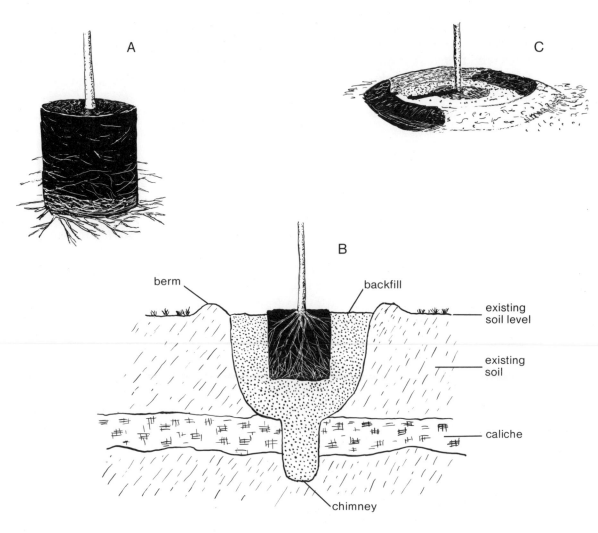

Figure 5-1. Planting a containerized plant. (A) Remove plant from container and inspect roots. Carefully free any long, winding roots. (B) Place root ball in appropriate-sized planting hole with the top of the root ball flush with or slightly higher than the existing soil level. The chimney permits water to drain through the caliche. (C) Make a watering basin by constructing a berm around the base of the plant.

2. Add organic material such as forest mulch to the soil just excavated, so that it constitutes about one quarter to one third of the total backfill volume. More than this proportion is likely to cause drainage problems. In addition, a slow-release fertilizer can be added at this time, following label directions. Mix thoroughly.

3. Return some backfill to the bottom of the hole. Remove the plant from its container and gently free any circling or winding roots, being careful not to break the root ball. Place sufficient backfill into the hole so the top of the root ball is flush with the level of the soil.

4. Hold the root ball in place and refill the hole with backfill. When the hole is about a third filled, tamp the soil gently around the root ball to remove air pockets and prevent later settling. Some water added to the hole at this time helps to firm the soil. Continue to refill, tamping the fill occasionally.

5. After planting, construct a 2–3 in. (5–8 cm) high circular berm in the soil to provide a watering basin approximately reflecting the leaf canopy. Such a berm is helpful even with drip irrigation. Fill the basin and allow to drain, then water again. These two irrigations will soak the root ball thoroughly. Keep the soil moist until new growth is observed. Then follow the standard watering instructions. A couple of inches of mulch such as bark chips or decomposed granite in the watering basin helps maintain moisture levels.

WATERING

Often, a gardener brings a plant home along with the incomplete advice to water it every couple of days after planting. The plant looks happy for a few months, but it then begins to wilt and drop leaves despite the water and attention lavished upon it. Actually it is drowning—what was good for it those first few weeks is now killing it.

Watering practices probably top the list of cultural practices harmful to newly planted trees and shrubs. As plants grow, their water needs change. This holds true even for most arid-adapted plants. Gardeners should develop the habit of observing growth changes and water accordingly.

Following transplanting, plants undergo a period of establishment. They require more frequent watering at this stage to allow for root growth and to achieve a good top-to-root balance. Some species may take one to two years to become established in the landscape, so watering should be tapered back gradually. Begin by watering new plants every other day or so for the first couple of weeks, then reduce this to once or twice a week. Once drought-resistant plants are established, watering can be reduced dramatically.

Established plants with deep, well-developed root systems are much better able to survive a long drought period. Deep root systems are encouraged by deep watering. Apply water slowly so that it soaks in to a good depth instead of running off. Conditions vary, of course, but start by assuming that one to two hours of slow soaking will wet the average soil to a depth of 2 ft. (60 cm) and six to eight hours of slow soaking will reach 4–5 ft. (1.2–1.5 m).

Such deep watering also flushes salts from the root zone. Salt content of arid-region soils normally is quite high. One theory for the mysterious disappearance of the far-flung prehistoric Hohokam civilization from Arizona is that they didn't understand the process of salt accumulation arising from the intensive irrigation and cultivation practices they used. So their crops declined year after year, although they were otherwise excellent farmers. A deep, slow, supplemental watering once a year is good insurance for maintaining established plants in arid regions.

How often to water is one of the trickier questions and requires some practice. Agricultural scientists have developed equations for evapotranspiration rates (or ET) which factor in air temperatures, soil types and evaporation to calculate the amount of watering needed. Although these tables are useful for commercial operations, most gardeners use a trial and error approach to formulate their own watering schedules. It helps to know the signs of water stress: a dull, off-color leaf and wilting and curling of foliage which may lead to browning. New plants should be watered before they reach this stage; established plants can tolerate wilting, but will not grow as fast.

Once drought-resistant plants are established, can the water automatically be turned off? In certain cases, yes. If a tree has reached its desired size and can get by on natural rainfall, by all means stop watering it. Many drought-resistant plants are so defined because they can grow without supplemental irrigation. They may not, however, maintain the level of appearance that is desired in a landscape situation, and so may need infrequent watering to keep them looking good.

Other drought-resistant plants need occasional watering to survive the hottest months. In hot areas, such as the deserts and California's Central Valley, many plants require supplemental water to get through the summer, but little to none at other times of the year.

IRRIGATION SYSTEMS

In most cases the most convenient and time-saving method of watering a landscape is with an automatic irrigation system, eliminating the need to drag garden hoses to various locations. Most gardeners find the convenience alone is worth the installation cost.

Automatic systems vary in the way they deliver water. Most use a combination of sprinklers, bubblers and drip emitters. They operate manually or by an electric or solar-powered time clock.

In recent years, drip irrigation, first developed for commercial agricultural applications, has emerged as an effective system for watering arid landscapes. This system involves the slow application of water to the soil over a period of time, promoting penetration and deep rooting while minimizing or eliminating runoff and evaporation. Water is applied exactly where needed—to the roots of the plant—and little is wasted. Since large surface areas are not moistened, weed growth is retarded. On slopes, drip irrigation cuts down on soil erosion. A drip system is flexible and adaptable. For example, as trees grow larger and require more water, more emitters can be easily added.

However, clogged emitters are a common complaint and require the gardener's constant vigilance to avoid loss of plants. For this reason, some gardeners have switched to bubblers, since it is easier to observe if they are not operating. Bubblers apply large amounts of water to small areas in a short time.

Pressure-compensating emitters are recommended where elevation changes occur. They are designed to insure equal amounts of water from each emitter. On slopes, be sure to place emitters above the plant to properly wet the root zone.

The basic components of a drip system include a valve, pressure regulator, filter, hose, emitter (or "spaghetti") tubes and the emitters themselves. Water flows from the valve through the hose and out the emitters at a reduced rate of flow. Hose material consists of polyethylene or PVC. While more expensive, PVC has proven more durable and trouble-free than polyethylene for many landscape projects. And be aware that rabbits sometimes chew through flexible polyethylene tubing to get at the water and that sun and high temperatures shorten its life much faster than PVC.

Emitters differ in their water delivery rate, usually measured as gph, or gallons per hour, varying from 0.5 to 4 gph (2 to 15 liters per hour). Trees and shrubs usually require 1- or 2-gph emitters (4 to 7.5 lph). Emitters are also available as single or multi-outlet, so plants with different water requirements can be watered on the same line. Measure water needs carefully. There is little margin for error.

Do-it-yourself drip irrigation systems for homeowners are commonly available at nurseries and home improvement stores. These are suited for small, easy jobs and are relatively easy to install. For more complex projects, consult an irrigation specialist.

While drip may be effective for trees and shrubs, and in some cases, even ground covers, sprinklers and spray heads remain the best choice for lawns and flower beds as they apply water evenly over a large surface area. Where lawns and beds are combined with trees and shrubs, as in most landscapes, drip, bubbler and sprinkler systems can be operated on different valves.

Good maintenance is mandatory for a smoothly operating irrigation system. Get in the habit of observing the system frequently while it is on so as to catch existing or potential problems. Repair or replace broken or nonworking components. Watering schedules, if run from a clock, need seasonal adjustments, so plants are not being overwatered during the cool season and vice versa.

In many cases a single application of water over a long period with automatic systems is not feasible, so watering is divided into two or three cycles during the day. Often these cycles are spread out too far over the day, resulting in a shallow area of soil being re-wet over and over. Running cycles closer together results in deeper penetration of water and healthier rooting. Computer-directed devices, obtainable for around $100, facilitate the timing process.

How long to run a system depends on location—obviously, water will have to be applied longer in Phoenix than in a similar landscape in Los Angeles. Soil type also is significant in figuring watering time. Plants grown in sandy soil require more frequent watering than those in clay soils, given equivalent temperatures and evapotranspiration factors. Soil types must also be considered to avoid problems such as runoff and erosion.

Plants are more adequately watered if they are grouped according to their water requirements. Trees and shrubs that have high (or low) requirements should be placed together, so they will tend not to be over- or underwatered. Although this practice is occasionally difficult to achieve in a particular landscape situation, it should always remain a leading objective.

FERTILIZING

Arid-adapted plants usually need little fertilizer. After all, most come from areas where soil nitrogen is low. Many horticultural experts believe that stimulating growth by fertilizing reduces the lifespan of many arid-adapted species.

If a landscape is providing the growth and appearance sought, there is really no need to fertilize the plants in it. Overfertilizing, in fact, promotes fast, weak top growth, leading to an imbalance with the root system. As plants increase their growth rate, they require more water and more maintenance, such as pruning. Also, excess soil salts can build up with too much fertilizer.

Fertilizing may help those plants which are growing too slowly, those whose leaves are off-color or those in decline and looking poor. But it is best to first determine the underlying cause of poor growth as other factors such as inadequate drainage might be the cause.

Sixteen elements are essential to plant growth. Plants take oxygen, hydrogen and carbon primarily from air or water. The remainder are absorbed mainly by the plant roots. The so-called primary nutrients are nitrogen, potassium and phosphorus, often referred to as N-P-K and, by law, the first three numbers on a bag of fertilizer (such as 10–6–4).

The secondary nutrients are sulfur, magnesium and calcium. The micronutrients are iron, zinc, copper, manganese, molybdenum, boron and chlorine. Since they are needed in only small amounts, they often are referred to as trace elements. Regardless of the amounts used, however, all 16 elements are essential to plants.

Nitrogen is the one element consistently low in most arid-region soils because the sparsity of vegetation leaves too little organic matter being recycled into the soil. Of course, foliage and other parts dropped by plants contain nitrogen, but not 100 percent is recycled, so adding a little fertilizer from time to time often proves beneficial. But less fertilizer is always better than too much. The descriptions for individual plant species advise recommended amounts. Again, less is always better than too much.

Nitrogen fertilizers are available in several different formulations. In alkaline soils, ammonium sulfate is a good nitrogen source that also helps to keep soil pH down. Inexpensive and readily available, it contains 21 percent nitrogen and 24 percent sulfur. As a general rule, a fourth to a half cup (57–115 g) of ammonium sulfate is sufficient for a good-sized shrub. Organic sources of nitrogen, such as manure and compost, are much lower in nitrogen content, but provide a steady, low output of nutrients as well as improving soil tilth. Manure contains salts and should be used with some caution in alkaline soils.

The soil's pH (hydrogen potential) is a most important consideration. The pH scale is logarithmic and ranges from 1 to 14, with 1 being the most acid, 14 the most alkaline and 7 neutral. In the acid-soil regions of the world, including much of the United States, gardeners apply lime to raise the pH level, which is lowered over the winter by rain and snow leaching. However, alkaline soils, which receive infrequent rain and which are typical of desert environments, require sulfur to lower the pH alkalinity. The idea in applying either lime or sulfur is the same—to provide the best possible pH level and therefore growing conditions. Most native, arid-adapted plants handle the alkaline, local soils.

Newly planted trees and shrubs benefit from slow-release fertilizer mixed in the planting hole. A slow, steady, balanced supply of nutrients is available as plants begin to grow. If slow-release fertilizer is not included in the backfill material, wait a couple of months until roots begin growing to apply fertilizers.

Again, established plants may or may not need any fertilizer. Once trees and shrubs reach their desired size, fertilizing should be curtailed unless specific problems develop. Some western United States natives such as *Eriogonum* and *Penstemon* prefer lean soils. Many leguminous plants, including some acacias, fix nitrogen when grown in their native soil. Other flowering plants such as verbena respond to balanced or nitrogen fertilizers with prolonged flowering.

In warm climates, early spring after the chance of frosts has passed is generally the best time to fertilize most evergreen plants. Winter warm spells induce growth late frosts can damage, particularly if fertilizer has been applied. Deciduous trees and shrubs may be fertilized in late winter as these forms are usually not stimulated into growth by warm weather.

Chlorosis

Some plants are prone to iron chlorosis, the symptoms of which are green veins on leaves with yellowing elsewhere. While few native plants develop the problem, which is caused by unavailable iron, many of the exotics do. If the condition develops, do not rush to apply iron chelates. First review irrigation practices to make certain that plants are not being kept overly wet and that irrigation is deep and infrequent.

Roots absorb iron through a very active oxygen-transfer process. Permanently wet soil allows less oxygen to enter the soil from the air, so less oxygen is available to carry iron to the plants. Furthermore, iron is reduced chemically in wet soil—that is, reduced as opposed to oxidized—which is a less easily used form.

Replacing unsatisfactory plants with better-adapted species is the ultimate answer. But if a gardener prefers ornamentals common to more temperate regions and does not want to convert an existing landscape, iron deficiency can become quite a problem. Advanced symptoms are marked by the dieback of branches or the production of very small leaves, often presaging the death of the plant due to progressive weakening of the plant until other factors—like insects or disease—complete the job.

Chelated irons can help. They usually are sold in formulations such as Fe 138 or Fe 330. Follow label directions carefully and, as with all iron supplements, do not spill on anything you don't want stained, such as concrete or clothing. Do not use chelates until chlorosis symptoms are observed and wait to apply them until soil temperatures are above 60°F (16°C).

PRUNING

Plants require pruning for several reasons. Proper pruning not only improves the health and function of many plants but also can transform an ordinary-looking specimen into one with a striking form and outline. Good pruning requires a knowledge of how plants grow, and an eye for bringing out natural beauty also helps. Unfortunately, examples of poor and botched pruning jobs are not hard to find.

It is important to recognize not only when a young plant needs pruning but how to prune that particular species so that it responds the way the gardener wants it to as well. To minimize pruning later on, select plants well-suited to the site, both in their mature size and in their place in the landscape.

The major reasons for pruning landscape plants are:

1. Training trees. Young trees often require some pruning to direct their growth and develop a strong framework of branches.

2. Controlling plant size. Trees, shrubs and ground covers may need cutting back when they become too large for the spaces provided them.

3. Removing dead, diseased, broken or crowded branches. Prune to minimize these problems in early spring after the chance of frost has passed. But remove diseased twigs or branches as soon as symptoms develop to protect the remainder of the plant and its neighbors.

4. Stimulating flowering. Pruning flowering plants in the right season encourages greater flower production.

5. Rejuvenating plants in decline. Plants that are growing poorly not infrequently respond to severe pruning with new growth.

6. Restoring balance. Prune young trees after transplanting if their roots have been damaged in the process. This pruning helps restore a balance between top and root growth but will retard overall growth a year or two.

Culture

The best time to prune varies from species to species. Most evergreen shrubs should be pruned in the early spring after the possibility of frost. This timing precludes the stimulation of new growth susceptible to cold damage. Shrubs which flower in spring on last year's growth should be pruned immediately after flowering. Prune shrubs which bloom in the summer on the current year's wood in early spring before growth resumes. Winter is usually the best time to prune deciduous plants as any problems are easily visible at this time.

Two types of pruning cuts are used:

1.   Heading (Figure 5-2). Young growth or large branches are cut back to a node.

2.   Thinning (Figure 5-3). This cut reduces the density of leaves to give better air circulation and allow more light to reach the interior of the plant. A branch is removed at its point of origin or at the ground. Thinning is the most desirable way to prune trees.

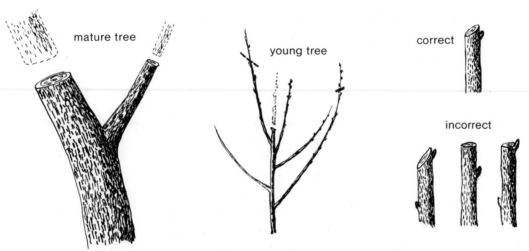

Figure 5-2. Heading-type pruning cuts for mature and young trees. Correct and incorrect cuts on young branches are shown.

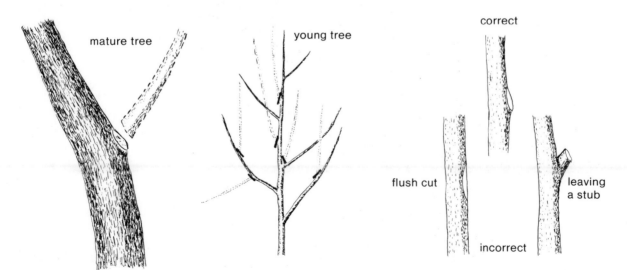

Figure 5-3. Thinning-type pruning cuts for mature and young trees. Incorrect cuts include flush cuts or leaving a stub.

Training Young Trees

Young trees often require training in their first few years to develop strong branch structure and so avoid problems later on. Some tree species naturally having irregular or sprawling growth habits should not be pruned for training. Oaks, for example, do best with minimal pruning. For most species, however, it is desirable to control and direct growth. In training (Figure 5-4):

1. Select a strong leader, that is, the principal branch out of and around which other branches will emerge.

2. Identify the other permanent framework branches, known as the scaffold branches, and remove all those not selected. The scaffold branches should be healthy and well-spaced both vertically and radially.

3. Remove crossing and crowded branches.

4. Allow some weaker, small-caliper branches to remain on the trunk below the lowest permanent branch, for they help to nourish and strengthen the trunk of a young tree while encouraging it to develop taper.

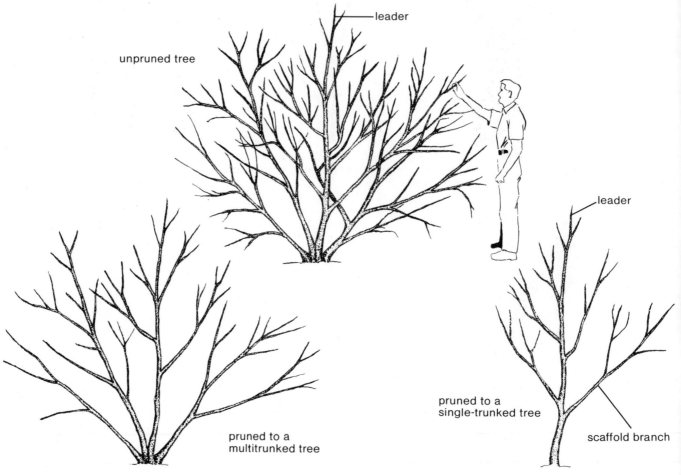

Figure 5-4. Training a young tree. Many trees make attractive, multitrunked specimens. For a single-trunked tree, select a strong leader and scaffold branches.

Pruning Mature Trees

As trees mature, they may outgrow the space they occupy and require trimming. Street trees usually need a regular pruning program to control their size and as a safety measure. Dead or diseased branches should be removed to protect a tree's health. Thin out excessively crowded branches if more light is needed in the interior or lower portions. Prune wind-damaged branches promptly.

Pruning needs will differ according to tree species. Some genera such as eucalyptus and pines do not respond well to heavy pruning. Others, such as olive and mulberry, withstand it very well. How trees are used also affects pruning. For example, many desert trees—such as palo verdes and mesquites—should have the lower branches removed if being used as shade trees but they also can be left in their natural, more shrublike form if being used for screening.

Pruning Shrubs

Shrubs may require pruning to control their size, stimulate flowering, or rejuvenate them. Shearing is sometimes necessary for maintaining hedges but results in a "meatball" look when used on individual shrubs. A combination of heading and thinning cuts maintains a more natural, appealing look (Figure 5-5).

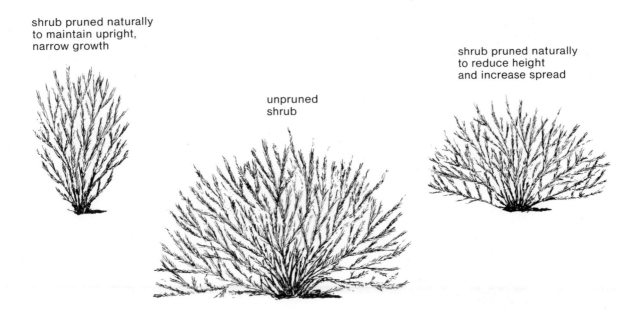

shrub pruned naturally to maintain upright, narrow growth

unpruned shrub

shrub pruned naturally to reduce height and increase spread

Figure 5-5. Informal pruning to control the shape and size of shrubs.

STAKING

Trees that have just been planted are often staked to hold them upright and keep them from falling over until the root system is fully developed. However, it is not necessary to stake all newly planted trees, particularly if a natural-looking landscape is desired. Staking is often desirable in formal landscapes, such as along roads, surrounding commercial buildings where space is often restricted, and in exposed, windy sites.

The trunks of trees growing in the wild are usually well tapered, which is why they don't need staking. Their diameter is greatest at the base and gets smaller as one moves up the trunk. This taper allows for equal weight distribution along the entire height of the tree, enabling the tree to stay upright. It has been shown experimentally that their strong taper is caused by the gentle swaying motion of the tree trunks in the wind.

Field-grown nursery trees have this desirable taper and usually need no staking after transplanting. Nurseries that grow trees in containers are given to rigidly staking them to increase production space. This practice results in trees with weak, spindly trunks. Unfortunately, when such trees are transplanted, the improper, nursery-style staking is often continued in the landscape and the unnatural growth habit continues.

If a tree should be staked, do so correctly, using two stakes. This usually means reworking the nursery-style staking. Improper staking slows trunk development, delays top growth and can delay the good root development necessary to anchor the tree. The stakes of properly staked trees are anchored outside the root ball. They should be attached at only one point on the trunk with a flexible tie so the tree can move in the wind and develop properly (Figure 5-6).

Fast-growing trees such as eucalyptus almost always require staking. Some species such as conifers, bottle trees (*Brachychiton*) and silk oak (*Grevillea*) generally do not need staking. Multitrunked trees have good wind resistance so seldom need staking unless it is required to maintain a particular effect. In this case, guying between trunks is usually the best practice.

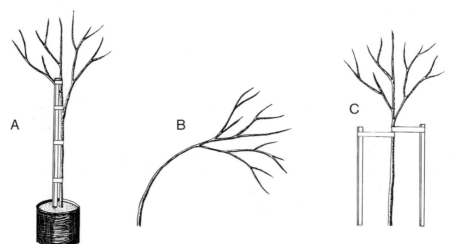

Figure 5-6. Proper staking of a container-grown tree. (A) Trees grown in containers are often rigidly staked at the nursery. These stakes must be removed when the trees are transplanted. (B) However, removing the stake causes the trunk to bend. Notice that the tree always bends away from the stake. (C) Proper staking requires two shorter stakes placed outside the root ball and only one point of attachment to the tree. This point is the lowest position at which the trunk stands upright, plus 4–6 in. (10–15 cm). Attach with flexible ties, not wire or nylon rope.

PROPAGATION

Growing your own plants can be one of the most rewarding and challenging experiences for a gardener. And with some patience, it can be an inexpensive way to supply plants for a home landscape.

Plants can be started from seeds (called sexual propagation) or cuttings (asexual or vegetative propagation). Most plants, and especially trees and shrubs, grown from seed vary genetically. These genetic differences are often readily visible in a plant's physical traits. Vegetatively propagated plants—started from a vegetative or asexual part of the plant—carry on the genetic traits of the mother plant. Vegetative propagation has been quite useful in the landscape industry to select and increase plants with desirable characteristics.

There are also other means of vegetative propagation such as layering, grafting, root division and tissue culture. But this discussion will concentrate on seeds and cuttings, the major methods of propagating most plants in this book.

Seeds

Most plants ensure their reproduction by producing seeds within the ovary after flowering. Others do not produce seeds at all but have other means of reproducing, such as offsets.

Many types of seeds, especially those of annuals, can simply be scattered on the ground and, with some rainfall, will germinate and grow without much more effort from the gardener. Others require special conditions before they germinate. Since plants grow in many different environments, the requirements for seed germination can also vary. Many seeds undergo a period of dormancy which enables the seeds to survive until conditions are right for germination.

One kind of such dormancy is called seed-coat dormancy. The seed coat covers and protects the inner seed tissues that will form the plant. In many cases, the seed coat forms a hardened, impenetrable layer that keeps out water and oxygen necessary for germination. Legumes such as palo verdes and acacias are prime examples. The first few years after these trees have been transplanted, the seeds they produce do not germinate. Eventually, seedlings may begin to sprout, not from the freshest seed crop, but from the earlier ones. In nature, seed-coat dormancy is overcome due to weathering and other environmental factors which break down the seed coat.

For the gardener, countering seed-coat dormancy through weathering is impractical, so mechanical means of scarification, or cutting through the seed coat, are necessary. Scratching the seed coat with a file, knife or similar object just enough to break through it accomplishes this.

Commercial growers often use sulfuric acid to scarify batches of seed. However, acid scarification must be done with care since there is great danger from the chemical both to humans and to the embryo within the seed.

Seeds with a hard seed coat may also be boiled to soften the outer layer. Seeds are briefly placed in boiling water, removed from the heat and left to soak for a day or so before sowing.

A second kind of dormancy is known as embryo dormancy. In this case, seeds do not germinate due to factors in the embryo. Such seeds require a chilling period before they can germinate. Seeds are stratified, or layered in cold, moist conditions in a light medium such as peat or vermiculite for 1 to 12 weeks. This is similar to what occurs in nature when seeds mature in the fall. By spring, their dormancy has been broken, and they germinate.

Some chaparral plants require both treatment for hard seed coats and stratification for embryo dormancy. Ceanothus and manzanitas possess such double dormancy. Certain other species even require high heat treatment such as fire to break dormancy. Propagators pile straw atop a seed bed and set it afire to duplicate the periodic fires normal in the chaparral.

Leaching is required of seeds that contain chemical inhibitors. Seeds of desert plants such as creosote bush and guayule (*Parthenium argentatum*) are soaked in running water for several hours to remove inhibitors.

When seeds are ready, sow in a light medium if planting in flats or pots. A commercial potting mix or a mixture of 50 percent sand and 50 percent peat works well. Direct sowing in the ground is successful with some species. Using only native soil in containers is usually not recommended. If the soil contains a lot of clay, it will crust and crack as it dries and this can injure the emerging seedlings. The standard rule is to plant the seed at twice the depth of its narrowest width. Very small seed should just barely be covered. Water well using a fine spray so as not to disrupt the seeds. Keep them moist but not flooded with water as they germinate.

Cuttings

Cuttings can be made from several plant parts: stems, roots and sometimes leaves. Stem cuttings are the most commonly used for asexual propagation, and include softwood, semihardwood and hardwood cuttings.

Softwood cuttings are made from the new, soft, tip growth a plant makes in spring and early summer. Many plants, especially shrubs, are successfully grown from softwood cuttings. Clip off about a 4-in. (10-cm) section of new tip growth. Remove the leaves on the bottom half of the cutting, leaving a few to several on the top portion.

The cutting is now ready to be treated with a rooting hormone. This step is optional for the home grower trying a few cuttings. Products such as Hormodin and Rootone can be purchased at garden centers for more ambitious projects. These are available as powders and contain plant hormones known as auxins, such as indole butyric acid (IBA) and/or naphthalene acetic acid (NAA), which stimulate rooting. Dip the base of the cutting in the powder. Commercial growers use rooting hormones routinely and often make their own.

Experts swear by various planting media for cuttings. Basically what is needed is a very light, porous media that new roots can grow into. A 50:50 mixture of perlite and vermiculite or perlite and peat is popular. Such a mixture retains moisture but is also well-aerated. Peat moss can also be added to the perlite-vermiculite mix. Even sand alone may work for the do-it-yourselfer. Put the mix in a shallow container and place cuttings in it (leaves should remain above the mix).

A moist environment is needed. Add enough water to the mix so that it drains through the bottom. In addition, leaves need high humidity to absorb moisture since no roots are present. Commercial growers use "mist benches" to grow cuttings. These benches use an irrigation mist system that turns on at timed intervals to keep moisture and humidity levels high. The home owner can create a humid environment by erecting a clear plastic cover over the container and periodically misting the cuttings. Clear plastic wrap such as that used for food storage works well. The cover should not be airtight.

Bottom heat of 75–80°F (24–27°C) supplied by heating cables increases the rooting percentage of many species. Again, this is more useful and practical for the commercial grower. Roots usually become visible in a period of two to three weeks. However, some plants may take less time, others longer.

Some plants are more successfully grown from semihardwood cuttings taken in midsummer or fall when growth is not as succulent as in spring. Most of the manzanitas propagate best this way. Semihardwood cuttings are prepared much the same way as softwood cuttings.

Hardwood cuttings are made from wood taken in the dormant season. Ash and olive trees and roses can be started from hardwood cuttings. Typically, these cuttings are about 6–12 in. (15–30 cm) long and the width of a small finger. However, cottonwoods can grow from even baseball bat-sized cuttings stuck in the ground. Bury hardwood cuttings directly in the ground in late fall or winter with just 1 or 2 nodes or buds above ground. Irrigate once a week in the absence of rainfall. After two to three months, roots will form at the nodes that are buried.

Once cuttings have adequate roots, transplant them into an appropriate-sized container of potting mix and water thoroughly. After the roots become well-developed in the container, the plants will be ready for the garden.

CHAPTER 6

Individual
Plant Descriptions

Plants are listed alphabetically by their botanical names, such as *Elaeagnus angustifolia*. An informal guide to pronounciation is provided for botanical names, with the stressed syllable in italics. The common name or names—in this case, Russian olive—follow. Common names are cross-referenced against botanical names in the Appendix.

The individual plant descriptions detail the plant's physical features, including form, leaf characteristics and outstanding qualities, and help in identification. Following is an explanation of the terms used in these plant descriptions:

Family: A broad designation of plants which share some general physical characteristics.

Deciduous: Drops all leaves on an annual basis.

Evergreen: Foliage remains green throughout the year.

Semideciduous: May be evergreen all year with mild winter conditions; will drop some to all leaves with colder temperatures.

Evergreen to deciduous: Shrubs and vines that lose foliage or die back with frost but are likely to be evergreen in mild winter areas.

Perennial: Lifespan of more than two years but not long-lived and lacking woody stems.

Height: The likely height—such as 20–25 ft. (6–7.5 m)—under average conditions, depending on where planted, how watered, and so on.

Spread: The likely width of the canopy—such as 15–20 ft. (4.5–6 m)—under average conditions, depending on where planted, how watered, and so on.

Rate of growth: Fast = for shrubs, reaching full size within two growing seasons; for trees, an annual growth of around 3 ft. (1 m). Moderate = for shrubs, reaching full size in 3–5 growing seasons; for trees, an annual growth of about 1–2 ft. (30–60 cm). Slow = for shrubs and trees, annual growth of less than 1 ft. (30 cm). These are rough guidelines, based on average cultural conditions, but they are a good indication of what to expect from a particular plant.

Light requirement: Sun = plant needs a minimum of 6–8 hours a day. Partial shade = plant needs less than 6 hours of sun daily, or grows well under trees or a filtered canopy. Shade = plant itself is in the shade, such as under an overhang or tree or under open sky against a north wall.

Native to: Geographical area and/or plant community (such as chaparral or coastal sage-scrub) of native habitat, often a clue to a plant's cultural needs or possible problems.

Flower and fruit: Physical descriptions of flowers and fruits and the season when they usually are present. Note, however, that in warm climates flowering can occur almost any time of year. For example, palo verdes can bloom in late summer after heavy summer rains. Those plants which have toxic fruit or flowers are noted.

Landscape uses: The best ways to use the plant, for example, as a shade tree, as a specimen or as a large shrub for screening in exposed, difficult sites.

Climate adaption: Provides a plant's cold hardiness range, its heat tolerance and areas in which it grows well.

Culture: Watering, fertilizing, pruning and propagation recommendations. Plants which have no special soil needs are listed as having minimal soil requirements. In the case of watering, recommendations are for a plant already established in the landscape (a process which usually requires a year or two after planting) and growing in average soil. Light, sandy soils will require more frequent watering; heavy soils, or those with poor drainage, will need less frequent watering. See Chapter 5 for more specific details.

Possible problems: Suggests the difficulties gardeners may experience, or points to why it might be wise to avoid a plant under certain circumstances. For example, a short-lived tree may die after growing normally in the landscape for 20 years or so, which will be a problem if the gardener has not anticipated this. Some plants may self-propagate, or naturalize, when this is not desirable. Also listed are common and often fatal diseases of the Southwest landscape such as oak root fungus, Texas root rot and verticillium wilt.

Acacia

PRONOUNCER: ah-*kay*-sha
FAMILY: Leguminosae

The acacias include about 1,200 species of trees or shrubs with diverse foliage and form. Many are widely used as landscape ornamentals. One reason, of course, is their showy, puffball blooms—actually compact heads of tiny flowers. But in arid regions, many also have proven rugged and drought-resistant, providing shade, shelter and color with minimal attention.

Acacia foliage falls into two categories: they have either bipinnate (twice-divided, feathery-type) leaves or phyllodes. Phyllodes are modified leaf stalks performing the role of true leaves and are thought to have been an adaption to conserve water. They occur on most acacias native to Australia.

Acacias vary greatly in their tolerance of soil conditions. Some thrive only in acid soils, some need alkaline conditions while others are quite adaptable. In landscapes in arid regions, those species whose native habitat is sandy soils require good drainage. Others survive in areas of low rainfall and clay soil because the soil never becomes saturated. A few also show a marked tolerance for waterlogged soils, enabling them to withstand periods of flooding.

Nitrogen fertilization of acacias is not recommended, unless plants are growing poorly and need stimulation. Many acacias naturally fix nitrogen, thus enriching the surrounding soil, although such nitrogen fixation does not occur in all soils. Due to their generally fast rate of growth, excess nitrogen often stimulates rank, weak growth and may even cause premature death. Some species are naturally short-lived, dying after 20–30 years, and overfertilizing accentuates this trait.

Limit pruning to removing lower branches to create an overhead canopy (important for thorny species in traffic areas), light shaping, or occasional thinning of interior branches. Heavy pruning overstimulates growth and can shorten lifespan.

Except for the infrequent, deep irrigation most of them like, the following acacias—if planted in the right situation—are basically low maintenance, trouble-free and usually best left to their own growth processes.

Acacia abyssinica　　　PLATE 1

PRONOUNCER: ah-*kay*-sha ab-ah-*sin*-i-cah
COMMON NAME: Abyssinian acacia

Semideciduous. Height: 20–30 ft. (6–9 m). Spread: 25–30 ft. (7.5–9 m). Rate of growth: Moderate. Light requirement: Sun. Native to Africa.

A graceful tree with finely textured, medium green foliage that provides a lush tropical look and light shade; has an open, airy canopy with upright branch structure; feathery leaves are 5–11 in. (13–28 cm) long and are divided into tiny leaflets; the smooth gray bark becomes rough and dark in maturity; thornless.

FLOWER AND FRUIT: Creamy white-to-yellow, mildly fragrant puffball flowers in the spring, followed by brown pods about 5 in. (13 cm) long.

LANDSCAPE USES: A specimen tree for patio or lawn, or in groups for a grove effect; foliage creates a cooling, oasis feel; a better—hardier—choice than jacaranda, which it resembles.

CLIMATE ADAPTION: Hardy to around 20°F (−6.5°C) but may lose some leaves if the temperatures drop suddenly; heat tolerant; best in low- and mid-elevation deserts and inland southern California.

CULTURE: Needs good drainage; tolerates alkaline soil. Minimal water requirement but looks best with deep, supplemental amounts every 2–3 weeks in the low desert during the warmest months. Minimal fertilizer. Needs training to make a single trunk; trim lower branches frequently while raising the crown above head level. Propagate by scarified seeds.

POSSIBLE PROBLEMS: Sucker growth in its interior; litter from leaves and pods.

Acacia acuminata

PRONOUNCER: ah-*kay*-sha ah-kew-mi-*nah*-tah
COMMON NAME: raspberry jam wattle

Evergreen. Height: 10–15 ft. (3–4.5 m). Spread: 8–12 ft. (2.5–3.5 m). Rate of growth: Fast. Light requirement: Sun. Native to Australia.

A small, upright tree with pendulous, long, narrow phyllodes that are medium green and up to 10 in. (25 cm) in length; gray bark and branches.

FLOWER AND FRUIT: Bright yellow flowers in 1-in. (2.5-cm) spikes in the spring, followed by slender pods.

LANDSCAPE USES: Provides light shade in patio areas or in background plantings.

CLIMATE ADAPTION: Best for coastal and inland southern California and California's Central Valley, where it is frost tolerant.

CULTURE: Needs good drainage; tolerates alkaline soil. Minimal water requirement; likes infrequent, summer watering in warmest areas. Little to no fertilizer. Prune to shape as needed. Propagate by scarified seeds.

POSSIBLE PROBLEMS: May be hard to find.

Acacia aneura　　　　PLATE 2

PRONOUNCER: ah-*kay*-sha ah-*nur*-ah
COMMON NAME: mulga

Evergreen. Height: 15–20 ft. (4.5–6 m). Spread: 12–15 ft. (3.5–4.5 m). Rate of growth: Moderate. Light requirement: Sun. Native to Australia.

A large shrub or a small, spreading tree with an airy canopy of silvery gray-green foliage; narrow phyllodes tend to vary from needlelike to flat to cylindrical and are 1–3 in. (2.5–8 cm) long.

FLOWER AND FRUIT: Yellow flowers in 0.75-in. (2-cm) spikes in the spring are followed by 1-in. (2.5-cm), flat, light brown pods.

LANDSCAPE USES: The foliage and flowers combine to make this a striking accent plant; or use as a large screen, hedge, space divider or specimen for a patio.

CLIMATE ADAPTION: Some branch damage around 20°F (−6.5°C) but recovers well in the spring; heat tolerant; widely adaptable but not for the higher desert.

CULTURE: Needs good drainage; tolerates alkaline soils. Drought tolerant; infrequent water in the summer or other periods of prolonged drought will keep it looking its best. Minimal fertilizer. Lightly trim lower branches to raise the leaf canopy above head level, if so desired. Propagate by scarified seeds.

POSSIBLE PROBLEMS: Heavy pod formation makes for unkempt look.

Acacia baileyana　　　　PLATE 3

PRONOUNCER: ah-*kay*-sha bay-lee-*ah*-nah
COMMON NAME: Bailey acacia

Evergreen. Height: 20–30 ft. (6–9 m). Spread: 20–40 ft. (6–12 m). Rate of growth: Fast. Light requirement: Sun. Native to Australia.

A spreading tree with a dense, round canopy; attractive, soft foliage is very finely divided, blue-green to silver-gray.

FLOWER AND FRUIT: Massive display of fragrant clusters of yellow puffballs in late winter; seed pods.

LANDSCAPE USES: Excellent specimen and shade tree for typical residential landscape; along roadsides or on banks. A much-used tree in California.

CLIMATE ADAPTION: Hardy in the 16–20°F (−9 to −6.5°C) range; best for coastal and inland southern California and California's Central Valley; not the best choice for desert conditions.

CULTURE: Needs good drainage. Needs occasional deep watering during the warmest months. Little to no fertilizer. Prune regularly to

shape, after flowering. Propagate by scarified seeds.

POSSIBLE PROBLEMS: Brittle wood; naturalizes; short lived.

Acacia baileyana 'Purpurea' has attractive, purplish new growth, but otherwise is the same.

Acacia berlandieri

PRONOUNCER: ah-*kay*-sha burr-lan-dee-*air*-eye
COMMON NAME: guajillo

Semideciduous. Height: 15–20 ft. (4.5–6 m). Spread: 18–20 ft. (5.5–6 m). Rate of growth: Moderate. Light requirement: Sun. Native to Texas and Mexico.

A large shrub or small, broad-crowned tree with delicate, feathery foliage; medium green leaves are 4–6 in. (10–15 cm) long and divided into tiny leaflets; bark is gray, becoming somewhat fissured on older trees.

FLOWER AND FRUIT: Fragrant, creamy to yellow spring flowers turn orange as they mature; flat pods 4–6 in. (10–15 cm) long in the summer are covered with minute, velvety hairs.

LANDSCAPE USES: Group for a barrier screen or use as an individual specimen for light shade in patio areas. Some are thorny so determine the projected use before selecting.

CLIMATE ADAPTION: Hardy to 10°F (−12°C); takes heat well; widely adaptable except for coastal areas.

CULTURE: Needs good drainage. Minimal water requirement but looks best with deep, monthly irrigation in the summer. Minimal fertilizer. Prune in late winter to train as a tree or to shape. Propagate by scarified seeds.

POSSIBLE PROBLEMS: Litter from pod shed.

Acacia constricta

PRONOUNCER: ah-*kay*-sha con-*strik*-tah
COMMON NAME: white thorn acacia, mescat acacia

Deciduous. Height: 10–18 ft. (3–5.5 m). Spread: 10–18 ft. (3–5.5 m). Rate of growth: Moderate. Light requirement: Sun. Native from Arizona to Texas and Mexico.

A large shrub or small tree with an open, airy habit; medium green leaves are finely divided, about 1–2 in. (2.5–5 cm) long. White thorns occur in pairs at the leaf nodes; the bark varies from gray to dark brown.

FLOWER AND FRUIT: Fragrant, small, yellow, ball-shaped flowers in clusters in spring and fall, followed by elongated seed pods that are constricted between the seeds.

LANDSCAPE USES: A large, informal hedge; for screening; as a background barrier shrub or, with supplemental watering and training, an attractive, small tree. Suitable for minimum maintenance areas.

CLIMATE ADAPTION: Hardy to 0°F (−18°C); heat tolerant; best in the deserts.

CULTURE: Minimal soil requirement. Drought tolerant; will leaf out more quickly during dry springs with supplemental irrigation and looks better with once-a-month deep watering in summer. Minimal fertilizer. Prune to shape in winter. Propagate by scarified seeds.

POSSIBLE PROBLEMS: Following a dry winter a plant may remain leafless until summer rains develop; thorns near walkways; naturalizes.

Acacia craspedocarpa   PLATE 4

PRONOUNCER: ah-*kay*-sha *crass*-ped-oh-car-pah

COMMON NAME: leatherleaf acacia, broadleaf mulga

Evergreen. Height: 9–12 ft. (2.75–3.5 m). Spread: 6–8 ft. (2–2.5 m). Rate of growth: Slow. Light requirement: Sun. Native to Australia.

A compact shrub with dense, upright branches and a rounded habit; oval, gray-green phyllodes are about 0.75 in. (2 cm) long and very leathery.

FLOWER AND FRUIT: Sulfur yellow puffball flowers in spikes about 0.5 in. (1.3 cm) long in spring, followed by flat, tan, 2-in. (5-cm) pods.

LANDSCAPE USES: An effective, sturdy shrub for hedges, screening, background settings or areas receiving minimal maintenance. Can be trained as a small tree.

CLIMATE ADAPTION: Moderately frost tolerant; no heat problems; best for low- and mid-elevation deserts and California's Central Valley.

CULTURE: Needs good drainage. Very drought tolerant; survives without extra water once established, but once-a-month supplemental watering in summer increases its growth rate and improves its appearance. Minimal fertilizer. Prune after bloom, but this is not required unless training or to control size. Propagate by scarified seeds.

POSSIBLE PROBLEMS: Slow growth.

Acacia cyclops   PLATE 5

PRONOUNCER: ah-*kay*-sha *sy*-klops

COMMON NAME: round-seeded acacia

Evergreen. Height: 10–15 ft. (3–4.5 m). Spread: 12–20 ft. (3.5–6 m). Rate of growth: Fast. Light requirement: Sun to part shade. Native to Australia.

A wide-spreading, dense shrub with a billowy appearance; narrow, light green phyllodes are up to 3.5 in. (9 cm) long.

FLOWER AND FRUIT: Small, yellow puffballs in the early spring; brown pods, 2.5–4 in. (6–10 cm) long.

LANDSCAPE USES: Attractive screen or tall hedge for parks, roadsides or as windbreaks; vigorous and adaptable.

CLIMATE ADAPTION: Best for coastal and inland southern California and California's Central Valley, where it is frost tolerant; not for the deserts.

CULTURE: Minimal soil requirement. Drought tolerant but likes occasional summer watering in warmest areas. Little to no fertilizer. Tolerates shearing. Propagate by seeds or cuttings.

POSSIBLE PROBLEMS: Can become invasive.

Acacia decurrens

PRONOUNCER: ah-*kay*-sha de-*kur*-enz

COMMON NAME: green wattle

Evergreen. Height: 30–50 ft. (9–15 m). Spread: 30–50 ft. (9–15 m). Rate of growth: Fast. Light requirement: Sun. Native to Australia.

A spreading tree with lush-appearing, dark green canopy; feathery, finely divided leaves.

FLOWER AND FRUIT: Attractive display of golden yellow puffballs, February–March; narrow pods with constrictions between seeds.

LANDSCAPE USES: A specimen or shade tree that is most effective in larger residential and public areas.

CLIMATE ADAPTION: Hardy in the 16–20°F (−9 to −6.5°C) range; best for inland southern California and California's Central Valley; give it a protected location in coastal areas; does not like desert heat.

CULTURE: Minimal soil requirement; tolerates alkalinity. Needs occasional deep watering in summer in warmest areas. No fertilizer needed. Prune to shape after flowering, as necessary. Propagate by scarified seeds.

POSSIBLE PROBLEMS: Litter; invasive roots; young trees need protection from frost; short lived.

Acacia farnesiana. See A. smallii

Acacia greggii

PRONOUNCER: ah-*kay*-sha *greg*-ee-eye

COMMON NAME: catclaw

Deciduous. Height: 15–20 ft. (4.5–6 m). Spread: 12–15 ft. (3.5–4.5 m). Rate of growth: Moderate. Light requirement: Sun. Native to the Southwest and adjoining Mexico.

A multibranched, open, spreading tree or shrub with rough, dark bark; feathery, gray-green foliage with 1–3 in. (2.5–8 cm) leaves; tenacious prickles similar to a cat's claw are scattered along the branches.

FLOWER AND FRUIT: Lightly fragrant, creamy flower spikes in the late spring and sometimes in the fall; in nonirrigated situations, flowers only after a moist winter; curved, brown, 3-in. (8-cm) pods; quails love the seeds.

LANDSCAPE USES: A barrier shrub or, with supplemental irrigation and training, an attractive specimen or shade tree with distinctive character. Avoid planting close to areas with heavy foot-traffic.

CLIMATE ADAPTION: Hardy to about 0°F (−18°C); heat tolerant; best for the deserts.

CULTURE: Needs good drainage. Minimal water requirement; looks best with a monthly soaking in the warmer months. Minimal fertilizer. Prune the lower branches to shape in January; accentuate the natural outline and structure. Propagate by scarified seeds.

POSSIBLE PROBLEMS: Thorny twigs and branches.

Acacia longifolia

PRONOUNCER: ah-*kay*-sha lon-ji-*foh*-lee-ah
COMMON NAME: Sydney golden wattle

Evergreen. Height: 10–20 ft. (3–6 m). Spread: 15–20 ft. (4.5–6 m). Rate of growth: Fast. Light requirement: Sun. Native to Australia.

A vigorous, spreading, large shrub or small tree with leathery, narrow, bright green phyllodes 3–6 in. (8–15 cm) long; roots along the ground and can spread quite a distance.

FLOWER AND FRUIT: Bright yellow spikes in the early spring; leathery pods to 5 in. (13 cm).

LANDSCAPE USES: Effective for screening or erosion control, especially in sandy areas; good for roadside plantings; resistant to oak root fungus.

CLIMATE ADAPTION: Best for coastal and inland southern California and California's Central Valley, where it is frost tolerant; not for the deserts.

CULTURE: Prefers good drainage. Likes a deep watering every 2–3 weeks in summer in warmest areas. Little to no fertilizer. Prune to shape or to keep in bounds after bloom. Propagate by cuttings or seeds.

POSSIBLE PROBLEMS: Can become invasive; short life span.

Acacia minuta. See A. smallii

Acacia pendula   PLATE 6

PRONOUNCER: ah-*kay*-sha *pen*-dyoo-lah
COMMON NAME: weeping acacia, weeping myall

Evergreen. Height: 20–25 ft. (6–7.5 m). Spread: 12–15 ft. (3.5–4.5 m). Rate of growth: Slow. Light requirement: Sun. Native to Australia.

A small, graceful tree with a rounded crown and willowlike, weeping branches and foliage; handsome, silvery blue-gray phyllodes are narrow, lance-shaped and about 1.5–4 in. (4–10 cm) long.

FLOWER AND FRUIT: Yellow puffballs in spring, followed by winged pods.

LANDSCAPE USES: This slow growing, long-lived tree in time develops into a refined and elegant specimen; it deserves a special place in the garden where its beauty can be easily observed and appreciated; the foliage provides a soft textural and color contrast and a cascade effect over walls.

CLIMATE ADAPTION: Frost and heat tolerant except for the higher deserts.

CULTURE: Prefers good drainage. Drought tolerant but likes monthly, deep irrigation in the summer in the warmest areas. Minimal fertilizer needed. Remove lower branches to shape in the spring. Propagate by seeds; limited success with cuttings.

POSSIBLE PROBLEMS: Becomes chlorotic in heavier soils; slow growth.

Acacia pennatula

PRONOUNCER: ah-*kay*-sha pen-nah-*too*-lah
COMMON NAME: coquete

Semideciduous. Height: 10–25 ft. (3–7.5 m). Spread: 15–25 ft. (4.5–7.5 m). Rate of growth: Slow. Light requirement: Sun. Native to the Sonoran Desert of Mexico south into northern South America.

A graceful, small, spreading tree with beautiful, very fine, feathery foliage; light green leaves are 5–7 in. (13–18 cm) long and divided into minute leaflets; bark is rough, dark gray; thorny.

FLOWER AND FRUIT: Rounded, yellow puffballs, February–July; flat, dark, 2.5–6 in. (6–15 cm) pods follow.

LANDSCAPE USES: Provides a dramatic, subtropical effect in locations sheltered from heavy frost; the fine foliage adds a soft texture to the landscape.

CLIMATE ADAPTION: Some frost damage around 25°F (−4°C); best for milder areas of the low desert; no heat problems.

CULTURE: Needs good drainage. Moderately drought tolerant; needs supplemental water every 2–3 weeks during the warmest months. Minimal fertilizer needed. Prune to shape in early spring. Propagate by seeds.

POSSIBLE PROBLEMS: Slow recovery from cold damage and may need heavy pruning of frost-damaged branches.

Acacia podalyriifolia   PLATE 7

PRONOUNCER: ah-*kay*-sha poh-dah-leer-ee-eye-*foh*-lee-ah
COMMON NAME: pearl acacia

Evergreen. Height: 12–20 ft. (3.5–6 m). Spread: 10–15 ft. (3–4.5 m). Rate of growth:

Fast. Light requirement: Sun. Native to Australia.

A rounded, large shrub or small tree with an upright to spreading form; densely covered with oval to oblong, light gray phyllodes, 1.5 in. (4 cm) long.

FLOWER AND FRUIT: Yellow flower clusters, November–March, followed by flat, 2–3 in. (5–8 cm) pods.

LANDSCAPE USES: Works well as a specimen or a background plant; combine with other plants to contrast its attractive foliage.

CLIMATE ADAPTION: Best for coastal and inland southern California and California's Central Valley, where it is frost and heat tolerant.

CULTURE: Prefers good drainage. Drought tolerant, but likes a deep soaking every 3–4 weeks in summer in hotter locations. Little to no fertilizer. Prune after flowering to shape, control growth, or train as a tree. Propagate by seeds.

POSSIBLE PROBLEMS: Wind damage.

Acacia redolens   PLATES 8 AND 9

PRONOUNCER: ah-*kay*-sha *red*-o-lenz
COMMON NAME: ongerup acacia, trailing acacia
Evergreen. Height: 1–5 ft. (30 cm–1.5 m). Spread: 8–10 ft. (2.5–3 m). Rate of growth: Very fast. Light requirement: Sun. Native to Australia.

A horizontal-spreading to rounded shrub; leathery, narrow, gray-green, 1–4 in. (2.5–10 cm) leaves; the growth habit and leaf size can be quite variable, especially among seed-grown plants.

FLOWER AND FRUIT: Tiny, yellow flower balls in early spring; 1–2 in. (2.5–5 cm), light brown pods follow.

LANDSCAPE USES: A tough, drought- and heat-resistant plant for bank and slope plantings and erosion control; often planted en masse as a ground cover, but the potential height can sometimes be a problem when used that way. Effective as a barrier; combines well with other arid-type plants. Space 6 ft. (2 m) apart as the plants fill in rapidly. A new cultivar, 'Desert Carpet', developed and trademarked by Mountain States Nursery in Phoenix, is much lower growing than the species.

CLIMATE ADAPTION: Hardy to about 20°F (−6.5°C); thrives in heat; widely adaptable except for the higher deserts, where plants show variations in their cold tolerance.

CULTURE: Minimal soil requirement; accepts alkaline or saline soils. Drought tolerant; does best with deep watering every 3–4 weeks in the summer in the hottest areas. Minimal fertilizer needed. Prune to shape in the early spring; can be clipped as a low hedge. Propagate by cuttings or seeds.

POSSIBLE PROBLEMS: Short lived with poor drainage.

Acacia salicina   PLATE 10

PRONOUNCER: ah-*kay*-sha sal-i-*see*-nah
COMMON NAME: willow acacia
Evergreen. Height: 20–30 ft. (6–9 m). Spread: 12–18 ft. (3.5–5.5 m). Rate of growth: Fast. Light requirement: Sun. Native to Australia.

Pendulous branchlets and medium green, smooth, somewhat glossy foliage give it an overall willowlike appearance; narrow, 5–6 in. (13–15 cm) phyllodes have undulating margins; bark is gray becoming rough on older trees.

FLOWER AND FRUIT: Subtly fragrant, cream-colored clusters of puffballs in spring; light brown seed pods follow.

LANDSCAPE USES: As a single specimen or in groups or rows for screening; adapts well to narrow areas such as entryways and patios. Not for planting in lawns as shallow watering encourages surface rooting which increases likelihood of being blown over. Attractive, shimmering foliage with little leaf and pod shed.

CLIMATE ADAPTION: Hardy to about 20°F (−6.5°C); heat tolerant; widely adaptable except for higher deserts.

CULTURE: Prefers heavier soils and good drainage; no problem with alkaline soils. Withstands long periods of drought but looks best with monthly, deep irrigation in the summer. Fertilize minimally with ammonium sulfate in the early spring; overfertilizing can cause excessive top growth. Prune lower branches to provide headroom and visibility. Propagate by scarified seeds.

POSSIBLE PROBLEMS: Young trees are more cold sensitive.

Acacia saligna   PLATE 11

PRONOUNCER: ah-*kay*-sha sah-*lig*-nah
COMMON NAME: goldwreath acacia
Evergreen. Height: 18–20 ft. (5.5–6 m). Spread: 15–20 ft. (4.5–6 m). Rate of growth: Very fast. Light requirement: Sun to part shade. Native to Australia.

A thornless tree with a dense, rounded canopy; the deep lustrous green foliage has a clean look; the phyllodes are narrow, lance-shaped, 6–7 in. (15–18 cm) long and somewhat variable in width.

FLOWER AND FRUIT: Masses of puffball, golden yellow flowers in March; papery, light brown pods follow.

LANDSCAPE USES: One of the showiest acacias in bloom; a fine choice also for quick shade. The canopy creates an ideal privacy screen; plant in rows or groups about 15 ft. (4.5 m) apart or as a single specimen. Dark green foliage imparts lush quality to the landscape; provides erosion control.

CLIMATE ADAPTION: Frost and heat tolerant except for the higher deserts.

CULTURE: Minimal soil requirement. Looks best with deep, monthly irrigation in the summer in the hottest areas. No fertilizer needed. Prune to shape in the spring. Propagate by scarified seeds.

POSSIBLE PROBLEMS: Short lived.

Acacia schaffneri PLATE 12

PRONOUNCER: ah-*kay*-sha *shaf*-ner-eye
COMMON NAME: twisted acacia

Semideciduous. Height: 20–25 ft. (6–7.5 m). Spread: 20–25 ft. (6–7.5 m). Rate of growth: Moderate. Light requirement: Sun. Native to the Chihuahuan Desert of Texas and Mexico and to South America.

A distinctive tree with an interesting, somewhat gnarled-looking habit; branches seem to reach down and twist around, creating a striking silhouette. Dark green, feathery, divided leaves are up to 1.75 in. (4.5 cm) long and held closely to the thorny branches; the dark brown to black bark has deep ridges.

FLOWER AND FRUIT: Fragrant, yellow flower balls about 0.5 in. (1.3 cm) across in the spring; slender, dark brown pods, about 3–5 in. (8–13 cm) long follow.

LANDSCAPE USES: A unique specimen tree with a strong character; place it where its irregular growth habit and twisted branches are set off; the dense, spreading canopy provides good shade; also excellent as a screen or barrier plant.

CLIMATE ADAPTION: Loses leaves around 20°F (−6.5°C) but survives in temperatures an additional 10°F (−5°C) lower; does fine in heat; best for the low- and mid-elevation deserts.

CULTURE: Needs good drainage. Drought tolerant, but appreciates supplemental, deep watering monthly during the warmest months. Minimal fertilizer needed. Prune to shape in winter. Propagate by seeds.

POSSIBLE PROBLEMS: Young trees tend to be more cold sensitive.

Acacia smallii PLATE 13

PRONOUNCER: ah-*kay*-sha *small*-ee-eye
COMMON NAME: sweet acacia, huisache

Semideciduous. Height: 20–30 ft. (6–9 m). Spread: 25–30 ft. (7.5–9 m). Rate of growth: Fast. Light requirement: Sun to partial shade. Native from west Texas to southern California.

Description: An attractive, large shrub or single- or multitrunked, small tree with a dense, umbrellalike canopy; bright green, finely divided leaves, 1–4 in. (2.5–10 cm) long; 1-in. (2.5-cm) thorns in pairs at the leaf bases. Also known as *A. farnesiana* and *A. minuta*.

FLOWER AND FRUIT: Small, yellow flower balls in spring and fall are fragrant and ornamental; thick, dark brown pods, 2–3 in. (5–8 cm) long follow.

LANDSCAPE USES: Excellent as a street, shade or patio tree; plant in rows 15 ft. (4.5 m) apart for a dense screen; the lush, feathery foliage creates an oasis effect in the desert landscape.

CLIMATE ADAPTION: Hardy to about 10°F (−12°C); drops leaves during cold winters; thrives in heat; best for the deserts although some cold damage is possible at higher elevations.

CULTURE: Prefers good drainage; tolerates alkalinity. Can survive on only rainfall but looks better with monthly irrigation in the summer. Minimal fertilizer needed. Keep lower branches trimmed, especially near people-traffic areas; looks best if grown as a multitrunked tree; try to accentuate its natural vase-shaped habit. Propagate by scarified seed.

POSSIBLE PROBLEMS: Pod shed looks messy in well-maintained areas.

Acacia stenophylla PLATE 14

PRONOUNCER: ah-*kay*-sha sten-*off*-i-lah
COMMON NAME: shoestring acacia

Evergreen. Height: 20–40 ft. (6–12 m). Spread: 15–20 ft. (4.5–6 m). Rate of growth: Fast. Light requirement: Sun. Native to Australia.

A slender, upright tree with an attention-demanding silhouette and a weeping effect; shoestringlike, gray-green phyllodes about 1 ft. (30 cm) long hang from the branches; reddish brown bark contrasts nicely with the light-colored foliage.

FLOWER AND FRUIT: Creamy white puffballs, few in number, in the fall and the spring; slender, tan pods resembling a string of beads follow.

LANDSCAPE USES: A fine specimen tree or grouped in small groves as a visual screen; a good choice for poor soil and drought conditions; generally pest and disease free.

CLIMATE ADAPTION: Hardy to about 20°F (−6.5°C); heat tolerant; widely adaptable except for the higher deserts.

CULTURE: Prefers good drainage; takes alkaline soils. Drought tolerant; does best with monthly, summer irrigation. Minimal fertilizer needed.

Remove lower branches as desired to provide headroom. Propagate by seeds.

POSSIBLE PROBLEMS: Young trees often look sparse.

Acacia willardiana   PLATE 15

PRONOUNCER: ah-*kay*-sha will-ard-ee-*ah*-nah

COMMON NAME: palo blanco

Deciduous. Height: 10–25 ft. (3–7.5 m). Spread: 5–15 ft. (1.5–4.5 m). Rate of growth: Fast. Light requirement: Sun. Native to the Sonoran Desert of Mexico.

A distinctive small tree with peeling, silver-white bark and sparse, weeping foliage; medium green leaves have flattened petioles and are divided into small leaflets; thornless.

FLOWER AND FRUIT: Eye-catching white puffballs in the spring are followed by 4–8 in. (10–20 cm) pods.

LANDSCAPE USES: A specimen tree with a light, airy effect or for small groupings.

CLIMATE ADAPTION: Best for the mainly frost-free areas of the low desert.

CULTURE: Needs good drainage. Drought tolerant; likes monthly, deep watering in summer. Minimal fertilizer needed. Lightly trim lower branches until trunk growth reaches head level. Propagate by seeds.

POSSIBLE PROBLEMS: Cold sensitivity.

Agave

PRONOUNCER: ah-*gah*-vee

FAMILY: Agavaceae

Agaves are bold-appearing inhabitants of arid landscapes and make stunning accent plants with their fleshy, succulent leaves arising spirally in a rosette. Most are of easy culture in warm climates providing the soil drains well. They prefer light or rocky soil. Heavy clay conditions are a problem.

Often called century plants, many agaves literally take decades to produce blooms. When they do flower, they send up tall stalks that grow very rapidly. In many species, flower and seed production result in the death of the mother plant, but she already has ensured reproduction through offshoots at her base.

Heat and drought pose no problems for most agave species, although some of the larger forms suffer in the low desert's sun. Cold tolerance varies. In hot climates, heavy watering at the time the flowering stalk appears encourages flower development. Otherwise, water once a month should be sufficient in warm weather. They need no irrigation in cold weather.

Agaves are subject to sudden collapse due to two dissimilar pests: agave snout weevil and gophers. Fortunately, these problems seldom arise simultaneously. Gophers eat the short, central stem, which is full of soft, succulent tissue. Larvae of the black, 0.5-in. (1.3-cm) weevil eat the soft tissue as well as carry a harmful fungus. Native species seem to be resistant. Scattering granular insecticide in the spring around the base provides a control.

Agave americana   PLATE 16

PRONOUNCER: ah-*gah*-vee ah-mer-i-*cah*-nah

COMMON NAME: century plant

Evergreen. Height: 5–6 ft. (1.5–2 m). Spread: 5–6 ft. (1.5–2 m). Rate of growth: Slow. Light requirement: Sun. Native to Mexico but it is cultivated in Mediterranean-type climates around the world.

A large, commonly used agave with bluish gray leaves 5–6 ft. (1.5–2 m) long, 6–9 in. (15–23 cm) wide, lined with prominent teeth. Some varieties or cultivars have leaves with white or yellow margins or stripes.

FLOWER AND FRUIT: Flowers after 10 years or more with a 15–40 ft. (4.5–12 m) flower stalk that produces yellowish flowers, after which the mother plant dies; brown seed capsules. The common name derives from the erroneous notion that the plant requires 100 years to flower.

LANDSCAPE USES: A very bold, striking appearance that harmonizes well with other succulents, or contrasts well with soft-textured shrubs; needs space to develop so not suitable for the typical residential landscape; keep it away from foot-traffic areas.

CLIMATE ADAPTION: May suffer some frost damage after extended periods around 20°F (−6.5°C); those with marginated leaves are much less cold hardy.

CULTURE: Minimal soil requirement, even accepts shallow soils. Low water user, but needs small amounts in the warmest months to look its best. No fertilizer. Prune to groom by removing lower, browning leaves. Propagate by seeds or offsets.

POSSIBLE PROBLEMS: Space requirements; wind may bend the flower stalk in the middle; agave snout weevil; produces many offsets; gophers.

Agave deserti

PRONOUNCER: ah-*gah*-vee *dez*-ert-eye

COMMON NAME: desert agave

Evergreen. Height: 1–2 ft. (30–60 cm). Spread: 1.5–2.5 ft. (45–75 cm). Rate of growth: Slow. Light requirement: Sun. Native to the Mojave and Sonoran deserts.

A small agave often found growing in large

colonies; gray-green to bluish leaves, 6–16 in. (15–40 cm) long with a prominent terminal spine.

FLOWER AND FRUIT: Yellow flowers on tall stalks develop after about 12 years; thick-walled seed capsules.

LANDSCAPE USES: Most effective in groups for rock and succulent gardens, or combined with shrubs. Once a food staple for Indians, who ate parts of the leaves, flowers and stalks.

CLIMATE ADAPTION: Hardy to at least 20°F (−6.5°C); heat tolerant; widely adaptable except for the higher desert.

CULTURE: Prefers good drainage. Very drought tolerant; grows more rapidly with summer watering. Wait a month after transplanting before watering to avoid fungus problems. Minimal fertilizer. Prune to groom. Propagate by seeds or offsets.

POSSIBLE PROBLEMS: Suckers; invasive; wildlife like to browse; gophers.

Agave gracilipes is frequently found growing in the wild with *A. lechuguilla*; it reaches about 1 ft. (30 cm) tall with an equal spread and is hardy to at least 10°F (−12°C) and quite heat tolerant.

Agave lechuguilla

PRONOUNCER: ah-*gah*-vee lech-oo-*gwee*-ah
COMMON NAME: lechuguilla

Evergreen. Height: 1–2 ft. (30–60 cm). Spread: 2–3 ft. (60–90 cm). Rate of growth: Slow. Light requirement: Sun. Native to southern New Mexico and western Texas, south into Mexico; an indicator plant for the Chihuahuan Desert.

A small, upright plant often seen in extensive clumps; the narrow, stiff, yellow- to gray-green leaves have small, sharp spines along the margins.

FLOWER AND FRUIT: Yellow to white flowers on a 3–12 ft. (1–3.5 m) flower stalk; blooms a few years after planting and does not always die after bloom; seed capsules are brown to black.

LANDSCAPE USES: A nice, low, understory plant; use in small groupings in borders and rock gardens or as a ground cover. Leaves are important commercially as a source of hard fibers used in brushes and rope.

CLIMATE ADAPTION: Hardy to at least 15°F (−9°C); best for the deserts.

CULTURE: Likes dry, alkaline and limestone soils. Very drought tolerant; extra water monthly in dry summer periods keeps the leaves plump. No fertilizer. Prune to groom. Propagate by offsets.

POSSIBLE PROBLEMS: Poisonous leaves; suckers widely.

Agave lophantha is a close relative of *A. lechuguilla* with a more attractive, spreading habit and darker green leaves; it is not widely available.

Agave murpheyi

PRONOUNCER: ah-*gah*-vee *murf*-ee-eye
COMMON NAME: Murphey agave

Evergreen. Height: 2–2.5 ft. (60–75 cm). Spread: 3–3.5 ft. (about 1 m). Rate of growth: Slow. Light requirement: Sun. Native to the Sonoran Desert of Arizona and Mexico.

A medium-sized agave with light green leaves 1.5–2 ft. (45–60 cm) long and 2–3 in. wide (5–8 cm); very little variation among plants; expands by freely suckering rosettes.

FLOWER AND FRUIT: Flower clusters with purplish to brownish tips on a thick, 10–12 ft. (3–3.5 m) stalk that often starts growing in the winter. Flowers in 12–15 years. Beaked seed capsules.

LANDSCAPE USES: Accent plant or in small groupings.

CLIMATE ADAPTION: Suffers some damage around 25°F (−4°C); best for low desert.

CULTURE: Needs good drainage. Minimal water and fertilizer required. Prune to groom. Propagate by bulbils, the small bulbs that grow on the stalk.

POSSIBLE PROBLEMS: Slow growth; cold sensitivity; gophers.

Agave parryi var. huachucensis   PLATE 17

PRONOUNCER: ah-*gah*-vee *pair*-ee-eye watch-oo-*sen*-sis
COMMON NAME: Huachuca agave

Evergreen. Height: 2–3 ft. (60–90 cm). Spread: 2–3 ft. (60–90 cm). Rate of growth: Moderate. Light requirement: Sun. Native to the Huachuca Mountains of Arizona.

A compact, very symmetrical agave with light gray-green leaf blades up to 1 ft. (30 cm) wide at the base with a prominent spine at the leaf tip.

FLOWER AND FRUIT: Greenish yellow blossoms occur on 6–15 ft. (2–4.5 m) stalks in the summer; plants bloom after 25 years or so; fruit is a capsule.

LANDSCAPE USES: Combine with other succulents or desert plants; neat, compact habit; one of the most attractive agaves.

CLIMATE ADAPTION: Hardy to about 10–15°F (−12 to −9°C); best for the deserts.

CULTURE: Needs good drainage. Very drought tolerant; give supplemental water only during long periods of drought. No fertilizer or pruning required. Propagate by seeds or offsets.

POSSIBLE PROBLEMS: Gophers.

49

Aloe barbadensis

Agave parryi var. *truncata* is a small, short-stemmed, light gray plant well-suited to containers and rock gardens; blooms in about 20 years.

Agave shawii   PLATE 18
PRONOUNCER: ah-*gah*-vee *shaw*-ee-eye
COMMON NAME: Shaw's century plant
Evergreen. Height: 2–3 ft. (60–90 cm). Spread: 3–4 ft. (about 1 m). Rate of growth: Slow. Light requirement: Sun. Native to Baja California but rare in California's adjacent San Diego County.
A small agave with dark green, glossy blades edged with prominent white teeth.
FLOWER AND FRUIT: Greenish to orange flowers on stalks to 12 ft. (3.5 m) high; seeds in capsules.
LANDSCAPE USES: Plant in small groupings or in borders; good scale for residential yards; handsome foliage.
CLIMATE ADAPTION: Hardy to about 24°F (−4°C); best for coastal and inland southern California, where it thrives on foggy conditions and higher humidity; not for the deserts.
CULTURE: Needs good drainage. Needs monthly watering in summer in warmer areas. No fertilizer. Prune as needed to groom. Propagate by seeds or offsets.
POSSIBLE PROBLEMS: Cold sensitivity; gophers.

Agave vilmoriniana   PLATE 19
PRONOUNCER: ah-*gah*-vee vil-mor-in-ee-*ah*-nah
COMMON NAME: octopus agave
Evergreen. Height: 3–4 ft. (about 1 m). Spread: 4–6 ft. (1.2–2 m). Rate of growth: Slow. Light requirement: Sun. Native to frost-free cliffs of Mexico's Sierra Madre.
Twisted, arching leaves 3 in. (8 cm) wide give this succulent the look of an octopus, which accounts for the common name; pale green rosettes with smooth leaf margins, single spine at leaf tip; very attractive.
FLOWER AND FRUIT: White or yellow flowers after about 15 years; seed capsules.
LANDSCAPE USES: Unusual accent or specimen plant for arid landscapes; group for dramatic effect; better than other agaves near people-traffic areas.
CLIMATE ADAPTION: Hardy to about 20°F (−6.5°C); best for the low- and mid-elevation deserts and coastal and inland southern California.
CULTURE: Needs good drainage. Likes monthly supplemental water in hottest areas. No fertilizer or pruning. Propagate by seeds or offsets.
POSSIBLE PROBLEMS: Gophers.

Aloe
PRONOUNCER: *al*-oh
FAMILY: Liliaceae
The aloes make striking accent plants for milder areas and are eye-catching in bloom. Their succulent rosettes bear fleshy flowers on tall stalks which last for several weeks in the landscape. They have been grown in the mid-elevation deserts with some success, if they are placed in a sheltered spot.

Aloe arborescens   PLATE 20
PRONOUNCER: *al*-oh ar-bor-*ess*-enz
COMMON NAME: giant aloe
Evergreen. Height: 9–18 ft. (2.75–5.5 m). Spread: 5–9 ft. (1.5–2.75 m). Rate of growth: Slow. Light requirement: Sun to part shade. Native to South Africa.
This succulent eventually develops a treelike appearance with a branched trunk supporting leaf rosettes; dull green leaves with red, spiny margins taper narrowly to a point.
FLOWER AND FRUIT: Tall, vertical stalks are tipped with orange flowers in spring; seed capsules follow.
LANDSCAPE USES: A striking accent plant; particularly effective in rock gardens. Combine with other succulents or tropical-looking plants.
CLIMATE ADAPTION: Cold damage occurs around 30°F (−1°C) but may survive lower temperatures; best for coastal and mild inland areas of southern California.
CULTURE: Needs good drainage. Wants only small to moderate amounts of supplemental watering. Little to no fertilizer needed. Remove old flower stalks to maintain the plant's appearance. Propagate by seeds or offsets.
POSSIBLE PROBLEMS: Cold sensitivity; branches somewhat brittle.

Aloe barbadensis   PLATE 21
PRONOUNCER: *al*-oh bar-bah-*den*-sis
COMMON NAME: aloe vera
Evergreen. Height: 1–1.5 ft. (30–45 cm). Spread: 5–8 ft. (1.5–2.5 m) clumps. Rate of growth: Slow. Light requirement: Sun to partial shade. Native to North Africa.
A succulent with upright, spiky, narrow, gray-green leaves in a rosette.
FLOWER AND FRUIT: Large, narrow, yellow or orange flowers on a 3-ft. (1-m) stalk in the spring; seed capsules follow.
LANDSCAPE USES: Provides a quite dramatic point in desert landscapes; is handsome in containers, rock gardens, or in combinations with other desert plants. The sap has been used since ancient times to treat burns and skin problems.

CLIMATE ADAPTION: Hardy to about 25°F (−4°C); no heat problems; best for the low deserts and the coastal and inland areas of southern California.

CULTURE: Minimal soil requirement. Minimal water requirement but looks better in the low desert with supplemental water every three weeks in the summer. Apply 2 oz. (57 g) ammonium sulfate in the spring after the plant is established. Groom after it blooms. Propagate by offsets or seeds.

POSSIBLE PROBLEMS: Thrips sometimes deform leaves; cold sensitivity.

Aloe saponaria PLATE 22

PRONOUNCER: *al*-oh sap-oh-*nar*-ee-ah

COMMON NAME: African aloe

Evergreen. Height: 8–15 in. (20–38 cm). Spread: 4–5 ft. (1.2–1.5 m) clumps. Rate of growth: Slow. Light requirement: Sun to partial shade. Native to South Africa.

A clumping succulent with spiky, sometimes mottled leaves in a rosette form; the leaves are pale to medium green with brown teeth around the edges; plants are greener when grown in the shade.

FLOWER AND FRUIT: Striking, fleshy, red or orange flowers atop a 20-in. (50-cm) stalk provide a long period of color in the spring and occasionally the fall; seed capsules follow.

LANDSCAPE USES: A color- and textural-accent plant for desert groupings; effective with other succulent-type plants.

CLIMATE ADAPTION: Frost tender, but recovers quickly in the spring; takes heat; best for the low deserts and mild inland and coastal areas of southern California.

CULTURE: Needs a loose soil with good drainage. Quite minimal water requirement but needs an occasional, supplemental irrigation to produce plump leaves. Apply 2 oz. (57 g) ammonium sulfate after the first year in the landscape. Prune to remove flower stalks and to groom. Divide clumps that have spread too widely. Propagate by seeds or offsets.

POSSIBLE PROBLEMS: Thrips occasionally deform plants; may become scraggly due to spreading or cold.

Ambrosia

PRONOUNCER: am-*bro*-zha

FAMILY: Compositae

The bursages are hardy and abundant natives of the Southwest. The white bursage, *Ambrosia dumosa*, together with creosote bush, forms a large plant community in the Sonoran Desert.

Where moisture is less limiting, the triangle-leaf bursage, *A. deltoidea*, appears. These drought-hardy shrubs survive extreme temperatures and aridity in the wild by limiting their growing season to those occasions when moisture is readily available and temperatures moderate.

In the landscape, drought-dormancy can be prevented by periodic watering. Plants become lush with supplemental water and light fertilizer. While bursages can go nearly unnoticed, they provide a natural, rugged and authentic desert appearance and are useful for native gardens, nonirrigated or naturalized areas, roadsides and land reclamation sites.

Their common name is derived from the small, burrlike fruit they produce. Plants have separate male and female flowers and are wind pollinated. The pollen triggers allergies in some people.

Ambrosia deltoidea PLATE 23

PRONOUNCER: am-*bro*-zha del-*toy*-dee-ah

COMMON NAME: triangle-leaf bursage, burrobush

Evergreen. Height: 2–3 ft. (60–90 cm). Spread: 2–3 ft. (60–90 cm). Rate of growth: Slow to moderate. Light requirement: Sun. Native to Sonoran Desert, where it commonly is seen in association with the palo verde.

A low, rounded shrub with gray-green, narrow triangular leaves that are 0.5–1.5 in. (1.3–4 cm) long and covered with fine, woolly hairs; branches are erect, whitish.

FLOWER AND FRUIT: Insignificant, tiny, whitish flowers lacking petals, December–April; burr-like fruits with flattened spines follow.

LANDSCAPE USES: A natural to combine with plants such as brittlebush, cassia, fairy duster and palo verde; use along roadsides, transitional or naturalized (wild-growing) areas.

CLIMATE ADAPTION: Not as cold hardy as *A. dumosa*; tolerant of intense heat; best for low- and mid-elevation deserts.

CULTURE: Needs soil with good drainage. Very drought tolerant; becomes quite lush with supplemental water every three weeks through summer months. Minimal fertilizer but responds to small amounts of nitrogen during growing periods. Prune lightly in spring if needed. Propagate by softwood cuttings or seeds.

POSSIBLE PROBLEMS: Wind pollination of flowers triggers allergies in some people; drought brings on dormancy which makes plants appear quite straggly.

Ambrosia dumosa

PRONOUNCER: am-*bro*-zha doo-*moh*-sah
COMMON NAME: white bursage, burrobush

Evergreen. Height: 8 in.–2 ft. (20–60 cm). Spread: 1–3 ft. (30–90 cm). Rate of growth: Slow to moderate. Light requirement: Sun. Very common plant in Sonoran Desert, extending into Mojave Desert, from low to mid-elevations.

Low, densely branched shrub with rounded habit; white branches bear deeply lobed, gray-green leaves about 1 in. (2.5 cm) long.
FLOWER AND FRUIT: Insignificant, small, petalless flower clusters in spring and fall; small burrlike fruits with flattened spines.
LANDSCAPE USES: As low cover in naturalized areas, combined with creosote bush and similar natives.
CLIMATE ADAPTION: Cold and heat hardy from low to higher deserts.
CULTURE: Needs good drainage. Very drought tolerant, but looks best with supplemental water every three weeks in summer. Minimal fertilizer but does better with small amounts of nitrogen during the growing season. No pruning required. Propagate by softwood cuttings or seeds.
POSSIBLE PROBLEMS: Browsed by sheep and burros; pollen causes allergies; can look straggly during drought.

Anisacanthus thurberi

PRONOUNCER: ah-nis-ah-*can*-thus *thur*-bur-eye
FAMILY: Acanthaceae
COMMON NAME: desert honeysuckle, desert chuparosa

Evergreen to deciduous. Height: 3–8 ft. (1–2.5 m). Spread: 4–5 ft. (1.2–1.5 m). Rate of growth: Slow. Light requirement: Sun. Native to canyons and along washes at 2,500–5,500 ft. (760–1,670 m) in Arizona, New Mexico, and south into northern Mexico.

A long-blooming shrub with light green foliage on erect branches; leaves are oblong to lance-shaped, 0.5–2 in. (1.3–5 cm) long; gray to white, peeling bark.
FLOWER AND FRUIT: Showy, 1.5 in. (4 cm), tubular, orange-red flowers with long stamens in spring and intermittently throughout the rest of the year; small, flat fruit capsules follow.
LANDSCAPE USES: Mix with other desert plants or plant in small groups to provide long periods of color in the landscape; does well in minimum-maintenance areas.
CLIMATE ADAPTION: Best in deserts; may lose foliage or die back in frost but recovers in spring; excellent heat tolerance.

CULTURE: Quite tolerant of soil conditions. Minimal water requirement; for best appearance, water deeply twice a month in the summer. Minimal fertilizer. Prune in early spring to remove any frost damage, or following bloom to promote bushiness. Propagate by cuttings or seeds.
POSSIBLE PROBLEMS: Can look somewhat twiggy and sparse without occasional pruning.

Antigonon leptopus   PLATE 24

PRONOUNCER: an-*tig*-o-non *lep*-toh-pus
FAMILY: Polygonaceae
COMMON NAME: queen's wreath, coral vine

Evergreen to deciduous. Height: 10–40 ft. (3–12 m). Spread: 20–30 ft. (6–9 m). Rate of growth: Very fast. Light requirement: Sun. Native to Mexico.

In warm areas with a long growing season, queen's wreath becomes a vigorous, spreading vine with tropical-looking foliage and brilliant flowers; bright green leaves are about 4 in. (10 cm) long, arrowhead-shaped. Climbs by tendrils so needs support. Reaches the size noted above if not cut back periodically by frost.
FLOWER AND FRUIT: Flower sprays usually pink but a white 'Album' and a deep pink-red cultivar 'Baja Red' are available; blooms from midsummer through fall, followed by abundant seeds that look much like buckwheat.
LANDSCAPE USES: Low-maintenance shade-cover for trellis or on south- or west-facing fences and walls; good late summer color.
CLIMATE ADAPTION: Widely adaptable; loves heat but frosts limit size and roots need protective mulching at about 20°F (−6.5°C); remains evergreen to about 28°F (−2°C).
CULTURE: Quite tolerant of soil conditions. Minimal water requirement, but moderate amounts in the summer every 7–14 days provide more flowers in the low desert. Minimize fertilizer: too much produces vegetative growth at the expense of flowering. Remove dead growth caused by frost. Propagate by seeds or cuttings.
POSSIBLE PROBLEMS: Flowers attract bees; plants need support; self-sows.

Arbutus unedo   PLATE 25

PRONOUNCER: ar-*bew*-tus yoo-*nee*-doh
FAMILY: Ericaceae
COMMON NAME: strawberry tree

Evergreen. Height: 15–30 ft. (4.5–9 m). Spread: 15–30 ft. (4.5–9 m). Rate of growth: Slow to moderate. Light requirement: Sun, except needs shade in hottest areas. Native to the Mediterranean region.

Large shrub or small tree with dense canopy of rich, dark green foliage; oblong, 2–3 in. (5–8 cm) leaves with toothed margins; trunk with reddish brown, shredding bark; becomes gnarled, picturesque with age. Dwarf cultivars available.

FLOWER AND FRUIT: White, urn-shaped flowers in clusters in fall; distinctive, red, strawberrylike, edible fruits are present into winter.

LANDSCAPE USES: Handsome specimen tree; suitable for lawn situations; also for screens or background plantings. Fall and winter decorative fruits. Resistant to oak root fungus. Dwarfs do well in large containers.

CLIMATE ADAPTION: Widely adaptable; hardy to at least 10°F (−12°C); thrives in cooler climates of coastal, inland and interior California; withstands desert heat if planted in shade.

CULTURE: Prefers good drainage, otherwise quite tolerant of soil conditions. Minimal water requirement but accepts moderate amounts if soil drains well. Apply 4 oz. (115 g) of ammonium sulfate in early spring to speed growth. Remove lower branches to train as a tree and expose attractive trunk. Propagate by seeds or semihardwood cuttings.

POSSIBLE PROBLEMS: Somewhat slow to develop; fruit litter.

Arctostaphylos

PRONOUNCER: ark-toh-*staff*-i-los
FAMILY: Ericaceae

The manzanitas are among the most picturesque native plants of the western United States. Their leathery leaves and small, dainty flowers appear atop thick, gnarled branches possessing a distinctive, smooth, deep red to brown surface.

There are 40 or so species of these woody evergreens in California alone, where they occur in coastal, chaparral, and foothill woodland communities. They hybridize readily in the wild and many forms and cultivars have been developed for horticultural use. Growth habit varies from large, treelike forms to medium-high, spreading shrubs to low, carpetlike ground covers.

They are inappropriate for desert landscapes where the high heat and low humidity overwhelm them. In coastal, inland, and interior California, they are hardy and drought tolerant.

The foliage always appears clean and neat. Leaves range in color from deep green to pale gray and emerge vertically around the stem.

New growth regularly adds attractive tinges of red or bronze. Winter and early spring bring white to pinkish clusters of bell-shaped flowers at the branch ends. The small, applelike fruits which follow give the plant its common name, manzanita, or "little apple" in Spanish.

Their growth cycle offers important clues about their planting and care. Winter and early spring are active periods of flowering and vegetative growth. As growth stops in the spring, next year's flower buds are formed. They remain dormant until the following season. Landscape planting is therefore best done in the fall just before growth begins. Winter and early spring are the best time to fertilize if needed. Propagation by cuttings also coincides with this cycle. Any pruning required to shape plants should be done immediately after flowering, so that this year's growth and next year's flower buds are not removed.

Once established, they require little care. Most benefit from well-spaced irrigation during the summer months or periods of long drought. Keep them away from lawn sprinklers. Many species and hybrids are quite adaptable to different soil conditions, provided their care corresponds to those conditions.

Arctostaphylos densiflora 'Howard McMinn'

PRONOUNCER: ark-toh-*staff*-i-los den-si-*flor*-ah
COMMON NAME: McMinn manzanita

Evergreen. Height: 4–6 ft. (1.2–2 m). Spread: 5–6 ft. (1.5–2 m). Rate of growth: Moderate. Light requirement: Sun to partial shade. A selection of *A. densiflora*.

A dense, rounded to spreading shrub with bright green, leathery, oval leaves held on reddish twigs; neat, clean foliage.

FLOWER AND FRUIT: Small, urn-shaped, white to pinkish flowers in the late winter and early spring, followed by small, fleshy berries.

LANDSCAPE USES: Quite adaptable and dependable for screening, on slopes or as a specimen; handsome foliage combines with a neat growth habit; does well under oaks. Generally disease free.

CLIMATE ADAPTION: Hardy to about 15°F (−9°C); best for coastal and inland southern California; needs afternoon shade in California's Central Valley; not for the deserts.

CULTURE: Likes a heavy loam soil. Needs deep watering every 3–4 weeks in the summer in the warmest areas. Fertilize iightly from late fall through early spring, as needed. Prune to shape immediately following bloom; tip-prune to encourage denser growth. Propagate by semihardwood cuttings.

POSSIBLE PROBLEMS: Overwatering; lighter soils tend to cut lifespan.

Arctostaphylos edmundsii
PRONOUNCER: ark-toh-*staff*-i-los ed-*munz*-ee-eye
COMMON NAME: Little Sur manzanita

Evergreen. Height: 3–4 ft. (1 m). Spread: 3–5 ft. (1–1.5 m). Rate of growth: Slow. Light requirement: Sun to part shade. Native to Monterey County, California.

A very refined-looking, small manzanita; bright green, rounded leaves to 1 in. (2.5 cm) long with reddish margins on spreading branches; plants root along the ground.
FLOWER AND FRUIT: Dainty, creamy pink blossoms are abundant, December-February; small, brown berries.
LANDSCAPE USES: Nice for massing or for mixed borders; does well under oaks.
CLIMATE ADAPTION: Best for coastal and inland southern California; appreciates part shade in warmer, inland locations; not for the deserts or California's Central Valley.
CULTURE: Likes a heavy loam soil. Needs deep watering every 2–3 weeks in the summer in inland areas. Little to no fertilizer. Prune to shape immediately following bloom; responds to shearing. Propagate by semihardwood cuttings.
POSSIBLE PROBLEMS: Overwatering.

Arctostaphylos edmundsii 'Carmel Sur' has gray-green foliage and good garden tolerance.

Arctostaphylos 'Emerald Carpet'   PLATE 26
COMMON NAME: emerald carpet manzanita

Evergreen. Height: 1–1.5 ft. (30–45 cm). Spread: 3–6 ft. (1–2 m). Rate of growth: Moderate to fast. Light requirement: Sun to part shade. Cultivar.

A ground-hugging manzanita with neat, compact growth; rich green, glossy leaves are 0.5-in. (1.3-cm) ovals that densely cover the prostrate branches.
FLOWER AND FRUIT: The small, pale pink flowers in the spring are relatively limited; small berries.
LANDSCAPE USES: Attractive ground cover for small areas, or massed for larger plantings and slopes; a natural for rock gardens. Handsome foliage has a deep, lustrous quality that offsets other plants well; good choice under oaks. Less susceptible to manzanita branch dieback.
CLIMATE ADAPTION: Hardy to about 15°F (−9°C); best for coastal and inland southern California and California's Central Valley; needs partial shade in the warmest areas.
CULTURE: Best with good drainage; does not like alkaline soil. Needs deep watering every 2–3 weeks in the warmest areas. Little to no fertilizer. Prune as needed immediately after bloom to keep within bounds. Propagate by semihardwood cuttings.
POSSIBLE PROBLEMS: Soil requirement.

Arctostaphylos manzanita   PLATE 27
PRONOUNCER: ark-toh-*staff*-i-los man-zah-*nee*-tah
COMMON NAME: common manzanita

Evergreen. Height: 6–20 ft. (2–6 m). Spread: 6–12 ft. (2–3.5 m). Rate of growth: Moderate. Light requirement: Sun to part shade. Native to the foothills and chaparral of the Sierra Nevada and the interior side of the Coast Range of California.

A large shrub that often assumes a treelike form with thick, crooked, reddish brown branches; rounded leaves are 1.5 in. (4 cm) long and vary from pale to dark green.
FLOWER AND FRUIT: Abundant, drooping clusters of white to pink flowers, February-April; white berries later turn red.
LANDSCAPE USES: Tree-form plants make attractive specimens with bold character, or use as a high, informal screen; long lived.
CLIMATE ADAPTION: Frost tolerant; best for coastal and inland southern California and California's Central Valley; not for the deserts.
CULTURE: Minimal soil requirement. Drought tolerant but likes occasional watering every 4–6 weeks through dry summer months in the warmest areas. Little to no fertilizer. Tip-prune immediately after bloom for denser foliage; shape to accentuate unique form, as desired. Propagate by semihardwood cuttings.
POSSIBLE PROBLEMS: Not as adaptable to garden conditions as some of the cultivars.

Arctostaphylos manzanita 'Dr. Hurd' is smaller, with light green leaves, and adapts well to landscape conditions.

Arctostaphylos pajaroensis
PRONOUNCER: ark-toh-*staff*-i-los *pah*-hah-roh-en-sis
COMMON NAME: Pajaro manzanita

Evergreen. Height: 3–10 ft. (1–3 m). Spread: 4–10 ft. (1.2–3 m). Rate of growth: Moderate. Light requirement: Sun to partial shade. Native to Monterey County, California.

A picturesque, upright shrub with dark red, exfoliating bark; oval to triangle-shaped leaves are gray-green and to 1.25 in. (3 cm) long; new growth has an attractive pinkish tinge.
FLOWER AND FRUIT: White to pink, dense flower clusters, December–January; light red fruits

0.25 in. (0.5 cm) across.

LANDSCAPE USES: As a specimen or background shrub or for screening; foliage creates a handsome contrast with many other plants.

CLIMATE ADAPTION: Frost tolerant; best for coastal and inland southern California; needs afternoon shade in California's Central Valley; not for the deserts.

CULTURE: Minimal soil requirement; accepts clay soil with good drainage. Likes deep watering every 2–3 weeks in summer in warmest areas. Little to no fertilizer. Prune only lightly, and then immediately after flowering. Propagate by cuttings in spring.

POSSIBLE PROBLEMS: Hard to find in nurseries.

Arctostaphylos rudis

PRONOUNCER: ark-toh-*staff*-i-los *roo*-dis
COMMON NAME: shagbark manzanita

Evergreen. Height: 2–5 ft. (60 cm–1.5 m). Spread: 2–4 ft. (60 cm–1.2 m). Rate of growth: Moderate. Light requirement: Sun to part shade. Native to San Luis Obispo and Santa Barbara counties of California.

A rounded shrub with shredding, reddish brown bark and gray branchlets; elliptic to oval, medium green leaves are 0.5–1.2 in. (1.3–3 cm) long.

FLOWER AND FRUIT: Pinkish flower clusters, November–February; the small, rounded fruits are brownish red.

LANDSCAPE USES: A durable shrub for low screens and borders or for mass plantings.

CLIMATE ADAPTION: Best for coastal and inland southern California; good choice for California's Central Valley, where it does best with afternoon shade; not for the deserts.

CULTURE: Needs good drainage. Needs summer watering every 3–4 weeks in interior areas. Little to no fertilizer. Prune to shape, immediately after flowering. Propagate by semihardwood cuttings.

POSSIBLE PROBLEMS: Overwatering.

Artemisia

PRONOUNCER: ar-tuh-*meezh*-ee-ah
FAMILY: Compositae

Sagebrush is one of those terms that seems synonymous with the western United States. And, for good reason, since the grayish, sometimes silvery, shrubs cover vast areas of the West's arid terrain. Several of these artemisias are very valuable in landscape plantings thanks to their foliage characteristics, informal appeal and durability. The often finely cut foliage is handsomely set off by other plants. Most require full sun and rapid-draining soils but are generally pest free and need little to no fertilizer.

Artemisia californica   PLATE 28

PRONOUNCER: ar-tuh-*meezh*-ee-ah cal-i-*for*-ni-cah
COMMON NAME: California sagebrush

Evergreen. Height: 2–5 ft. (60 cm–1.5 m). Spread: 3–6 ft. (1–2 m). Rate of growth: Fast. Light requirement: Sun. Native to coastal northern California south to Baja.

Shallow-rooting shrub with narrow, dull, gray-green leaves; very commonly found in California's coastal sage-scrub community. The cultivar 'Canyon Gray' forms a dense, silvery-gray mat less than 1 ft. (30 cm) high and 3 ft. (1 m) across.

FLOWER AND FRUIT: Tiny, greenish flowers are not showy, from late summer into early winter; one-seeded fruits follow.

LANDSCAPE USES: Useful for erosion control on slopes, for revegetation sites, in naturalized areas mixed with other plants, or as a low hedge or divider.

CLIMATE ADAPTION: Best in coastal and inland California.

CULTURE: Minimal soil requirement. Drought tolerant, but requires summer water in inland areas every 3–4 weeks to prevent dropping of leaves. Little to no fertilizer. Prune in the winter for denser growth. Propagate by seeds or cuttings.

POSSIBLE PROBLEMS: Sometimes has scrubby appearance; not for areas subject to fire.

Artemisia caucasica

PRONOUNCER: ar-tuh-*meezh*-ee-ah caw-*cas*-i-cah
COMMON NAME: silver spreader

Evergreen. Height: 3–6 in. (8–15 cm). Spread: 1–2 ft. (30–60 cm). Rate of growth: Moderate. Light requirement: Sun. Native to Caucasus Mountains of USSR.

Very low shrub that forms a ground-hugging, silvery green mound; leaves are very finely dissected.

FLOWER AND FRUIT: Small, yellow flowers in summer.

LANDSCAPE USES: Good for borders and rock gardens mixed with other plants in small areas; not suitable for mass planting. Fire resistant.

CLIMATE ADAPTION: Takes heat and cold of Southwest coastal areas to low deserts.

CULTURE: Minimal soil requirement. Drought tolerant but needs occasional summer water in low deserts. Little to no fertilizer. Remove old flower heads and any dead limbs. Propagate by seeds.

POSSIBLE PROBLEMS: Short lived; can die back.

PLATE 1. *Acacia abyssinica*

PLATE 2. *Acacia aneura*

PLATE 3. *Acacia baileyana*

PLATE 4. *Acacia craspedocarpa*

PLATE 5. *Acacia cyclops*

PLATE 6. *Acacia pendula*

PLATE 7. *Acacia podalyriifolia*

PLATE 8. *Acacia redolens*

PLATE 9. *Acacia redolens* 'Desert Carpet'

PLATE 10. *Acacia salicina*

PLATE 11. *Acacia saligna*

PLATE 12. *Acacia schaffneri*

PLATE 13. *Acacia smallii*

PLATE 14. *Acacia stenophylla*

PLATE 16. *Agave americana*

PLATE 15. *Acacia willardiana*

PLATE 17. *Agave parryi* var. *huachucensis*

PLATE 18. *Agave shawii*

PLATE 19. *Agave vilmoriniana*

PLATE 20. *Aloe arborescens*

PLATE 21. *Aloe barbadensis*

PLATE 22. *Aloe saponaria*

PLATE 23. *Ambrosia deltoidea*

PLATE 24. *Antigonon leptopus*

PLATE 25. *Arbutus unedo*

PLATE 26. *Arctostaphylos* 'Emerald Carpet'

PLATE 27. *Arctostaphylos manzanita*

PLATE 28. *Artemisia californica*

PLATE 29. *Artemisia ludoviciana*

PLATE 30. *Artemisia pycnocephala*

PLATE 31. *Artemisia tridentata*

PLATE 32. *Asparagus densiflorus* 'Sprengeri'

PLATE 33. *Atriplex canescens*

PLATE 34. *Atriplex semibaccata*

PLATE 35. *Baccharis* 'Centennial'

PLATE 36. *Baccharis pilularis* 'Twin Peaks'

PLATE 37. *Baccharis sarothroides*

PLATE 38. *Bougainvillea* 'Barbara Karst'

PLATE 39. *Brachychiton acerifolius*

PLATE 40. *Brachychiton populneus*

PLATE 41. *Brahea armata*

PLATE 42. *Buddleia marrubiifolia*

PLATE 43. *Butia capitata*

PLATE 44. *Caesalpinia cacalocoa*

PLATE 46. *Caesalpinia mexicana*

PLATE 45. *Caesalpinia gilliesii*

PLATE 47. *Caesalpinia pulcherrima*

PLATE 48. *Calliandra californica*

PLATE 49. *Calliandra eriophylla*

PLATE 51. *Carissa macrocarpa*

PLATE 50. *Callistemon phoeniceus*

PLATE 52. *Cassia artemisioides*

PLATE 53. *Cassia didymobotrya*

PLATE 54. *Cassia nemophila*

PLATE 56. *Cassia sturtii*

PLATE 55. *Cassia phyllodinea*

PLATE 57. *Cassia wislizenii*

PLATE 58. *Casuarina cunninghamiana*

PLATE 59. *Ceanothus* 'Blue Jeans'

PLATE 60. *Ceanothus* 'Concha'

PLATE 61. *Ceanothus* 'Dark Star'

PLATE 63. *Ceanothus* 'Joyce Coulter'

PLATE 62. *Ceanothus hearstiorum*

PLATE 64. *Ceanothus* 'Julia Phelps'

PLATE 65. *Ceanothus ramulosus* var. *fascicularis*

PLATE 66. *Ceanothus* 'Ray Hartman'

PLATE 67. *Ceanothus rigidus* 'Snowball'

PLATE 68. *Celtis pallida*

PLATE 69. *Ceratonia siliqua*

PLATE 70. *Cercidium floridum*

PLATE 71. *Cercidium microphyllum*

PLATE 72. *Cercidium praecox*

PLATE 74. *Cercocarpus betuloides*

PLATE 73. *Cercis occidentalis*

PLATE 75. *Chamaerops humilis*

PLATE 76. *Chilopsis linearis*

PLATE 77. *Cistus purpureus*

PLATE 78. *Comarostaphylis diversifolia*

PLATE 79. *Convolvulus cneorum*

PLATE 80. *Cordia boissieri*

PLATE 81. *Cordia parvifolia*

PLATE 82. *Cotoneaster buxifolius*

PLATE 83. *Cupressus arizonica*

PLATE 84. *Dalbergia sissoo*

PLATE 85. *Dalea bicolor* var. *argyraea*

PLATE 86. *Dalea greggii*

PLATE 87. *Dalea spinosa*

PLATE 88. *Dalea versicolor*

PLATE 89. *Dasylirion wheeleri*

PLATE 90. *Dendromecon harfordii*

PLATE 91. *Dietes vegeta*

PLATE 92. *Diplacus longiflorus*

PLATE 93. *Dodonaea viscosa*

PLATE 94. *Drosanthemum floribundum*

PLATE 95. *Elaeagnus angustifolia*

PLATE 96. *Encelia californica*

PLATE 97. *Encelia farinosa*

PLATE 98. *Eriogonum arborescens*

PLATE 99. *Eriogonum crocatum*

PLATE 100. *Eriogonum fasciculatum*

PLATE 101. *Eriogonum giganteum*

PLATE 103. *Eucalyptus calophylla*

PLATE 102. *Erythrina flabelliformis*

PLATE 104. *Eucalyptus citriodora*

PLATE 105. *Eucalyptus formanii*

PLATE 106. *Eucalyptus leucoxylon* 'Rosea'

PLATE 107. *Eucalyptus microtheca*

PLATE 108. *Eucalyptus nicholii*

PLATE 109. *Eucalyptus papuana*

PLATE 110. *Eucalyptus polyanthemos*

PLATE 111. *Eucalyptus spathulata*

PLATE 112. *Feijoa sellowiana*

PLATE 113. *Fouquieria splendens*

PLATE 114. *Fraxinus velutina*

PLATE 115. *Fremontodendron californicum*

PLATE 116. *Fremontodendron* 'California Glory'

PLATE 117. *Garrya elliptica*

PLATE 118. *Geijera parviflora*

PLATE 119. *Genista aethnensis*

PLATE 120. *Grevillea lanigera*

PLATE 121. *Grevillea robusta*

PLATE 122. *Hesperaloe parviflora*

PLATE 123. *Heteromeles arbutifolia*

PLATE 124. *Isomeris arborea*

PLATE 125. *Juniperus sabina* 'Tamariscifolia'

PLATE 126. *Justicia californica*

PLATE 127. *Justicia candicans*

PLATE 128. *Justicia spicigera*

PLATE 129. *Lantana camara* 'Radiation'

PLATE 131. *Larrea tridentata*

PLATE 130. *Lantana montevidensis*

PLATE 132. *Lavandula angustifolia*

PLATE 133. *Lavandula stoechas*

PLATE 134. *Leptospermum laevigatum*

PLATE 135. *Leptospermum scoparium* 'Ruby Glow'

PLATE 136. *Leucaena retusa*

PLATE 137. *Leucophyllum candidum* 'Silver Cloud'

PLATE 138. *Leucophyllum frutescens*

PLATE 139. *Leucophyllum laevigatum*

PLATE 140. *Lupinus albifrons*

PLATE 141. *Lysiloma thornberi*

PLATE 142. *Macfadyena unguis-cati*

PLATE 143. *Mahonia* 'Golden Abundance'

PLATE 144. *Mahonia nevinii*

PLATE 145. *Mahonia pinnata*

PLATE 146. *Mascagnia macroptera*
DON PINKAVA

PLATE 147. *Melampodium leucanthum*

PLATE 148. *Mimosa dysocarpa*

PLATE 149. *Muhlenbergia dumosa*

PLATE 150. *Myoporum parvifolium*

PLATE 151. *Myrtus communis*

PLATE 152. *Nandina domestica*

PLATE 153. *Nerium oleander* 'Petite Pink'

PLATE 154. *Nolina microcarpa*

PLATE 155. *Oenothera berlandieri*

PLATE 156. *Oenothera caespitosa*

PLATE 157. *Olea europaea*

PLATE 158. *Olneya tesota*

PLATE 159. *Parkinsonia aculeata*

PLATE 160. *Pennisetum setaceum* 'Cupreum'

PLATE 161. *Penstemon eatoni*

PLATE 162. *Penstemon palmeri*

PLATE 163. *Penstemon parryi*

PLATE 164. *Penstemon pseudospectabilis*

PLATE 165. *Penstemon spectabilis*

PLATE 166. *Phoenix dactylifera*

PLATE 167. *Pinus eldarica*

PLATE 168. *Pinus roxburghii*

PLATE 169. *Pistacia chinensis*

PLATE 170. *Pithecellobium flexicaule*

PLATE 171. *Pittosporum phillyraeoides*

PLATE 172. *Podranea ricasoliana*

PLATE 173. *Prosopis glandulosa*

PLATE 174. *Prosopis* hybrid

PLATE 175. *Punica granatum*

PLATE 176. *Quercus agrifolia*

PLATE 177. *Quercus lobata*

PLATE 178. *Quercus virginiana* 'Heritage'

PLATE 179. *Rhamnus californica*

PLATE 180. *Rhus integrifolia*

PLATE 181. *Rhus lancea*

PLATE 182. *Rhus trilobata*

PLATE 183. *Ribes speciosum*

PLATE 184. *Romneya coulteri*

PLATE 185. *Rosmarinus officinalis* 'Collingwood Ingram'

PLATE 186. *Ruellia peninsularis*

PLATE 188. *Salvia clevelandii*

PLATE 187. *Salvia chamaedryoides*

PLATE 189. *Salvia farinacea*

PLATE 190. *Salvia greggii*

PLATE 191. *Salvia leucantha*

PLATE 192. *Santolina chamaecyparissus*

PLATE 193. *Sophora secundiflora*

PLATE 194. *Tabebuia impetiginosa*
TERRY MIKEL

PLATE 195. *Tagetes lemmonii*

PLATE 196. *Tecoma stans* var. *angustata*

PLATE 197. *Teucrium fruticans* var. *compactum*

PLATE 198. *Trichostema lanatum*

PLATE 199. *Ungnadia speciosa*

PLATE 200. *Vauquelinia californica*

PLATE 201. *Verbena gooddingii*

PLATE 202. *Verbena rigida*

PLATE 203. *Verbena tenuisecta*

PLATE 204. *Viguiera dentata*

PLATE 205. *Viguiera laciniata*

PLATE 206. *Vitex agnus-castus*

PLATE 207. *Washingtonia filifera*

PLATE 208. *Washingtonia robusta*

PLATE 209. *Xylosma congestum* 'Compacta'

PLATE 210. *Yucca brevifolia*

PLATE 211. *Yucca elata*

PLATE 212. *Yucca recurvifolia*

PLATE 213. *Yucca rigida*

PLATE 214. *Yucca schidigera*

PLATE 215. *Yucca whipplei*

PLATE 216. *Zauschneria cana*

PLATE 217. *Zauschneria latifolia*

PLATE 218. *Zinnia grandiflora*

PLATE 219. *Ziziphus obtusifolia canescens*

55

Asparagus densiflorus 'Sprengeri'

Artemisia ludoviciana PLATE 29

PRONOUNCER: ar-tuh-*meezh*-ee-ah lood-oh-vis-ee-ah-nah
COMMON NAME: prairie sage

Evergreen. Height: 2–3 ft. (60–90 cm). Spread: 3–6 ft. (1–2 m). Rate of growth: Moderate to fast. Light requirement: Sun to part shade. Widespread in foothills and mountains west of Mississippi River.

Low-growing, spreading perennial with silvery gray-green leaves that are sometimes lobed and to 2 in. (5 cm) long; upright branches.
FLOWER AND FRUIT: Small, greenish flowers in 2-in. (5-cm) heads in summer and fall; one-seeded fruit follows.
LANDSCAPE USES: Attractive edging and low border plant, or ground cover; silvery foliage nice for contrast.
CLIMATE ADAPTION: Widely adaptable and very cold hardy; does better in low deserts with some afternoon shade.
CULTURE: Minimal soil requirement. Drought tolerant, but water occasionally in hottest weather. Little to no fertilizer. Prune to shape or contain. Propagate by cuttings or seeds.
POSSIBLE PROBLEMS: None.

Artemisia pycnocephala PLATE 30

PRONOUNCER: ar-tuh-*meezh*-ee-ah pik-no-*sef*-ah-lah
COMMON NAME: sandhill sage

Evergreen. Height: 1–2 ft. (30–60 cm). Spread: 3–4 ft. (about 1 m). Rate of growth: Fast. Light requirement: Sun to part shade. Native to coastal northern California and Oregon.

Low shrubby perennial; attractive, silvery gray leaves are finely dissected, 0.5–1 in. (1.3–2.5 cm) long.
FLOWER AND FRUIT: Small, yellow flowers on spikes occur in late spring and summer; small, brown seed heads follow.
LANDSCAPE USES: Creates handsome low border; soft texture and foliage color provide interesting contrasts. Useful as a revegetation plant.
CLIMATE ADAPTION: Best for coastal and inland southern California and California's Central Valley; requires partial shade in the hottest areas.
CULTURE: Tolerates light or heavy soils. Drought tolerant, but likes supplemental summer water every 2–3 weeks in warmest areas. Little to no fertilizer. Remove old flower heads. Propagate by seeds.
POSSIBLE PROBLEMS: Short lived; must be replaced about every three years.

Artemisia tridentata PLATE 31

PRONOUNCER: ar-tuh-*meezh*-ee-ah try-den-*tah*-tah
COMMON NAME: big sagebrush

Evergreen. Height: 1.5–6 ft. (45 cm-2 m) or more. Spread: 4–6 ft. (1.2–2 m). Rate of growth: Moderate to fast. Light requirement: Sun. Native to West and Southwest, becoming dominant in large areas of the Great Basin Desert at elevations from 1,500 to 10,600 ft. (450–3,300 m).

Rounded, gray-green shrub; strongly aromatic, wedge-shaped leaves are 0.5–1.5 in. (1.3–4 cm) long with usually three teeth at the tip; deep rooted.
FLOWER AND FRUIT: Small flower heads, August–October, not showy; small seed heads.
LANDSCAPE USES: Effective in naturalized areas; as specimen for foliar contrast or for erosion control on slopes and hillsides.
CLIMATE ADAPTION: Widely adaptable; takes extremes of heat and cold.
CULTURE: Needs good drainage. Very drought tolerant, but benefits from monthly deep watering in hotter areas during long periods of drought. Little to no fertilizer. Prune lightly to tidy plants or to expose interesting branch structure. Occasional heavy pruning stimulates growth. Propagate by seeds or with cuttings taken in spring.
POSSIBLE PROBLEMS: Pollen can trigger allergies; many animals and birds eat foliage and seeds.

Asparagus densiflorus 'Sprengeri' PLATE 32

PRONOUNCER: us-*pair*-uh-gus den-si-*flor*-us spren-gur-eye
FAMILY: Liliaceae
COMMON NAME: Sprenger asparagus

Evergreen. Height: 1–2 ft. (30–60 cm). Spread: 2–5 ft. (60 cm–1.5 m). Rate of growth: Moderate. Light requirement: Sun to part shade. Native to Africa.

A low, fernlike plant becoming a mound of light green, narrow, shiny leaves on trailing stems; very attractive. Thick, fleshy roots.
FLOWER AND FRUIT: Small, whitish flowers in the spring; red berries in the fall.
LANDSCAPE USES: Good choice for a lush focal point near entryways, as a ground cover in semishady locations, or in flower or raised-planting beds, and other protected areas. Attractive in containers. The foliage is much used in floral arrangements. A favorite plant of many generations.
CLIMATE ADAPTION: Plants freeze back about 25°F (−4°C) but recover quickly in the spring; best for coastal and inland southern California

where it can be grown in full sun. Likes some shade in California's Central Valley and in low- and mid-elevation deserts.

CULTURE: Likes good drainage and soil with added organic matter. Can take some drought but for best appearance, water every 1–2 weeks in the summer in warmer areas. Apply 2 oz. (57 g) ammonium sulfate in the spring; plants in alkaline soils may need added iron. Trim dead growth in spring; plants can also be cut back hard to rejuvenate. Propagate by fresh seeds or division of clumps.

POSSIBLE PROBLEMS: Iron chlorosis; occasional foliage dieback.

Atriplex

PRONOUNCER: *at*-ri-plex
FAMILY: Chenopodiaceae

The saltbushes are among the toughest plants for extremes of heat, drought and saline soil conditions. Found throughout the arid regions of the world, *Atriplex* grows on plains, along washes, and in alkali flats or sinks, sometimes becoming the dominant shrub in such areas. Their light gray foliage covered with scurfy scales reduces evapotranspiration while their roots and stems store moisture against prolonged periods of heat and drought.

In the landscape, saltbushes have an informal appeal and work well with other desert plants, especially as transition, boundary or barrier plants. They are valuable for erosion control and revegetation of disturbed, alkaline soil sites.

Give them regular watering as they get established. Once they are, they can survive on natural rainfall, but look healthier if given occasional deep irrigation during the driest months. Minimal nitrogen fertilizer speeds the growth of the slower-growing species; otherwise, fertilizer is not essential. Saltbushes can assume a rangy appearance with time, which is best corrected by occasional pruning to shape plants.

Atriplex canescens   PLATE 33

PRONOUNCER: *at*-ri-plex cah-*nes*-enz
COMMON NAME: four-wing saltbush

Evergreen. Height: 3–5 ft. (90 cm–1.5 m). Spread: 3–7 ft. (90 cm–2.2 m). Rate of growth: Slow. Light requirement: Sun. Widespread in the West, from California east into Texas; from eastern Washington to South Dakota; northern Mexico.

Tough, deep-rooted shrub with silvery gray foliage that varies from dense to sparse; narrow, linear leaves 1–2 in. (2.5–5 cm) long on erect branches.

FLOWER AND FRUIT: Insignificant flowers in summer, with male and female blooms on separate plants; clusters of yellow fruit in summer become papery, forming tiny, four-wing structures that persist into winter.

LANDSCAPE USES: Best for mass plantings in minimum-maintenance areas; space 4 ft. (1.2 m) apart for informal hedge or low screen; useful for erosion control and revegetation purposes; fire resistant.

CLIMATE ADAPTION: Good heat tolerance; cold hardy to −30°F (−34°C); widely adaptable from coastal and interior areas to low-, mid- and high-elevation deserts.

CULTURE: Likes good drainage but adapts to difficult soil conditions; tolerates soil salts. Very drought tolerant, but looks better with deep irrigation every 3–4 weeks in hottest weather. To promote growth, apply 2 oz. (57 g) ammonium sulfate in early spring for plants in the ground more than a year. Prune to shape, at any time. Propagate by seeds or cuttings.

POSSIBLE PROBLEMS: Can become unsightly if not watered during long, dry spells, but rebounds nicely with extra water and some pruning; browse plant for many animals; litter from seeds borne on female plants.

Atriplex hymenelytra

PRONOUNCER: *at*-ri-plex hi-men-e-*lee*-tra
COMMON NAME: desert holly

Evergreen. Height: 1–3 ft. (30 cm–90 cm). Spread: 3–4 ft. (about 1 m). Rate of growth: Moderate. Light requirement: Sun. Native to lower elevations of the Mojave Desert, south into Mexico.

Low, compact shrub with lovely, silvery foliage that resembles holly in form; broad, soft leaves with toothed margins 1.5 in. (4 cm) long on white stems.

FLOWER AND FRUIT: Small flower clusters in spring, with male and female flowers occurring separately on the same plant; flat, round, papery fruit form conspicuous clusters.

LANDSCAPE USES: Decorative, silver foliage contrasts well with other plants; use it for maximum effect; plant in small groupings for border or low barrier. Good wind tolerance. Often used for Christmas season decorations.

CLIMATE ADAPTION: Severe damage around 20°F (−6.5°C); no heat problems; best in low deserts.

CULTURE: Good drainage necessary; prefers alkaline soils. Very drought tolerant; give it deep irrigation every 3–4 weeks in summer to keep foliage at its best, but be careful about overwatering. Minimal fertilizer; responds to 2 oz. (57 g) ammonium sulfate each spring until fully grown. Prune to shape, in early spring. Propagate by seeds or cuttings.

POSSIBLE PROBLEMS: Short lived; becoming somewhat rare in wild.

Atriplex lentiformis

PRONOUNCER: *at*-ri-plex len-ti-*form*-is
COMMON NAME: quail bush, big saltbush

Deciduous. Height: 5–10 ft. (1.5–3 m). Spread: 8–12 ft. (2.5–3.5 m). Rate of growth: Moderate. Light requirement: Sun. Native to alkali sinks of the San Joaquin Valley, California; Mojave Desert; Arizona; north into Utah; and south into Mexico.

Sprawling shrub with dense, blue-gray foliage; oval to triangle-shaped leaves 0.5–2 in. (1.3–5 cm) long and scaly. The quite similar Brewer saltbush, *A. lentiformis* 'Breweri', has dense, gray leaves, is smaller, slower growing and better adapted to coastal areas.

FLOWER AND FRUIT: Tassel-like spikes of flowers in summer followed by clusters of yellow fruit at branch ends.

LANDSCAPE USES: Suitable as screen, hedge or windbreak; can be grouped for informal background plantings or minimum-maintenance areas; well-adapted to desert conditions, but give it room.

CLIMATE ADAPTION: Excellent cold and heat tolerance; best for low to higher deserts and the Central Valley of California.

CULTURE: Needs good drainage; highly tolerant of alkaline soils. Minimal water requirement but looks best with deep watering every 3–4 weeks in summer. Apply 2 oz. (57 g) of ammonium sulfate in late winter for faster growth. Prune to shape, in winter through summer, or to remove old seed heads. Propagate by semihardwood cuttings or seeds.

POSSIBLE PROBLEMS: Odor may be objectionable; forage for many animals and cover for wild birds.

Atriplex nummularia

PRONOUNCER: *at*-ri-plex num-yoo-*lair*-ee-ah
COMMON NAME: old man saltbush

Evergreen. Height: 4–6 ft. (1.2–2 m). Spread: 7–9 ft. (2.2–2.75 m). Rate of growth: Fast. Light requirement: Sun. Native to Australia.

Dense, rounded shrub with attractive, roundish, blue-gray leaves to 2 in. (5 cm) that are covered with tiny scales.

FLOWER AND FRUIT: Insignificant, tiny flowers in summer are followed by brown fruits with winged bracts.

LANDSCAPE USES: Tough plant for screening along roadsides and other difficult sites; plant in transitional and naturalized gardens where it has plenty of room; can be sheared as a hedge; bluish gray foliage forms an attractive backdrop for flowering shrubs with deeper green foliage such as rosemary, autumn sage, fairy duster and mountain marigold.

CLIMATE ADAPTION: Hardy to about 22°F (−5°C); no heat problems; has naturalized in inland valleys of southern California.

CULTURE: Minimal soil requirement; does well in clay soils. Very drought resistant, but appreciates once-a-month watering in the hottest months in the warmest areas. No fertilizer. Trim occasionally to shape, control size; withstands shearing. Propagate by cuttings or seeds.

POSSIBLE PROBLEMS: Pollen causes allergies.

Atriplex semibaccata   PLATE 34

PRONOUNCER: *at*-ri-plex sem-eye-bah-*kah*-tah
COMMON NAME: Australian saltbush

Evergreen. Height: 6–12 in. (15–30 cm). Spread: 4–6 ft. (1.2–2 m). Rate of growth: Fast. Light requirement: Sun. Native to Australia but has naturalized in Southwest.

Dense ground cover that forms a tight mat as it roots along the ground; gray-green, oval leaves are 0.5–1.5 in. (1.3–4 cm) long. The cultivar 'Corto' shows more uniformity and greater cold tolerance.

FLOWER AND FRUIT: Small flower clusters in summer are inconspicuous, followed by small, fleshy, red fruits in the fall.

LANDSCAPE USES: Excellent for erosion control on banks and slopes, seminaturalized or transitional areas, revegetation and other difficult sites. Fire resistant.

CLIMATE ADAPTION: Damaged by cold at 20°F (−6.5°C), but recovers in the spring; good heat tolerance; best for low deserts and coastal and inland southern California.

CULTURE: Likes good drainage; if planted in heavier soil, use care not to overwater. Drought tolerant but looks lusher in the low desert with some irrigation every two weeks in summer. Minimal to no fertilizer. Prune in early spring to remove cold damaged or dead growth. Propagate by seeds.

POSSIBLE PROBLEMS: Reseeds; older growth sometimes becomes scraggly; rabbits love to nibble.

Baccharis

PRONOUNCER: *bak*-er-is
FAMILY: Compositae

Several baccharis species are very valuable for landscaping in warm, dry regions. As shrubs and ground covers, they adapt to a wide range of

58

conditions. They tolerate heavy as well as light, porous soils, need little to moderate amounts of water, and seem at ease in both exposed, difficult sites and the residential garden.

Male and female flowers occur on separate plants. The female produces a fluffy, cottony flower and seed that is easily carried by the wind. While in flower the females take on an attractive, soft, whitish glow, but they are considered messy by some. Thus, cutting-grown, male selections are recommended for more formal or manicured areas.

Baccharis 'Centennial'   PLATE 35
COMMON NAME: centennial baccharis
Evergreen. Height: 2–3.5 ft. (60 cm–1 m). Spread: 8–10 ft. (2.5–3 m). Rate of growth: Fast. Light requirement: Sun. Hybrid.

Compact, low-growing shrub created from a cross of *B. sarothroides* and *B. pilularis*; dark green, narrow to oblong leaves are up to 0.75 in. (2 cm) long. All plants are female.
FLOWER AND FRUIT: Small, white flower heads in fall; few to no seeds.
LANDSCAPE USES: Rugged and adaptable ground cover that withstands heat, cold and drought; useful for street and highway plantings, home landscapes and slopes for erosion control. Space 3–5 ft. (1–1.5 m) apart.
CLIMATE ADAPTION: Hardy to −10°F (−23°C); takes extreme heat; best for deserts.
CULTURE: Minimal soil requirement. Drought tolerant but does better with monthly irrigation in summer. Responds to light applications of nitrogen. Prune as needed in early spring. Propagate by cuttings.
POSSIBLE PROBLEMS: Flowers are messy.

Baccharis pilularis   PLATE 36
PRONOUNCER: *bak*-er-is pill-yoo-*lair*-is
COMMON NAME: coyote brush
Evergreen. Height: 1–3 ft. (30–90 cm). Spread: 3–13 ft. (1–4 m). Rate of growth: Moderate to fast. Light requirement: Sun to light shade. Native to coastal northern California.

Prostrate, matlike shrub with woody base and dense foliage; planted en masse, makes undulating mounds of green; 0.75-in. (2-cm) oval, coarsely toothed leaves vary from dull to dark green. Cultivar 'Twin Peaks' is a fast-growing, male selection with small, bright green leaves; reaches a height of 2 ft. (60 cm) and a spread of 6 ft. (2 m). 'Pigeon Point' has light green leaves; is lower growing than 'Twin Peaks' and is better suited to northern California. *Baccharis pilularis* ssp. *consanguinea* (chaparral broom) is an evergreen shrub, 3–12

ft. (1–3.5 m) high that blooms in early spring and has an extensive root system that is ideal for erosion control.
FLOWER AND FRUIT: Attractive, off-white pistillate (female) flowers produce cottony fruits considered messy by many; male flowers are yellowish; usually August–December.
LANDSCAPE USES: Outstanding ground cover for mass plantings on slopes, roadsides, parking areas and residential gardens; fire resistant, very adaptable and worthwhile.
CLIMATE ADAPTION: Hardy to about 15°F (−9°C); widely adaptable but needs protection from afternoon sun in hottest areas.
CULTURE: Minimal soil requirement. Drought tolerant, but give it deep, summer watering every 2–3 weeks in the hottest areas. Responds to light applications of nitrogen. Trim, clip or mow for more formal appearance; rejuvenate by cutting out old woody centers in late winter to early spring before growth starts. Propagate by seeds or cuttings; cuttings from male plants produce seedless, male offspring.
POSSIBLE PROBLEMS: Female plants produce messy seeds; susceptible to dieback; spider mites.

Baccharis sarothroides   PLATE 37
PRONOUNCER: *bak*-er-is sair-uh-*throy*-deez
COMMON NAME: desert broom
Evergreen. Height: 3–9 ft. (1 m–2.75 m). Spread: 6–9 ft. (2–2.75 m). Rate of growth: Fast. Light requirement: Sun. Native to southern California east into New Mexico; Mexico.

A rounded shrub with broomlike appearance due to its many bright green, narrow, photosynthesizing branchlets; true leaves are few and scalelike, almost inconspicuous; habit varies from dense to open, depending on conditions.
FLOWER AND FRUIT: Females produce small, plumelike buds that open in the fall with countless white, silky seeds which float off in the slightest breeze; males have inconspicuous flowers.
LANDSCAPE USES: Rugged plant for massing in informal screens or hedges, or use as a specimen in desert plantings; deep rooted and effective for erosion control.
CLIMATE ADAPTION: Hardy to at least 15°F (−9°C); no heat problems; best for deserts.
CULTURE: Minimal; takes alkaline conditions. Minimal water requirement but looks best with supplemental water every 4–6 weeks in the summer. No fertilizer. Prune lightly to make a denser plant; takes shearing and can be trimmed as a hedge; cut back hard to rejuvenate. Propagate by cuttings from the usually

preferred male plants.

POSSIBLE PROBLEMS: Short lived; floating seeds from female plants create a mess in pools; interior sometimes looks sparse.

Bougainvillea PLATE 38

PRONOUNCER: boo-gan-*vee*-ah
FAMILY: Nyctaginaceae
COMMON NAME: bougainvillea

Evergreen to deciduous. Height: 3–20 ft. (1–6 m). Spread: 3–20 ft. (1–6 m). Rate of growth: Fast. Light requirement: Sun to part shade. Native to Brazil.

Woody, tropical vine with bright green, heart-shaped leaves on thorny branches; some varieties are shrublike. All burst with stunning color during hot weather. Cultivars include: 'Barbara Karst'—an all-around favorite, especially in the low deserts, with bright magenta bracts. 'San Diego Red'—deep red bracts, tends to stay evergreen. 'Superstition Gold'—a shrubby variety with gold and orange-pink blooms; suggested for low deserts. 'Orange King'—coppery-orange bracts; not frost tolerant; does best with long, hot summers.

FLOWER AND FRUIT: True flowers are small and insignificant but are surrounded by bright-colored bracts in a variety of brilliant colors.

LANDSCAPE USES: Best for south- and west-facing walls where intense sunlight and heat promote the best color displays. They make excellent focal points for street and home entryways; blend well in arid landscapes and provide lasting, spectacular summer color. Use shrubby forms in a sunny bed.

CLIMATE ADAPTION: Relishes heat; drops leaves and may die back as temperatures approach freezing. Best for areas without heavy frosts such as low deserts and coastal and inland areas of southern California. Survives with protection in mid-elevation desert.

CULTURE: Likes good drainage. Moderately drought tolerant. In the warmest areas, appreciates a once-a-week watering during the spring growing months, but blooms heaviest if water is tapered back to about every three weeks in the summer. Apply 4 oz. (115 g) of balanced fertilizer, such as 10–6–4, in the spring. Prune to shape or train; wait to spring to see extent of frost damage. Propagate by cuttings.

POSSIBLE PROBLEMS: Vine types need support to climb; use extreme care to not break root ball at planting time; cold sensitivity.

Brachychiton

PRONOUNCER: bray-key-*kye*-ton
FAMILY: Sterculiaceae

The unusual, bottle-shaped, stout trunks of *Brachychiton* are the distinguishing feature of these Australian natives. The bottletree has proven quite adaptable in the low- and mid-elevation deserts. The flame tree has spectacular flowers and does better in more moderate climate conditions.

Brachychiton acerifolius PLATE 39

PRONOUNCER: bray-key-*kye*-ton ace-er-i-*foh*-lee-us
COMMON NAME: flame tree

Deciduous. Height: 40–50 ft. (12–15 m). Spread: 30–50 ft. (9–15 m). Rate of growth: Slow. Light requirement: Sun. Native to Australia.

A stout-trunked tree which produces an outstanding floral display before the new leaves appear. The large, broad leaves are up to 10 in. (25 cm) wide, have deep lobes, and are a shiny, bright green; the bark is smooth and green.

FLOWER AND FRUIT: Large clusters of light to deep red, tubular flowers from late spring to early summer; the large, woody, dark brown fruit pods are often used in dried flower arrangements.

LANDSCAPE USES: A handsome specimen tree; good along streets, in parking areas and other large landscapes.

CLIMATE ADAPTION: Hardy to about 25°F (−4°C); best for coastal and inland areas of southern California; not for the deserts.

CULTURE: Does best in deep soils with good drainage. Moderately drought tolerant; prefers supplemental watering every 2–3 weeks in the warmest months. Fertilize only minimally. Prune to shape or to train in youth, as necessary. Propagate by seeds.

POSSIBLE PROBLEMS: Slow growth; litter.

Brachychiton populneus PLATE 40

PRONOUNCER: bray-key-*kye*-ton pop-ul-*nee*-us
COMMON NAME: bottletree

Evergreen. Height: 30–40 ft. (9–12 m). Spread: 20–30 ft. (6–9 m). Rate of growth: Fast. Light requirement: Sun. Native to Australia.

This tree often grows as much as 4 ft. (1.2 m) a year during its first 4–5 years in the landscape; pyramidal in youth, becoming rounded with age. Shiny, 3-in. (8-cm) leaves shimmer in the breeze like a poplar's; variable in shape, some having deep lobes. Most people seem to prefer the pointed types. The trunk is covered with patterned, greenish bark; it tapers from a large

2,22,2,2 2 2 2 2 2 2 2 2 2 2 2 2 2 2 2 2 2 2 2 2 2 2 2 2 2 2 2 2 2 2 2 2 2 2 2 2 2 2 2 2 2 2 2 2 2 2 2 2 2

round trunk inward several feet above ground.

FLOWER AND FRUIT: Clusters of pink, bell-shaped, small flowers in the late spring are followed by woody seed pods shaped like 3-in. (8-cm) canoes.

LANDSCAPE USES: A specimen, street or background screen tree for residential as well as public landscapes. The foliage adds a refreshing, bright green to desert landscapes.

CLIMATE ADAPTION: The foliage is damaged at about 18°F (−8°C) but recovers rapidly in the spring; widely adaptable but not for the higher deserts.

CULTURE: Needs good drainage. Drought tolerant, but likes deep soakings every 2–3 weeks; seems to be able to handle a planting site in lawns. Minimal fertilizer needed. Prune to shape. Propagate by seeds.

POSSIBLE PROBLEMS: Texas root rot; the fragile root system requires careful handling in transplanting; fuzz from the seed pods is irritating to the skin; roots lift paving and sidewalks.

Brahea armata PLATE 41

PRONOUNCER: bra-*hee*-ah ar-*mah*-tah

FAMILY: Palmae

COMMON NAME: Mexican blue palm

Evergreen. Height: 23–30 ft. (7–9 m). Spread: 8–12 ft. (2.5–3.5 m). Rate of growth: Slow. Light requirement: Sun to partial shade. Native to Baja California.

Very adaptable and attractive palm with bluish gray, fan-shaped fronds that form a wide-spreading crown above a stout trunk.

FLOWER AND FRUIT: Fragrant, creamy-white flowers form along long strands hanging below the foliage in spring; fruit is brown and berrylike.

LANDSCAPE USES: A striking accent plant with strong foliar contrast; use as an individual specimen, for silhouette effect, or in rows along streets and property boundaries. Imparts a bold, tropical feel; quite in scale for the typical home landscape. Good in containers. Wind tolerant.

CLIMATE ADAPTION: Hardy to 15–18°F (−9 to −8°C); takes heat well; best in low- and mid-elevation deserts, coastal and inland southern California.

CULTURE: Needs good drainage; tolerates alkaline soil conditions. Drought resistant; deep summer watering once a month will do. Apply 1 lb. (0.45 kg) of ammonium sulfate in early spring to large, established tree; adjust for younger ones. Remove old fronds and flower structures after bloom. Propagate by seeds.

POSSIBLE PROBLEMS: Slow growth.

Brahea edulis, the Guadalupe fan palm, is similar but with greener leaves.

Buddleia marrubiifolia PLATE 42

PRONOUNCER: *bud*-lee-ah mah-roo-bee-eye-*foh*-lee-ah

FAMILY: Loganiaceae

COMMON NAME: woolly butterfly bush

Evergreen. Height: 3–5 ft. (1–1.5 m). Spread: 2–5 ft. (60 cm–1.5 m). Rate of growth: Moderate. Light requirement: Sun. Native along the Rio Grande in Texas and Mexico.

A compact, silvery white, rounded shrub; thick, feltlike oval to elliptic leaves with scalloped margins; young stems are also covered with brownish, downy hair.

FLOWER AND FRUIT: Unusual, 0.5-in. (1.3-cm) round heads tightly hold tiny, orange flowers in the summer and fall; fruit capsules with numerous seeds follow.

LANDSCAPE USES: Combines nicely with other arid-adapted plants; foliage color makes a lovely contrast with shrubs such as creosote bush; neat, compact growth is another desirable feature.

CLIMATE ADAPTION: No heat problems; best for low- and mid-elevation deserts; freezes to ground in higher deserts but usually recovers in spring.

CULTURE: Minimal soil requirement; prefers good drainage. Very drought tolerant; supplemental water in summer every 3–4 weeks keeps it looking its best and increases growth rate. No fertilizer. Prune in early spring as needed to keep a compact form. Propagate by seeds in spring or softwood cuttings through summer.

POSSIBLE PROBLEMS: Overwatering in summer may cause root rot; becomes leggy in even partial shade; rabbits like to nibble.

Butia capitata PLATE 43

PRONOUNCER: *bew*-tee-ah cap-i-*tah*-tah

FAMILY: Palmae

COMMON NAME: pindo palm

Evergreen. Height: 10–20 ft. (3–6 m). Spread: 10–15 ft. (3–4.5 m). Rate of growth: Slow. Light requirement: Sun to partial shade. Native to Brazil and Argentina.

A small palm with graceful, feathery, blue-green fronds; trunk when trimmed of old leaves has an attractive texture.

FLOWER AND FRUIT: Tiny, yellow to red flowers; large clusters of orange, edible fruit.

LANDSCAPE USES: Adaptable and attractive choice for small areas or public spaces such as parks;

the foliage color and trunk make it a nice accent plant.

CLIMATE ADAPTION: Hardy to about 15°F (−9°C); heat tolerant; widely adaptable except for the higher desert.

CULTURE: Needs good drainage. Moderately drought tolerant; likes deep watering every 2–3 weeks in the warmest months in the warmest areas; taper off in coolest months. Light nitrogen applications speed growth. Prune old leaf bases to create trunk pattern. Propagate by seeds.

POSSIBLE PROBLEMS: Slow growth.

Caesalpinia

PRONOUNCER: seez-al-*pin*-ee-ah

FAMILY: Leguminosae

When in bloom, the exotic-flowered bird of paradise makes a garden come alive with color. Its large, brightly hued racemes accent the landscape over a long period in attractive shades of yellow, or in the case of *Caesalpinia pulcherrima*, in a fiery red, orange and yellow combination. In contrast to the bold look of its flowers, bird of paradise has feathery foliage that creates a lacy pattern.

These evergreen to deciduous shrubs or small trees thrive in the desert heat. All are drought tolerant and can survive on little to no supplemental irrigation. Watering plants deeply every two weeks during the summer bloom period keeps flowers plentiful and plants in attractive condition. But plants accept more or less water than this.

Birds of paradise are quite tolerant of varying soil conditions, but do best in well-drained sites. Heavier soils sometimes bring on chlorosis, so iron chelate may be required. Adjust nitrogen applications according to watering scheme as quick bursts of growth demand more water. The deciduous types can be pruned back hard during the winter when they look their worst. They recover quickly in spring in a more compact, rounded form.

Caesalpinia cacalocoa PLATE 44

PRONOUNCER: seez-al-*pin*-ee-ah kah-kah-*loh*-koh-ah

COMMON NAME: Mexican bushbird

Evergreen. Height: 10–18 ft. (3–5.5 m). Spread: 12–15 ft. (3.5–4.5 m). Rate of growth: Fast. Light requirement: Sun. Native to Mexico.

Small, multitrunked, vase-shaped tree with dark green foliage and spectacular blooms; leaves divided into oval leaflets about 1 in. (2.5 cm) long; branches lined with curved prickles similar to a rose's.

FLOWER AND FRUIT: Showy, large, yellow flower clusters crown the tree in fall.

LANDSCAPE USES: Good choice for a small tree in natural, desert landscapes; plant along walkways as a barrier or in lawns; flowers when many other plants begin to look drab.

CLIMATE ADAPTION: Hardy to at least 20°F (−6.5°C); does best in low- and mid-elevation deserts.

CULTURE: Needs good drainage. Minimal water requirement, but appreciates extra every 2–3 weeks in hottest months and when blooming. After 5–6 in. (13–15 cm) of new growth (usually in May), apply 2 oz. (57 g) ammonium sulfate. Prune to shape in early spring; can be trained in youth to single trunk. Propagate by scarified seeds.

POSSIBLE PROBLEMS: Drainage; Texas root rot; poisonous pods and seeds.

Caesalpinia gilliesii PLATE 45

PRONOUNCER: seez-al-*pin*-ee-ah gill-*is*-ee-eye

COMMON NAME: desert or yellow bird of paradise

Deciduous. Height: 6–10 ft. (2–3 m). Spread: 4–6 ft. (1.2–2 m). Rate of growth: Moderate. Light requirement: Sun. Native to South America but has naturalized in Southwest and Mexico.

Medium-sized shrub with striking, festive flowers and light green, ferny foliage; bipinnate leaves are 3–5 in. (8–13 cm) long on somewhat irregular branches.

FLOWER AND FRUIT: Large, terminal clusters of yellow flowers with showy, red, protruding stamens in spring and summer followed by small brown pods.

LANDSCAPE USES: Dramatic effect in mass plantings, as individual specimen or in rows; foliage texture and showy flowers add tropical feel to oasis areas, arid landscapes; good roadside plant.

CLIMATE ADAPTION: Revels in heat; hardy to about 10°F (−12°C); widely adaptable except for coastal areas.

CULTURE: Quite tolerant of soil conditions but watch drainage. Minimal water requirement but flowers betters with some supplemental water every 2–3 weeks in hottest months in low desert. After 5–6 in. (13–15 cm) of new growth (usually in May), apply 2 oz. (57 g) ammonium sulfate. Minimize pruning except to shape; can be cut back sharply in winter for bushier plant. Propagate by scarified seeds.

POSSIBLE PROBLEMS: Drainage; Texas root rot; reseeds; poisonous pods and seeds.

Caesalpinia mexicana PLATE 46
PRONOUNCER: seez-al-*pin*-ee-ah mex-i-*cah*-nah
COMMON NAME: Mexican bird of paradise

Semideciduous. Height: 6–18 ft. (2–5.5 m). Spread: 8–10 ft. (2.5–3 m). Rate of growth: Fast. Light requirement: Full sun. Native to northern Mexico.

Lush, deep green foliage distinguishes this large shrub from some of the other birds of paradise; 4–6 in. (10–15 cm) leaves are divided into oval leaflets; evergreen in warmest areas.

FLOWER AND FRUIT: Fragrant, rounded clusters of yellow flowers in racemes 3–6 in. (8–15 cm) long spring through fall; light brown, 2-in. (5-cm) pods follow.

LANDSCAPE USES: Flowering accent and oasis plant; maximum effect for tropical, natural and desert landscapes.

CLIMATE ADAPTION: No problems with heat but may be damaged around 20°F (−6.5°C); best for low- and mid-elevation deserts.

CULTURE: Does best with good drainage. Looks best with supplemental water every other week during bloom; little or none other times. After 5–6 in. (13–15 cm) of new growth (usually in May), apply 2 oz. (57 g) ammonium sulfate. Prune to shape in early spring. Propagate by scarified seeds.

POSSIBLE PROBLEMS: Drainage; watch for Texas root rot; may escape from cultivation; poisonous pods and seeds.

Caesalpinia pulcherrima PLATE 47
PRONOUNCER: seez-al-*pin*-ee-ah pull-*chair*-i-mah
COMMON NAME: red bird of paradise

Deciduous. Height: 6–12 ft. (2–3.5 m). Spread: 5–8 ft. (1.5–2.5 m). Rate of growth: Fast. Light requirement: Sun. Native to Mexico.

Outstanding, summer-blooming shrub with fiery blossoms and lush, feathery, medium green leaves 8–15 in. (20–38 cm) long.

FLOWER AND FRUIT: Profuse, orange-red-yellow flowers in upright clusters followed by flat, 3–6 in. (8–15 cm) brownish pods.

LANDSCAPE USES: Specimen or in mass plantings for bright color all summer long; maximum effect for tropical, natural and desert landscapes.

CLIMATE ADAPTION: Freezes to the ground when temperatures stay around 30°F (−1°C), but recovers rapidly in spring; loves heat; excellent for low- and mid-elevation deserts, also hot inland valleys of southern California.

CULTURE: Quite tolerant of soil conditions but needs good drainage. Avoid supplemental watering November–April; accepts moderate to ample water the rest of the year but gets along fine with little, even in summer, although flowers best with some every 2–3 weeks. After 5–6 in. (13–15 cm) of new growth (usually in May), apply 2 oz. (57 g) of ammonium sulfate. When it becomes unsightly, November–December, can be cut to within 5–6 in. (13–15 cm) of the ground; or prune to shape after possibility of last frost. Propagate by scarified seeds.

POSSIBLE PROBLEMS: Drainage; Texas root rot; reseeds; pods and seeds poisonous.

Calliandra
PRONOUNCER: kal-ee-*an*-drah
FAMILY: Leguminosae

The showy blossoms of *Calliandra,* the fairy dusters, are actually long, protruding stamens which form pink to deep red, pincushionlike balls. Both the flowers and finely textured foliage have a delicate, charming appeal. They are best when observed at close range.

Of these, *C. eriophylla* is the most tolerant of cold, heat and drought, but drops its leaves in the summer if not provided with supplemental water.

Calliandra californica PLATE 48
PRONOUNCER: kal-ee-*an*-drah cal-i-*for*-ni-cah
COMMON NAME: California fairy duster

Evergreen. Height: 4–5 ft. (1.2–1.5 m). Spread: 3–5 ft. (1–1.5 m). Rate of growth: Slow to moderate. Light requirement: Sun. Native to Baja California.

A small, open shrub with slender branches that hold lacy, medium green, divided foliage.

FLOWER AND FRUIT: Deep red flowers, 1–1.5 in. (2.5–4 cm) across in the fall and winter and intermittently during other periods of the year; seed pods 1.5–2.5 in. (4–6 cm) long.

LANDSCAPE USES: A flowering accent in the landscape which combines well with other arid-adapted plants. Give it a close-up spot where its blooms can be enjoyed.

CLIMATE ADAPTION: Hardy to about 20°F (−6.5°C); widely adaptable except for the higher deserts.

CULTURE: Needs good drainage. Drought tolerant, but water twice a month in the hottest areas in summer. No fertilizer. Prune after flowering, as necessary to shape. Propagate by scarified seed.

POSSIBLE PROBLEMS: Can look leggy after bloom or without summer watering.

Calliandra eriophylla PLATE 49
PRONOUNCER: kal-ee-*an*-drah air-ee-*off*-i-lah
COMMON NAME: fairy duster, huajillo

Semideciduous. Height: 2–3 ft. (60–90 cm). Spread: 3–4 ft. (1–1.2 m). Rate of growth: Slow to moderate. Light requirement: Sun. Native from west Texas to California and south into Mexico.

A petite, compact shrub with intricate branching and attractive flowers; the foliage is finely divided into tiny leaflets.

FLOWER AND FRUIT: Rose pink balls about 1.5 in. (4 cm) in diameter in late winter and spring followed by 2-in. (5-cm), slender pods.

LANDSCAPE USES: Provides a delicate touch to banks, borders and group plantings; does well in street medians. A most striking plant in flower; good winter color. May be used as a ground cover if spaced 3 ft. (1 m) apart.

CLIMATE ADAPTION: Hardy to at least 10°F (−12°C), no heat problems; best for the deserts and inland southern California.

CULTURE: Prefers good drainage. Very drought resistant; watering every 3–4 weeks improves appearance during the hottest months and in long, dry periods. Apply 2 oz. (57 g) ammonium sulfate in the early spring for more vigorous growth. No pruning. Propagate by scarified seed.

POSSIBLE PROBLEMS: Deer like the foliage.

Calliandra tweedii

PRONOUNCER: kal-ee-*an*-drah *twee*-dee-eye
COMMON NAME: Trinidad flame bush

Evergreen. Height: 8–10 ft. (2.5–3 m). Spread: 6–8 ft. (2–2.5 m). Rate of growth: Moderate. Light requirement: Sun. Native to South America.

A large, fine-textured shrub with the leaves divided into tiny, lacy leaflets; rounded, mounded shape.

FLOWER AND FRUIT: Spectacular, deep red flower sprays in early spring and fall, and other times of year; followed by seed pods.

LANDSCAPE USES: Flowering accent and specimen shrub, or for informal screening. Leaves offer pleasing contrast to the flowers.

CLIMATE ADAPTION: Top hardy to around 25°F (−4°C); best for coastal and inland areas of southern California; freezes back, then regrows in colder areas, including the low desert.

CULTURE: Needs good drainage. Drought tolerant, but likes occasional deep watering during the warmest months. Little to no fertilizer needed. Prune to shape after spring bloom. Propagate by seeds.

POSSIBLE PROBLEMS: Cold sensitivity.

Callistemon phoeniceus

PLATE 50

PRONOUNCER: cal-*iss*-stih-mun fo-*nee*-shus
FAMILY: Myrtaceae
COMMON NAME: fiery bottlebrush

Evergreen. Height: 6–8 ft. (2–2.5 m). Spread: 6–8 ft. (2–2.5 m). Rate of growth: Moderate. Light requirement: Full sun best. Native to western Australia.

Most spectacular blooming and adaptable of the bottlebrushes; narrow, gray-green leaves on arching branches; lower growing with tighter foliage than the more commonly seen *C. citrinus* and *C. viminalis*. *Callistemon phoeniceus* 'Prostrata' is lower growing.

FLOWER AND FRUIT: 4-in. (10-cm), dark red flower clusters appear mainly in the spring and resemble the brushes used to clean bottles; hummingbirds love them; fruits are tiny, brown capsules which persist on the stems in an interesting, attractive fashion.

LANDSCAPE USES: Accent plant or massed in informal hedges or screens; excellent around a swimming pool, fronting a cement-block wall, or in tropical and desert landscaping. Avoid planting in lawns.

CLIMATE ADAPTION: Hardy to about 20°F (−6.5°C), no heat problems; best for coastal and inland southern California, the low deserts, and protected locations in California's Central Valley and mid-elevation deserts.

CULTURE: Needs good drainage; avoid highly alkaline soil. Drought resistant but likes about 2 in. (5 cm) of supplemental watering monthly in the warmest periods; iron-deficiency chlorosis can be a major problem if plants are overwatered. Apply a cupful (225 g) of ammonium sulfate in early spring for a plant that is 4 ft. (1.2 m) high with an equal spread, adjusting proportionally for larger or smaller plants. If plants become chlorotic, first check watering procedures; if okay, add iron chelate, following label carefully. Gracefulness may be improved with occasional thinning or heading back after flowering. Propagate by semihardwood cuttings.

POSSIBLE PROBLEMS: Chlorosis; slow to recover if frozen; do not attempt to transplant once a plant is established in the landscape.

Carissa macrocarpa

PLATE 51

PRONOUNCER: cah-*riss*-ah mak-roh-*car*-pah
FAMILY: Apocynaceae
COMMON NAME: Natal plum

Evergreen. Height: 2–6 ft. (60 cm–2 m). Spread: 2–4 ft. (60 cm–1.2 m). Rate of growth: Medium. Light requirement: Sun to partial shade. Native to South Africa.

A handsome shrub with dark green foliage, fragrant flowers and edible fruit; 2–3 in. (5–9 cm), leathery leaves; distinctive thorns are split much like a snake's forked tongue. Also known as *C. grandiflora*. More compact cultivars include: 'Boxwood Beauty', thornless and about 2 × 2 ft. (60 × 60 cm); 'Green Carpet', about 1 × 4 ft. (30 cm × 1.2 m); and 'Tuttle', which grows 2–3 ft. (60–90 cm) high and 3–5 ft. (90 cm–1.5 m) wide.

FLOWER AND FRUIT: White, star-shaped, 2-in. (5-cm), five-petaled flowers in late spring and early summer are followed by 1-in. (2.5-cm), red, plumlike fruit.

LANDSCAPE USES: Good barrier plant and for screening or hedges. Dwarf cultivars make good ground covers.

CLIMATE ADAPTION: Loves heat but tender to frost, often damaged around 28°F (−2°C), although it usually recovers in the spring; best for coastal and inland southern California and low-desert plantings in a south or west exposure under an overhang.

CULTURE: Needs good drainage. Looks best with moderate to ample amounts of water every 1–2 weeks during the hottest months; however, avoid keeping roots continually wet. Scatter 2 oz. (57 g) of an all-purpose fertilizer such as 10–6–4 on soil surface in March, May and August for the first 2–3 years in the landscape; thereafter 4 oz. (115 g) in May. Prune to shape and contain or to remove cold-damaged growth in spring. Propagate by cuttings.

POSSIBLE PROBLEMS: Foliage browning in cold weather; dies if overwatered.

Cassia

PRONOUNCER: *cass*-ee-ah
FAMILY: Leguminosae

Cassias native to the warm regions of North America and Australia offer considerable variety and color for the landscape. Most have divided, fine-textured foliage and long periods of bloom. These shrubs range from evergreen to deciduous and vary somewhat in their degree of cold hardiness. Plant them in rapidly draining soil if possible. They tolerate heavier soils if given more infrequent, but deep irrigation. As cassias produce seeds prolifically, it is best to prune them after flowering to reduce seed pod formation and promote a rounded, bushy form. Fertilize minimally or not at all.

Cassia artemisioides PLATE 52

PRONOUNCER: *cass*-ee-ah ar-tuh-miz-ee-*oy*-deez
COMMON NAME: feathery cassia

Evergreen. Height: 4–6 ft. (1.2–2 m). Spread: 3–5 ft. (1–1.5 m). Rate of growth: Fast. Light requirement: Sun to partial shade. Native to Australia.

Rounded, gray-green foliage provides an airy, attractive look year-round; floral display in spring is spectacular and fragrant; leaves are divided into 6–8 needlelike leaflets about 1 in. (2.5 cm) long.

FLOWER AND FRUIT: Yellow, 0.5-in. (1.3-cm) flowers in clusters in spring and sometimes other seasons, followed by 3-in. (8-cm) flat pods.

LANDSCAPE USES: As a specimen, in mass plantings or as an informal screen; one of the desert's earliest bloomers, much as forsythia is in colder areas.

CLIMATE ADAPTION: Hardy to about 20°F (−6.5°C); no problems with heat; best in low- and mid-elevation deserts and coastal and inland areas of southern California.

CULTURE: Needs good drainage. Minimal water requirement, but looks better in low desert with supplemental water every 2–3 weeks in summer. Little to no fertilizer. Light pruning to remove seed pods and to promote a rounded, bushy form. If older plants need rejuvenation, trim back hard in spring and allow to regrow. Propagate by scarified seeds.

POSSIBLE PROBLEMS: Frost may damage flowers just before opening; occasionally develops iron-deficiency chlorosis; heavy seed set and litter can be unattractive.

Cassia didymobotrya PLATE 53

PRONOUNCER: *cass*-ee-ah did-ee-mo-*bot*-ree-ah
COMMON NAME: popcorn cassia

Evergreen. Height: 6–10 ft. (2–3 m). Spread: 6–10 ft. (2–3 m). Rate of growth: Fast. Light requirement: Sun. Native of East Africa.

A tall-growing shrub, rounded to rangy in form, with large, lush foliage; bright green, 2-in. (5-cm), rounded leaflets form about 1-ft. (30-cm) long leaves; its common name, popcorn cassia, comes from aroma of flowers and leaves when crushed.

FLOWER AND FRUIT: Very showy, large, upright clusters of yellow, 2-in. (5-cm) flowers in winter and early spring; black pod to 4 in. (10 cm) long.

LANDSCAPE USES: Strong specimen or accent plant; bold foliage, flowers and form provide a wild, tropical appearance in landscape; provides winter color.

CLIMATE ADAPTION: Hardy to about 26°F (−3°C); thrives in desert heat; best for low deserts, mild inland areas in southern California.

CULTURE: Needs good drainage. Minimal water requirement but looks better in desert with some supplemental water every two weeks in summer or extended dry periods. Avoid fertilizing. After flowering, can be headed back to control form and size or to remove cold-damaged branches. Propagate by seeds.

POSSIBLE PROBLEMS: Some people find scent of flowers and leaves disagreeable, and not everyone agrees smell is like popcorn; tends to naturalize.

Cassia nemophila   PLATE 54

PRONOUNCER: *cass*-ee-ah nem-*off*-i-lah

COMMON NAME: desert cassia

Evergreen. Height: 5–8 ft. (1.5–2.5 m). Spread: 4–6 ft. (1.2–2 m). Rate of growth: Moderate to fast. Light requirement: Sun. Native to Australia.

Medium, rounded shrub with soft, fresh effect; medium green leaves are divided into needlelike leaflets 1 in. (2.5 cm) long.

FLOWER AND FRUIT: Masses of yellow, 0.5-in. (1.3-cm) flowers in early spring and sometimes fall, followed by papery, brown pods about 3 in. (8 cm) long.

LANDSCAPE USES: An attractive, tough plant for screening or barriers, for mass plantings or combined with other desert plants; foliage provides a nice contrast with grayer hues. More cold hardy than *C. artemisioides* or *C. sturtii*.

CLIMATE ADAPTION: Hardy to at least 20°F (−6.5°C); takes heat well; best in low- and mid-elevation deserts, California's Central Valley, and inland areas of southern California.

CULTURE: Prefers good drainage but seems to tolerate heavy soils. Minimal water requirement but deep, once-a-month, summer watering improves appearance. Little to no fertilizer. Prune as needed after flowering to remove seed pods or control size. Propagate by scarified seeds.

POSSIBLE PROBLEMS: Seed pods.

Cassia phyllodinea   PLATE 55

PRONOUNCER: *cass*-ee-ah fy-lo-*din*-ee-ah

COMMON NAME: silverleaf cassia

Evergreen. Height: 3–6 ft. (1–2 m). Spread: 3–5 ft. (1–1.5 m). Rate of growth: Moderate to fast. Light requirement: Sun. Native to Australia.

Medium-sized, rounded shrub providing a ripple effect in wind due to the silvery foliage; narrow, 1–3 in. (2.5–8 cm), phyllode-type leaves are curved; stems whitish.

FLOWER AND FRUIT: Yellow, 0.5-in. (1.3-cm) flowers

in early spring and sometimes late fall; seed pods follow. Bloom not as heavy as from other Australian cassias.

LANDSCAPE USES: Excellent shrub for borders, street and median plantings, or mixed with other flowering shrubs; attractive flowers and clean foliage.

CLIMATE ADAPTION: Hardy to 20°F (−6.5°C); no heat problems; best for low- and mid-elevation deserts, California's Central Valley and inland areas of southern California.

CULTURE: Needs good drainage. Minimal water requirement but looks better with supplemental water every 2–3 weeks in summer. Little to no fertilizer. Prune after flowering to shape or as necessary to control size. Propagate by scarified seeds.

POSSIBLE PROBLEMS: Seed pods.

Cassia sturtii   PLATE 56

PRONOUNCER: *cass*-ee-ah *ster*-tee-eye

COMMON NAME: Sturt's cassia

Evergreen. Height: 5–8 ft. (1.5–2.5 m). Spread: 4–6 ft. (1.2–2 m). Rate of growth: Moderate to fast. Light requirement: Sun. Native to Australia.

A rounded shrub with soft foliage that is gray-green above and almost whitish underneath; leaves are divided into narrow leaflets about 1 in. (2.5 cm) long; quite variable due to hybridization.

FLOWER AND FRUIT: Clusters of bright yellow flowers in spring and fall, followed by brown seed pods.

LANDSCAPE USES: Screening or specimen plant, or combined with other arid-type plants.

CLIMATE ADAPTION: Hardy to about 22°F (−5°C); no heat problems; best for low deserts and warm inland areas of southern California.

CULTURE: Likes good drainage. Drought tolerant, but looks best with supplemental water every 2–3 weeks in summer. Little to no fertilizer. Needs regular trimming after flowering to remove pods and control size. Propagate by scarified seeds.

POSSIBLE PROBLEMS: Not as cold hardy as *C. nemophila* or *C. artemisioides*; occasional chlorosis; becomes lanky without regular pruning.

Cassia wislizenii   PLATE 57

PRONOUNCER: *cass*-ee-ah wis-li-*zen*-ee-eye

COMMON NAME: shrubby senna

Deciduous. Height: 4–8 ft. (1.2–2.5 m). Spread: 3–6 ft. (1–2 m). Rate of growth: Slow. Light requirement: Sun to partial shade. Native to southeastern Arizona, New Mexico, west

Texas and Mexico.

Open, spreading shrub that is spectacular when in bloom; dark branches with deep green, lacy leaves divided into small, rounded leaflets about 1.5 in. (4 cm) long; wood is very hard.

FLOWER AND FRUIT: Rounded, yellow flowers about 1 in. (2.5 cm) in large clusters in late summer and occasionally other times of the year, followed by slender, dark brown pods up to 6 in. (15 cm) long.

LANDSCAPE USES: Flowering accent or specimen shrub in desert-type landscapes; mix with other native and arid-adapted plants.

CLIMATE ADAPTION: No heat or cold problems in desert Southwest.

CULTURE: Needs good drainage; tolerant of salty soil. Needs little water but stops blooming if too dry; once-a-month supplemental watering should do it. Apply 2 oz. (57 g) ammonium sulfate in late winter to speed growth. Shape by pruning in early spring. Propagate by scarified seeds.

POSSIBLE PROBLEMS: Poor appearance except when blooming.

Casuarina
PRONOUNCER: kazh-ur-*eye*-nah
FAMILY: Casuarinaceae

From a distance, the she oaks are often mistaken for pines. Their long, weeping "needles" are actually jointed branchlets, with the tiny, almost unnoticeable leaves occurring in whorls about the joints. They even produce a woody cone, which contains flat, winged seeds.

These plants are angiosperms, or true flowering plants. Male and female flowers occur separately on the same plant, or on different plants. The tiny flowers are inconspicuous, but sometimes give the tree a brownish cast.

About 65 species of *Casuarina* occur in southeast Asia and the southwest Pacific, with many in Australia. Some species produce very hard wood that has been used for making furniture. Of the three most commonly seen in the Southwest, the horsetail tree is the most widely used.

The she oaks are noted for their ability to tolerate difficult conditions, including heat, drought and poor soils. Thanks to these virtues, they are often relegated to marginal areas. But with a little water and care, they are fine choices for parks, streets and other public spaces.

Casuarina cunninghamiana   PLATE 58
PRONOUNCER: kazh-ur-*eye*-nah kuh-ning-ham-ee-*ah*-nah
COMMON NAME: Australia pine, river she oak

Evergreen. Height: 50–70 ft. (15–21.5 m). Spread: 25–30 ft. (7.5–9 m). Rate of growth: Fast. Light requirement: Sun. Native to Australia.

Large, finely textured tree with dense covering of very slender, dark green branchlets; rough, gray bark.

FLOWER AND FRUIT: Insignificant flowers; fruit a small, woody cone about 0.3 in. (1 cm) in diameter.

LANDSCAPE USES: Good shade and screen tree for streets, highways and parks or group in rows for a large windbreak. Sturdiest and most attractive of the casuarinas.

CLIMATE ADAPTION: Hardy to about 20°F (−6.5°C); heat tolerant; widely adaptable from California's coast, inland and interior regions into low- and mid-elevation deserts.

CULTURE: Minimal soil requirement; tolerates alkaline and saline soils. Drought tolerant, but looks best with monthly, supplemental, summer water in warmer areas. Little to no fertilizer. Prune to shape, in youth. Propagate by seeds.

POSSIBLE PROBLEMS: Interior branch dieback with age.

Casuarina equisetifolia
PRONOUNCER: kazh-ur-*eye*-nah eh-kwi-sec-ti-*foh*-lee-ah
COMMON NAME: horsetail tree

Evergreen. Height: 40–50 ft. (12–15 m). Spread: 20–25 ft. (6–7.5 m). Rate of growth: Fast. Light requirement: Sun. Native to Asia and Australia, but has naturalized in Southwest.

Slender tree with long, drooping, gray-green, needlelike branchlets; often confused with *C. cunninghamiana.*

FLOWER AND FRUIT: Insignificant flowers; fruit is an olive-sized, woody cone.

LANDSCAPE USES: Good resistance to smog; useful for erosion control and revegetation purposes in coastal areas as well as inland; of easy cultivation.

CLIMATE ADAPTION: Cold damage after prolonged temperatures below 25°F (−4°C); takes heat well; widely adaptable from coastal and inland California into low- and mid-elevation deserts.

CULTURE: Minimal soil requirement; tolerates alkaline and saline conditions. Drought tolerant; monthly, supplemental irrigation during the summer in warmer areas improves appearance. Little to no fertilizer. Prune to train in youth. Propagate by seeds.

POSSIBLE PROBLEMS: shallow rooted; litter.

Casuarina stricta

PRONOUNCER: kazh-ur-*eye*-nah *strik*-tah
COMMON NAME: she oak

Evergreen. Height: 20–30 ft. (6–9 m). Spread: 10–15 ft. (3–4.5 m). Rate of growth: Fast. Light requirement: Sun. Native to Australia.

Small, slender tree with open growth of dark green, narrow branchlets.

FLOWER AND FRUIT: Flowers insignificant; 0.5-in. (1.3-cm) woody cones.

LANDSCAPE USES: For marginal conditions calling for a specimen tree in small gardens or along streets, background plantings.

CLIMATE ADAPTION: Hardy to about 20°F (−6.5°C); widely adaptable but not for higher deserts.

CULTURE: Minimal soil requirement. Minimal water needs but looks better with deep, monthly irrigation during warmest months. Apply 2 oz. (57 g) ammonium sulfate in early spring to young trees. Prune to remove dead branches and shape. Propagate by seeds.

POSSIBLE PROBLEMS: Sparse appearance as it ages; litter; shallow rooted.

Ceanothus

PRONOUNCER: see-uh-*noh*-thus
FAMILY: Rhamnaceae

The "wild lilacs," native to North America, mainly California, have been cultivated ornamentally for years and remain some of the most popular and useful plants in Southwest landscapes.

Their chief horticultural value is the heavenly clusters of tiny, soft-scented flowers colored in a rich variety of shades from powdery blues and violets to deep purple-blues. And their clean, often dark green foliage provides a most restful element in the landscape. They are tree-sized to low spreaders in form.

With the exception of one or two, *Ceanothus* is best suited to coastal, inland and interior regions of California. Its natural range is, after all, concentrated in the mountains and foothills, particularly near the coast, of that state. Most species prefer cooler growing conditions, but some can endure the hot summers of the interior, provided they are given a semishady location.

Overwatering is a quick and certain way to kill them. Although some of the newer cultivars tolerate heavy soils, as well as general garden conditions, they by and large require good drainage and do best when planted on slopes. Even in the hot summers of the interior, plants should be watered only infrequently to avoid root rot. Siting plants outside of regularly irrigated areas is a good landscape strategy.

They are also susceptible to insect pests such as aphids, whiteflies and ceanothus stem gall moth, which distorts branch growth.

Although most ceanothus are short lived, they remain quite valuable in both natural and formal settings as screen, border and background plantings.

Ceanothus arboreus

PRONOUNCER: see-uh-*noh*-thus ar-*bor*-ee-us
COMMON NAME: Catalina ceanothus

Evergreen. Height: 12–20 ft. (3.5–6 m). Spread: 12–15 ft. (3.5–4.5 m). Rate of growth: Slow to moderate. Light requirement: Sun to part shade. Native to the Channel Islands of California.

A large shrub or small tree with smooth, gray branches; shiny, dark green, oval to elliptic leaves up to 3 in. (8 cm) long have three prominent veins extending from the base to the top with a dense covering of white hairs underneath.

FLOWER AND FRUIT: Large, pale blue clusters up to 6 in. (15 cm) long, February–May; dark, triangle-shaped, small fruits.

LANDSCAPE USES: A ceanothus for larger spaces; specimen shrub or tree; also useful as a tall background or slope plant.

CLIMATE ADAPTION: Frost tolerant; adapts to coastal and inland areas; needs partial shade in California's Central Valley.

CULTURE: Needs good drainage. Looks best with once-a-month, deep watering in the summer in the warmest areas; avoid overwatering. Little to no fertilizer. Prune after bloom to shape, as needed. Propagate by cuttings or by seeds treated with hot water and then cold stratified.

POSSIBLE PROBLEMS: Susceptible to damage by ceanothus stem gall moth.

Ceanothus 'Blue Jeans'   PLATE 59

COMMON NAME: blue jeans ceanothus

Evergreen. Height: 6–8 ft. (2–2.5 m). Spread: 6–8 ft. (2–2.5 m). Rate of growth: Fast. Light requirement: Sun. Cultivar.

A vigorous, erect to rounded, spreading shrub with small, glossy, dark green leaves to 0.5 in. (1.3 cm).

FLOWER AND FRUIT: Profuse clusters of heatherlike, pale blue to lavender flowers in the spring; small capsules.

LANDSCAPE USES: An attractive specimen, screen or hedge plant. Tolerates garden conditions well; resistant to deer.

CLIMATE ADAPTION: Best for coastal and inland southern California; does not like the summer

heat of the Central Valley.

CULTURE: Tolerates heavy soils. Likes summer irrigation every 3–4 weeks in the warmer, inland areas. Little to no fertilizer. Prune to shape after bloom; accepts shearing into hedge. Propagate by cuttings.

POSSIBLE PROBLEMS: Overwatering.

Ceanothus 'Concha' PLATE 60

COMMON NAME: concha ceanothus

Evergreen. Height: 5–7 ft. (1.5–2.2 m). Spread: 5–7 ft. (1.5–2.2 m). Rate of growth: Fast. Light requirement: Sun to part shade. Cultivar.

A medium-sized shrub with rich, dark green, 1-in. (2.5-cm) leaves densely covering the mounding branches.

FLOWER AND FRUIT: Profuse, dark blue, 1-in. (2.5-cm) flower clusters in March–May; fairly long bloom period; small capsule.

LANDSCAPE USES: An outstanding specimen shrub with good garden tolerance; also useful for screening, borders and mixed plantings. One of the more adaptable ceanothus with nice form, foliage and flowers; generally disease resistant.

CLIMATE ADAPTION: Hardy to 15°F (−9°C); best for coastal and inland southern California and an especially good choice for California's Central Valley.

CULTURE: Tolerates heavy soils. Likes summer watering every 2–3 weeks in the warmest areas. Little to no fertilizer. Prune after flowering to shape, as necessary. Propagate by cuttings.

POSSIBLE PROBLEMS: Overwatering.

Ceanothus 'Dark Star' PLATE 61

COMMON NAME: dark star ceanothus

Evergreen. Height: 5–6 ft. (1.5–2 m). Spread: 8–12 ft. (2.5–3.5 m). Rate of growth: Moderate. Light requirement: Sun. Cultivar.

A medium-sized, spreading shrub with narrow, crinkled, dark green leaves 0.25 in. (0.5 cm) long.

FLOWER AND FRUIT: Intense, dark blue, 1.5-in. (4-cm) flower clusters cover plants in the spring; small capsule follows.

LANDSCAPE USES: An excellent flowering accent plant; also useful in borders or as a medium screen; deerproof.

CLIMATE ADAPTION: Best for coastal and inland southern California and California's Central Valley.

CULTURE: Tolerates clay to sandy soils. Needs deep, summer watering every 2–4 weeks except on the coast, where its needs are minimal. Little to no fertilizer. Prune lightly after flowering. Propagate by cuttings.

POSSIBLE PROBLEMS: Overwatering.

Ceanothus 'Frosty Blue'

COMMON NAME: frosty blue ceanothus

Evergreen. Height: 6–10 ft. (2–3 m). Spread: 8–12 ft. (2.5–3.5 m). Rate of growth: Fast. Light requirement: Sun to partial shade. Cultivar.

A large shrub densely covered with shiny, small, dark green leaves with deep veins.

FLOWER AND FRUIT: Bright blue and white flower clusters are 3.5 in. (9 cm) long and have a frosted look, April–June; small capsule.

LANDSCAPE USES: A good choice for screening or on slopes; can be trained as an attractive specimen or a small tree. Combines well with darker-flowered ceanothus species. Tolerates garden conditions.

CLIMATE ADAPTION: Hardy to about 15°F (−9°C); best for coastal and inland southern California.

CULTURE: Tolerates heavy soils. Looks best with summer watering every 4–6 weeks in warmer, inland areas. Little to no fertilizer. Prune to shape or train as a small tree, after bloom. Propagate by cuttings.

POSSIBLE PROBLEMS: Becomes rangy without pruning.

Ceanothus greggii

PRONOUNCER: see-uh-*noh*-thus *greg*-ee-eye

COMMON NAME: Mojave ceanothus

Evergreen. Height: 3–6 ft. (1–2 m). Spread: 4–8 ft. (1.2–2.5 m). Rate of growth: Slow to moderate. Light requirement: Sun. Native to the Mojave Desert east to Arizona and Utah.

An erect, open shrub with gray-green, narrow, oval leaves up to 0.5 in. (1.3 cm) long held rigidly on stiff, gray branches; some variation exists within the species.

FLOWER AND FRUIT: Creamy white or sometimes bluish or pinkish flowers in small clusters, May–June; small, round capsules.

LANDSCAPE USES: A slope cover, barrier or divider plant in naturalized areas.

CLIMATE ADAPTION: Frost tolerant but does not like low-desert heat; best for mid- and higher-elevation deserts.

CULTURE: Needs good drainage. Drought tolerant; infrequent, deep watering every 4–6 weeks in the summer or during periods of long drought improves its appearance. No fertilizer. Prune to shape after flowering, as desired. Propagate by seeds or semihardwood cuttings.

POSSIBLE PROBLEMS: Can look straggly; flowers not as showy as other ceanothus.

Ceanothus greggii 'Perplexans'

has a denser habit, medium green foliage and abundant white flowers.

Ceanothus griseus

PRONOUNCER: see-uh-*noh*-thus *gris*-ee-us
COMMON NAME: Carmel ceanothus

Evergreen. Height: 3–10 ft. (1–3 m). Spread: 3–10 ft. (1–3 m). Rate of growth: Fast. Light requirement: Sun to partial shade. Native to California's Coast Range, Santa Barbara to Mendocino counties.

An upright, medium-sized shrub with broad, glabrous, dark green leaves to 1.75 in. (4.5 cm) long; resembles *C. thyrsiflorus*.

FLOWER AND FRUIT: Dense panicles to 2 in. (5 cm) long are violet-blue, March–May; roundish, tiny black capsules.

LANDSCAPE USES: As a specimen, in background plantings or on slopes; does well under oaks.

CLIMATE ADAPTION: Frost tolerant; best for coastal and inland southern California; needs partial shade in California's Central Valley.

CULTURE: Needs good drainage. Minimal watering in coastal areas but likes well-spaced irrigations, every 3–4 weeks in the summer in inland and interior locations. Little to no fertilizer. Prune to shape after flowering, as desired. Propagate by seeds or cuttings.

POSSIBLE PROBLEMS: Overwatering.

Ceanothus griseus var. *horizontalis*, the Carmel creeper, forms a dense, low carpet 1.5–2.5 ft. (45–75 cm) high, spreading 5–15 ft. (1.5–4.5 m), with light blue flowers.

Ceanothus hearstiorum   PLATE 62

PRONOUNCER: see-uh-*noh*-thus herst-ee-*or*-um
COMMON NAME: Hearst's ceanothus

Evergreen. Height: 4–8 in. (10–20 cm). Spread: 6–8 ft. (2–2.5 m). Rate of growth: Moderate. Light requirement: Sun to partial shade. Native to San Luis Obispo County, California.

A matlike ground cover that spreads over a large area; the small oblong leaves are medium to bright green and crinkled, covering prostrate branches.

FLOWER AND FRUIT: Bright blue flower clusters cover plants, March–April; small capsules.

LANDSCAPE USES: An attractive and adaptable ground cover for slopes, banks and borders.

CLIMATE ADAPTION: Best for coastal and inland southern California and California's Central Valley.

CULTURE: Needs good drainage. Needs summer watering every 2–4 weeks in the warmest areas. No fertilizer. Prune to keep in bounds as necessary after bloom. Propagate by cuttings.

POSSIBLE PROBLEMS: Weed invasions before plants become established.

Ceanothus impressus

PRONOUNCER: see-uh-*noh*-thus im-*press*-us
COMMON NAME: Santa Barbara ceanothus

Evergreen. Height: 6–8 ft. (2–2.5 m). Spread: 10–12 ft. (3–3.5 m). Rate of growth: Moderate. Light requirement: Sun. Native to Santa Barbara and San Luis Obispo counties, California.

A spreading, dense shrub with small, roundish, dark green leaves 0.5 in. (1.3 cm) long, with prominent veins; young growth covered with hairs.

FLOWER AND FRUIT: Dense clusters of dark blue flowers, March–April; small, rounded capsules.

LANDSCAPE USES: A slope or bank cover; good for large areas mixed with other ceanothus and native plants.

CLIMATE ADAPTION: Hardy to about 15°F (−9°C); best for coastal and inland southern California.

CULTURE: Needs porous soil with good drainage. Little to no summer irrigation required in coastal areas but likes some water every 4–6 weeks in the warmest, inland areas. Little to no fertilizer. Prune to shape. Propagate by seeds or cuttings.

POSSIBLE PROBLEMS: Somewhat fussy under garden conditions.

Ceanothus integerrimus

PRONOUNCER: see-uh-*noh*-thus in-te-*jer*-i-mus
COMMON NAME: deer brush

Semideciduous. Height: 3–10 ft. (1–3 m). Spread: 5–10 ft. (1.5–3 m). Rate of growth: Moderate. Light requirement: Sun to partial shade. Native to mountainous areas of the Southwest and West.

A somewhat open, medium to large shrub with broad, light green leaves to 3 in. (8 cm) long held on green branches; plants vary in leaf characteristics and flower color.

FLOWER AND FRUIT: Compound clusters of flowers to 6 in. (15 cm) long that vary from white to pink to deep blue in the spring; small, crested capsules.

LANDSCAPE USES: Looks best in naturalized or wild gardens and transitional areas, or as a slope or background plant. A valuable browse plant for livestock.

CLIMATE ADAPTION: Widely adaptable except for low deserts, where the summers are too hot.

CULTURE: Needs good drainage. Likes supplemental water in summer every 3–4 weeks in warmer locations. No fertilizer. Prune to shape and to promote denser habit in young plants. Propagate by seeds or cuttings.

POSSIBLE PROBLEMS: Somewhat straggly with age; flowers not as showy as those of other ceanothus.

Ceanothus 'Joyce Coulter' PLATE 63
COMMON NAME: Joyce Coulter ceanothus
Evergreen. Height: 3–5 ft. (1–1.5 m). Spread: 6–12 ft. (2–3.5 m). Rate of growth: Fast. Light requirement: Sun to partial shade. Cultivar.
A medium-sized, wide-spreading shrub with a mounding habit; deep green, narrow leaves about 1–2 in. (2.5–5 cm) long.
FLOWER AND FRUIT: Medium blue flower clusters are 3–5 in. (8–13 cm) long in April; small capsules.
LANDSCAPE USES: Along borders, roadsides, or on banks. An attractive shrub that is adaptable and tolerant of garden conditions.
CLIMATE ADAPTION: Hardy to at least 20°F (−6.5°C); best for coastal and inland southern California; appreciates some shade in California's Central Valley.
CULTURE: Tolerates heavy soils. Moderately drought tolerant; plants in interior locations require deep watering up to twice a month during the summer. Little to no fertilizer. Prune to shape or control size, as necessary. Propagate by cuttings.
POSSIBLE PROBLEMS: Overwatering.

Ceanothus 'Julia Phelps' PLATE 64
COMMON NAME: Julia Phelps ceanothus
Evergreen. Height: 4–6 ft. (1.2–2 m). Spread: 6–10 ft. (2–3 m). Rate of growth: Moderate. Light requirement: Sun to partial shade. Cultivar.
A medium-sized shrub with dense, stiff branches and small, dark green, deeply veined leaves.
FLOWER AND FRUIT: Abundant and beautiful dark blue, 1-in. (2.5-cm) flower clusters in April; small capsules.
LANDSCAPE USES: Attractive mixed with other native and low-water-use plants, including flannel bush, manzanita and mahonia. Ideal for slopes; provides outstanding floral display.
CLIMATE ADAPTION: Hardy to about 15°F (−9°C); best for coastal and inland southern California; does not like heat.
CULTURE: Needs good drainage. May need summer watering every 4–6 weeks in the warmest inland locations but does not tolerate regular irrigation. Little to no fertilizer. Prune lightly to shape after bloom, as desired. Propagate by cuttings.
POSSIBLE PROBLEMS: Overwatering.

Ceanothus maritimus
PRONOUNCER: see-uh-*noh*-thus ma-*rit*-i-mus
COMMON NAME: maritime ceanothus
Evergreen. Height: 1–3 ft. (30–90 cm).

Spread: 3–8 ft. (1–2.5 m). Rate of growth: Moderate. Light requirement: Sun to partial shade. Native to San Luis Obispo County, California.
A low, spreading shrub with numerous, rigid, dense branches; glossy, thick leaves are 0.5 in. (1.3 cm) long, dark green above and whitish beneath.
FLOWER AND FRUIT: White to lavender or light blue flowers in 0.5-in. (1.3-cm) clusters, January–March; small capsules.
LANDSCAPE USES: A low border or ground cover in small areas; or cascading over boulders or low walls.
CLIMATE ADAPTION: Best for coastal and inland southern California and California's Central Valley; needs partial shade in inland and interior areas.
CULTURE: Needs good drainage. Needs infrequent, deep summer watering in warmer areas. No fertilizer. Prune to shape or keep in bounds after flowering, as necessary. Propagate by seeds or cuttings.
POSSIBLE PROBLEMS: Weed infestations.

Ceanothus ramulosus var. **fascicularis** PLATE 65
PRONOUNCER: see-uh-*noh*-thus ram-ewe-*loh*-sus fah-sik-ewe-*lair*-is
COMMON NAME: Lompoc ceanothus
Evergreen. Height: 3–8 ft. (1–2.5 m). Spread: 5–10 ft. (1.5–3 m). Rate of growth: Moderate. Light requirement: Sun. Native to Santa Barbara and San Luis Obispo counties, California.
A rounded to spreading shrub with arching branches; soft, billowy appearance in bloom; elliptic leaves to 0.75 in. (2 cm) are bright green and glossy.
FLOWER AND FRUIT: Breathtaking display of lavender to light blue flower clusters, March–April; small capsules.
LANDSCAPE USES: Specimen shrub, for screening or to cascade over banks.
CLIMATE ADAPTION: Hardy to about 15°F (−9°C); best for coastal and inland southern California.
CULTURE: Needs good drainage. Looks best with 3–4 summer irrigations in inland areas. Little to no fertilizer. Prune lightly to shape as desired after bloom. Propagate by seeds or cuttings.
POSSIBLE PROBLEMS: Overwatering.

Ceanothus 'Ray Hartman' PLATE 66
COMMON NAME: Ray Hartman ceanothus
Evergreen. Height: 12–16 ft. (3.5–5 m). Spread: 12–16 ft. (3.5–5 m). Rate of growth: Fast. Light requirement: Sun to partial shade. Cultivar.
A large, vigorous shrub or small tree with

erect to spreading branches; large, 2–3 in. (5–8 cm), shiny, dark green leaves.

FLOWER AND FRUIT: Abundant, medium blue flower spikes are 3–5 in. (8–13 cm) long in April; small capsules.

LANDSCAPE USES: Handsome, spring-flowering accent plant; good in background or naturalized settings; can also be trained as a small tree. Needs room. Combine with darker-flowered ceanothus. One of the older cultivars, but a reliable and beautiful one.

CLIMATE ADAPTION: Widely adaptable in California except for the deserts; one of the best for the Central Valley.

CULTURE: Needs good drainage. Likes a monthly, deep watering in summer in the warmest areas. Little to no fertilizer. Prune to shape or to train as a single- or multitrunked tree. Propagate by cuttings.

POSSIBLE PROBLEMS: Tends to be rangy.

Ceanothus rigidus 'Snowball'   PLATE 67

PRONOUNCER: see-uh-*noh*-thus *ri*-ji-dus

COMMON NAME: Monterey ceanothus

Evergreen. Height: 4–6 ft. (1.2–2 m). Spread: 4–10 ft. (1.2–3 m). Rate of growth: Moderate. Light requirement: Sun to partial shade. A selected form of *C. rigidus*.

A round to spreading, dense shrub with small, smooth, dark green leaves.

FLOWER AND FRUIT: Small, tight clusters of white flowers cover plants, March–April; small capsules.

LANDSCAPE USES: Good slope or screen plant; a flowering accent to mix with other plants or dark-flowered varieties of ceanothus; quite handsome and long lived.

CLIMATE ADAPTION: Hardy to about 15°F (−9°C); best for coastal and inland southern California and California's Central Valley, where it needs afternoon shade.

CULTURE: Needs good drainage. Water deeply in summer every 3–4 weeks in the warmest locations. Little to no fertilizer. Prune to control size or shape, as desired. Propagate by seeds or cuttings.

POSSIBLE PROBLEMS: Overwatering.

Ceanothus thyrsiflorus

PRONOUNCER: see-uh-*noh*-thus thir-si-*flor*-us

COMMON NAME: blueblossom

Evergreen. Height: 6–20 ft. (2–6 m). Spread: 8–10 ft. (2.5–3 m). Rate of growth: Moderate. Light requirement: Sun to partial shade. Native to California's Coast Range.

A large shrub or small tree with angular branches bearing oval, dark green leaves to 2 in.

(5 cm) long.

FLOWER AND FRUIT: 3-in. (8-cm), pale to deep blue flower clusters, March–May, followed by small, roundish capsules.

LANDSCAPE USES: A specimen shrub or small tree, or mixed with other plants for backgrounds, barriers and slopes.

CLIMATE ADAPTION: Frost tolerant; best for coastal southern California; needs partial shade in inland southern California and California's Central Valley.

CULTURE: Needs good drainage. Likes deep waterings every 3–4 weeks in summer in the warmest areas. Little to no fertilizer. Prune to shape, or to train in youth as a tree. Propagate by seeds or cuttings.

POSSIBLE PROBLEMS: Overwatering.

Ceanothus thyrsiflorus 'Skylark' is 6–8 ft. (2–2.5 m) with dark blue flowers in June; tolerates moderate watering.

Ceanothus thyrsiflorus 'Snow Flurry' is a heavy bloomer with large, white flower clusters. Grows to 6–10 ft. (2–3 m).

Celtis

PRONOUNCER: *sell*-tis

FAMILY: Ulmaceae

The rugged hackberries are ideal for transitional or informal areas of the landscape. They attract an abundance of wildlife, including birds and small mammals that relish their fruit. The netleaf hackberry requires moister conditions than the desert hackberry and even tolerates lawn situations.

Celtis pallida   PLATE 68

PRONOUNCER: *sell*-tis *pal*-lid-ah

COMMON NAME: desert hackberry

Evergreen to deciduous. Height: 5–12 ft. (1.5–3.5 m). Spread: 5–10 ft. (1.5–3 m). Rate of growth: Slow. Light requirement: Sun. Native from western Texas to Arizona and northern Mexico.

Large, sprawling, thorny shrub or small tree with dense, irregular branching habit; deep green, oval leaves have coarsely toothed margins and a sandpapery texture.

FLOWER AND FRUIT: Tiny spring flowers and orange berries in the fall.

LANDSCAPE USES: Dense screen or barrier plant; informal or transitional areas. Valuable for erosion control.

CLIMATE ADAPTION: Cold hardy but may lose leaves under 20°F (−6.5°C); no heat problems;

best for deserts.

CULTURE: Minimal soil requirement. Minimal water requirement, but grows faster with some supplemental water about once a month in summer. Apply 2 oz. (57 g) ammonium sulfate in early spring to promote growth. Prune as desired to control size. Propagate by seeds.

POSSIBLE PROBLEMS: Thorns.

Celtis reticulata

PRONOUNCER: *sell*-tis reh-ti-kew-*lah*-tah

COMMON NAME: netleaf hackberry, western hackberry

Deciduous. Height: 25–30 ft. (7.5–9 m). Spread: 25–30 ft. (7.5–9 m). Rate of growth: Moderate. Light requirement: Sun. Native from Arizona to Colorado, Texas and south into Mexico at elevations of 2,500 to 6,000 ft. (760–1,830 m).

A spreading tree with irregular form and pendulous branches; rough, dark green leaves are asymmetrical, oval to lanceolate, 1–3 in. (2.5–8 cm) long, with smooth margins; bark is gray to reddish brown.

FLOWER AND FRUIT: Tiny flowers in spring not showy; tiny red to orange berries in fall.

LANDSCAPE USES: Specimen or shade tree or for informal areas where it provides shelter and berries for birds and animals.

CLIMATE ADAPTION: Hardy to about −20°F (−29°C); no heat problems; best for deserts and Central Valley of California.

CULTURE: Needs good drainage. Does not tolerate extended drought; requires deep watering every 3–4 weeks in warmest months. Apply 1 lb. (0.45 kg) ammonium sulfate in late winter per 100 sq. ft. (9 sq. m) under leaf canopy. Prune in winter to shape and expose interesting form. Propagate by seeds.

POSSIBLE PROBLEMS: Leaf galls caused by insects can be unsightly; looks rangy and messy if not maintained; reseeds.

Ceratoides lanata

PRONOUNCER: sair-ah-*toy*-deez lah-*nah*-tah

FAMILY: Chenopodiaceae

COMMON NAME: winterfat

Semideciduous. Height: 1–3 ft. (30–90 cm). Spread: 1–1.5 ft. (30–45 cm). Rate of growth: Fast. Light requirement: Sun. Widespread throughout western United States.

A small, erect shrub which in fall becomes an attractive, cloudy mass of white seed heads; pale blue-green leaves to 2 in. (5 cm) long are covered with whitish hairs; many stems, woody at the base; deeply rooted.

FLOWER AND FRUIT: Inconspicuous flowers in the spring and summer are followed by white, woolly seed heads in the fall.

LANDSCAPE USES: Good plant for contrast, both foliage and ornamental fruits; mix with other plants in a border or plant in naturalized areas. Useful for erosion control; important forage plant.

CLIMATE ADAPTION: Hardy to below 0°F (−18°C); widely adaptable from coastal areas to high deserts.

CULTURE: Minimal soil requirement but likes alkaline soil. Very drought tolerant; survives without supplemental water. No fertilizer. For compact growth, cut back in late winter. Propagate by seeds.

POSSIBLE PROBLEMS: Attracts birds; browsed by livestock, deer and rabbits.

Ceratonia siliqua   PLATE 69

PRONOUNCER: sair-ah-*tone*-ee-ah sil-*ee*-quah

FAMILY: Leguminosae

COMMON NAME: carob tree

Evergreen. Height: 25–30 ft. (7.5–9 m). Spread: 20–35 ft. (6–10.5 m). Rate of growth: Fast. Light requirement: Sun. Native to Mediterranean region.

A very broad-canopied tree with dense foliage providing deep shade; dark green compound leaf 8 in. (20 cm) or more long with rounded leaflets about 1 × 2 in. (2.5 × 5 cm); the heavy trunk becomes somewhat gnarled and picturesque with age.

FLOWER AND FRUIT: White flower clusters on males in spring; females have small, red flower clusters that produce chocolate brown, slender, 6–12 in. (15–30 cm) long, edible pods; pods sold commercially in health-food stores.

LANDSCAPE USES: If space is available, a good landscape tree where dense shade is needed; can produce a 25-ft. (7.5-m) tree with 20-ft. (6-m) spread within 10 years, with single or multiple trunks.

CLIMATE ADAPTION: Hardy to about 20°F (−6.5°C); loves heat; best for low deserts and coastal and inland areas of southern California.

CULTURE: No special soil requirement but avoid continual moisture around the base, a condition favoring crown rot. While drought resistant, it does best with monthly, deep watering in warm months in hotter locations. Apply an all-purpose fertilizer such as 10–6–4 in early spring at the rate of one cupful (225 g) for each year the tree has been in the landscape. Remove suckers as they develop; minimize pruning cuts of large limbs as wounds are very slow to heal. Propagate by seeds or air layering in summer.

73

Cercidium praecox

POSSIBLE PROBLEMS: Roots heave pavement if planted too close; litter from females; unpleasant odor from male flowers; root rot; wind breakage.

Cercidium

PRONOUNCER: sir-*sid*-ee-um
FAMILY: Leguminosae

The palo verdes are common inhabitants of the valleys, arroyos and foothills of the Southwest deserts and Mexico. They are easily recognized by their green to blue-green bark and branches which carry on photosynthesis when leaves are not present. They tolerate high summer desert temperatures well and make fine specimen and filtered-shade trees. They are a beautiful sight in spring when their branches burst into clouds of yellow flowers.

Cercidium floridum   PLATE 70

PRONOUNCER: sir-*sid*-ee-um *flor*-i-dum
COMMON NAME: blue palo verde

Deciduous. Height: 15–25 ft. (4.5–7.5 m). Spread: 15–30 ft. (4.5–9 m). Rate of growth: Moderate to fast. Light requirement: Sun. Native to washes and floodplains of Sonoran Desert in Arizona, California and Mexico.

A small tree with a spreading habit and attractive blue-green foliage and bark; usually, the first palo verde to bloom in the spring; leaves are divided into small oval leaflets on spiny branches.
FLOWER AND FRUIT: Pale to bright yellow flowers appear before new leaves, filling the entire canopy, followed by 3-in. (8-cm) seed pods that the Indians used as food.
LANDSCAPE USES: A small specimen tree for desert landscapes; blue-green foliage and bark make for a handsome contrast with more deeply colored plants; provides filtered shade.
CLIMATE ADAPTION: Hardy to about 12°F (−11°C); no heat problems; best for low- and mid-elevation deserts.
CULTURE: Needs good drainage, prefers a sandy soil. Likes deep watering once a month in the summer; drops its leaves during extreme dry spells; grows larger with more irrigation, sometimes reaching 35 ft. (10 m). Apply 1 lb. (0.45 kg) ammonium sulfate per 100 sq. ft. (9 sq. m) of leaf canopy in February for faster growth. Young trees need training; keep lower branches pruned up. Propagate by scarified seeds.
POSSIBLE PROBLEMS: May die after 20–25 years; litter; older trees are not as attractive as when young; mistletoe infestations; palo verde beetle larvae may kill.

Cercidium microphyllum   PLATE 71

PRONOUNCER: sir-*sid*-ee-um my-cro-*fil*-um
COMMON NAME: foothill palo verde, little-leaf palo verde

Deciduous. Height: 10–15 ft. (3–4.5 m) or more. Spread: 15–20 ft. (4.5–6 m). Rate of growth: Slow. Light requirement: Sun. Native to dry, rocky slopes, 4,000 ft. (1,218 m) or lower, of Sonoran Desert, Arizona, California, south into Mexico and Baja California.

This smallest and probably most rugged of the palo verdes produces yellow-green foliage and bark and an irregular, multitrunked form; leaves are divided into tiny rounded leaflets; branch ends are spiny.
FLOWER AND FRUIT: Pale to bright yellow flowers in spring, followed by 2-in. (5-cm) pod with a characteristic sharp beak.
LANDSCAPE USES: With some training, it makes an attractive specimen tree that fits into desert landscaping well; in nature, often found growing near blue palo verde, *C. floridum*.
CLIMATE ADAPTION: Hardy to about 15°F (−9°C); no heat problems; best in low- and mid-elevation deserts.
CULTURE: Needs good drainage. Minimal water requirements but does best with a monthly, deep irrigation in summer; drops its leaves if drought stressed. Apply 1 lb. (0.45 kg) ammonium sulfate per 100 sq. ft. (9 sq. m) of leaf canopy in February for faster growth. Remove lower branches and thin to expose branch structure. Propagate by scarified seeds.
POSSIBLE PROBLEMS: Litter from flowers and seed pods; palo verde beetle larvae may kill; mistletoe infestations.

Cercidium praecox   PLATE 72

PRONOUNCER: sir-*sid*-ee-um *pray*-cox
COMMON NAME: palo brea, Sonoran palo verde

Deciduous. Height: 15–25 ft. (4.5–7.5 m). Spread: 15–25 ft. (4.5–7.5 m). Rate of growth: Moderate. Light requirement: Sun. Native to Mexico.

Considered by many as the Sonoran Desert's most beautiful tree. Smooth, green bark on the trunk and branches; fine, light green foliage gives it a leafier look than other palo verdes; strong lateral branch habit creates an interesting silhouette; thorny.
FLOWER AND FRUIT: Masses of bright yellow flowers in spring followed by small, oblong, brown seed pods.
LANDSCAPE USES: Choice selection as a small specimen tree or in groupings or rows; provides summer shade and winter sun.
CLIMATE ADAPTION: Hardy to about 20°F (−6.5°C);

no heat problems; best in the low desert; sometimes frost damaged in the mid-elevation desert.

CULTURE: Needs good drainage. Rainfall normally meets its water needs, but it looks best with deep irrigation once a month during the growing season. Apply 1 lb. (0.45 kg) ammonium sulfate in February for each 100 sq. ft. (9 sq. m) of leaf canopy. Prune every January to develop head-high canopy and accentuate strong branch structure. Cut out infestations of mistletoe, a parasitic plant, or a dense, rounded mass known as "witches' broom" (caused by eriophyid mites), whenever either occur. Propagate by scarified seeds.

POSSIBLE PROBLEMS: Young trees need protection during frosts; short lived, 25–30 years; root borer may kill.

Cercis occidentalis PLATE 73

PRONOUNCER: *sair*-sis ox-i-den-*tal*-is
FAMILY: Leguminosae
COMMON NAME: western redbud

Deciduous. Height: 10–20 ft. (3–6 m). Spread: 10–15 ft. (3–4.5 m). Rate of growth: Moderate. Light requirement: Sun to light shade. Native mainly to California's foothills and canyons, but also to parts of Arizona, Nevada and Utah.

A large, open shrub or small tree with year-round seasonal interest; attractive, rounded to heart-shaped leaves to 3.5 in. (9 cm) wide, light green on spreading branches.

FLOWER AND FRUIT: Showy clusters of bright magenta flowers line the branches, February–April, before the leaves appear; seed pods are reddish, to 3 in. (8 cm) long.

LANDSCAPE USES: Handsome flowering accent for mixed plantings, slopes and backgrounds; effective with plants requiring light shade. Provides brilliant, early spring color and some yellow to red color in the fall; resistant to oak root fungus.

CLIMATE ADAPTION: Hardy to about 10°F (−12°C); best for inland southern California and California's Central Valley.

CULTURE: Minimal soil requirement. Drought tolerant but needs once-a-month, deep watering in the summer in the hottest areas. No fertilizer. Prune after bloom to shape or to train as a tree; try to maintain an open, spreading form. Propagate by seeds after hot water treatment and stratification for two months.

POSSIBLE PROBLEMS: Flower set may vary from plant to plant; reseeds.

Cercocarpus betuloides PLATE 74

PRONOUNCER: sair-koh-*kar*-pus bet-ewe-*loy*-deez
FAMILY: Rosaceae
COMMON NAME: western mountain mahogany

Evergreen. Height: 6–20 ft. (2–6 m). Spread: 8–12 ft. (2.5–3.5 m). Rate of growth: Moderate to fast. Light requirement: Sun to partial shade. Native to California's chaparral and woodlands, north to Oregon and south into Baja California.

Usually seen as a large shrub to about 12 ft. (3.5 m) high but sometimes becomes a 20-ft. (6-m) tree; erect to spreading, smooth, gray branches; dark green, oval, birchlike leaves to 1 in. (2.5 cm) long have conspicuous veins and toothed upper margins; quite variable.

FLOWER AND FRUIT: Small, whitish flowers in clusters of 2–3, March–May; distinctive fruits have a twisted, feathery style attached.

LANDSCAPE USES: Open branch structure makes an attractive background tree or shrub, or mix with other native plants; good for slopes.

CLIMATE ADAPTION: Hardy to at least 15°F (−9°C); best for coastal and inland southern California; needs part shade in California's Central Valley; does not like desert heat.

CULTURE: Minimal soil requirement; tolerates alkaline conditions. Needs supplemental water every 3–4 weeks in the summer in the warmest areas. No fertilizer. Needs little pruning; if necessary, maintain the natural framework. Propagate by seeds.

POSSIBLE PROBLEMS: Poor appearance of older plants.

Cercocarpus betuloides var. *blancheae* from the Channel Islands of California is more symmetrical and more adaptable.

Cercocarpus montanus, the mountain mahogany, is deciduous, smaller, more useful in colder climates.

Chamaerops humilis PLATE 75

PRONOUNCER: *kam*-er-ops *hu*-mi-lis
FAMILY: Palmae
COMMON NAME: Mediterranean fan palm

Evergreen. Height: 10–20 ft. (3–6 m). Spread: 10–15 ft. (3–4.5 m). Rate of growth: Very slow. Light requirement: Sun or shade. Native to Mediterranean area.

Attractive, clumping palm with gracefully curved trunks topped with green, fan-shaped leaves, 3–4 ft. (about 1 m) across; persistent leaf bases along the trunk give it an appealing, rough texture.

FLOWER AND FRUIT: Inconspicuous flowers

followed by small, shiny black fruit that clusters around the trunk just below the leaf stalks.

LANDSCAPE USES: Accent or focal plant producing a tropical look; use near entryways, at corners, and combined with other accent plants, such as yuccas and agaves. Probably the best palm for the average-sized home landscape since it grows only about 6 in. (15 cm) a year. Always looks good, great around swimming pools or in containers. Excellent wind resistance.

CLIMATE ADAPTION: Hardy to about 6°F (−14°C); takes desert heat; widely adaptable from coastal areas to deserts.

CULTURE: Tolerant of soil conditions but likes rich soil. Moderate drought tolerance; likes deep irrigation in warmest months—4–6 inches (10–15 cm) at three-week intervals—but survives on little; apply same amount every six weeks in winter. To speed growth, apply 1 lb. (0.45 kg) ammonium sulfate to large, established tree in February and June; water deeply afterwards. Offsets may be removed if a single-trunked form is desired; remove old fronds. Propagate by seeds and offsets.

POSSIBLE PROBLEMS: Thorns; offsets; somewhat susceptible to heart rot fungus when humidity is high; young trees are frost tender.

Chilopsis linearis   PLATE 76

PRONOUNCER: chill-*op*-sis lin-ee-*air*-is
FAMILY: Bignoniaceae
COMMON NAME: desert willow

Deciduous. Height: 15–30 ft. (4.5–9 m). Spread: 10–15 ft. (3–4.5 m). Rate of growth: Fast. Light requirement: Sun to partial shade. Native to dry washes of the Southwest and Mexico.

A large shrub or small tree with open, ascending branch habit and weeping appearance; glossy, willowlike leaves are usually 3–5 in. (8–13 cm) long but can vary according to native habitat; not a true willow despite appearance; deep rooted. Cultivars include 'Barranca', a more upright form with deeper lavender flowers; 'Tejas', with pink and reddish purple flowers; 'Marfa Lace', with semidouble pink and rose flowers, and 'Alpine', which has wider leaves and very large, pink flowers.

FLOWER AND FRUIT: Showy, trumpet-shaped flowers in the spring and summer range in color from white to purple and look somewhat like orchids; 4–8 in. (10–20 cm) narrow pods hang on through winter; blooms the first year after planting.

LANDSCAPE USES: A graceful, small tree or large shrub; use as a specimen or in groups; spectacu-

lar in bloom and fast growing, often 3 ft. (1 m) a year before it matures. Blends well with other desert plants. Useful for erosion control on slopes or washes. Handsome when grown as a naturally multitrunked tree.

CLIMATE ADAPTION: Hardy to at least 10°F (−12°C); takes heat; best in deserts.

CULTURE: Needs good drainage. Minimal water requirement but twice-monthly, deep watering at flowering time improves bloom. Minimal fertilizer needs but flourishes with a cup (225 g) of ammonium sulfate in late winter after the first year in the landscape. If forming a single-trunked tree, choose a strong central leader and remove lower branches as it grows; otherwise, prune to shape. Roots produce frequent suckers, which must be removed. Propagate by seeds or hardwood as well as semihardwood cuttings.

POSSIBLE PROBLEMS: Pods produce some litter and can be unsightly hanging from bare branches in the winter; suckers.

Cistus

PRONOUNCER: *sis*-tus
FAMILY: Cistaceae

Cistus hybridus (C. corbariensis) is shrubby, 2–5 ft. (60 cm–1.5 m) high with abundant white flowers 1.5 in. (4 cm) across in the spring and summer.

Cistus ladanifer has 4 in. (10 cm) long, narrow, dark green leaves and white flowers with a purple spot at the base of the petals in summer; about 3 ft. (1 m) high.

Cistus purpureus   PLATE 77

PRONOUNCER: *sis*-tus pur-pur-*ay*-us
COMMON NAME: orchid rockrose

Evergreen. Height: 3–4 ft. (about 1 m). Spread: 3–4 ft. (about 1 m). Rate of growth: Fast. Light requirement: Sun. Native to the Mediterranean region.

A rounded, flowering shrub with narrow, crinkly leaves, 2–3 in. (5–8 cm) long that are dark green above, gray-green and hairy below.

FLOWER AND FRUIT: Reddish purple, 3-in. (8-cm) flowers have five petals with a distinctive blotch at the base of each petal, June–July; seed capsule.

LANDSCAPE USES: Colorful in masses, for borders, on slopes, or as a specimen shrub; provides erosion control.

CLIMATE ADAPTION: Hardy to about 15°F (−9°C); best for coastal southern California, where it takes the wind and salt spray, and inland southern California and California's Central Valley; marginal in desert heat.

CULTURE: Needs good drainage. Drought tolerant; requires watering every 2–3 weeks during the summer in inland and interior areas. Apply light amounts of a balanced fertilizer before flowering. Tip-prune after bloom to stimulate bushy growth; occasionally thin out the oldest branches. Propagate by seeds or softwood cuttings.

POSSIBLE PROBLEMS: Be careful not to overwater.

Cistus salviifolius is a low, spreading shrub to 6 ft. (2 m) across with 1.5-in. (4-cm), white flowers with yellow spots at the base of the petals in the spring.

Comarostaphylis diversifolia   PLATE 78

PRONOUNCER: kom-air-oh-*staff*-i-lis di-ver-si-*foh*-lee-ah

FAMILY: Ericaceae

COMMON NAME: summer holly

Evergreen. Height: 15–20 ft. (4.5–6 m). Spread: 15–20 ft. (4.5–6 m). Rate of growth: Slow to moderate. Light requirement: Sun to part shade. Native to dry slopes from Santa Barbara County, California, south into Baja California.

An attractive, rounded, large shrub or small tree with a dense, neat look; oaklike, dark green leaves are leathery, oblong, to 3.5 in. (9 cm) long, and lined with sharp teeth.

FLOWER AND FRUIT: Whitish, urn-shaped flowers in clusters, May–June; showy, red berry clusters follow in late summer and fall.

LANDSCAPE USES: Dark, clean foliage makes it ideal for more formal areas of landscape; also useful for screening or as a background plant. Provides a neat look year-round as well as seasonal color by virtue of its flowers and fruit.

CLIMATE ADAPTION: Hardy to about 15°F (−9°C) but does not take high temperatures; best for coastal and inland southern California; needs some shade in California's Central Valley.

CULTURE: Needs good drainage. Water once a month in summer. Little to no fertilizer. Prune to shape or train as a tree. Propagate by seeds.

POSSIBLE PROBLEMS: Slow to get going; not widely available.

Convolvulus cneorum   PLATE 79

PRONOUNCER: con-*vol*-vew-lus nee-*or*-um

FAMILY: Convolvulaceae

COMMON NAME: bush morning glory, silverbush

Evergreen. Height: 1–2 ft. (30–60 cm). Spread: 3–4 ft. (about 1 m). Rate of growth: Moderate. Light requirement: Sun to part shade. Native to southern Europe.

A compact ground cover with narrow leaves that are 2.5 in. (6 cm) long, gray-green above and silvery white below.

FLOWER AND FRUIT: White to pink flowers like the common morning glory's appear spring through summer and year-round in milder areas.

LANDSCAPE USES: Tough plant for street medians as well as garden displays; use in small masses or mixed with other low-growing shrubs; foliar and flowering accent.

CLIMATE ADAPTION: Hardy to at least 10°F (−12°C); no heat problems; widely adaptable.

CULTURE: Needs light, rapidly draining soil. Minimal water requirement but in the summer likes supplemental water every 2–3 weeks in hottest areas. Does not tolerate overhead watering. Little to no fertilizer. Prune hard occasionally to rejuvenate and promote compact growth. Propagate by cuttings.

POSSIBLE PROBLEMS: Can die out with overwatering; becomes leggy in deep shade.

Cordia

PRONOUNCER: *kor*-dee-ah

FAMILY: Boraginaceae

The white-flowering cordias offer desert gardens a combination of color and durability. The little-leaf cordia, *C. parvifolia*, appears quite unremarkable in the off season, but becomes a showy springtime beauty when in bloom. Flowers appear on and off through the summer. It is more drought and heat tolerant than Texas olive, *C. boissieri*, thriving in roadside landscapes, though Texas olive has a lusher look with its large, dark green leaves. Both are cold hardy throughout the warm-arid Southwest and need little maintenance.

Cordia boissieri   PLATE 80

PRONOUNCER: *kor*-dee-ah boy-see-*air*-eye

COMMON NAME: Texas olive, anacahuite

Deciduous. Height: 15–20 ft. (4.5–6 m). Spread: 12–18 ft. (3.5–5.5 m). Rate of growth: Moderate. Light requirement: Sun. Native to southern Texas and Mexico.

A large shrub or small tree valued for its lovely, rhododendronlike clusters of flowers and the textural contrast of its foliage; dark green, velvety-soft leaves are oblong, 1–5 in. (2.5–13 cm) long on stout branches.

FLOWER AND FRUIT: Funnel-shaped, white flowers 2 in. (5 cm) across in terminal clusters in spring and summer; 1-in. (2.5-cm), berrylike fruit, yellowish in summer, brown in fall.

LANDSCAPE USES: Flowering accent; as specimen; background or in small groups.

CLIMATE ADAPTION: Cold hardy to about 10°F (−12°C); no problems with heat; best for deserts.

CULTURE: Prefers good drainage. Requires moderate water during bloom period; twice monthly, deep irrigation through summer in low desert. Apply 2 oz. (57 g) ammonium sulfate in February to speed growth. Prune after bloom to shape or train as a tree. Propagate by seeds or softwood or semihardwood cuttings. Fresh seeds germinate quickly but stored seeds need stratification.

POSSIBLE PROBLEMS: Foliage sometimes damaged by late-season frost.

Cordia parvifolia   PLATE 81

PRONOUNCER: *kor*-dee-ah par-vi-*foh*-lee-ah

COMMON NAME: little-leaf cordia

Deciduous. Height: 5–8 ft. (1.5–2.5 m). Spread: 6–10 ft. (2–3 m). Rate of growth: Moderate. Light requirement: Sun. Native to Chihuahuan and Sonoran deserts.

Spring-flowering shrub with open, spreading form; medium to gray-green leaves are 0.25 in. (0.5 cm) long, oval, with toothed margins.

FLOWER AND FRUIT: Lovely, white, crepelike flowers are cup-shaped, 2 in. (5 cm) across, in spring and summer; small, fleshy fruit.

LANDSCAPE USES: Flowering accent in small groupings; mixes well with desert shrubs. Flowers and foliage make an attractive cascade over low walls. Tough enough for roadside and highway plantings.

CLIMATE ADAPTION: Cold hardy to at least 15°F (−9°C); heat tolerant; best in deserts.

CULTURE: Needs good drainage. Minimal water requirement but looks best with irrigation every 2–3 weeks through bloom period. Minimal fertilizer. Prune following bloom to shape or control size. Propagate by seeds or cuttings.

POSSIBLE PROBLEMS: May drop leaves if it becomes too dry in summer.

Cotoneaster buxifolius   PLATE 82

PRONOUNCER: kuh-toe-nee-*as*-ter buk-si-*foh*-lee-us

FAMILY: Rosaceae

COMMON NAME: bright-bead cotoneaster

Evergreen. Height: 1–2 ft. (30–60 cm). Spread: 3–6 ft. (1–2 m). Rate of growth: Slow. Light requirement: Sun to partial shade. Native to western China.

A low, sprawling shrub with arching or stiff, gray-green branches and small, gray-green leaves. Formerly known as *C. glaucophyllus*.

FLOWER AND FRUIT: Small, white flowers in dense clusters in the spring followed in the fall by small, reddish orange berries.

LANDSCAPE USES: Ground cover or space definer in arid landscapes; nice in planters.

CLIMATE ADAPTION: Widely adaptable; hardy to about 10°F (−12°C); needs afternoon shade in the desert.

CULTURE: Requires loose, well-drained soil with humus. Prefers to be irrigated deeply at widely spaced intervals. To promote growth, apply 2 oz. (57 g) ammonium sulfate in early spring. Prune to size or remove dead wood. Propagate by leafy cuttings in spring or summer or by layering.

POSSIBLE PROBLEMS: Texas root rot; iron chlorosis in alkaline soils; fireblight.

Cotoneaster lacteus, the red clusterberry, and *C. pannosus*, the silverleaf cotoneaster, are larger but equally attractive.

Cowania mexicana

PRONOUNCER: cow-*ay*-nee-ah mex-i-*cah*-nah

FAMILY: Rosaceae

COMMON NAME: cliffrose

Evergreen. Height: 4–6 ft. (1.2–2 m). Spread: 4–6 ft. (1.2–2 m). Rate of growth: Moderate. Light requirement: Sun. Native to Mojave Desert, east to Texas and into Mexico.

A spreading, much-branched shrub; small, thick, dark green leaves with 3–5 deep lobes and about 0.5 in. (1.3 cm) long.

FLOWER AND FRUIT: White or yellowish, single-rose type, 1-in. (2.5-cm) flowers in spring are very fragrant; feathery, long, narrow fruit follows in fall. May bloom in the fall in warmer areas.

LANDSCAPE USES: Flowers and fruit are rather showy so it can be used as an accent plant; suitable for screening or for erosion control on slopes.

CLIMATE ADAPTION: Best for middle and high deserts; questionable in low-desert heat; cold tolerant.

CULTURE: Likes dry-soil environment, good drainage. Minimal water requirement; likes deep watering every 3–4 weeks in summer, but overwatering produces weak growth. Minimal

fertilizer; fixes nitrogen. Prune after flowering to shape or obtain more compact growth. Propagate by seeds or cuttings.
POSSIBLE PROBLEMS: Wild animals like to browse; hybridizes with related plants, *Purshia tridentata* and *Fallugia paradoxa*.

Cupressus arizonica   PLATE 83
PRONOUNCER: coo-*press*-us air-i-*zo*-ni-cah
FAMILY: Cupressaceae
COMMON NAME: Arizona cypress
  Evergreen. Height: 20–30 ft. (6–9 m). Spread: 12–15 ft. (3.5–4.5 m). Rate of growth: Fast. Light requirement: Sun. Native from west Texas to southern Arizona and northern Mexico.
  A dense, pyramid-shaped conifer with silvery, gray-green foliage; dark-fissured bark. The cultivars 'Gareei' and 'Pyramidalis' have more uniform growth. Smooth-barked forms often sold as *C. glabra*.
FLOWER AND FRUIT: Tiny flowers in spring, 1-in. (2.5-cm) cones.
LANDSCAPE USES: Specimen tree or in groups for windbreak, screening or tall background. Space 15 ft. (4.5 m) apart for dense screen.
CLIMATE ADAPTION: Hardy to −20°F (−29°C); best for deserts and California's Central Valley; sometimes suffers in low-desert heat.
CULTURE: Minimal soil requirement. Minimal water requirement, but likes monthly, deep irrigation, which also encourages deeper rooting. Avoid fertilizing because of potential nitrogen damage. Prune lower foliage as desired to reveal trunk. Propagate by cuttings.
POSSIBLE PROBLEMS: Shallow rooted if watered too frequently and can blow over; short lived; bark beetles; nitrogen fertilizer injury.

Cytisus praecox
PRONOUNCER: *sit*-i-sus *pray*-cox
FAMILY: Leguminosae
COMMON NAME: Warminster broom
  Deciduous. Height: 3–5 ft. (1–1.5 m). Spread: 3–5 ft. (1–1.5 m). Rate of growth: Fast. Light requirement: Sun. Native to southern Europe.
  A small shrub with broomlike, green stems bearing early deciduous leaves.
FLOWER AND FRUIT: Profuse clusters of light yellow to whitish, pealike blooms in the spring, followed by narrow pods.
LANDSCAPE USES: A bright-flowering accent for borders or small groupings. Not as prone to naturalizing as are other brooms such as Scotch broom, *C. scoparius,* and Spanish broom, *Spartium junceum.*

CLIMATE ADAPTION: Hardy to at least 0°F (−18°C); best for coastal and inland southern California and California's Central Valley; there are better choices for the deserts.
CULTURE: Needs good drainage. Looks best with summer watering every 2–3 weeks in the warmest areas. No fertilizer. Prune after flowering, to shape and remove the forming pods. Propagate by cuttings or seeds.
POSSIBLE PROBLEMS: May be invasive; odor of the flowers is disagreeable to some.

Cytisus praecox 'All Gold' has bright yellow flowers.

Dalbergia sissoo   PLATE 84
PRONOUNCER: dal-*ber*-jee-ah *sis*-soo
FAMILY: Leguminosae
COMMON NAME: sissoo tree
  Deciduous. Height: 65–80 ft. (20–24.5 m). Spread: 20–30 ft. (6–9 m) wide. Rate of growth: Fast. Light requirement: Sun. Native to India.
  A large tree with glossy leaves somewhat resembling those of a poplar; leaves divided into rounded, medium green leaflets; rough, gray bark.
FLOWER AND FRUIT: Small, creamy flowers in spring, followed by 2-in. (5-cm), flat, light brown pods.
LANDSCAPE USES: Good shade tree for larger spaces; effective in groves.
CLIMATE ADAPTION: Hardy to about 20°F (−6.5°C); best in low desert and coastal and inland southern California; expect some frost damage in mid-elevation deserts.
CULTURE: Minimal soil requirement. Drought tolerant; looks best with deep watering monthly in summer in noncoastal areas. Minimal to no fertilizer. Prune in winter, to shape or as needed. Propagate by seeds or cuttings.
POSSIBLE PROBLEMS: Sensitive to frost.

Dalea
PRONOUNCER: *day*-lee-ah
FAMILY: Leguminosae
  "Soft and subtle" describes daleas. They can go almost unnoticed when not in bloom, but as the flower clusters appear, it is as if someone brushed the garden with watercolor hues of lavender and purple.
  The blooming season varies among the species, and there seems to be a shrub-type dalea in bloom almost any time of the year. There is also a small tree that is usually leafless but blooms spectacularly. The leaves of the shrubby daleas are divided into small leaflets,

giving the plants a fine, lacy texture. Some have silvery foliage covered with silky hairs that are quite handsome in full sunlight.

Fortunately, more species are being tested and becoming available through nurseries. They offer a delicate contrast to the striking and bold textures of many Southwestern plants.

Dalea bicolor var. *argyraea*   PLATE 85
PRONOUNCER: *day*-lee-ah *by*-cul-er ar-*jeer*-ee-ah
COMMON NAME: silver dalea

Evergreen. Height: 2–3 ft. (60–90 cm). Spread: 2–3 ft. (60–90 cm). Rate of growth: Fast. Light requirement: Sun. Native to Chihuahuan Desert in New Mexico, Texas and Mexico.

A small shrub with rounded habit and silvery gray foliage; leaves are divided into small leaflets covered with tiny hairs.

FLOWER AND FRUIT: Rose-purple flowers on dense spikes in the fall; small, one-seeded fruit.
LANDSCAPE USES: Fall-flowering and foliar accent plant for borders or other mixed plantings.
CLIMATE ADAPTION: Hardy to about 15°F (−9°C); best in low-and mid-elevation deserts.
CULTURE: Needs good drainage. Water every 1–2 weeks in summer, tapering off to once a month in the winter. No fertilizer. Prune to shape in early spring, as needed. Propagate by seeds and cuttings.
POSSIBLE PROBLEMS: Rabbits like to nibble young plants.

Dalea bicolor var. *orcuttiana*, the Baja dalea, grows to 4 ft. (1.2 m), with gray-green foliage, purplish pink, fall flowers. Less cold hardy than silver dalea.

Dalea greggii   PLATE 86
PRONOUNCER: *day*-lee-ah *greg*-ee-eye
COMMON NAME: trailing or dwarf indigo bush

Evergreen. Height: 0.5–1 ft. (15–30 cm). Spread: 4–5 ft. (1.2–1.5 m). Rate of growth: Fast. Light requirement: Sun. Native to rocky hillsides of west Texas and Mexico.

Fast spreading, dense ground cover that forms soft, low mounds; the attractive, silvery foliage is finely divided into oval, 0.25-in. (0.5-cm) leaflets; long, trailing branches root at leaf nodes as they grow.

FLOWER AND FRUIT: Tiny, rose-lavender flower heads in the late winter and early spring followed by small, pealike pods.
LANDSCAPE USES: Excellent, fast-growing ground cover for banks, slopes, or erosion control; performs well in exposed, tough sites; decorative foliage blends well with other desert plants. Space 4 ft. (about 1 m) apart for a ground cover.

A dependable performer.
CLIMATE ADAPTION: Frost and heat tolerant; best for deserts, but freezes back and regrows at higher desert locations.
CULTURE: Minimal soil requirement; does well in rocky and alkaline soils. Looks better if watered deeply every 2–3 weeks in summer but do not irrigate in winter. No fertilizer. Prune as needed to control size. Propagate by cuttings or seeds.
POSSIBLE PROBLEMS: Roots rot and tops die back from overwatering.

Dalea pulchra
PRONOUNCER: *day*-lee-ah *pul*-krah
COMMON NAME: bush dalea

Evergreen. Height: 4–5 ft. (1.2–1.5 m). Spread: 4–5 ft. (1.2–1.5 m). Rate of growth: Fast. Light requirement: Sun. Native to southeast Arizona and adjoining Mexico.

An open, rounded shrub with small, silvery gray leaves divided into 2–4 pairs of leaflets. Foliage is similar to silver dalea.

FLOWER AND FRUIT: Profuse rose or pink-purple bracts on 1.5–3 in. (4–8 cm) flowering spikes, March–April.
LANDSCAPE USES: Blends well with other spring-flowering desert plants; handsome foliage and delicate flower spikes.
CLIMATE ADAPTION: Hardy to at least 10°F (−12°C); no heat problems; best in the desert.
CULTURE: Prefers soil enriched with organic matter and needs good drainage. In summer give plants a deep watering every 1–2 weeks for best appearance. No fertilizer. Prune lightly to shape after bloom, as necessary. Propagate by seeds or cuttings.
POSSIBLE PROBLEMS: Protect young plants from rabbits.

Dalea spinosa   PLATE 87
PRONOUNCER: *day*-lee-ah spy-*no*-sah
COMMON NAME: smoke tree

Deciduous. Height: 12–20 ft. (3.5–6 m). Spread: 8–12 ft. (2.5–3.5 m). Rate of growth: Slow. Light requirement: Sun. Native to southwestern Arizona, southern California, adjoining Mexico.

An unusual, small tree with open growth and ashy branches that make it appear like a cloud of smoke from a distance; small, sparse leaves are absent much of the year; spiny.

FLOWER AND FRUIT: Showy, blue clusters of pealike flowers in spring followed by pods with one seed.
LANDSCAPE USES: A distinctive specimen in informal or naturalized areas; blends well with cactuses and palms.

CLIMATE ADAPTION: Hardy to about 20°F (−6.5°C); no heat problems; best in low desert.

CULTURE: Needs good drainage. Very drought tolerant; survives on natural rainfall, but tolerates infrequent, supplemental water. Apply 2 oz. (57 g) ammonium sulfate in late winter to speed growth after the first year in the landscape. Prune to shape or to improve natural appearance. Propagate by seeds.

POSSIBLE PROBLEMS: Thorns; overwatering.

Dalea versicolor PLATE 88
PRONOUNCER: *day*-lee-ah *vir*-si-cul-er
COMMON NAME: indigo bush

Evergreen. Height: 3–4 ft. (about 1 m). Spread: 3–4 ft. (about 1 m). Rate of growth: Fast. Light requirement: Sun. Native to rocky hills of southeastern Arizona and south into Mexico.

A spreading shrub with soft, gray foliage divided into small, oval to elliptic leaflets in 4–12 pairs.

FLOWER AND FRUIT: Cylindrical, lavender to purple spikes, 2 in. (5 cm) long throughout the spring; small seed pods.

LANDSCAPE USES: Blends nicely in arid plantings; try with winter-spring bloomers like cassia and brittlebush. Softens walls and similar architectural features.

CLIMATE ADAPTION: Frost and heat tolerant; best for the deserts.

CULTURE: Likes good drainage. Looks best with deep watering every two weeks in summer; taper off in cooler months. Little to no fertilizer. Prune as needed after bloom to keep bushy. Propagate by cuttings or seeds.

POSSIBLE PROBLEMS: Overwatering.

Dasylirion
PRONOUNCER: das-i-*leer*-ee-on
FAMILY: Agavaceae

Dasylirion acrotriche, the green desert spoon, resembles *D. wheeleri* but has medium green leaf blades; native to the Chihuahuan Desert.

Dasylirion wheeleri PLATE 89
PRONOUNCER: das-i-*leer*-ee-on *wheel*-ur-eye
COMMON NAME: desert spoon, sotol

Evergreen. Height: 3–5 ft. (1–1.5 m). Spread: 3–5 ft. (1–1.5 m). Rate of growth: Slow to moderate. Light requirement: Sun. Native from west Texas to Arizona and south into northern Mexico.

A boldly textured plant with blue-gray, sword-shaped leaves carried in a rosette; sharply toothed leaf blades are about 1 in. (2.5 cm) wide and curve to form a striking silhouette. Base of leaf is broad, giving the appearance of a long-handled spoon. Southwest Indians used this plant to make an alcoholic beverage called sotol.

FLOWER AND FRUIT: A plume of tiny, cream-colored flowers rises on a stalk 5 ft. (1.5 m) or more above foliage in late spring and summer; small capsules follow.

LANDSCAPE USES: Provides a bold accent in rock gardens and desert landscapes; combine with other succulents and cactuses. While it resembles its relative the yuccas, it is not attacked by the agave snout weevil.

CLIMATE ADAPTION: Hardy to around 0°F (−18°C); loves heat; best for deserts.

CULTURE: Needs good drainage. Minimal water requirement but grows faster with infrequent, supplemental irrigation during warmest months. Apply 2 oz. (57 g) ammonium sulfate in early spring to speed growth. Remove old flower stalks and dead lower leaves. Propagate by fresh seeds in spring or separate young plants in late winter from parent clump for easy transplanting.

POSSIBLE PROBLEMS: Slow to establish; due to the sharp-pointed leaves, avoid planting near foot-traffic areas.

Dendromecon harfordii PLATE 90
PRONOUNCER: den-*dro*-me-kon har-*ford*-ee-eye
FAMILY: Papaveraceae
COMMON NAME: island bush poppy

Evergreen. Height: About 7–20 ft. (2.2–6 m). Spread: 7–15 ft. (2.2–4.5 m). Rate of growth: Moderate. Light requirement: Sun to partial shade. Native to California's Channel Islands.

A large, rounded shrub or small tree with bright, poppylike flowers against bluish green foliage; leaves are oval to elliptic, up to 3 in. (8 cm) long.

FLOWER AND FRUIT: Golden yellow flowers up to 3 in. (8 cm) across provide a long display, April–July; fruit is a narrow capsule.

LANDSCAPE USES: A colorful, flowering accent; good mixed with other native plants on slopes and in naturalized areas.

CLIMATE ADAPTION: Frost tolerant; best for coastal and inland southern California and California's Central Valley.

CULTURE: Needs good drainage. Drought tolerant; water plants infrequently during the summer at warmer inland and interior locations; avoid watering in coastal areas. No fertilizer. Can be pruned lightly after bloom, but avoid heavy pruning. Somewhat difficult to propagate; stem cuttings taken in winter and spring may be the most successful method; fire-treated seed cold-stratified for 1.5–3 months also yields results.

POSSIBLE PROBLEMS: Fleshy taproot makes transplanting difficult; hard to find in nurseries.

Dendromecon rigida, which is found in California's chaparral, is smaller and has narrow, gray-green leaves. It is more difficult to propagate and grow.

Dietes vegeta   PLATE 91

PRONOUNCER: die-*ee*-teez *ve*-je-tah

FAMILY: Iridaceae

COMMON NAME: fortnight lily

Evergreen. Height: 2–3 ft. (60–90 cm). Spread: 2–3 ft. (60–90 cm). Rate of growth: Moderate. Light requirement: Sun or light shade. Native to South Africa.

Low grower with narrow, swordlike, light green leaves that grow fanlike from the base of the plant to form a clump; formerly known as *Morea iridioides* or *D. iridioides*. They are available in several other flower colors, notably a yellow one, but *D. vegeta* usually is the most satisfactory.

FLOWER AND FRUIT: Large white petals are marked with yellow, brown and purple; fruit is a 0.5-in. (1.3-cm), greenish capsule. Bursts of bloom come about every two weeks, mainly in the spring and fall; flowers last only a day.

LANDSCAPE USES: Adds form and contrast to the landscape; outstanding when massed, particularly around a swimming pool or as a specimen in a tropical setting with palms and nandinas; interesting shadow effects in daytime or when backlighted at night.

CLIMATE ADAPTION: Hardy to about 10°F (−12°C); no heat problems; widely adaptable.

CULTURE: Needs good drainage. Twice-monthly watering needed in the warmest months for best flowering; accepts lawn-sprinkler situations but be careful water does not stand around roots. In the early spring and summer, apply 2 oz. (57 g) of an all-purpose fertilizer such as 10–6–4 to a plant that has 1.5-ft. (45-cm) leaves and a 6-in. (15-cm) spread at the base; adjust proportionally to the size of other plants. Dead leaves persist and must be removed by hand pruning in late winter or early spring. Caution: Do not cut the entire flower stalk, which lasts from year to year. Increase flower production by snapping off seed pods. Propagate by dividing clumps every few years in the fall.

POSSIBLE PROBLEMS: Pruning requirements.

Diospyros texana

PRONOUNCER: die-*os*-per-ohs tex-*ah*-nah

FAMILY: Ebenaceae

COMMON NAME: Texas persimmon

Evergreen. Height: 30–40 ft. (9–12 m). Spread: 15–20 ft. (4.5–6 m). Rate of growth: Slow. Light requirement: Sun. Native to Texas and northern Mexico.

A smooth-barked tree or large shrub; leathery, dark green leaves are 1–3 in. (2.5–8 cm) long on gnarled branches and form a handsome canopy.

FLOWER AND FRUIT: Male and female flowers greenish white, small, not showy, occur on separate plants; black, pulpy fruits are about 1 in. (2.5 cm) long, sweet and relished by wildlife.

LANDSCAPE USES: Specimen, shade or patio tree; attractive white bark.

CLIMATE ADAPTION: No heat or cold problems; best for the deserts.

CULTURE: Needs good drainage. Looks best with monthly deep watering in the summer. Fertilize to speed growth, if desired. Prune to train as single- or multitrunked tree; remove lower branches to expose bark. Propagate by seeds.

POSSIBLE PROBLEMS: Slow growth.

Diplacus longiflorus   PLATE 92

PRONOUNCER: *dip*-la-kus lon-ji-*flor*-us

FAMILY: Scrophulariaceae

COMMON NAME: southern bush monkey flower

Perennial. Height: 1–3 ft. (30–90 cm). Spread: 2–3 ft. (60–90 cm). Rate of growth: Fast. Light requirement: Sun to part shade. Native to San Luis Obispo County, California, south into Baja California.

A shrubby plant with a long blooming season; blooms in a variety of bright colors; narrow, medium long, green leaves are resinous. It has many natural and man-made hybrids. This species is often sold as *Mimulus longiflorus*.

FLOWER AND FRUIT: Showy, tubular flowers, 1–3 in. (2.5–8 cm) long in red, yellow, salmon and cream, April–July.

LANDSCAPE USES: For massing in color displays or mixing in borders with other native plants having similar water requirements; good for dry, semishady areas such as under oaks.

CLIMATE ADAPTION: Best for coastal and inland southern California; marginal in California's Central Valley, where plants become summer dormant.

CULTURE: Minimal soil requirement. Moderately drought tolerant; water occasionally, especially through bloom period; stop irrigating when plants cease to bloom and become dormant in hotter areas. Minimal fertilizer. Prune severely after flowering to reinvigorate. Propagate by cuttings.

POSSIBLE PROBLEMS: Unattractive summer appearance in warmer areas.

Dodonaea
PRONOUNCER: doh-duh-*nay*-ah
FAMILY: Sapindaceae

Dodonaea microzyga, the red wing hopbush, a Southwest native, grows 3–4 ft. (about 1 m) high with an equal spread. It is best in the low desert.

Dodonaea viscosa   PLATE 93
PRONOUNCER: doh-duh-*nay*-ah vis-*koh*-sah
COMMON NAME: hopseed bush
Evergreen. Height: 4–10 ft. (1.2–3 m). Spread: 6–12 ft. (2–3.5 m). Rate of growth: Fast. Light requirement: Sun to part shade. Native to the dry slopes of southern and central Arizona as well as Australia and South Africa.

Large, informal shrub with willowlike, bright green foliage; leaves are 1–5 in. (2.5–13 cm) long on upright stems. The cultivar 'Purpurea' has a purplish appearance, is more symmetrical, less dense and less cold hardy.

FLOWER AND FRUIT: Insignificant, light green flowers in spring produce very attractive, papery, seed capsules.

LANDSCAPE USES: Tough shrub for a clipped hedge, screen or specimen with minimal maintenance problems; space plants 6 ft. (2 m) apart to make an informal screen; provides restful appearance in desert landscapes.

CLIMATE ADAPTION: May be damaged around 20°F (−6.5°C); revels in heat; widely adaptable except for the higher deserts.

CULTURE: Prefers good drainage. Likes monthly, deep irrigations but will survive on average rainfall; reaches its maximum growth with moderate watering. Minimal fertilizer needed. Prune leaders to promote bushiness. Propagate by seeds.

POSSIBLE PROBLEMS: Can be set back by a long, hard freeze.

Drosanthemum floribundum   PLATE 94
PRONOUNCER: droh-*san*-the-mum flor-i-*bun*-dum
FAMILY: Aizoaceae
COMMON NAME: rosea ice plant
Evergreen. Height: 3–6 in. (8–15 cm). Spread: 3–4 ft. (about 1 m). Rate of growth: Fast. Light requirement: Sun. Native to South Africa but has naturalized in southern California.

A ground-hugging, flowering succulent with silvery, gray- green, fleshy, narrow leaves to 1 in. (2.5 cm) long that shimmer in the sunlight.

FLOWER AND FRUIT: Pink or purple flowers about 1 in. (2.5 cm) across in spring and summer; fleshy capsules.

LANDSCAPE USES: A colorful plant in rock gardens or as a fine-textured ground cover; good on slopes for erosion control or to drape over a low wall.

CLIMATE ADAPTION: Frost sensitive but heat tolerant; best for coastal and inland southern California and the low desert.

CULTURE: Requires rapidly draining soil; add gravel or sand at planting time to loosen soil, as needed. Needs occasional water in the summer in hot areas but less in cooler months and areas; water only when the soil is very dry since overwatering leads to root rot. Minimal fertilizer. Prune to keep in bounds, if needed. Propagate by cuttings.

POSSIBLE PROBLEMS: Rotting from overwatering, especially in the low desert; will not accept foot traffic.

Drosanthemum speciosum spreads quickly to 3 ft. (1 m) across with hot pink flowers; blooms in spring in low deserts. Other useful ice plants include the *Malephora* spp. and *Cephalophyllum* 'Red Spike'.

Elaeagnus
PRONOUNCER: ee-lee-*ag*-nuss
FAMILY: Elaeagnaceae
Elaeagnus make valuable plants by virtue of their handsome foliage, which is usually covered with silvery scales that shimmer in sunlight. They are quite useful as large shrubs and, with some training, the Russian olive makes a good specimen tree, particularly for colder desert locations.

Elaeagnus angustifolia   PLATE 95
COMMON NAME: Russian olive
PRONOUNCER: ee-lee-*ag*-nuss an-goos-ti-*foh*-lee-ah
Deciduous. Height: 20–25 ft. (6–7.5 m). Spread: 15–20 ft. (4.5–6 m). Rate of growth: Fast. Light requirement: Sun. Native to southern Europe and western Asia, but has naturalized in the western United States.

A large shrub or small tree that resembles the olive (*Olea europaea*) with its gray foliage; lance-shaped leaves are 1.5–3 in. (4–8 cm) long and silvery below; dark rough bark; variably spiny branches.

FLOWER AND FRUIT: Fragrant, small, yellowish flowers in early summer; yellow, inedible berries follow.

LANDSCAPE USES: Effective as a specimen or as a large shrub for screening in exposed, difficult sites; tolerates wind. Can be trained as an attractive shade tree in more formal locations.

CLIMATE ADAPTION: No problems with heat or cold in Southwest deserts but not satisfactory in coastal and inland southern California.

CULTURE: Tolerates poor soils. Water deeply once a month through hottest months. No fertilizer needed. Train as a tree in youth or shape as desired when older; can be pruned as a hedge. Propagate by hardwood cuttings in early spring or by seeds.

POSSIBLE PROBLEMS: May be shortlived in milder areas; invasive, escaping cultivation easily.

Elaeagnus pungens

PRONOUNCER: ee-lee-*ag*-nuss *pun*-genz
COMMON NAME: silverberry

Evergreen. Height: 6–12 ft. (2–3.5 m). Spread: 6–10 ft. (2–3 m). Rate of growth: Moderate. Light requirement: Sun to partial shade. Native to Europe.

A dense, sprawling shrub; olive green, wavy-edged, 2–3 in. (5–8 cm) leaves with tiny, brownish dots; sparkles in the wind. The larger-leaved cultivar 'Fruitlandia' is preferred. The cultivar 'Maculata' is a variegated form.

FLOWER AND FRUIT: Tiny white flowers in the fall, followed by 0.5-in. (1.3-cm) edible, reddish fruit.

LANDSCAPE USES: Individual specimen or massed as a tall screening hedge; good around swimming pools; easy to train.

CLIMATE ADAPTION: Hardy to about 0°F (−18°C); widely adaptable but sometimes suffers in low-desert heat.

CULTURE: Minimal soil requirements. Minimal water required but welcomes weekly, deep irrigation in low deserts during the summer if in full sun. Apply 4 oz. (115 g) ammonium sulfate in early spring. Prune to shape in early spring. Propagate by seeds or cuttings in fall.

POSSIBLE PROBLEMS: Summer irrigation needs in the low desert.

Encelia

PRONOUNCER: en-*see*-lee-ah
FAMILY: Compositae

These small, gray-leaved shrubs are covered with bright yellow daisies many months of the year. Brittlebush, in particular, becomes a nearly solid mass of yellow when in bloom. Combine them with the purple and pink of ceanothus, verbena or salvia for vibrant color displays. They appreciate some summer irrigation to keep them looking their best.

Encelia californica   PLATE 96

PRONOUNCER: en-*see*-lee-ah cal-i-*for*-ni-cah
COMMON NAME: bush sunflower

Evergreen. Height: 2–5 ft. (60 cm–1.5 m). Spread: 2–5 ft. (60 cm–1.5 m). Rate of growth: Fast. Light requirement: Sun. Native to the coastal sage scrub and chaparral of southern California and the Channel Islands.

A rounded, flowering shrub with gray-green, oval leaves to 2.5 in. (6 cm) long.

FLOWER AND FRUIT: Showy, 2–3 in. (5–8 cm), bright yellow daisies with reddish brown centers, mainly February–June but sometimes other months.

LANDSCAPE USES: Provides a sunny, flowering accent for mixed plantings and borders, banks and streets; useful for revegetating disturbed soils.

CLIMATE ADAPTION: Hardy to about 20°F (−6.5°C); best for coastal and inland southern California and California's Central Valley; does not tolerate desert heat.

CULTURE: Minimal soil requirement. Drought tolerant, but looks best with summer irrigation every 3–4 weeks in the warmest areas. Little to no fertilizer needed. Prune after blooming to shape. Propagate by seeds.

POSSIBLE PROBLEMS: Looks poor with neglect.

Encelia farinosa   PLATE 97

PRONOUNCER: en-*see*-lee-ah fair-i-*no*-sah
COMMON NAME: brittlebush, incienso

Evergreen. Height: 2–3 ft. (60–90 cm). Spread: 3–4 ft. (about 1 m). Rate of growth: Fast. Light requirement: Sun. Native to dry, rocky slopes throughout the Southwest.

A mounding, low shrub with silver-gray, triangular leaves about 3 in. (8 cm) long that almost cover a plant growing in favorable conditions.

FLOWER AND FRUIT: Masses of yellow, daisylike, 1-in. (2.5-cm) flowers cover the plant in early spring and sometimes other months following rains.

LANDSCAPE USES: Good contrast plant in the desert or natural garden, either as a specimen or in groups; looks good with verbena. Plant 3 ft. (1 m) apart for a mass effect.

CLIMATE ADAPTION: Hardy to around 15°F (−9°C); although sometimes frost-damaged in the 20s°F (−2 to −6.5°C), recovery is usually rapid in the spring; widely adaptable except for coastal southern California.

CULTURE: Needs good drainage. Drought tolerant, but becomes lush with moderate watering in the summer months. Apply 2 oz. (57 g) ammonium sulfate in the early spring. Remove old blossoms; can be cut back after flowering to stimulate new growth. Propagate by cuttings or seeds.

POSSIBLE PROBLEMS: Dieback in colder weather; older plants sometimes become sparse and require replacement; may go dormant in the summer without watering.

Ericameria laricifolia

PRONOUNCER: air-i-cuh-*mer*-ee-ah lar-i-si-*foh*-lee-ah

FAMILY: Compositae

COMMON NAME: turpentine bush

Evergreen. Height: 1–3 ft. (30–90 cm). Spread: 2.5–3 ft. (75–90 cm). Rate of growth: Moderate to fast. Light requirement: Sun. Native to rocky slopes and canyons, 3,500–6,500 ft. (1,000–2,000 m), from the Mojave Desert east to west Texas and Mexico.

Low, rounded shrub with tan branches densely covered with narrow, 0.5–1 in. (1.3–2.5 cm) green leaves bearing glandular dots; the odor of crushed foliage is similar to turpentine. Formerly known as *Haplopappus laricifolius*.

FLOWER AND FRUIT: Masses of golden yellow flowers, August–November, turn an attractive tan as they dry; tiny, one-seeded fruit.

LANDSCAPE USES: Bright green foliage makes it an attractive plant for borders and edging; or group more informally; good for naturalized areas; one of a few fall bloomers.

CLIMATE ADAPTION: Best for deserts, as it is cold and heat tolerant.

CULTURE: Minimal soil requirement. Needs twice-a-month watering in summer. Little to no fertilizer. Prune to shape or invigorate growth in spring. Softwood cuttings best for propagation; seeds.

POSSIBLE PROBLEMS: Looks poor with neglect.

Eriogonum

PRONOUNCER: air-ee-*og*-uh-num

FAMILY: Polygonaceae

The wild buckwheats are a large group of perennials and shrubs native mostly to western North America. Several are cultivated for their ornamental qualities. In some, the leaves are clustered around the base of the plant and in others, they arise along the stems. The blooms bring a lacy, airy quality to the summer landscape. Flower stalks bearing clusters of small, cream-colored to yellow to pink flowers rise well above the foliage. These dry to an attractive rust color, persist on the plant a long while and are prized for dry floral arrangements.

Eriogonum arborescens   PLATE 98

PRONOUNCER: air-ee-*og*-uh-num ar-bor-*ess*-ens

COMMON NAME: Santa Cruz Island buckwheat

Evergreen. Height: 2–6 ft. (60 cm–2 m). Spread: 4–5 ft. (1.2–1.5 m). Rate of growth: Moderate. Light requirement: Sun to partial shade. Native to California's Channel Islands.

A medium-sized, spreading shrub. The narrow, gray-green leaves are up to 1.5 in. (4 cm) long in clusters at the ends of the rugged branches, giving the look of miniature trees; the bark is shreddy.

FLOWER AND FRUIT: Dense, terminal, pinkish clusters, May–September; tiny, one-seeded fruit.

LANDSCAPE USES: Attractive in small groupings and mixed with other natives and low-water-use plants.

CLIMATE ADAPTION: Best for coastal and inland southern California; needs afternoon shade in California's Central Valley; not for deserts.

CULTURE: Needs good drainage. Drought tolerant but likes supplemental watering every 2–3 weeks in the summer in warmer areas. No fertilizer. Prune to shape as desired or to accentuate interesting form in early spring. Propagate by seeds.

POSSIBLE PROBLEMS: Can naturalize; overwatering.

Eriogonum crocatum   PLATE 99

PRONOUNCER: air-ee-*og*-uh-num crow-*cah*-tum

COMMON NAME: saffron buckwheat

Evergreen. Height: 6–12 in. (15–30 cm). Spread: 1–2 ft. (30–60 cm). Rate of growth: Moderate. Light requirement: Sun. Native to Ventura County, California.

A low-growing perennial with 1-in. (2.5-cm), oval, whitish leaves densely covered with hairs above and below.

FLOWER AND FRUIT: Sulfur yellow, flat flower clusters, April–July; one-seeded fruit.

LANDSCAPE USES: For borders, rock gardens; provides summer color.

CLIMATE ADAPTION: Hardy to about 15°F (−9°C); best for coastal and inland southern California; does not like the heat of California's Central Valley or the deserts.

CULTURE: Best with good drainage. Drought tolerant; give it infrequent or no summer water, especially in heavier soils. No fertilizer. Prune after flowering, if grooming is needed. Propagate by seeds.

POSSIBLE PROBLEMS: Somewhat fussier to grow than other buckwheats.

Eriogonum fasciculatum   PLATE 100

PRONOUNCER: air-ee-*og*-uh-num fuss-ik-ewe-*lah*-tum

COMMON NAME: California buckwheat

Evergreen. Height: 1–3 ft. (30–90 cm). Spread: 2–4 ft. (60 cm–1.2 m). Rate of growth: Moderate to fast. Light requirement: Sun. Native to southern California, Arizona, Nevada and Baja California.

A small, spreading shrub with light green, linear, 0.5–0.75 in. (1.3–2 cm) leaves. There are a number of subspecies which vary in adaptability outside their native area.

FLOWER AND FRUIT: Rounded, pinkish beige clusters, May–October and sometimes at other times of the year; light brown, one-seeded fruit. Flower clusters turn rust color as they dry.

LANDSCAPE USES: Ideal for rock gardens, borders, or as a ground cover for erosion control. Provides a soft-textured look.

CLIMATE ADAPTION: Hardy to about 15°F (−9°C); best for coastal and inland southern California, California's Central Valley and the mid-elevation desert.

CULTURE: Likes good drainage. Drought tolerant, but appreciates infrequent summer watering in hottest areas. No fertilizer. Prune to groom. Propagate by seeds.

POSSIBLE PROBLEMS: Reseeds; variable adaptability of some subspecies.

Eriogonum fasciculatum 'Theodore Payne' is a dependable, low- growing cultivar.

Eriogonum giganteum   PLATE 101

PRONOUNCER: air-ee-*og*-uh-num jy-*gan*-tee-um

COMMON NAME: St. Catherine's lace

Evergreen. Height: 1–4 ft. (30 cm–1.2 m). Spread: 1–4 ft. (30 cm–1.2 m). Rate of growth: Fast. Light requirement: Sun to part shade. Native to Santa Catalina and San Clemente islands, California.

A rounded shrub that is hard to miss when it flowers; silver gray, oval leaves 1.5–3 in. (4–8 cm) long, with whitish, feltlike hairs below.

FLOWER AND FRUIT: Numerous lacy flower heads form flat, creamy white clusters above plants, May–August; rust-colored dried flowers are useful for arrangements; one-seeded fruit.

LANDSCAPE USES: Attractive shrub for borders or to mix with other flowering native and drought-tolerant plants. Provides a long, attractive floral display. Use foliage for accent or contrast.

CLIMATE ADAPTION: Hardy to about 15°F (−9°C); best for coastal and inland southern California; needs afternoon shade in California's Central Valley.

CULTURE: Minimal soil requirement. Drought tolerant but likes occasional summer watering in warmer areas; avoid wetting the foliage, which can lead to fungal diseases. No fertilizer. Prune to shape in the early spring. Propagate by seeds.

POSSIBLE PROBLEMS: Tends to become rangy without pruning.

Eriogonum umbellatum

PRONOUNCER: air-ee-*og*-uh-num um-bel-*ah*-tum

COMMON NAME: sulfur buckwheat

Evergreen. Height: 1–3 ft. (30–90 cm). Spread: 2–4 ft. (60 cm–1.2 m). Rate of growth: Fast. Light requirement: Sun to part shade. Native to the higher elevations of California, Arizona, Nevada, Oregon.

A small, shrubby perennial with oval, light green leaves clustered around the stem ends.

FLOWER AND FRUIT: Bright yellow flower clusters on stalks up to 1 ft. (30 cm) cover the plants June–August, later turning rust color; one-seeded fruit.

LANDSCAPE USES: Attractive in rock gardens, borders and edgings, and as a foreground in mixed plantings; good summer color.

CLIMATE ADAPTION: Excellent cold tolerance; best for coastal and inland southern California and California's Central Valley, where it needs part shade.

CULTURE: Likes porous soils with good drainage. Drought tolerant but needs occasional supplemental water in the summer in warmest locations. No fertilizer. Prune to groom. Propagate by seeds or cuttings.

POSSIBLE PROBLEMS: Overwatering cuts lifespan.

Erythrina

PRONOUNCER: air-uh-*thrine*-ah

FAMILY: Leguminosae

The coral trees' unusual, bold flowers steal the show when they burst into brilliant red or orange bloom in the spring. The plants in this genus range from trees to shrubs with a strong branch structure and prickly stems. The leaves are divided into fan-shaped leaflets which provide a tropical look. Several are adaptable to mild, coastal climates. Western coral bean is best in the desert.

Erythrina coralloides
PRONOUNCER: air-uh-*thrine*-ah core-ah-*loy*-deez
COMMON NAME: naked coral tree

Deciduous. Height: 20–25 ft. (6–7.5 m). Spread: 25–30 ft. (7.5–9 m). Rate of growth: Moderate to fast. Light requirement: Sun. Native to Mexico.

A small tree or large shrub; yellow- to medium green foliage; compound leaf with three heart-shaped leaflets, each about 2 in. (5 cm) long and 3 in. (8 cm) wide; foliage appears translucent when backlighted; usually defoliates completely before blooming.

FLOWER AND FRUIT: Before opening in spring, the flower buds look something like a 6-in. (15-cm) red pine cone; fingerlike flowers unfurl from the buds.

LANDSCAPE USES: Fine patio tree providing ample shade in the warmer months; can reach 15 ft. (4.5 m) with an equal spread in 10 years or less; the spectacular flowers usually appear at a time when there is little other color in the landscape.

CLIMATE ADAPTION: Hardy to about 25°F (−4°C); no heat problems; best for coastal and mild inland areas of southern California.

CULTURE: Needs good drainage. Water deeply once a month in the summer to encourage deep root penetration. Apply an all-purpose fertilizer, such as 10–6–4, in July at a ratio of one cupful (225 g) for each year in the landscape. Prune to correct any tendency to lopsided growth. Propagate by seeds.

POSSIBLE PROBLEMS: Thorns; irregular growth; may lose some foliage in hot winds.

Erythrina crista-galli is a small tree to about 20 ft. (6 m), or a perennial shrub in colder areas, with pink to deep red flowers.

Erythrina flabelliformis
PLATE 102
PRONOUNCER: air-uh-*thrine*-ah fla-bell-i-*for*-mis
COMMON NAME: western coral bean

Deciduous. Height: 6–15 ft. (2–4.5 m). Spread: 6–10 ft. (2–3 m). Rate of growth: Moderate. Light requirement: Sun. Native to the dry slopes of Arizona, New Mexico and Mexico.

A large shrub or in mild areas, a small tree with spiny, short-lived branches; bright green, triangular leaflets about 3 in. (8 cm) long and 5 in. (13 cm) wide at the base.

FLOWER AND FRUIT: Spectacular, bright red flowers in the spring, often before the leaves appear, followed by a 4–10 in. (10–25 cm) pod with red seeds. The seeds are poisonous. The flowers attract hummingbirds.

LANDSCAPE USES: A flowering accent, background planting or where climate permits, a specimen tree.

CLIMATE ADAPTION: Stems freeze at 24–28°F (−4 to −2°C) but the plant usually regrows in the spring; best for low- and mid-elevation deserts; prefers afternoon shade in the low desert.

CULTURE: Prefers good drainage. Needs supplemental irrigation every 1–2 weeks in summer months for best growth. No fertilizer needed. Requires shaping to grow as a tree. Propagate by scarified seeds.

POSSIBLE PROBLEMS: Poisonous seeds; long deciduous period.

Eucalyptus
PRONOUNCER: ewe-ka-*lip*-tus
FAMILY: Myrtaceae

Many eucalyptus species are grown in the Southwest as shade and windbreak trees. In California, where the plants sometimes escape cultivation and in areas where they have been extensively planted, the air becomes heavy with the odor of their foliage after rain.

Introduced in the 1800s from Australia, they range in size from the small, sprawling shrubs known as mallees to statuesque trees exceeding 100 ft. (30.5 m) in height. Their common characteristics of pungent foliage, peeling bark, and informal habit charm many people. The same attributes elicit only scorn from others.

But whatever one's view of them, the eucalypts are an extraordinarily valuable group of plants thanks to their fast growth, adaption to a wide range of climates and tolerance of adverse conditions.

More good news is that a number of new eucalypt species relating better to the scale of typical gardens have been and continue to be introduced. These smaller eucalypts also widen the variety of foliage texture and color, growth habit, and bark characteristics available. For example, in *E. spathulata*, the typical gray-green foliage is replaced by narrow, dark green leaves that create a fine-textured, billowy canopy while the dark green *E. populnea* bears poplarlike foliage on a very erect form.

Newly planted eucalypts require adequate moisture their first year in the ground and should be staked for good trunk and root development. Once established, watering can be cut back to a moderate to low regime, and they generally need little maintenance. Spring through midsummer is a good period to do any pruning necessary to control size or remove wayward or dying branches.

For all their toughness and versatility,

eucalypts do, however, experience some problems. Some species have a tendency to become chlorotic in shallow, alkaline soils or when overwatered. Rather than endlessly applying iron chelate, select species better adapted to such conditions. Nitrogen fertilizer helps establish these fast-growing plants but is not necessary after the first year. In fact, eucalypts do best with a minimum of fertilizer; excess nitrogen only produces rapid, weak top growth out of balance with the root system.

In recent years, eucalypts in southern and central California have become infested with the eucalyptus longhorn borer, a pest imported from their native Australia. The female adult beetle lays its eggs on the bark of stressed and unhealthy trees. The larvae (borers) burrow through the bark into the cambium and wood. Healthy trees, on the other hand, produce plentiful amounts of gum if attacked, so thwarting the attack in most cases. Clearly, it is important to keep trees healthy. While trees in this genus can take a certain amount of drought, they should be watered on a regular basis during such periods to keep them in top shape to ward off pests.

Eucalyptus calophylla   PLATE 103
PRONOUNCER: ewe-ka-*lip*-tus cal-*off*-i-lah
COMMON NAME: Marri red gum
Evergreen. Height: 30–50 ft. (9–15 m). Spread: 30–40 ft. (9–12 m). Rate of growth: Fast. Light requirement: Sun.

A distinctive, dark-leaved eucalypt with a broad, rounded canopy and dense foliage; oval leaves are dark green, glossy above, pale green beneath, and 4–7 in. (10–18 cm) long; the bark on trunks is rough, gray and persistent, that on the branches reddish brown.
FLOWER AND FRUIT: Striking, large flower clusters 1 ft. (30 cm) across in white, pink, and red occur much of the year; the oval seed capsules, 1.5 in. (4 cm) across are attractive in dried flower arrangements.
LANDSCAPE USES: A handsome specimen and shade tree for larger areas; use for roadsides, streets, public areas; attractive foliage and flowers.
CLIMATE ADAPTION: Hardy to around 25–28°F (−4 to −2°C); best for coastal and inland southern California; cold tender in California's Central Valley.
CULTURE: Minimal soil requirement; withstands sandy to heavier soils. Moderate drought tolerance, but maintain even moisture. Little to no fertilizer. Prune to shape in youth, if neces-

sary. Propagate by seeds.
POSSIBLE PROBLEMS: Cold sensitive.

Eucalyptus calophylla 'Rosea' reaches 30–40 ft. (9–12 m) and has light pink to deep red flowers.

Eucalyptus camaldulensis
PRONOUNCER: ewe-ka-*lip*-tus cum-ald-ewe-*len*-sis
COMMON NAME: red gum
Evergreen. Height: To 80–120 ft. (24.5–36.5 m). Spread: 25–35 ft. (7.5–10.5 m). Rate of growth: Very fast. Light requirement: Sun.

A giant with weeping branches, long, slender, gray-green leaves and mottled, white to gray trunk; quite variable.
FLOWER AND FRUIT: Tiny, yellow flowers in summer followed by tiny seed capsules.
LANDSCAPE USES: Only for situations where a massive tree is needed; for windbreaks, highways, and large properties. This tree often grows 10–15 ft. (3–4.5 m) a year before reaching its eventual height, so it is obviously not for the average residential landscape.
CLIMATE ADAPTION: Hardy to 15°F (−9°C); no heat problems; widely adaptable except in the higher deserts.
CULTURE: Requires good drainage; deep soils promote best growth. Minimal water requirement but likes a monthly, deep soaking in summer. No fertilizer. Pruning is best left to professionals after a couple of years. Propagate by seeds.
POSSIBLE PROBLEMS: Prone to iron chlorosis in alkaline soils; litter from leaves, bark and seed capsules; eventual size.

Eucalyptus camaldulensis var. *obtusa*, with broader leaves, is not as prone to chlorosis and is better suited for the desert and other areas with alkaline soils.

Eucalyptus citriodora   PLATE 104
PRONOUNCER: ewe-ka-*lip*-tus sit-ree-oh-*dor*-ah
COMMON NAME: lemon-scented gum
Evergreen. Height: 75–100 ft. (23–30.5 m). Spread: 20–30 ft. (6–9 m). Rate of growth: Fast. Light requirement: Sun.

A handsome, tall, slender tree with beautiful, smooth, white to almost pinkish bark on trunk and branches; light green, narrow leaves are 3–7 in. (8–18 cm) long; when crushed, they give off a strong lemon scent.
FLOWER AND FRUIT: Tiny, cream-colored flower clusters in winter; tiny seed capsules.
LANDSCAPE USES: The striking vertical form and presence are highlighted by the white trunk; plant near buildings to accent vertical lines;

ideal for narrow areas, in rows along roadsides, or in groves.

CLIMATE ADAPTION: Hardy to 24–28°F (−4 to −2°C); best for coastal and inland southern California; not for California's Central Valley or the deserts.

CULTURE: Needs good drainage. Minimal water requirement but responds to moderate amounts in the warmest months. Little to no fertilizer. Shape in youth to develop structural strength. Propagate by seeds.

POSSIBLE PROBLEMS: Requires staking; cold sensitive.

Eucalyptus cladocalyx

PRONOUNCER: ewe-ka-*lip*-tus klad-oh-*kale*-ix
COMMON NAME: sugar gum

Evergreen. Height: 60–80 ft. (18–24.5 m). Spread: 35–65 ft. (10.5–20 m). Rate of growth: Fast. Light requirement: Sun.

A large tree with an open, rounded canopy; the lance-shaped to oval leaves, 3–5 in. (8–13 cm) long, have a reddish tinge; smooth, tan bark exfoliates to expose whitish patches.

FLOWER AND FRUIT: The cream-colored flower clusters in summer are not showy; seed clusters follow.

LANDSCAPE USES: Handsome silhouette tree, good for large areas such as roadsides, parks and other public spaces. Wind tolerant.

CLIMATE ADAPTION: Hardy to about 25°F (−4°C); heat tolerant; best for coastal and inland southern California.

CULTURE: Accepts poor and alkaline soils. Minimal water requirement; likes a deep, monthly watering in summer. Little to no fertilizer. Prune as desired for bushier growth. Propagate by seeds.

POSSIBLE PROBLEMS: Cold sensitive.

Eucalyptus cladocalyx 'Nana' grows to 20–25 ft. (6–7.5 m). A good tree for residential gardens.

Eucalyptus erythrocorys

PRONOUNCER: ewe-ka-*lip*-tus er-ith-roh-*kor*-eez
COMMON NAME: red-cap gum

Evergreen. Height: 20–25 ft. (6–7.5 m). Spread: 10–15 ft. (3–4.5 m). Rate of growth: Fast. Light requirement: Sun.

An attractive, small, often multitrunked tree with an open habit and attractive flower buds and flowers; the thick, narrow to broad leaves are a glossy, bright green, 4–7 in. (10–18 cm) long; the gray to white bark peels in flakes.

FLOWER AND FRUIT: Distinctive, red, four-part flower-bud caps give rise to bright yellow flower clusters from fall to early spring; woody

seed capsules follow.

LANDSCAPE USES: Fine choice for a small tree for small spaces.

CLIMATE ADAPTION: Hardy to 23°F (−5°C); best for coastal and inland southern California and the low desert.

CULTURE: Prefers sandy or clay-loam soils; needs good drainage; tolerates alkaline conditions. Moderately drought tolerant; water every 2–3 weeks in the hottest months in the desert. Little to no fertilizer. Prune in youth to encourage tight growth and greater wind tolerance. Propagate by seeds.

POSSIBLE PROBLEMS: Cold sensitive; wind can damage.

Eucalyptus erythronema

PRONOUNCER: ewe-ka-*lip*-tus er-ith-roh-*nee*-mah
COMMON NAME: red-flowered mallee

Evergreen. Height: 15–30 ft. (4.5–9 m). Spread: 15–20 ft. (4.5–6 m). Rate of growth: Fast. Light requirement: Sun.

A small, clean-looking tree with distinctive, smooth bark in shades of white, pink, gray and brown; drooping, narrow leaves are light green, and 2–3 in. (5–8 cm) long.

FLOWER AND FRUIT: Abundant red or sometimes yellow flowers in clusters followed by capsules.

LANDSCAPE USES: A neat-growing shade or street tree; wind tolerant.

CLIMATE ADAPTION: Hardy to 17–22°F (−8 to −5°C); heat tolerant; widely adaptable except for the higher deserts.

CULTURE: Minimal soil requirement. Drought tolerant; water once a month in summer in warmer areas. Little to no fertilizer needed. Prune in youth to shape to tree form. Propagate by seeds.

POSSIBLE PROBLEMS: Pruning requirements.

Eucalyptus erythronema var. *marginata* is like the type but has especially attractive, smooth, white, powdery bark.

Eucalyptus formanii   PLATE 105

PRONOUNCER: ewe-ka-*lip*-tus for-*man*-ee-eye
COMMON NAME: Forman's mallee

Evergreen. Height: 15–30 ft. (4.5–9 m). Spread: 15–20 ft. (4.5–6 m). Rate of growth: Moderate. Light requirement: Sun.

A rounded, bushy tree or large shrub with fine, light green foliage having a reddish tinge on the new growth on the branches; the narrow, linear leaves are 2–3.5 in. (5–9 cm) long; the bark on the lower trunk is rough and gray, becoming smooth and gray-brown higher up.

FLOWER AND FRUIT: Profuse, creamy clusters in

summer; small, round seed capsules.

LANDSCAPE USES: Specimen, background plant or spaced 8–10 ft. (2.5–3 m) apart for screening; narrow leaves create a fine texture unlike most eucalypts.

CLIMATE ADAPTION: Hardy to at least 15°F (−9°C); widely adaptable except for the higher deserts.

CULTURE: Likes good drainage; tolerates alkaline soils. Drought resistant; once established, it can survive on rainfall in average years; looks best with a monthly, summer watering in hottest areas. Little to no fertilizer needed. Prune to train as a tree, if desired. Propagate by seeds.

POSSIBLE PROBLEMS: Be careful not to break root ball during planting; pay special attention to keeping soil moist around roots for the first few months.

Eucalyptus leucoxylon, with white flowers, tends to grow much higher than *E. leucoxylon* 'Rosea'— perhaps to 80 ft. (24.5 m).

Eucalyptus leucoxylon 'Purpurea' is similar to 'Rosea'.

Eucalyptus leucoxylon 'Rosea' PLATE 106
PRONOUNCER: ewe-ka-*lip*-tus loo-*cox*-i-lon row-*zay*-ah
COMMON NAME: white ironbark

Evergreen. Height: 25–30 ft. (7.5–9 m). Spread: 15–20 ft. (4.5–6 m). Rate of growth: Fast. Light requirement: Sun.

An ornamental tree with striking blossoms; shreds its smooth, white bark, leaving an attractive, mottled trunk that combines with the gray-green leaves to make a particularly pleasing appearance.

FLOWER AND FRUIT: Showy, deep pink flowers from fall through winter; seed capsules are about 0.25 in. (0.5 cm).

LANDSCAPE USES: Excellent, smaller-sized tree for groups or in rows planted 15 ft. (4.5 m) apart; a good choice for the residential garden. Wind tolerant.

CLIMATE ADAPTION: Hardy to about 18°F (−8°C); widely adaptable except for the coldest parts of the higher deserts.

CULTURE: Minimal soil requirement; accepts alkaline conditions. Drought tolerant; likes watering every 3–4 weeks in the hottest areas in summer. Little fertilizer needed. Prune new plants to remove poorly placed branches and produce a good form; otherwise, minimal pruning. Propagate by seeds.

POSSIBLE PROBLEMS: Growth habit can be irregular.

Eucalyptus microtheca PLATE 107
PRONOUNCER: ewe-ka-*lip*-tus my-cro-*thee*-cah
COMMON NAME: coolibah tree

Evergreen. Height: 30–40 ft. (9–12 m). Spread: 20–30 ft. (6–9 m). Rate of growth: Moderate to fast. Light requirement: Sun.

A handsome, medium-sized tree with pendulous branches and a thick canopy of gray-green, narrow leaves up to 8 in. (20 cm) long; a slender form in youth, becoming broader with age; single- or multitrunked. Trunks are smooth and white in youth becoming rough and cracked when older.

FLOWER AND FRUIT: Creamy white, insignificant flowers; very tiny seed capsules in clusters.

LANDSCAPE USES: Probably the best eucalyptus for desert conditions. Fine shade tree, as a specimen or as a windbreak. Not as susceptible to wind damage as other species. Space 15 ft. (4.5 m) apart for screening, 30 ft. (9 m) for shade.

CLIMATE ADAPTION: Hardy to at least 5°F (−15°C); takes heat well; widely adaptable.

CULTURE: Needs good drainage; tolerates alkaline soils. Drought tolerant; likes a monthly soaking in summer but needs no supplemental watering in an average rainfall year; adapts to moister conditions as well. Minimal fertilizer. More attractive as a multitrunked form, it can be trained to a single trunk. Propagate by seeds.

POSSIBLE PROBLEMS: Single-trunked trees need staking; in selecting nursery-container stock, make sure to get one that is not rootbound.

Eucalyptus nicholii PLATE 108
PRONOUNCER: ewe-ka-*lip*-tus nick-*oh*-lee-eye
COMMON NAME: willow peppermint, Nichol's willow-leafed peppermint

Evergreen. Height: 30–40 ft. (9–12 m). Spread: 15–25 ft. (4.5–7.5 m). Rate of growth: Fast. Light requirement: Sun.

A medium-sized tree with narrow to spreading canopy of weeping branches and foliage; gray-green leaves are 3–5 in. (8–13 cm) long, very narrow and produce a peppermint smell when bruised; persistent, brown, fibery bark on a vertical trunk.

FLOWER AND FRUIT: Tiny, white flowers in summer are not showy; small seed capsules.

LANDSCAPE USES: A fine specimen or street tree, cleaner than many eucalypts due to persistent bark. Plant as a screen in rows, or in groves. Gray-green, finely textured foliage has a refined look and contrasts well with the bark. Wind tolerant.

CLIMATE ADAPTION: Hardy to 12–15°F (−11 to −9°C); widely adaptable but not the best choice for the deserts.

CULTURE: Needs good drainage; planting in alkaline soils is likely to result in iron chlorosis. Moderately drought tolerant; likes a deep watering every 3–4 weeks in the warmest months. Needs little to no fertilizer. Prune to shape as desired. Propagate by seeds.

POSSIBLE PROBLEMS: Iron chlorosis.

Eucalyptus papuana   PLATE 109

PRONOUNCER: ewe-ka-*lip*-tus pop-oo-*ah*-nah

COMMON NAME: ghost gum

Evergreen. Height: 40–50 ft. (12–15 m). Spread: 26–50 ft. (8–15 m). Rate of growth: Fast. Light requirement: Sun.

A medium-sized tree with spreading crown atop a smooth, white, often crooked trunk; lime green, glossy, narrow leaves are 2–5 in. (5–13 cm) long on drooping branches; a narrow habit in youth.

FLOWER AND FRUIT: Small, fragrant, white flower clusters in summer; seed capsules.

LANDSCAPE USES: Nice background tree; in groves on larger properties, or along roadsides.

CLIMATE ADAPTION: Hardy to 22°F (−5°C); best for coastal and inland areas of southern California and in the low deserts.

CULTURE: Likes good drainage. Minimal water requirement, but does better with a monthly, deep watering in the summer in the hottest areas. Little to no fertilizer needed. Prune lightly to shape or train in youth. Propagate by seeds.

POSSIBLE PROBLEMS: Light frost can cause foliar damage, although the tree recovers in the spring.

Eucalyptus polyanthemos   PLATE 110

PRONOUNCER: ewe-ka-*lip*-tus pol-ee-*an*-the-mose

COMMON NAME: silver dollar gum

Evergreen. Height: 20–60 ft. (6–18 m). Spread: 20–30 ft. (6–9 m). Rate of growth: Fast. Light requirement: Sun.

A much-used tree that is vertical in youth but spreads with age. The ornamental, juvenile leaves are roundish, gray-green, 2–3 in. (5–8 cm) across, often used in flower arrangements; mature leaves on older trees are narrower. Scaly, gray bark on trunks is somewhat variable in form.

FLOWER AND FRUIT: Cream-colored flower clusters 0.5 in. (1.3 cm) wide, followed by seed capsules.

LANDSCAPE USES: Large screen or shade tree; avoid lawn situations, as frequent watering causes chlorosis.

CLIMATE ADAPTION: Hardy to 14–18°F (−10 to −8°C); heat tolerant; best for coastal and inland southern California and California's Central Valley; tends to become chlorotic in deserts.

CULTURE: Needs good drainage; limited tolerance of alkaline conditions. Looks best with a monthly, deep watering in Central Valley. Little to no fertilizer needed. Prune to shape in youth, if necessary. Propagate by seeds.

POSSIBLE PROBLEMS: Select uniform, vigorous plants as they are variable; chlorosis; not the best choice for interior, arid areas; tends to be brittle.

Eucalyptus polyanthemos 'Polydan' has a more even growth habit and narrower, pointed leaves. Appears, however, to be less drought tolerant.

Eucalyptus populnea

PRONOUNCER: ewe-ka-*lip*-tus pop-ul-*nee*-ah

COMMON NAME: poplar box, bimble box

Evergreen. Height: 20–25 ft. (6–7.5 m). Spread: 12–15 ft. (3.5–4.5 m). Rate of growth: Fast. Light requirement: Sun.

A small tree with an erect form and dense crown; shiny, dark green, poplarlike leaves are 2–5 in. (5–13 cm) ovals; bark is light gray-brown and does not shed.

FLOWER AND FRUIT: Small, white flower clusters occur in late summer; seed capsules.

LANDSCAPE USES: Attractive specimen or shade tree that is in a good scale to the average home; effective in small groves or rows. Large, glossy leaves provide color and textural contrasts; clean bark.

CLIMATE ADAPTION: Hardy to 22°F (−5°C); does fine in heat; best for the low desert and inland areas of southern California.

CULTURE: Minimal soil requirement; tolerates heavy clay. Drought tolerant but appreciates supplemental watering once or twice a month in the summer. Little to no fertilizer needed. Minimal pruning. Propagate by seeds.

POSSIBLE PROBLEMS: Prone to suckering.

Eucalyptus rudis

PRONOUNCER: ewe-ka-*lip*-tus *roo*-dis

COMMON NAME: flooded gum

Evergreen. Height: 30–60 ft. (9–18 m). Spread: 30–40 ft. (9–12 m). Rate of growth: Fast. Light requirement: Sun.

A vigorous, medium to large tree with a spreading head; gray-green, oval to elliptic leaves are 4–6 in. (10–15 cm) long; lower bark is gray to brown, rough, with smooth, white branches above.

FLOWER AND FRUIT: Whitish flower clusters in spring and summer; seed clusters about 0.3 in. (1 cm) wide.

LANDSCAPE USES: A tough tree for shade and shelter in large groves and coastal plantings; good windbreak. Not for the average home landscape, however, because it needs room.
CLIMATE ADAPTION: Hardy to 16°F (−9°C); takes heat; best for coastal and inland southern California and California's Central Valley. There are better choices for the deserts.
CULTURE: Needs good drainage; often develops chlorosis in desert soils. Water once a month in the hottest areas in the summer. Little to no fertilizer and pruning required. Propagate by seeds.
POSSIBLE PROBLEMS: Chlorosis; eventual size; litter.

Eucalyptus sargentii

PRONOUNCER: ewe-ka-*lip*-tus sar-*jen*-tee-eye
COMMON NAME: salt river gum or mallet
Evergreen. Height: 25–35 ft. (7.5–10.5 m). Spread: 15–25 ft. (4.5–7.5 m). Rate of growth: Moderate. Light requirement: Sun.
A rugged tree with a dense, spreading canopy on a short trunk; rough, dark bark; narrow, linear leaves are dark green, 2–3 in. (5–8 cm) long, and give the tree a somewhat smoky appearance.
FLOWER AND FRUIT: Creamy white flowers in clusters in spring, followed by woody capsules.
LANDSCAPE USES: Specimen, screening or street tree, especially in poor-soil areas; fine-textured foliage.
CLIMATE ADAPTION: Hardy to about 22°F (−5°C); no problems with heat; best for the low desert and inland southern California.
CULTURE: Tolerates poor drainage and saline and alkaline soils. Drought resistant but looks best with once-a-month, summer watering in desert areas. Little to no fertilizer needed. Accepts heavy pruning. Propagate by seeds.
POSSIBLE PROBLEMS: Becomes extremely chlorotic with excess water.

Eucalyptus sideroxylon

PRONOUNCER: ewe-ka-*lip*-tus sid-er-*ox*-il-on
COMMON NAME: pink ironbark, red ironbark
Evergreen. Height: 20–50 ft. (6–15 m). Spread: 15–25 ft. (4.5–7.5 m). Rate of growth: Fast. Light requirement: Sun.
A slender tree with attractive, deep reddish brown bark that contrasts nicely with its blue-gray foliage; narrow, lance-shaped leaves with red stems; tree size and form often vary.
FLOWER AND FRUIT: Showy, hanging clusters of light to deep pink flowers from fall through spring; small seed capsules.
LANDSCAPE USES: As a specimen or street tree, or

in groves; flowers and bark are the key landscape features.
CLIMATE ADAPTION: Hardy to about 20°F (−6.5°C); best for coastal and inland southern California.
CULTURE: Avoid shallow or alkaline soils. Occasional deep watering in summer. Minimal fertilizer and pruning needed. Propagate by seeds.
POSSIBLE PROBLEMS: Iron chlorosis; does poorly in desert areas.

Eucalyptus spathulata

PLATE 111
PRONOUNCER: ewe-ka-*lip*-tus spath-ewe-*lah*-tah
COMMON NAME: swamp mallee, narrow-leaved gimlet
Evergreen. Height: 20–25 ft. (6–7.5 m). Spread: 12–18 ft. (3.5–5.5 m). Rate of growth: Moderate to fast. Light requirement: Sun.
A graceful, small, single- or multitrunked tree with a billowy canopy; reddish gray trunk with smooth, peeling bark; narrow, dark green, glossy leaves 2–3 in. (5–8 cm) long.
FLOWER AND FRUIT: Creamy flowers in the spring and early summer with small capsules following.
LANDSCAPE USES: Excellent tree for small or narrow areas, including streets, patios and entryways; very adaptable; plant 8 ft. (2.5 m) apart for screen; appealing fine texture.
CLIMATE ADAPTION: Hardy to about 20°F (−6.5°C); no heat problems; widely adaptable except in the higher deserts.
CULTURE: Despite the common name of swamp mallee, this plant is quite adaptable in all soils. Drought tolerant but needs deep watering every 2–4 weeks during the warmest months or in long, dry periods; accepts moderate amounts but use care not to overwater. Apply 2 oz. (57 g) ammonium sulfate in the early spring after the first year in the ground. Prune to shape in youth or to train as a single-trunked tree. Propagate by seeds.
POSSIBLE PROBLEMS: Overwatering, but be careful that newly planted trees are kept moist.

Eucalyptus torquata

PRONOUNCER: ewe-ka-*lip*-tus tor-*kah*-tah
COMMON NAME: coral gum
Evergreen. Height: 15–25 ft. (4.5–7.5 m). Spread: 15–20 ft. (4.5–6 m). Rate of growth: Fast. Light requirement: Sun.
A graceful tree with vertical to spreading form, lovely in bloom; pale, gray-green leaves vary from slender to broad, up to 4 in. (10 cm) long, and sometimes have a yellowish cast; rough, gray bark and reddish young branchlets.
FLOWER AND FRUIT: Exquisite flowers in bursts of red to coral in the winter and summer, or occa-

sionally at other times of the year; capsules cylindrical.

LANDSCAPE USES: Excellent for small or narrow areas, such as streets, patios, along entryways or walkways. Small groves give maximum effect. Long flowering period is a special plus.

CLIMATE ADAPTION: Hardy to about 22°F (−5°C); widely adaptable; best for coastal and inland areas of southern California and the low deserts.

CULTURE: Needs good drainage; tolerates alkalinity. Minimal watering except in the hottest locations, where it needs deep watering every 2–3 weeks in the summer. Little to no fertilizer needed. Usually needs some shaping, which is best done in the early spring after the last frosts. Propagate by seeds.

POSSIBLE PROBLEMS: Young trees require staking for good structural development; nursery plants are variable.

Eucalyptus woodwardii

PRONOUNCER: ewe-ka-*lip*-tus wood-*ward*-ee-eye
COMMON NAME: lemon-flowered gum

Evergreen. Height: 25–30 ft. (7.5–9 m). Spread: 15–20 ft. (4.5–6 m). Rate of growth: Moderate. Light requirement: Sun.

A slender, open tree with pendulous, whitish branches that bear distinctive, thick, silvery-gray leaves and bright flower clusters; broad leaves are 4–6 in. (10–15 cm) long; smooth, gray bark on trunk.

FLOWER AND FRUIT: Showy, large, lemon yellow clusters in spring and fall, followed by whitish gray fruit clusters; plant blooms when very young.

LANDSCAPE USES: Foliage and flowers make it an excellent accent tree; fits well in arid landscapes; good for small areas.

CLIMATE ADAPTION: Hardy to about 20°F (−6.5°C); best for low- and mid-elevation deserts, inland southern California and California's Central Valley.

CULTURE: Prefers good drainage but grows in heavier soils; accepts alkaline conditions. Minimal water needs but likes supplemental watering every 3–4 weeks in the deserts in the summer. Little to no fertilizer needed. Prune young trees to direct growth. Propagate by seeds.

POSSIBLE PROBLEMS: Pruning requirement due to natural growth habit of young trees; once-a-year shedding of bark.

Fallugia paradoxa

PRONOUNCER: fa-*looj*-ee-ah pair-ah-*dox*-ah
FAMILY: Rosaceae
COMMON NAME: Apache plume

Semideciduous. Height: 3–6 ft. (1–2 m). Spread: 6–8 ft. (2–2.5 m). Rate of growth: Slow to moderate. Light requirement: Sun. Native to higher elevations of the Southwest and Mexico.

Open shrub with flaky bark; leaves clustered, divided into linear segments, dark green above and rust colored below; often evergreen in the low desert.

FLOWER AND FRUIT: Showy, white flowers like single roses to 1.5 in. (4 cm) across, May–June; attractive, plumed, seed clusters are tan to pinkish and reflect the sun in the fall.

LANDSCAPE USES: Good erosion control for banks, or use in mixed plantings and naturalized areas.

CLIMATE ADAPTION: Hardy to at least 0°F (−18°C); no heat problems; best for deserts.

CULTURE: Minimal soil requirement. Good drought tolerance; give it monthly, deep water during hot and dry periods. No fertilizer. Prune lightly to shape in the winter; blooms on new growth; can be trimmed for a hedge. Propagate by seeds or cuttings.

POSSIBLE PROBLEMS: Deer and livestock browse foliage but rabbits dislike.

Feijoa sellowiana   PLATE 112

PRONOUNCER: fay-*jo*-ah sell-oh-ee-*ah*-nah
FAMILY: Myrtaceae
COMMON NAME: pineapple guava

Evergreen. Height: 12–25 ft. (3.5–7.5 m). Spread: 12–25 ft. (3.5–7.5 m). Rate of growth: Moderate. Light requirement: Best in sun. Native to Brazil.

Ornamental large shrub or small tree with edible fruit; light green, glossy leaves are silver-gray underneath, to 3 in. (8 cm) long. 'Nazemetz', 'Pineapple Gem' and 'Coolidge' are good, self-pollinating cultivars.

FLOWER AND FRUIT: White-petaled, 1-in. (2.5-cm) flowers with a showy spray of red stamens in late spring; edible, gray-green oval fruit to 3 in. (8 cm) long sweeter than the true guava, develops in summer. Fruit contains numerous, black edible seeds and is used for making jams and preserves; edible fleshy petals are often used in salads.

LANDSCAPE USES: Specimen, informal shrub or screen plant; tolerates a lawn situation.

CLIMATE ADAPTION: Hardy to about 15°F (−9°C); widely adaptable except in higher deserts; takes heat of low desert but fruit production and taste is inferior.

CULTURE: Quite tolerant of soil conditions but needs good drainage. Drought tolerant, but drops fruit if moisture stressed. Water deeply during flowering and fruiting season to increase yield. Spring application of a balanced fertilizer improves fruit production and speeds growth. Prune in late spring to shape and control size or to train as a tree; thin fruit set as desired. Propagate by semihardwood cuttings. Seedlings vary.
POSSIBLE PROBLEMS: Litter from blooms; branches may break under a large load of fruit.

Forestiera neomexicana

PRONOUNCER: for-ess-tee-*air*-ah nee-oh-mex-i-*cah*-nah
FAMILY: Oleaceae
COMMON NAME: desert olive, New Mexico privet
   Deciduous. Height: 10–15 ft. (3–4.5 m). Spread: 8–10 ft. (2.5–3 m). Rate of growth: Moderate. Light requirement: Sun. Native to much of the Southwest, 3,000 to 7,000 ft. (900–2,100 m).
   A large shrub or small tree with erect form; bright green, oval to oblong leaves to 1.5 in. (4 cm) long; smooth, white-gray bark.
FLOWER AND FRUIT: Fragrant clusters of white or yellow flowers in the spring before new leaves appear; birds love the olivelike, black fruit which ripens in the summer.
LANDSCAPE USES: Handsome when trained as a small specimen tree with a canopy of neat foliage; useful in narrow areas such as entryways or in large planters in urban settings. Plant about 6 ft. (2 m) apart for a screen. Can be pruned to an excellent hedge or used as a specimen shrub.
CLIMATE ADAPTION: Hardy to −25°F (−32°C); widely adaptable but suffers from the heat of the low desert.
CULTURE: Minimal soil requirement but does not like highly alkaline conditions. Drought resistant but drops its leaves if allowed to become too dry; faster, denser growth occurs with monthly, deep irrigation in the warmest periods. Young plants respond to a light application of nitrogen. Can be trained as a multitrunked tree or pruned as a hedge or shrub; accepts shearing. Propagate by seeds cold-stratified for 30 days or by hardwood cuttings.
POSSIBLE PROBLEMS: Chlorosis in alkaline soil.

Fouquieria splendens   PLATE 113

PRONOUNCER: foh-quee-*air*-ee-ah *splen*-dens
FAMILY: Fouquieriaceae
COMMON NAME: ocotillo

   Deciduous. Height: 5–20 ft. (1.5–6 m). Spread: 5–10 ft. (1.5–3 m). Rate of growth: Slow. Light requirement: Sun. Native to Southwest deserts.
   Ornamental shrub with spectacular flowers and many slender, rigid stems growing from its base; thorns cover each stem. Clusters of bright green leaves cover stems after rains, but most of the year stems are barren.
FLOWER AND FRUIT: Brilliant red to orange-red, tubular, 0.5–1 in. (1.3–2.5 cm) flowers in long clusters, March–June; fruit is a small capsule with numerous winged seeds.
LANDSCAPE USES: Specimen plant in arid landscapes or rock gardens; strong vertical effect; a common sight on dry hillsides in natural desert areas. Easy to develop into impenetrable living fence by planting stems into ground where they eventually root.
CLIMATE ADAPTION: Hardy to at least 10°F (−12°C); takes heat; best for deserts.
CULTURE: Needs good drainage. No water requirement but will need some irrigation if applying very light nitrogen to speed the growth of young plants. Best if never pruned; avoid topping. Propagate from stem cuttings.
POSSIBLE PROBLEMS: Thorns; plants may look shriveled in abnormally dry periods.

Fraxinus velutina   PLATE 114

PRONOUNCER: *frax*-i-nus vel-ewe-*tee*-nah
FAMILY: Oleaceae
COMMON NAME: Arizona ash
   Deciduous. Height: 30–40 ft. (9–12 m). Spread: 15–30 ft. (4.5–9 m). Rate of growth: Fast. Light requirement: Sun. Native from west Texas to southern California and Mexico.
   A medium-sized tree that is narrow when young but develops a broad canopy with age; light green leaves to 8 in. (20 cm) long are divided into 3–5 oval to elliptic leaflets. Gray furrowed bark; deep rooted.
FLOWER AND FRUIT: Tiny male and female flowers occur on separate plants in the early spring; clusters of 1-in. (2.5-cm), one-seeded, winged fruit.
LANDSCAPE USES: A nice shade tree for patios and public areas, but keep away from paving due to surface roots; tolerates lawn situations; useful in difficult areas; yellow fall color.
CLIMATE ADAPTION: Hardy to about −10°F (−23°C); heat tolerant; widely adaptable, including desert and coastal conditions.
CULTURE: Good drainage best. Once-a-month, deep watering in the summer will do. Young trees respond to a light application of nitrogen.

Prune to train or shape in the winter. Propagate by seeds.
POSSIBLE PROBLEMS: Susceptible to ash decline syndrome, verticillium wilt; invasive roots; litter; pollen allergenic to some.

Fraxinus velutina 'Modesto' has a more compact, symmetrical appearance and shinier leaves.

Fraxinus velutina 'Rio Grande', the fan-tex ash, is a durable selection with larger and darker green foliage and uniform growth.

Fremontodendron californicum   PLATE 115
PRONOUNCER: free-mon-toh-*den*-dron cal-i-*for*-ni-cum
FAMILY: Bombacaceae
COMMON NAME: flannel bush, fremontia
Evergreen. Height: 5–25 ft. (1.5–7.5 m). Spread: 6–30 ft. (2–9 m). Rate of growth: Moderate to fast. Light requirement: Sun to part shade. Native to California's chaparral and the dry slopes of central Arizona.
A shrub or small tree with open, spreading to upright branches; lobed leaves to 2 in. (5 cm) long have a rough texture; the lower surface is covered with dense, starlike hairs.
FLOWER AND FRUIT: 2-in. (5-cm) flowers lack true petals but have showy, bright yellow sepals, March–June; bristly capsules follow.
LANDSCAPE USES: Accent plant or for combining with other spring-flowering shrubs; background and hillside plantings.
CLIMATE ADAPTION: Frost tolerant but dislikes heat; best for coastal and inland southern California; needs afternoon shade in California's Central Valley; not for the deserts.
CULTURE: Needs good drainage. Water once a month or so in the summer but less in heavy soils; plants in coastal areas can do without. No fertilizer. Prune after flowering to shape, as necessary. Propagate by cold-stratified seeds and cuttings.
POSSIBLE PROBLEMS: Overwatering encourages root rot.

Fremontodendron californicum var. *decumbens* is a spreading plant reaching about 4 ft. (1.2 m) high and 10 ft. (3 m) across with reddish yellow flowers. It is difficult both to find and to grow.

Fremontodendron mexicanum, southern flannel bush, grows to 18 ft. (5.5 m) with yellow-orange flowers. Hybrids of this species and *F. californicum* include: 'California Glory' with larger flowers and heavier bloom; 'Pacific Sunset' with

orange-yellow flowers; and 'San Gabriel', with golden yellow flowers.   PLATE 116

Garrya
PRONOUNCER: *gair*-ee-ah
FAMILY: Garryaceae
There is no missing the silktassels when they bloom in the winter and spring. Their weeping, tassel-like flower clusters are quite beautiful. The leathery, evergreen foliage forms an attractive backdrop. They are dioecious, meaning male and female flowers occur on separate plants. Male plants with their longer catkins produce a more handsome display. Females produce dark-colored berries.
The genus *Garrya* includes 18 or so members which are found in western North America, Guatemala and the West Indies. The Southwest species commonly grow in chaparral and mixed forest communities. They prefer good drainage and sunny to partially shady exposures in the landscape. Given the right location and conditions, they require little care.

Garrya elliptica   PLATE 117
PRONOUNCER: *gair*-ee-ah e-*lip*-ti-cah
COMMON NAME: coast silktassel
Evergreen. Height: 6–20 ft. (2–6 m). Spread: 8–10 ft. (2.5–3 m). Rate of growth: Fast. Light requirement: Sun to partial shade. Native to the dry slopes of California's Coast Range from Ventura County north to Oregon.
A dense shrub or small tree with leathery, oval leaves that are dark green above, woolly-white below, and 1.5–2.5 in. (4–6 cm) long.
FLOWER AND FRUIT: Long, drooping, yellowish male catkins are 3–8 in. (8–20 cm) long; female catkins are 2–3.5 in. (5–9 cm) long; in January–March; females bear purple berry clusters covered with silky hairs in the summer.
LANDSCAPE USES: Good specimen, screen or background plant. The dark foliage provides an effective contrast with many other plants.
CLIMATE ADAPTION: Quite cold tolerant, but does not like desert heat; best for coastal and inland southern California and California's Central Valley; protect from sun and wind in warmer locations.
CULTURE: Needs good drainage. Looks best with summer watering every 2–3 weeks in warmer locations. Little to no fertilizer. Prune after bloom to shape or to train as a tree. Propagate by cold-stratified seeds or cuttings.
POSSIBLE PROBLEMS: Size of flower clusters varies.

Garrya elliptica 'James Roof' is showier, with heavier bloom and longer clusters.

Garrya flavescens, pale silktassel, is another adaptable Southwest species that grows to 6 ft. (2 m) high with gray, leathery foliage covered with silky hairs.

Garrya fremontii
PRONOUNCER: *gair*-ee-ah free-*mon*-tee-eye
COMMON NAME: Fremont silktassel
   Evergreen. Height: 5–10 ft. (1.5–3 m). Spread: 6–8 ft. (2–2.5 m). Rate of growth: Moderate. Light requirement: Sun to part shade. Native to dry slopes from southern California to southern Washington.
   An erect shrub with glossy, oblong, yellowish green leaves up to 2.5 in. (6 cm) long; leaf undersides are pale, but not white and woolly as in *G. elliptica*.
FLOWER AND FRUIT: Showy, male catkins are yellowish, 2.75–8 in. (7–20 cm) long, while female catkins are up to 2 in. (5 cm) long; January–April; purple to black berries.
LANDSCAPE USES: Nice screen or background shrub with attractive foliage and flowers. Hardier and more drought tolerant than *G. elliptica*.
CLIMATE ADAPTION: Quite cold tolerant, but does not accept desert heat; best for inland southern California and California's Central Valley, where it needs afternoon shade.
CULTURE: Likes good drainage. Prefers deep watering every 3–4 weeks in the summer in warmer locations. Little to no fertilizer. Prune to shape after bloom, as desired. Propagate by stratified seeds or cuttings.
POSSIBLE PROBLEMS: Tends to become leggy in the shade.

Garrya veatchii is native to the chaparral of southern California south into Baja California; it grows to 8 ft. (2.5 m) with dark green, narrow to broad leaves that are hairy below; suitable for southern California and north to the central coast.

Garrya wrightii
PRONOUNCER: *gair*-ee-ah *right*-ee-eye
COMMON NAME: Wright silktassel
   Evergreen. Height: 2–15 ft. (60 cm-4.5 m). Spread: 5–15 ft. (1.5–4.5 m). Rate of growth: Slow. Light requirement: Sun. Native to the dry slopes and canyons of west Texas, New Mexico, Arizona and Mexico.
   A shrub or small tree with light green, elliptic to oblong leaves, 0.75–2 in. (2–5 cm) long; leaves nearly glabrous.
FLOWER AND FRUIT: Loose catkins, the female to 3.5 in. (9 cm) long and the male to 5 in. (13 cm) long,

March–August; fruits are showy, bluish purple.
LANDSCAPE USES: On slopes for erosion control, as screening, or in background and transitional plantings.
CLIMATE ADAPTION: Excellent cold tolerance; best for mid-elevation and higher deserts; tends to suffer in low-desert heat.
CULTURE: Prefers good drainage. Quite drought tolerant but plants in hotter elevations require an occasional, deep, summer watering. Little to no fertilizer. Prune to shape after bloom, as necessary. Propagate by seeds, but seedlings are very susceptible to fungus.
POSSIBLE PROBLEMS: Flowers are not as showy as other silktassels; slow growing.

Geijera parviflora   PLATE 118
PRONOUNCER: jy-*jeer*-ah par-vi-*flor*-ah
FAMILY: Rutaceae
COMMON NAME: Australian willow
   Evergreen. Height: 15–25 ft. (4.5–7.5 m). Spread: 15–20 ft. (4.5–6 m). Rate of growth: Moderate. Light requirement: Sun. Native to Australia.
   A willowlike, weeping tree with a narrow to rounded form and medium green, fine-textured foliage; narrow, 3–5 in. (8–13 cm) leaves; deep rooted; a distant relative of citrus.
FLOWER AND FRUIT: Insignificant white flowers in the spring and possibly fall; tiny, rounded fruit.
LANDSCAPE USES: Small tree for patios, screening or in street plantings; provides light shade, tolerates lawn situations.
CLIMATE ADAPTION: No heat problems; may defoliate about 18°F (−8°C) but recovers; best in low desert and coastal and inland southern California.
CULTURE: Good drainage; tolerates alkaline soils. Drought tolerant, but give it a monthly, deep irrigation during the warmest months or prolonged dry periods. To speed growth, apply 1 lb. (0.45 kg) ammonium sulfate in early spring for every 200 sq. ft. (18 sq. m) under leaf canopy. Prune to shape, trim low-hanging branchlets. Propagate by seeds.
POSSIBLE PROBLEMS: Slow recovery from severe frost damage.

Genista
PRONOUNCER: je-*nis*-tah
FAMILY: Leguminosae
   The genistas are much less aggressive than other brooms, such as *Spartium* and *Cytisus* (see separate listings), which are likely to naturalize and crowd out other plants. The genistas need

sun and good drainage but otherwise are quite undemanding and are particularly attractive in flower. The three genera of broom are relatives and are often confused with each other.

Genista aethnensis   PLATE 119

PRONOUNCER: je-*nis*-tah eeth-*nen*-sis
COMMON NAME: Mt. Aetna broom
   Deciduous. Height: 10–20 ft. (3–6 m). Spread: 10–15 ft. (3–4.5 m). Rate of growth: Moderate. Light requirement: Sun. Native to Sicily and Sardinia.
   A small tree or large shrub with a heavy display of flowers; handsome, smooth green bark is much like a palo verde's; slender, drooping branches bear small, linear leaves that are few in number.
FLOWER AND FRUIT: Fragrant, golden yellow flowers in dense, terminal clusters in spring and summer; oval, 1–3 seeded pods.
LANDSCAPE USES: A wonderful, flowering accent plant for small spaces; deserves to be used more; open canopy provides filtered shade.
CLIMATE ADAPTION: Hardy to at least 20°F (−6.5°C); best for California's Central Valley and coastal and inland southern California.
CULTURE: Prefers good drainage. Likes infrequent summer watering in warmest areas. Little to no fertilizer. Looks best if trained as a tree. Propagate by seeds.
POSSIBLE PROBLEMS: Not widely available.

Genista hispanica

PRONOUNCER: je-*nis*-tah his-*pan*-i-cah
COMMON NAME: Spanish broom
   Evergreen. Height: 1–2 ft. (30–60 cm). Spread: 3–4 ft. (about 1 m). Rate of growth: Fast. Light requirement: Sun. Native from Spain to northern Italy.
   A low, wide-spreading shrub, densely branched and spiny, with narrow leaves about 0.5 in. (1.3 cm) long.
FLOWER AND FRUIT: Sweet scented, yellow flowers in terminal clusters in late spring and early summer; pods follow.
LANDSCAPE USES: A low barrier plant or a ground cover; good for slopes and banks.
CLIMATE ADAPTION: Hardy to at least 0°F (−18°C); widely adaptable.
CULTURE: Needs good drainage. Needs infrequent watering in summer in warmest areas. Little to no fertilizer. Prune to shape as needed. Propagate by seeds.
POSSIBLE PROBLEMS: Thorny branches.

Genista lydia, from Greece, is a heavy-flowering shrub to 3 ft. (1 m).

Grevillea

PRONOUNCER: gre-*vil*-ee-ah
FAMILY: Proteaceae
   There are about 200 species of grevilleas, mostly Australian natives ranging from shrubs to trees. While prized for their decorative qualities, they should be used with caution in the Southwest because disadvantages such as iron chlorosis in alkaline soils often outweigh their advantages. Shrubby types make good barrier or screen plants. The silk oak is useful where quick growth is desired.

Grevillea lanigera   PLATE 120

PRONOUNCER: gre-*vil*-ee-ah lan-*i*-jer-ah
COMMON NAME: woolly grevillea
   Evergreen. Height: 4–6 ft. (1.2–2 m). Spread: 6–10 ft. (2–3 m). Rate of growth: Moderate. Light requirement: Sun to part shade. Native to Australia.
   A spreading shrub with medium to gray-green, needlelike foliage.
FLOWER AND FRUIT: Red and cream-colored flowers in clusters in summer; small, woody fruit.
LANDSCAPE USES: A fine-textured barrier or screen plant; good on slopes.
CLIMATE ADAPTION: Hardy to about 24°F (−4°C); best for coastal and inland southern California.
CULTURE: Needs good drainage; becomes chlorotic in alkaline soils. Moderately drought tolerant; needs watering every 2–3 weeks in the warmest months and long, dry periods. Apply 2 oz. (57 g) ammonium sulfate in early spring. Prune to shape or contain size. Propagate by cuttings or seeds.
POSSIBLE PROBLEMS: Iron chlorosis.

Grevillea 'Canberra' is a large shrub to 10 ft. (3 m) that is reportedly more tolerant of alkaline soil.

Grevillea 'Noellii' grows to about 4 ft. (1.2 m), with red flowers in the spring; requires more water than the species.

Grevillea robusta   PLATE 121

PRONOUNCER: gre-*vil*-ee-ah row-*bus*-tah
COMMON NAME: silk oak
   Evergreen. Height: 30–100 ft. (9–30.5 m). Spread: 25–30 ft. (7.5–9 m). Rate of growth: Fast. Light requirement: Sun to partial shade. Native to Australia.
   A large, narrow, pyramidal tree with dark green, deeply cut, fernlike leaves with silvery-white undersides.
FLOWER AND FRUIT: Clusters of yellow-orange flowers in spring on leafless branches of old

wood, followed by small, woody pods with black seeds.

LANDSCAPE USES: A specimen or screen tree for large areas when a plant requiring little maintenance is needed.

CLIMATE ADAPTION: Older trees hardy to about 15°F (−9°C), but younger ones can be damaged around 24°F (−4°C); best for coastal and inland southern California and California's Central Valley; risky in the deserts, where it takes the heat but often develops chlorosis.

CULTURE: Needs good drainage; sensitive to alkaline soils. Tolerates drought but grows and looks best with monthly, deep irrigation in summer months; accepts ample water in lighter soils. Minimal fertilizer. Prune dead or unsightly branches; remove lower ones in traffic areas. Propagate by seeds.

POSSIBLE PROBLEMS: Quite susceptible to Texas root rot and iron chlorosis; litter; wind damage.

Hakea suaveolens

PRONOUNCER: *hay*-kee-ah swah-vee-*oh*-lenz
FAMILY: Proteaceae
COMMON NAME: sweet hakea

Evergreen. Height: 8–18 ft. (2.5–5.5 m). Spread: 6–15 ft. (2–4.5 m). Rate of growth: Moderate to fast. Light requirement: Sun. Native to Australia.

A dense, rounded shrub with needlelike foliage giving it a "conifer" appearance; medium green leaves 3–4 in. (8–10 cm) long are variable, with some divided and forklike.

FLOWER AND FRUIT: Fragrant, white flowers on dense spikes in late fall and early winter; pale brown to gray, 1-in. (2.5-cm) woody fruit.

LANDSCAPE USES: Sturdy yet soft-textured shrub; effective for barriers and screens.

CLIMATE ADAPTION: Moderately frost tolerant; best for coastal regions, as it withstands both wind and salt spray, and inland areas of southern California.

CULTURE: Needs good drainage; develops chlorosis in alkaline soils. Minimal water requirement; in light soils, needs supplemental irrigation every 2–3 weeks during long, dry periods. Little to no fertilizer needed. Prune to shape after bloom, or to train as a small tree. Propagate by cuttings or seeds.

POSSIBLE PROBLEMS: Iron chlorosis.

Hardenbergia

PRONOUNCER: har-den-*ber*-jee-ah
FAMILY: Leguminosae

Hardenbergia comptoniana is a more widely used species than *H. violacea*. It has pinkish blue flowers but is not as drought resistant or cold hardy as *H. violacea*.

Hardenbergia violacea

PRONOUNCER: har-den-*ber*-jee-ah vy-oh-*loss*-ee-ah
COMMON NAME: lilac vine

Evergreen. Height: 8–10 ft. (2.5–3 m). Spread: 5–10 ft. (1.5–3 m). Rate of growth: Moderate. Light requirement: Sun to part shade. Native to Australia.

A flowering vine with thin, twining stems; dark green, narrow, pointed leaves to 4 in. (10 cm). The 'Happy Wanderer' cultivar is more vigorous than the species.

FLOWER AND FRUIT: Bright purple to rose to white, pea-type flowers in clusters covering the plant in late winter to early spring; small, gray to brown pods.

LANDSCAPE USES: Provides a light cover for low walls and fences; grows well under the filtered shade of palo verdes and acacias in the low deserts. Needs support on a wall but twines up a tree trunk.

CLIMATE ADAPTION: Hardy to about 20°F (−6.5°C); widely adaptable except for the higher desert.

CULTURE: Needs good drainage. Needs supplemental watering in the low desert every two weeks through the spring and summer months; less in other areas. Responds to minimal fertilizer. Trim overgrown plants after flowering. Propagate by seeds or cuttings.

POSSIBLE PROBLEMS: Spider mites.

Hesperaloe

PRONOUNCER: hes-per-*al*-oh
FAMILY: Agavaceae

Hesperaloe funifera has white flowers and is slightly larger than *H. parviflora*.

Hesperaloe parviflora   PLATE 122

PRONOUNCER: hes-per-*al*-oh par-vi-*flor*-ah
COMMON NAME: red yucca

Evergreen. Height: 3–4 ft. (about 1 m). Spread: 3–4 ft. (about 1 m). Rate of growth: Very slow. Light requirement: Full sun is best. Native to Texas and Mexico.

One of the Southwest's gems. A dense, clumping plant with narrow, gray-green leaves to 4 ft. (1.2 m) long that curve up from the base, forming a stiff, rounded clump; distinctive fibrous threads occur along leaf margins.

FLOWER AND FRUIT: Very showy, fleshy, red to pink,

1-in. (2.5-cm) flowers in clusters on tall spikes in late spring and early summer; rounded fruit capsules follow.

LANDSCAPE USES: A striking accent plant that in bloom adds a real burst of color to the landscape; blends exceptionally well with palms, cactuses and similar plants. A rugged plant for roadsides and medians; effective in rock gardens and containers; provides a long period of bright color.

CLIMATE ADAPTION: Hardy to about 0°F (−18°C); loves heat; widely adaptable but best in deserts.

CULTURE: Minimal soil requirement. Does better with 1 in. (2.5 cm) of supplemental water once a month in summer in deserts. Apply 1 oz. (30 g) ammonium sulfate in early spring on established plants. Remove old flower spikes. Propagate by seeds or by dividing clumps.

POSSIBLE PROBLEMS: Slow growth.

Heteromeles arbutifolia   PLATE 123

PRONOUNCER: het-er-*om*-el-eez ar-bew-ti-*foh*-lee-ah

FAMILY: Rosaceae

COMMON NAME: toyon, California holly

Evergreen. Height: 10–25 ft. (3–7.5 m). Spread: 10–25 ft. (3–7.5 m). Rate of growth: Moderate. Light requirement: Sun to part shade. Native to chaparral from northern California to Baja California.

Large shrub or small tree with dark green, leathery, oblong leaves with toothed margins, to 4 in. (10 cm) long; open to dense growth, depending on sunlight; deep rooted. Formerly known as *Photinia arbutifolia.*

FLOWER AND FRUIT: Large terminal clusters of small, white flowers in early summer; decorative berry clusters turn red in the fall and last through most of the winter.

LANDSCAPE USES: Versatile and handsome plant that can be used as a winter accent, for screening or as a background plant; popular for roadsides and slopes where its deep roots provide erosion control. Can be trained as a specimen tree. Winter berries attract birds.

CLIMATE ADAPTION: Best for coastal and inland areas of southern California; needs part shade in California's Central Valley, where it is not always happy; marginal in deserts.

CULTURE: Needs good drainage. Deep-water monthly in summer. Minimal fertilizer. Prune to shape or train as a tree in the winter or early spring. Propagate by fresh seeds or semihardwood cuttings.

POSSIBLE PROBLEMS: Fireblight; oak root fungus.

Isomeris arborea   PLATE 124

PRONOUNCER: eye-*som*-er-is ar-*bor*-ee-ah

FAMILY: Capparidaceae

COMMON NAME: bladderpod

Evergreen. Height: 3–5 ft. (1–1.5 m). Spread: 4–6 ft. (1.2–2 m). Rate of growth: Moderate. Light requirement: Sun. Native to the deserts and coastal sage-scrub community of southern California and south into Mexico.

A rounded shrub with pungent, gray-green foliage divided palmately into three narrow leaflets. Quite variable in foliage and fruit.

FLOWER AND FRUIT: Yellow flowers with four petals and prominent stamens from the spring through much of the year; unusual, 1–2 in. (2.5–5 cm) fruits are inflated, giving the plant its common name.

LANDSCAPE USES: An informal, flowering shrub for mixed plantings or naturalized areas or as a low screen; similar in effect to the Australian cassias.

CLIMATE ADAPTION: Hardy to at least 20°F (−6.5°C); widely adaptable, but not for the higher deserts.

CULTURE: Needs good drainage. Drought tolerant, but looks best with monthly watering in the warmest months. Little to no fertilizer. Minimal pruning. Propagate by seeds.

POSSIBLE PROBLEMS: Pungent smell of foliage at close range.

Juniperus

PRONOUNCER: june-*ip*-er-us

FAMILY: Cupressaceae

Junipers are available in many sizes, habits and foliage colors. Most are versatile and widely adaptable from coastal regions to the deserts. They lend themselves to well-mannered areas such as oriental gardens as well as informal settings, but sometimes their physical features do not blend well with Southwestern native plants. They are sensitive to too frequent watering and high-nitrogen fertilizer, which can burn the roots. Three have proven themselves in the Southwest.

Juniperus chinensis 'Pfitzeriana'

PRONOUNCER: june-*ip*-er-us chi-*nen*-sis fit-zer-ee-*ah*-nah

COMMON NAME: Pfitzer juniper

Evergreen. Height: 5–8 ft. (1.5–2.5 m). Spread: 8–10 ft. (2.5–3 m). Rate of growth: Moderate. Light requirement: Sun to partial shade. Cultivar.

A shrub with sharp-to-touch, needlelike, usually gray-green foliage on spreading, upward-arching branches.

FLOWER AND FRUIT: Insignificant, tiny flowers; round, brownish, berrylike cones about 0.3 in. (1 cm) across.

LANDSCAPE USES: In many ways, this is the lazy gardener's dream: a plant requiring minimal maintenance but providing outstanding focal points. Ideal for softening corners, on hillsides in mass plantings, as a specimen, informal hedge or background for floral displays. Can be held at just about any size desired with occasional pruning, but do not shear.

CLIMATE ADAPTION: Hardy to about 0°F (−18°C); widely adaptable.

CULTURE: Needs good drainage; avoid planting where soil stays wet, such as near lawns. For the first couple of years in the landscape, water thoroughly once a week in the warmest months and cut back in cooler months. Thereafter, water deeply every 1–2 weeks in the hottest areas in the summer. Apply only low-nitrogen fertilizers in late winter for deeper, richer color. When the plant reaches the desired size, remove the main leaders inside the foliage each January. Avoid shearing or heavy pruning as plants have difficulty recovering. Propagate by cuttings.

POSSIBLE PROBLEMS: Bermuda grass invasion, which can be controlled by trimming the lower branches high enough to permit spraying grass killers without hitting the juniper foliage; spider mites.

Juniperus chinensis 'Pfitzeriana Compacta' is a low-growing form to 2 ft. (60 cm) high with a spread of about 4 ft. (1.2 m).

Juniperus sabina 'Tamariscifolia'   PLATE 125
PRONOUNCER: june-*ip*-er-us sa-*bee*-nah tam-ar-is-i-*foh*-lee-ah
COMMON NAME: tam juniper

Evergreen. Height: 1–3 ft. (30–90 cm). Spread: 10–20 ft. (3–6 m). Rate of growth: Moderate. Light requirement: Sun. Cultivar.

A low, wide-spreading juniper with dark green foliage and a neat, dense growth habit.

FLOWER AND FRUIT: Insignificant flowers; small, woody cones.

LANDSCAPE USES: A durable ground cover and divider plant; its rich, dark foliage provides a wonderful contrast. Set plants about 6 ft. (2 m) apart.

CLIMATE ADAPTION: Hardy to about 0°F (−18°C); widely adaptable.

CULTURE: Needs good drainage; tolerates alkaline soil. Needs supplemental water every 1–2 weeks in the low desert; less in other regions; taper off in cooler months. Apply low-nitrogen

fertilizer lightly as needed for deeper color. Trim plants lightly in early spring by thinning branches; avoid shearing. Propagate by cuttings.

POSSIBLE PROBLEMS: Overwatering; nitrogen damage; spider mites; Bermuda grass invasions, which require handpulling.

Justicia
PRONOUNCER: jus-*tis*-ee-ah
FAMILY: Acanthaceae

The Southwestern justicias are ideal shrubs for providing color in the landscape as they flower throughout much of the year. The desert honeysuckle and red firecracker require regular watering; hummingbird bush can be used in naturalized areas but also tolerates occasional irrigation.

Justicia californica   PLATE 126
PRONOUNCER: jus-*tis*-ee-ah cal-i-*for*-ni-cah
COMMON NAME: chuparosa

Semideciduous. Height: 3–4 ft. (about 1 m). Spread: 4–5 ft. (1.2–1.5 m). Rate of growth: Moderate. Light requirement: Sun. Native to southern Arizona, southeastern California, northern Mexico.

Broad, mounding, densely branched shrub with gray-green foliage and stems accented much of the year with flowers; oval leaves vary in size from 0.5 to 2 in. (1.3–5 cm) in length, depending on moisture and light; known as *Beloperone californica* for years.

FLOWER AND FRUIT: 2-in. (5-cm), tubular, red flowers, mainly in spring, followed by small, club-shaped fruit with two seeds.

LANDSCAPE USES: Excellent flowering shrub for naturalized areas or as an informal hedge; hummingbirds love it.

CLIMATE ADAPTION: Hardy to about 25°F (−4°C); recovers quickly from frost setbacks; best for low deserts and protected locations in mid-elevation deserts; also adapts to inland southern California.

CULTURE: Needs good drainage. Very drought resistant; survives with natural rainfall, but drops its leaves during drought periods without supplemental water. Minimal to no fertilizer. Pinch tips to encourage bushiness. Propagate by softwood cuttings.

POSSIBLE PROBLEMS: Drainage; can look scraggly without extra moisture in summer.

Justicia candicans   PLATE 127
PRONOUNCER: jus-*tis*-ee-ah *can*-di-canz
COMMON NAME: red firecracker

Evergreen. Height: 3–4 ft. (about 1 m). Spread: 3–4 ft. (about 1 m). Rate of growth: Slow. Light requirement: Sun to light shade. Native to southern Arizona and northern Mexico.

A small shrub with an erect form and attractive spring flowers; oval, bright green leaves. Formerly known as *J. ovata.*

FLOWER AND FRUIT: Bright red, funnel-shaped flowers, 0.75 in. (2 cm) long in clusters in spring, followed by club-shaped fruit.

LANDSCAPE USES: In groups for border plantings or mixed with other flowering shrubs; does best under trees providing filtered shade.

CLIMATE ADAPTION: Frost damage around 25°F (−4°C); no heat problems; best for low deserts and inland southern California but survives in protected locations in the mid-elevation desert.

CULTURE: Prefers good drainage. Drought tolerant, but likes water every 1–2 weeks in the hottest areas during summer. Apply 2 oz. (57 g) ammonium sulfate in early spring. Cut back in spring after bloom for bushy, more compact growth. Propagate by softwood cuttings or seeds.

POSSIBLE PROBLEMS: Can become rangy.

Justicia spicigera　　　　　PLATE 128
PRONOUNCER: jus-*tis*-ee-ah spy-*sij*-ur-ah
COMMON NAME: desert honeysuckle

Evergreen. Height: 3–5 ft. (1–1.5 m). Spread: 4–6 ft. (1.2–2 m). Rate of growth: Moderate. Light requirement: Sun to part shade. Native to Mexico.

Colorful, rounded shrub with rich green foliage and bright flowers; oval leaves are 2–3 in. (5–8 cm) long.

FLOWER AND FRUIT: Clusters of slender, tubular, orange-red flowers, 1.5 in. (4 cm) long, appear mainly in spring but frequently show year-round; attractive to hummingbirds.

LANDSCAPE USES: Deservedly a popular desert shrub; use in small groupings or mixed with other flowering shrubs such as ruellias and salvias. Nearly year-round color; foliage provides bold accent. An ideal location in low deserts is near trees that provide partial shade.

CLIMATE ADAPTION: Freezes to the ground around 25°F (−4°C) but recovers with warm weather; best for the low desert and inland southern California; survives in mid-elevation desert locations.

CULTURE: Needs good drainage. Drought resistant, but flowers best with a moderate supply of water every 1–2 weeks during the warmest months. Apply 2 oz. (57 g) ammonium sulfate in the early spring after the first year. Pinch tips for bushiness in spring. Propagate by softwood cuttings.

POSSIBLE PROBLEMS: Sometimes develops chlorosis in heavy, alkaline soils; can look poor in cold weather.

Lantana
PRONOUNCER: lan-*tan*-ah
FAMILY: Verbenaceae

These tropical shrubs or perennials provide nearly year-round color in the warm-arid landscape. Both shrub and ground cover types come in a variety of colors. They are very heat tolerant, although flowering is reduced in the heat of summer in the low desert. They may be deciduous in colder weather. Group them with other moderate water users.

Lantana camara　　　　　PLATE 129
PRONOUNCER: lan-*tan*-ah cah-*mar*-ah
COMMON NAME: bush lantana

Evergreen to deciduous. Height: 2–4 ft. (60 cm–1.2 m). Spread: 3–6 ft. (1–2 m). Rate of growth: Moderate. Light requirement: Sun to partial shade. Native to Mexico.

Shrublike, flowering perennial; bright green leaves to 3 in. (8 cm) long with toothed margins. The best cultivars are 'Christine', to 6 ft. (2 m) with pink and yellow flowers; 'Radiation', 3–5 ft. (1–1.5 m), especially long-blooming with red-orange-yellow flowers; and 'Dwarf Yellow', a 2–4 ft. (60 cm–1.2 m) plant producing yellow flowers.

FLOWER AND FRUIT: Yellow, orange, red, pink or multicolored flowers, depending on cultivar, appear much of the year, followed by clusters of tiny, black berries, which are especially poisonous when green.

LANDSCAPE USES: Group for masses of color or as an informal, flowering hedge. Can be grown in containers. Dwarf selections make handsome, flowering ground covers, focal points for entryways.

CLIMATE ADAPTION: Foliage damage and leaf drop at around 27°F (−3°C); most plants recover in the spring; best in low- and mid-elevation deserts, coastal and mild inland valleys of southern California.

CULTURE: Best in enriched soil; tolerates alkaline conditions. Water about once a week in warmer months in hottest areas; needs very little otherwise. Apply 2 oz. (57 g) ammonium sulfate in early spring after the plant has been in the landscape at least a year. Cut back in early spring to shape and remove frost-damaged branches. Propagate by softwood cuttings.

101

Lavandula angustifolia

POSSIBLE PROBLEMS: Poisonous fruit; off-color appearance in winter; abrasive foliage; pungent smell; reseeds.

Lantana montevidensis   PLATE 130
PRONOUNCER: lan-*tan*-ah mon-te-vi-*den*-sis
COMMON NAME: trailing lantana

Evergreen to deciduous. Height: 8–12 in. (20–30 cm). Spread: 4–6 ft. (1.2–2 m). Rate of growth: Fast. Light requirement: Sun. Native to South America.

A ground cover providing fantastic color in warm weather with minimum effort from the gardener. Leaves are prickly, small, medium green. Stems root along the ground and it spreads quickly to great lengths.
FLOWER AND FRUIT: 1-in. (2.5-cm) clusters of purple flowers show almost constantly during the warmer months; tiny, black berries.
LANDSCAPE USES: Ground cover; particularly useful on mounds and banks; plant about 3 ft. (1 m) apart.
CLIMATE ADAPTION: Foliage damage and leaf drop at about 25°F (−4°C), recovers quickly in warm weather; widely adaptable except for higher deserts.
CULTURE: Minimal soil requirement. Looks best with moderate water during warmer months, every 7–10 days in low deserts; minimal otherwise. Little to no fertilizer. Prune to remove frost damage and control growth in early spring. Propagate by softwood cuttings.
POSSIBLE PROBLEMS: Poisonous fruit; prickly foliage; pungent smell; unwanted spreading.

Larrea tridentata   PLATE 131
PRONOUNCER: *lair*-ree-ah try-den-*tah*-tah
FAMILY: Zygophyllaceae
COMMON NAME: creosote bush, greasewood

Evergreen. Height: 5–8 ft. (1.5–2.5 m). Spread: 5–8 ft. (1.5–2.5 m). Rate of growth: Slow. Light requirement: Sun to partial shade. Native to Southwest deserts.

Open and airy, bright green foliage in rainy seasons changes to dark green at other times; density also varies. Small leaves glossy, resinous; pungent fragrance, especially after rain; extensive root system. Probably the most common shrub of Southwest deserts below 5,000 ft. (1,500 m), where it grows in large, often pure, stands.
FLOWER AND FRUIT: Numerous, 2–3 in. (5–8 cm), single, yellow flowers in the spring followed by small, white, fuzzy seed balls; sometimes blooms in the fall and winter following rains.

LANDSCAPE USES: A natural for desert landscapes. Combines well in informal groupings with other desert plants; excellent for screening. Plant away from regularly watered areas.
CLIMATE ADAPTION: Frost tolerant but varies somewhat according to original habitat so in the coldest areas it is best to purchase locally grown plants; needs a great deal of heat for an extended period to develop; best for deserts.
CULTURE: Prefers well-aerated soil, otherwise quite tolerant. Minimal water requirement, and may die from overwatering in heavy soils. In general, appreciates infrequent deep soakings but must be kept on the moist side for first six months in the landscape. Apply 2 oz. (57 g) ammonium sulfate in late winter after the plant has been in the landscape at least a year. Prune lightly in spring to control size, as desired. Propagate by seeds, but they are difficult; remove fuzzy hulls.
POSSIBLE PROBLEMS: Foliage odor may be objectionable; believed by some to poison soil around it for other plants; flowers attract bees.

Lavandula angustifolia   PLATE 132
PRONOUNCER: lav-*and*-ewe-lah an-goos-ti-*foh*-lee-ah
FAMILY: Labiatae
COMMON NAME: English lavender

Evergreen. Height: 3–4 ft. (about 1 m). Spread: 2–3 ft. (60–90 cm). Rate of growth: Fast. Light requirement: Sun to part shade. Native to the Mediterranean region.

A small, gray-green shrub with very aromatic foliage and flowers that are often used in perfumes and potpourris; linear leaves to 2 in. (5 cm) long have smooth margins. Dwarf cultivars 'Hidcote' and 'Munstead' are available.
FLOWER AND FRUIT: Lavender, tubular flowers about 0.5 in. (1.3 cm) on long, slender spikes throughout much of the year; tiny nutlets.
LANDSCAPE USES: A showy shrub in borders, mixed with other plants, especially other types of lavender, or for rock gardens.
CLIMATE ADAPTION: Hardy to at least 15°F (−9°C); best for coastal and inland southern California and California's Central Valley; marginal in desert heat.
CULTURE: Needs good drainage; prefers alkaline soil. Drought resistant, but likes occasional watering in the summer in warm areas. Little to no fertilizer. Remove old flower heads and trim plants after flowering to keep bushy. Propagate by cuttings or seeds.
POSSIBLE PROBLEMS: Flowers attract bees.

Lavandula dentata, French lavender, has gray, toothed leaves, light purple flowers.

Lavandula stoechas, Spanish lavender, grows to 3 ft. (1 m) with deep purple flowers; said to be the most drought resistant of the genus.   PLATE 133

Leptospermum
PRONOUNCER: lep-toh-*sper*-mum
FAMILY: Myrtaceae

A woman from the Midwest, seeing her first leptospermums, exclaimed, "These are really pretty!" It was springtime and they were presenting their annual floral show. But, in or out of flower, the "tea tree" makes an excellent landscape plant, except in the deserts. They need good drainage. Early explorers of Australia and New Zealand used the leaves to brew a tea.

Leptospermum laevigatum   PLATE 134
PRONOUNCER: lep-toh-*sper*-mum lay-vi-*gah*-tum
COMMON NAME: Australian tea tree
Evergreen. Height: 15–30 ft. (4.5–9 m). Spread: 15–25 ft. (4.5–7.5 m). Rate of growth: Slow. Light requirement: Sun. Native to Australia.

An attractive large shrub or small tree with pendulous branches and a twisted, gnarled trunk with fibery bark; light gray-green leaves are oval to oblong, about 0.5 in. (1.3 cm) long. Often seen as a multitrunked tree.
FLOWER AND FRUIT: Showy, small, numerous white flowers in late spring and early summer.
LANDSCAPE USES: Picturesque specimen, large screen or natural or clipped hedge; good bonsai subject.
CLIMATE ADAPTION: Best for southern California's coastal regions, where it tolerates salt spray, and inland valleys; less cold tolerant than *L. scoparium*; not for the deserts.
CULTURE: Needs good drainage; best in acid soils. Prefers infrequent, deep watering in the warmest months. Responds to light fertilizing in summer and fall. Prune to shape or to emphasize form and trunk. Propagate by cuttings or seeds.
POSSIBLE PROBLEMS: Root rot if overwatered.

Leptospermum laevigatum 'Compactum' is a rounded, spreading shrub to 8 ft. (2.5 m) with gray-green foliage and shredding bark; nice screening or background shrub.

Leptospermum scoparium
PRONOUNCER: lep-toh-*sper*-mum sko-*pair*-ee-um

COMMON NAME: New Zealand tea tree
Evergreen. Height: 6–8 ft. (2–2.5 m). Spread: 8–10 ft. (2.5–3 m). Rate of growth: Moderate. Light requirement: Sun. Native to New Zealand.

A flowering shrub with upright stems; needlelike leaves to 0.5 in. (1.3 cm), pointed, densely set. For the best floral show, pick one of the many cultivars, which range from ground covers to large shrubs.
FLOWER AND FRUIT: Large numbers of small, red or pink flowers from spring to summer; small, woody seed capsule.
LANDSCAPE USES: Specimen plant, flowering accent or for screening and backgrounds; the ground cover types do well on slopes.
CLIMATE ADAPTION: Hardy to about 25°F (−4°C); best for the coastal and inland valleys of southern California; does not like desert heat.
CULTURE: Needs good drainage; does not do well in alkaline soils. Drought resistant, but likes occasional water, especially in warmer months. Little to no fertilizer. Prune as needed after flowering to shape. Propagate by cuttings or seeds.
POSSIBLE PROBLEMS: Overwatering causes root rot.

Leptospermum scoparium 'Pink Cascade' is a low, spreading, 1 ft. (30 cm) tall shrub with light pink flowers.

Leptospermum scoparium 'Ruby Glow' is a 6–8 ft. (2–2.5 m), striking accent shrub with red flowers that give the entire plant a deep red appearance in winter and spring.   PLATE 135

Leucaena
PRONOUNCER: loo-*see*-na
FAMILY: Leguminosae

Leucaena pulverulenta, the Texas lead ball tree, is larger but has less attractive blooms than *L. retusa*.

Leucaena retusa   PLATE 136
PRONOUNCER: loo-*see*-na ray-*too*-sa
COMMON NAME: golden lead ball, yellow popinac
Deciduous. Height: 15–20 ft. (4.5–6 m). Spread: 12–15 ft. (3.5–4.5 m). Rate of growth: Moderate. Light requirement: Sun. Native to southwestern Texas, northern Mexico.

Multi- or single-trunked, small tree or large shrub with attractive, tropical-looking, bright green foliage and spectacular flowers; bipinnate leaves are divided into leaflets 0.5–1 in. (1.3–2.5 cm) long; bark varies from light gray to brown and is scaly on older trunks.

FLOWER AND FRUIT: Very showy and abundant, golden yellow puffballs 1 in. (2.5 cm) across, mainly in the spring but also in fall; 3–10 in. (8–25 cm) brown pods follow.

LANDSCAPE USES: Specimen for patio or similar settings and small areas; foliage has a lush quality for oasis areas; however, the floral show is reason enough for planting.

CLIMATE ADAPTION: Hardy to about 12°F (−11°C); best for deserts.

CULTURE: Best with good drainage; tolerates alkaline soils. Likes deep watering every 3–4 weeks in hottest months. Responds with faster growth to 2 oz. (57 g) ammonium sulfate applied in the spring. Needs shaping to grow as a tree; can be trained to single- or multitrunked form. Propagate by seeds; possible from semihardwood cuttings.

POSSIBLE PROBLEMS: Branches may snap in strong winds, so avoid planting near structures.

Leucophyllum

PRONOUNCER: loo-ko-*fil*-um
FAMILY: Scrophulariaceae

The versatile leucophyllums are among the best low-water-use plants. Give them first consideration when looking for a small to large evergreen shrub. Their major problem: overwatering. Death comes swiftly in soggy soil, so be sure of good drainage before planting and apply supplemental irrigation only during prolonged dry weather. Several new cultivars that add to the color palette have become available recently.

Leucophyllum frutescens   PLATES 137 AND 138

PRONOUNCER: loo-ko-*fil*-um froo-*tes*-ens
COMMON NAME: Texas sage, Texas ranger

Evergreen. Height: 5–8 ft. (1.5–2.5 m). Spread: 4–6 ft. (1.2–2 m). Rate of growth: Moderate. Light requirement: Sun. Native to Texas, New Mexico and northern Mexico.

Tough, versatile shrub with soft, silvery to gray-green foliage; oval leaves are covered with dense hairs. 'Compactum' is a smaller and denser cultivar. 'Green Cloud' has light green foliage, purplish flowers. 'White Cloud' has silvery-gray foliage and white flowers. Other related species include *L. candidum* 'Silver Cloud', small and silvery with deep purple flowers, and *L. zygophyllum,* a fast grower to 6 ft. (2 m) with bluish purple flowers.

FLOWER AND FRUIT: Showy, violet-purple, 1-in. (2.5-cm), bell-shaped flowers appear soon after

rains or irrigation; followed by tiny seed capsules.

LANDSCAPE USES: Outstanding choice as a space-defining shrub or used as a specimen, screen or clipped hedge; blends well with other evergreens; a low-maintenance plant for all arid landscapes.

CLIMATE ADAPTION: Hardy to about 5°F (−15°C); thrives in heat; best in deserts; can be marginal in California's Central Valley due to wetter winters. *Leucophyllum candidum* 'Silver Cloud' is not quite as cold hardy.

CULTURE: Needs good drainage; does well in alkaline soils. Minimal water requirement but may look scraggly; becomes almost succulent with supplemental watering but will die if overwatered; for best results, water every 2–4 weeks through summer or long periods of drought. No fertilizer. No pruning except to produce a desired effect or more compact growth or maintain as a hedge. Propagate by softwood cuttings or seeds collected before capsules open.

POSSIBLE PROBLEMS: Overwatering causes death from root rot.

Leucophyllum laevigatum   PLATE 139

PRONOUNCER: loo-ko-*fil*-um lay-vi-*gah*-tum
COMMON NAME: Chihuahuan Desert sage

Evergreen. Height: 3–4 ft. (about 1 m). Spread: 3–5 ft. (1–1.5 m). Rate of growth: Slow. Light requirement: Sun. Native to Chihuahuan Desert of Mexico.

Upright, mounding shrub with medium green foliage that is frequently obscured by flowers in the summer and fall after rain or irrigation.

FLOWER AND FRUIT: Striking, light purple-blue, 1 in. (2.5 cm) long, tubular flowers followed by 0.2-in. (3-mm), black seed pods.

LANDSCAPE USES: Accent plant that in bloom adds a soft, pastel hue to arid gardens; attractive in small groups or mixed with other low, flowering shrubs in a border.

CLIMATE ADAPTION: Hardy to at least 12°F (−11°C); best for deserts.

CULTURE: Needs good drainage. Minimal water requirement, but give it some extra every 2–3 weeks during prolonged dry periods in summer. To speed growth, apply 2 oz. (57 g) ammonium sulfate in early spring after the first year in the landscape. No pruning needed except to shape; in that case, early spring pruning improves summer bloom production. Propagate by cuttings.

POSSIBLE PROBLEMS: Dies if overwatered; mealybugs sometimes attack.

Lupinus

PRONOUNCER: loo-*py*-nus
FAMILY: Leguminosae

The best-known display of lupines in North America occurs in Texas in the spring, where the bluebonnet (*Lupinus texensis*) is the state flower. Those annual wildflowers are not to be confused with the shrubby plants discussed here. More than 100 species occur throughout much of the world, with many native to the western United States.

The perennial, shrubby lupines are attractive in their palmate foliage as well as in their purple, terminal racemes. Give them good drainage and occasional summer water in warmer, inland areas. Do not use them in the deserts. Locally adapted species usually outperform all others.

Lupinus albifrons   PLATE 140

PRONOUNCER: loo-*py*-nus *al*-bi-fronz
COMMON NAME: silver bush lupine

Evergreen. Height: 3–5 ft. (1–1.5 m). Spread: 3–6 ft. (1–2 m). Rate of growth: Moderate. Light requirement: Sun. Native to the dry hillsides of California's Coast Range and the Sierra Nevada foothills.

A rounded shrub with handsome, soft, silvery foliage divided palmately into narrow leaflets with silky hairs above and below.

FLOWER AND FRUIT: Showy, fragrant, blue, purple, pink or white flower clusters to 1 ft. (30 cm), March–July; flat pods.

LANDSCAPE USES: An accent shrub for mixed plantings, borders, or in groupings; the silvery foliage catches sunlight and contrasts well with more deeply hued plants. The silver bush is likely to perform better than the tree lupine for most gardeners.

CLIMATE ADAPTION: Good cold tolerance; best for coastal and inland southern California and the more moderate areas of California's Central Valley.

CULTURE: Needs good drainage. Prefers water every 2–3 weeks in the summer in the warmer areas; minimal other times and on the coast. No fertilizer. Prune to shape and remove old flower heads. Propagate by seeds.

POSSIBLE PROBLEMS: Short lived.

Lupinus arboreus

PRONOUNCER: loo-*py*-nus ar-*bor*-ee-us
COMMON NAME: tree lupine

Evergreen. Height: 3–6 ft. (1–2 m). Spread: 3–6 ft. (1–2 m). Rate of growth: Fast. Light requirement: Sun. Native to California coastal areas.

A dense, rounded shrub with gray-green leaves palmately divided into 6–9 leaflets, often covered with silky hairs.

FLOWER AND FRUIT: Showy flower spikes, 4–12 in. (10–30 cm) long in blue, yellow or white, March–June; light brown pods.

LANDSCAPE USES: As a specimen shrub, in mixed borders, or in mass plantings for floral effects; tolerates wind.

CLIMATE ADAPTION: Best for coastal and inland southern California.

CULTURE: Needs good drainage; prefers sandy soil. Minimal water requirement but tolerates moderate amounts. No fertilizer. Prune to tidy plants; remove old flower heads. Propagate by seeds.

POSSIBLE PROBLEMS: Susceptible to root rot; short lived.

Lysiloma thornberi   PLATE 141

PRONOUNCER: lie-suh-*lo*-ma *thorn*-bur-eye
FAMILY: Leguminosae
COMMON NAME: fern of the desert

Semideciduous. Height: 15–20 ft. (4.5–6 m). Spread: 15–20 ft. (4.5–6 m). Rate of growth: Moderate. Light requirement: Sun to partial shade. Native to southern Arizona and northern Mexico.

A graceful, large shrub or small tree with single or multiple trunk and rounded canopy; medium green, feathery foliage with finely divided leaves, 5 in. (13 cm) or more long.

FLOWER AND FRUIT: White puffballs appear in clusters with new leaves, usually in April and May; fruit is a flat, brownish, 4–8 in. (10–20 cm) seed pod.

LANDSCAPE USES: Handsome as a specimen or in background plantings; lush, soft foliage adds a tropical or oasis touch; good for patios and entryways, screening and to soften building corners.

CLIMATE ADAPTION: No heat problems but can be killed to the ground in very coldest winters; recovers quickly in the spring. Loses leaves around 25°F (−4°C), and branch damage begins around 20°F (−6.5°C); best for low-and mid-elevation deserts, mild inland valleys of southern California.

CULTURE: Needs good drainage. Looks best with deep, monthly watering in the summer but gets along with none; water deeply if growing as a tree. Responds to 4 oz. (115 g) ammonium sulfate in winter after a year in the landscape. Prune in the spring to shape as a tree, create canopy or remove frost-damaged branches. Propagate by scarified seeds.

POSSIBLE PROBLEMS: Cold sensitivity; some litter; becomes chlorotic if overwatered.

Lysiloma watsonii, the feather bush, is similar to *L. thornberi* but is deciduous rather than semideciduous.

Macfadyena unguis-cati   PLATE 142

PRONOUNCER: mac-fad-*yen*-ah *un*-gwee *cat*-eýe
FAMILY: Bignoniaceae
COMMON NAME: cat's claw

Evergreen. Height: 10–20 ft. (3–6 m). Spread: Up to 40 ft. (12 m). Rate of growth: Rapid. Light requirement: Sun. Native to Central America.

A dense, climbing vine with clawlike, hooked tendrils. Glossy green leaves are divided into two oval, 2-in. (5-cm) leaflets. Flowers and leaves tend to form at the end of the stems. The roots form large tubers. Formerly known as *Doxantha unguis-cati* and *Bignonia tweediana.*
FLOWER AND FRUIT: Spectacular, yellow, trumpetlike, 2-in. (5-cm) flowers mainly in spring but sometimes in summer, followed by slender seed pods.
LANDSCAPE USES: Wonderful to cover cement block walls and other unsightly surfaces in the hottest exposures; clings to just about any support in places nothing else survives. Important: keep far away from homes because of extreme invasive tendency, including ability to penetrate indoors through cracks. Virtually impossible to eradicate once established.
CLIMATE ADAPTION: Hardy to about 15°F (−9°C); relishes heat; widely adaptable.
CULTURE: Minimal soil requirement. Minimal water needs; looks better in low desert with deep watering every 3–4 weeks in the summer. No fertilizer. Stimulate new growth by cutting almost to the ground; recovers quickly. Propagate by layering, seeds, or tip cuttings during active growth.
POSSIBLE PROBLEMS: Can fall completely from support; very invasive; dead tendrils most difficult to remove from structures.

Mahonia

PRONOUNCER: mah-*hone*-ee-ah
FAMILY: Berberidaceae

Several species of *Mahonia* are native to the western United States. All are evergreen shrubs prized for their attractive, year-round appearance. Foliage, flower and fruit all provide seasonal interest in the landscape. Leaves are spiny and hollylike, ranging from rich, dark green to gray- and blue-green. The often grapelike berries attract birds. Some perform better under some shade in hotter locations. The genus *Mahonia* is sometimes included in the related *Berberis,* but the mahonias differ by having compound leaves and spineless stems.

Mahonia aquifolium

PRONOUNCER: mah-*hone*-ee-ah ah-kwi-*foh*-lee-um
COMMON NAME: Oregon grape

Evergreen. Height: 3–6 ft. (1–2 m). Spread: 3–6 ft. (1–2 m). Rate of growth: Slow to moderate. Light requirement: Sun to shade. Native to West Coast foothills.

Many-branched shrub with hollylike foliage; leaves 4–10 in. (10–25 cm) long with 5–9 leaflets on each leaf; leathery, spiny teeth on edges. The young growth is ruddy while mature foliage is generally a glossy dark green but sometimes duller. Spreads by underground stems. There are several shorter, more compact cultivars.
FLOWER AND FRUIT: Yellow flower clusters 2–4 in. (5–10 cm) long in the spring; grapelike, 0.3-in. (1-cm), blue-purple, edible berries ripen in the fall. State flower of Oregon.
LANDSCAPE USES: A handsome, versatile shrub for use in groups or as a specimen. It provides different foliage colors throughout the year, plus conspicuous flowers and berries. Makes an excellent, informal hedge.
CLIMATE ADAPTION: Hardy to below 0°F (−18°C), widely adaptable but often suffers in deserts and California's Central Valley unless grown in the shade.
CULTURE: Tolerates various soil types but does best with good drainage. Keep soil moist for the first two years; thereafter, deep-water once or twice a month in the warmest months. Apply one-third cup (90 g) all-purpose fertilizer such as 10–6–4 to a plant that is 3 ft. (1 m) high with 3–5 trunks in the early spring; adjust fertilizer quantities to size of plant. Uneven growth habits in young plants tend to fill out with maturity. Prune long shoots in spring to encourage compactness. Propagate by stratified seeds in the winter or leafy cuttings in the summer.
POSSIBLE PROBLEMS: Leaf margins are sharp; chlorosis in alkaline areas; caterpillars; oak root fungus.

Mahonia fremontii

PRONOUNCER: mah-*hone*-ee-ah free-*mon*-tee-eye
COMMON NAME: desert mahonia

Evergreen. Height: 3–8 ft. (1–2.5 m). Spread: 3–5 ft. (1–1.5 m). Rate of growth: Moderate. Light requirement: Sun to part shade. Native to higher elevations of the Southwest deserts.

A clumping, erect shrub with many stems

from the base. Foliage is gray-to-yellowish green with 3–5, thick, 1-in. (2.5-cm), short-petioled leaflets having sharp, spiny edges. Similar in appearance to *M. haematocarpa*.

FLOWER AND FRUIT: Yellow flowers in 1–1.5 in. (2.5–4 cm) clusters in late spring, followed by 0.5-in. (1.3-cm) blue to brown berries.

LANDSCAPE USES: Specimen plant; informal screen or background. Native craftsmen often use the wood for small articles.

CLIMATE ADAPTION: Hardy to around 0°F (−18°C); best for mid- and high-elevation deserts; welcomes afternoon shade in the low desert.

CULTURE: Needs good drainage. Looks best with some supplemental water every 3–4 weeks in the summer. Minimal water requirement. No fertilizer or pruning needed. Propagate by seeds or cuttings.

POSSIBLE PROBLEMS: Sharp leaves; looper caterpillar.

Mahonia 'Golden Abundance', a hybrid of *M. aquifolium* and *M. amplectans,* grows to about 8 ft. (2.5 m) tall, is denser and heavier blooming than the parents.   PLATE 143

Mahonia haematocarpa

PRONOUNCER: mah-*hone*-ee-ah hay-mat-oh-*car*-pah

COMMON NAME: red barberry

Evergreen. Height: 5–12 ft. (1.5–3.5 m). Spread: 5–8 ft. (1.5–2.5 m). Rate of growth: Slow. Light requirement: Sun to partial shade. Native from eastern Mojave Desert to west Texas, south into Mexico.

Decorative shrub with irregular habit and gray-green, hollylike foliage; stiff, spiny leaves are divided into 3–7 slender leaflets. Also known as *Berberis haematocarpa*.

FLOWER AND FRUIT: Fragrant, golden yellow clusters of small flowers in spring; red-purple berries ripen in the summer.

LANDSCAPE USES: Handsome, bold-textured foliage and irregular habit create a nice accent in the garden; makes a tough barrier or hedge when planted in rows; space 5–6 ft. (1.5–2 m) apart.

CLIMATE ADAPTION: Widely adaptable to desert conditions; not for other areas. Does better under part shade in the low desert.

CULTURE: Minimal soil requirement but needs good drainage. Looks best with some supplemental water every 3–4 weeks in summer in the low desert; minimal needs elsewhere. Apply 2 oz. (57 g) ammonium sulfate in late winter to promote growth. Prune to shape, as desired, in spring after bloom. Propagate by seeds.

POSSIBLE PROBLEMS: Slow growth.

Mahonia nevinii   PLATE 144

PRONOUNCER: mah-*hone*-ee-ah nev-*in*-ee-eye

COMMON NAME: Nevin's barberry

Evergreen. Height: 3–12 ft. (1–3.5 m). Spread: 8–12 ft. (2.5–3.5 m). Rate of growth: Slow to moderate. Light requirement: Sun. Native to southern California, where it has become rare in the wild.

A large, rounded to spreading, blue-green shrub with attractive flowers and fruits; leathery leaves divided into 3–5 spiny leaflets about 1–2 in. (2.5–5 cm) long.

FLOWER AND FRUIT: Loose, 1–2 in. (2.5–5 cm) racemes are bright yellow, March–April; bright red berry clusters follow.

LANDSCAPE USES: Nice barrier or background plant or specimen shrub. Plant on hillsides for erosion control. The red, summer berries are set off handsomely against the blue-green foliage. Resistant to oak root fungus.

CLIMATE ADAPTION: Hardy to about 15°F (−9°C); best for coastal and inland southern California and California's Central Valley; not for the deserts.

CULTURE: Minimal soil needs. Drought tolerant, but accepts moderate amounts of water. Fertilize lightly in the early spring to speed growth. Prune to shape, if desired. Propagate by cold-stratified seeds.

POSSIBLE PROBLEMS: Looper caterpillar.

Mahonia pinnata   PLATE 145

PRONOUNCER: mah-*hone*-ee-ah pin-*nah*-tah

COMMON NAME: shinyleaf barberry

Evergreen. Height: 3–10 ft. (1–3 m). Spread: 5–8 ft. (1.5–2.5 m). Rate of growth: Moderate. Light requirement: Sun to part shade. Native to the Coast Range from southern Oregon into Baja California.

An erect, medium to large shrub with stiff branches covered with shiny, bright green foliage; the leaves are thin, divided into 5–9, spiny, oval leaflets 1–2 in. (2.5–5 cm) long; colorful, reddish new growth; resembles *M. aquifolium*. Variety 'Ken Hartman' has a more uniform growth habit.

FLOWER AND FRUIT: Yellow flower clusters 1.5–2.5 in. (4–6 cm) long, March–May; bluish berries follow.

LANDSCAPE USES: Dense barrier plant, specimen or in mixed groupings.

CLIMATE ADAPTION: Best for coastal and inland southern California; requires afternoon shade in California's Central Valley; not for the deserts.

CULTURE: Needs good drainage. Minimal water requirement but looks best with deep watering

once a month in the summer. Minimal fertilizer required. Prune to shape, as necessary. Propagate by cold-stratified seed.
POSSIBLE PROBLEMS: Looper caterpillar.

Mahonia trifoliolata is, like *M. fremontii* and *M. haematocarpa*, another attractive Southwestern species. It reaches 7 ft. (2.2 m), with blue-green leaves divided into three-pointed leaflets.

Mascagnia
PRONOUNCER: mass-*kag*-nee-ah
FAMILY: Malpighiaceae

Mascagnia lilacina, the lilac orchid vine, is similar to *M. macroptera* and equally attractive.

Mascagnia macroptera   PLATE 146
PRONOUNCER: mass-*kag*-nee-ah mak-*rop*-ter-ah
COMMON NAME: yellow orchid vine, paper fruit vine
   Evergreen to deciduous. Height: 10–30 ft. (3–9 m). Spread: 10–30 ft. (3–9 m). Rate of growth: Fast. Light requirement: Sun. Native to Mexico.
   A vigorous vine with deep green, narrow, pointed leaves and green stems.
FLOWER AND FRUIT: Showy, orchidlike, yellow flowers 1 in. (2.5 cm) across with five fringed petals in spring; large paperlike, tan fruits.
LANDSCAPE USES: On walls it forms a lush, colorful backdrop to the garden; train on posts or trellises for summer shade; requires support on walls.
CLIMATE ADAPTION: Frost damage around 25°F (−4°C); regrows rapidly in spring; roots need protection by mulching in colder areas; heat loving; best for low- and mid-elevation deserts and inland southern California.
CULTURE: Minimal soil requirement. Looks best with twice-monthly watering in summer. No fertilizer needed. Cut back frost-damaged growth. Propagate by seeds.
POSSIBLE PROBLEMS: Cold sensitivity.

Melaleuca
PRONOUNCER: mel-ah-*loo*-kah
FAMILY: Myrtaceae

Melaleuca nesophila, the pink melaleuca, is a shrub or small tree to 20 ft. (6 m) with gray-green foliage accented much of the year with rosy pink blossoms; use as a specimen or screen.

Melaleuca quinquenervia
PRONOUNCER: mel-ah-*loo*-kah kwin-kwe-*ner*-vee-ah
COMMON NAME: cajeput tree
   Evergreen. Height: 20–40 ft. (6–12 m). Spread: 15–20 ft. (4.5–6 m). Rate of growth: Fast. Light requirement: Sun. Native to Australia.
   A slender, upright tree with graceful foliage and a distinctive, thick, tan bark that sheds in many thin layers; narrow, tapering leaves are dull green, 2–4 in. (5–10 cm) long, mostly alternate. Young growth is reddish when it opens. Formerly known as *M. leucadendron*.
FLOWER AND FRUIT: Clusters of creamy white flowers in summer and fall on 1.5–4 in. (4–10 cm) spikes; tiny, persistent, cup-shaped capsules.
LANDSCAPE USES: Good choice for specimen tree in difficult situations; for groves, in lawns or along roadways. Multitrunked forms provide fine accents. Resistant to smog and wind. Useful in erosion control.
CLIMATE ADAPTION: Hardy to about 25°F (−4°C); no heat problems; best for coastal and inland southern California and the low desert.
CULTURE: Minimal soil requirement; tolerates saline and alkaline conditions. Accepts drought but prefers deep, monthly watering. Little to no fertilizer. Prune young trees in the spring to develop a bushy crown. Prune by thinning only; be careful heading back branches since new growth will not develop from old wood. Propagate by seeds.
POSSIBLE PROBLEMS: May naturalize.

Melampodium leucanthum   PLATE 147
PRONOUNCER: mel-am-*pode*-ee-um loo-*can*-thum
FAMILY: Compositae
COMMON NAME: blackfoot daisy
   Evergreen. Height: 6–12 in. (15–30 cm). Spread: 1–1.5 ft. (30–45 cm). Rate of growth: Slow. Light requirement: Sun. Native from southern Arizona to Kansas, northern Mexico.
   A low, gray-green perennial with massive displays of flowers; woody base; leaves about 1.5 in. (4 cm), lance-shaped, sometimes toothed. Often reseeds.
FLOWER AND FRUIT: Very showy, white, 1-in. (2.5-cm) daisies with yellow centers in late spring and summer as well as in the winter months in the very warmest regions; one-seeded fruit.
LANDSCAPE USES: Effective as a massed contrast in desert plantings; as specimens in decomposed granite, or to create a colorful planting mix with

flowering perennials such as verbena, zinnia and mealycup sage.

CLIMATE ADAPTION: Hardy to about 0°F (−18°C); no heat problems; best in the desert, not for coastal areas.

CULTURE: Needs good drainage. Minimal water requirement but watering every two weeks in summer improves bloom. No fertilizer. Cut back in the fall if plant becomes scraggly. Propagate by seeds or cuttings.

POSSIBLE PROBLEMS: Short lived; flower damage from late-season frosts.

Mimosa
PRONOUNCER: mi-*moh*-sah
FAMILY: Leguminosae

Mimosa biuncifera, the chaparral catclaw, is a deciduous, white-to-pink-flowering shrub reaching a height of 6–8 ft. (2–2.5 m). Useful for erosion control.

Mimosa dysocarpa   PLATE 148
PRONOUNCER: mi-*moh*-sah dy-soh-*car*-pah
COMMON NAME: velvetpod mimosa
Deciduous. Height: 3–6 ft. (1–2 m). Spread: 4–6 ft. (1.2–2 m). Rate of growth: Moderate. Light requirement: Sun to partial shade. Native to the mountain canyons of Arizona, New Mexico, Texas and northern Mexico.

An open shrub with light green leaves divided into small leaflets covered with tiny hairs; numerous prickles occur on the short branches.

FLOWER AND FRUIT: Pink, showy, fragrant flowers on short spikes in summer; velvety, flat seed pods. Quail love the seeds.

LANDSCAPE USES: An informal, flowering, accent shrub or as a barrier or low hedge.

CLIMATE ADAPTION: Cold and heat tolerant in the deserts, where it is best suited.

CULTURE: Minimal soil requirement. Needs deep irrigation every 3–4 weeks in summer for best appearance. Little to no fertilizer. Prune to shape, as needed. Propagate by scarified seeds or semihardwood cuttings.

POSSIBLE PROBLEMS: Long taproot may make transplanting difficult; livestock browse foliage.

Muhlenbergia
PRONOUNCER: mew-len-*ber*-jee-ah
FAMILY: Gramineae

Muhlenbergia dumosa, bush muhlenbergia, reaches about 4 ft. (1.2 m) high with an equal spread; fast growing and evergreen with an airier appearance than *M. rigens.*   PLATE 149

Muhlenbergia rigens
PRONOUNCER: mew-len-*ber*-jee-ah *ry*-jens
COMMON NAME: deer grass
Evergreen. Height: 2.5–5 ft. (75 cm–1.5 m). Spread: 3–5 ft. (1–1.5 m). Rate of growth: Moderate to fast. Light requirement: Sun. Native to the chaparral in the Southwest and Mexico.

A grassy clump of dark green, long-lasting leaves forming a graceful, fountainlike display.

FLOWER AND FRUIT: 2–3 ft. (60–90 cm), slender flower stalks rise above foliage in early fall; wispy, white seed heads.

LANDSCAPE USES: Mixes well among boulders in dry creek beds, among subtropical plants or in a pasturelike setting. Consider to replace lilyturf, *Liriope* or *Ophiopogon.* Seed heads sway in light breeze.

CLIMATE ADAPTION: Cold and heat tolerant; widely adaptable.

CULTURE: Minimal soil requirement. Looks best with weekly watering in summer in the low desert but needs less elsewhere. Little to no fertilizer. Trim back in the winter for best appearance. Propagate by seeds.

POSSIBLE PROBLEMS: May not be widely available.

Myoporum parvifolium   PLATE 150
PRONOUNCER: my-ah-*por*-um par-vi-*foh*-lee-um
FAMILY: Myoporaceae
COMMON NAME: myoporum
Evergreen. Height: 6–8 in. (15–20 cm). Spread: 6–9 ft. (2–2.75 m). Rate of growth: Fast. Light requirement: Sun. Native to Australia.

Low, creeping ground cover with an attractive shadow pattern. Stems send down roots as they grow along the ground, forming a tight, dense cover. Bright green, lance-shaped leaves are about 1.5 in. (4 cm) long. Fleshy leaves and stems store moisture and are fire retardant.

FLOWER AND FRUIT: 0.5-in. (1.3-cm) starlike, white flowers cover the plants in spring and summer; tiny, purple berries follow.

LANDSCAPE USES: Ideal for use on mounds, banks, and for other erosion-control purposes. Can be planted along walks and entryways but requires occasional trimming to keep in bounds. In the desert landscape, provides refreshing islands of green.

CLIMATE ADAPTION: Hardy to about 20°F (−6.5°C); moderate heat tolerance but can suffer in the low desert; widely adaptable except in higher deserts.

CULTURE: Needs good drainage. Performs best with supplemental water every 1–2 weeks in hottest areas in the summer, but do not keep soil continually moist. No fertilizer. May require occasional edging near paving; otherwise, prune woody growth on older plants in the spring to improve appearance. Propagate by cuttings.

POSSIBLE PROBLEMS: Can not tolerate foot traffic; root rot if overwatered.

Myrtus communis   PLATE 151

PRONOUNCER: *mir*-tus cum-*ewe*-nis
FAMILY: Myrtaceae
COMMON NAME: myrtle

Evergreen. Height: 5–8 ft. (1.5–2.5 m). Spread: 5–6 ft. (1.5–2 m). Rate of growth: Slow. Light requirement: Sun to part shade. Native to southern Europe and western Asia.

A dense shrub with small, glossy, dark green leaves; aromatic scent when crushed. This is the classic myrtle. There are several cultivars, including 'Compacta', which is very slow growing to 2 × 3 ft. (60 × 90 cm) and 'Boetica', which is more rugged looking than the species, usually seen as a large shrub to about 12 ft. (3.5 m), and may be trained as a small, gnarled tree.

FLOWER AND FRUIT: Creamy white, 0.5-in. (1.3-cm) flowers in the summer; tiny, blue-black berries in the fall.

LANDSCAPE USES: A versatile, much-used shrub. Group or plant in rows as a clipped or informal hedge or screen; along walls as a foundation plant, or as a topiary subject. Highly resistant to Texas root rot.

CLIMATE ADAPTION: Hardy to about 20°F (−6.5°C); tolerates heat; widely adaptable.

CULTURE: Needs good drainage. Some drought tolerance but prefers deep, monthly irrigation; avoid shallow watering. Apply 2 oz. (57 g) all-purpose fertilizer such as 10–6–4 in late spring and early fall to a 12 × 18 in. (30 × 45 cm) plant, adjusting proportions to other-sized plants. Prune to shape or contain; accepts shearing. Propagate by softwood cuttings.

POSSIBLE PROBLEMS: Iron chlorosis; be careful not to allow soil to cover the main stem.

Nandina domestica   PLATE 152

PRONOUNCER: nan-*dee*-nah doh-*mess*-tih-cah
FAMILY: Berberidaceae
COMMON NAME: nandina, heavenly bamboo

Evergreen. Height: 6–8 ft. (2–2.5 m). Spread: 3–4 ft. (about 1 m). Rate of growth: Slow to moderate. Light requirement: Sun to partial shade. Native to Japan and China.

A graceful, erect shrub; lacy, 1–2 in. (2.5–5 cm) leaflets on canelike, multiple stems; turns reddish in fall.

FLOWER AND FRUIT: Clusters of white flowers in the spring on the terminal ends of the branches; shiny, orange-red, 0.3-in. (1-cm) berries follow. The berries turn blue to black and drop off with cold weather.

LANDSCAPE USES: An outstanding specimen shrub or in groups or hedges. Fall color is spectacular, but it shows well in every season. Excellent for large containers, narrow spaces, entrances and back-lighting at night. Low to no maintenance. There are several smaller cultivars, such as 'Compacta', 'Nana' and 'Purpurea Dwarf'.

CLIMATE ADAPTION: Hardy to at least 5°F (−15°C); widely adaptable. Needs protection from afternoon sun in the hottest desert areas but colors best in full sun elsewhere. May lose leaves around 10°F (−12°C).

CULTURE: Needs good drainage. Does best with an ample, monthly irrigation but withstands long periods of drought. Apply 4 oz. (115 g) all-purpose fertilizer in the spring for a plant 3 ft. (1 m) high; adjust the amount proportionally for larger or smaller plants. Apply iron chelate as needed for chlorosis. Prune 2–3 of the oldest canes in the winter to shape. Propagate by seeds planted in the fall.

POSSIBLE PROBLEMS: Sunburn in the hottest areas; iron-deficiency chlorosis in alkaline soils.

Nerium oleander   PLATE 153

PRONOUNCER: *near*-ee-um *oh*-lee-an-der
FAMILY: Apocynaceae
COMMON NAME: oleander

Evergreen. Height: 8–16 ft. (2.5–5 m). Spread: 8–10 ft. (2.5–3 m). Rate of growth: Fast. Light requirement: Sun. Native to the Mediterranean region.

An erect, large shrub or small tree with lance-shaped leaves that are leathery, dark green, 4–12 in. (10–30 cm). There are many cultivars. Dwarf forms, such as 'Petite Pink', 'Petite Salmon' and 'Little Red', are also available, although they are much less robust. The dwarfs reach about 5 ft. (1.5 m). In large sizes, 'Sister Agnes' is the more common, white form. 'Mrs. Roeding' has double pink flowers.

FLOWER AND FRUIT: White to shades of yellow, pink, salmon and red flowers, 2–3 in. (5–8 cm) wide, occur mainly in the summer but sometimes in the spring and fall and provide spectacular displays. Most cultivars have single flowers, but a number of double forms are available.

LANDSCAPE USES: Fine background hedge or screen, large specimen shrub, for corner or filler plantings. Can be trained into a single- or multi-trunked, small tree but requires considerable maintenance thereafter. If not trained, minimal maintenance is required. Good wind tolerance. Most problems with oleanders result from failure to give plants enough room.

CLIMATE ADAPTION: Often damaged below 15°F (−9°C) but recovers quickly in the spring; relishes heat; widely adaptable except for most of the dwarfs, which are more frost sensitive.

CULTURE: Minimal soil requirement. Drought resistant after the plant reaches a height of 4 ft. (1.2 m) but looks best with deep watering once or twice a month in the summer. No fertilizer. Remove any warty growths (galls) that develop, disinfecting the pruning shears after each cut. Can be pruned to shape in the early spring, but it dislikes heavy pruning; tip-prune to keep within bounds. Propagate by cuttings.

POSSIBLE PROBLEMS: All parts, including the sap, are poisonous and the smoke resulting from burning is dangerous; invasive roots; suckers; bacterial gall.

Nolina

PRONOUNCER: no-*lee*-nah
FAMILY: Agavaceae

The nolinas are durable and versatile performers in arid landscapes. Their green, grassy clumps are effective not only in making a lush oasis but also to naturalize areas, along dry streambeds or in street and median plantings. About 25 species are native to southwestern North America. Although agave relatives, they do not die after flowering and are generally cold hardy and pest free.

Nolina bigelovii, a Southwest species, usually reaches 2–3 ft. (60–90 cm) tall with about a 4-ft. (1.2-m) spread; 0.75-in. (2-cm) leaves have a bluish cast.

Nolina microcarpa   PLATE 154

PRONOUNCER: no-*lee*-nah my-cro-*car*-pah
COMMON NAME: bear grass

Evergreen. Height: 3–4 ft. (about 1 m). Spread: 4–6 ft. (1.2–2 m). Rate of growth: Slow. Light requirement: Sun. Native to the desert slopes of Arizona, New Mexico, Texas and Mexico.

Long leaves about 0.3 in. (1 cm) wide form a tight rosette from an underground stem; has the appearance of a large, coarse clump of grass. Leaf edges have tiny teeth. Indians used the leaves to weave baskets.

FLOWER AND FRUIT: Numerous clusters of white flowers on about a 6-ft. (2-m) stalk in early summer; winged capsules.

LANDSCAPE USES: An accent clump among boulders in dry landscapes or on slopes. Be sure to allow for full growth.

CLIMATE ADAPTION: Hardy to at least 10°F (−12°C); loves heat; best for the deserts and California's Central Valley.

CULTURE: Needs good drainage. Minimal water requirement but looks best with irrigation every 3–4 weeks in the summer. Responds with faster growth to 2 oz. (57 g) ammonium sulfate in the early spring. Remove dead stalks and leaves. Propagate by seeds.

POSSIBLE PROBLEMS: Eventual size.

Nolina parryi

PRONOUNCER: no-*lee*-nah *pair*-ee-eye
COMMON NAME: Parry's nolina

Evergreen. Height: 4–5 ft. (1.2–1.5 m). Spread: 3–4 ft. (about 1 m). Rate of growth: Moderate. Light requirement: Sun. Native to southern California.

A broad-trunked shrub topped by green leaves about 1 in. (2.5 cm) wide and 3 ft. (1 m) long spilling in a fountainlike display.

FLOWER AND FRUIT: Creamy white, small flowers on a 4–5 ft. (1.2–1.5 m) stalk, May–June; winged capsules.

LANDSCAPE USES: Blends well with its relatives such as yuccas and agaves in an arid landscape.

CLIMATE ADAPTION: Hardy to at least 15°F (−9°C); loves heat; widely adaptable except for the coldest parts of the high desert.

CULTURE: Needs good drainage. Minimal water requirement but looks best in the deserts with monthly irrigation in the summer. Little to no fertilizer. Remove dead leaves to tidy appearance. Propagate by seeds.

POSSIBLE PROBLEMS: Dies if overwatered or if drainage is poor.

Oenothera

PRONOUNCER: ee-no-*thair*-ah
FAMILY: Onagraceae

The evening primroses are among the most beautiful native North American plants. Their delicate appearance belies their durability in the landscape. Most can be used as ground covers. They produce cup-shaped, four-petaled flowers in colors ranging from white to yellow to pink. Many are native to one of the continent's most arid regions, the Gran Desierto of Mexico's Sonora, which often is called a sand sea.

Oenothera berlandieri PLATE 155
PRONOUNCER: ee-no-*thair*-ah burr-lan-dee-*air*-eye
COMMON NAME: Mexican primrose
Evergreen. Height: 6–12 in. (15–30 cm). Spread: 1–3 ft. (30–90 cm). Rate of growth: Fast. Light requirement: Sun to partial shade. Native to Texas and Mexico.

A low-growing, spreading perennial with a profusion of attractive flowers; oval, bright green leaves to 2 in. (5 cm); roots along the ground. Also known as *O. speciosa*.
FLOWER AND FRUIT: Pink, 1.5-in. (4-cm) flowers almost continuously present on slender stems from late spring through summer; blooms during the day; small seed capsules.
LANDSCAPE USES: For seasonal coloring or as a minimum-care ground cover, particularly for slopes.
CLIMATE ADAPTION: May be killed to the ground by frost but recovers quickly with warm weather; likes heat; widely adaptable.
CULTURE: Minimal soil requirement. Needs supplemental watering once a week in the low desert in summer; less often in other areas and times of year. No fertilizer needed. Clip almost to the ground after bloom. Can also be mowed in the spring. Propagate by cuttings or seeds.
POSSIBLE PROBLEMS: Unattractive when out of bloom; may become invasive; powdery mildew with too much moisture; flea beetles.

Oenothera caespitosa PLATE 156
PRONOUNCER: ee-no-*thair*-ah ses-pi-*toh*-sah
COMMON NAME: white evening primrose
Perennial. Height: 8–12 in. (20–30 cm). Spread: 1–1.5 ft. (30–45 cm). Rate of growth: Fast. Light requirement: Sun. Native from the Midwest through the Southwest.

A compact grower with dark green, lance-shaped, wavy-margined leaves to 5 in. (13 cm) long and about 0.5 in. (1.3 cm) wide; reddish underneath but the tops appears whitish in sunlight.
FLOWER AND FRUIT: White, fragrant, 2–4 in. (5–10 cm) flowers open late in the day and remain open until the following day's heat, mainly in the spring and fall. Green, linear seed capsules turn woody and straw-colored at maturity.
LANDSCAPE USES: A ground cover or in perennial beds, borders and rock gardens. Best used close to living areas, such as courtyards, to savor the floral display.
CLIMATE ADAPTION: Dies to the ground after frost but resprouts in the spring; widely adaptable but goes dormant in the summer heat of the low desert.
CULTURE: Needs good drainage. Drought tolerant but water twice a month during the blooming season in the warmest areas; avoid over-watering. No fertilizer. Remove old flower stalks. Propagate by seeds or cuttings; plants can be divided.
POSSIBLE PROBLEMS: Centers die out after a few years; root rot with too much moisture.

Oenothera calylophus var. *hartwegii* is a perennial from southeastern Arizona growing to 2 ft. (60 cm) across with bright yellow flowers that last much of the day.

Oenothera missouriensis
PRONOUNCER: ee-no-*thair*-ah mih-zoo-ree-*en*-sis
COMMON NAME: Missouri evening primrose
Perennial. Height: 6–14 in. (15–36 cm). Spread: 12–14 in. (30–36 cm). Rate of growth: Slow. Light requirement: Sun. Native from Missouri to Arizona.

A spreading, free-flowering plant with velvetlike, 4–5 in. (10–13 cm), narrow leaves.
FLOWER AND FRUIT: Yellow flowers 4–5 in. (10–13 cm) across on about 10-in. (25-cm) stems; prolific bloomer from about May to September; fragrant; opening in the evening.
LANDSCAPE USES: Flowers are perhaps the most striking and largest of all the night-blooming primroses; superb in rock gardens, in borders and along parking strips.
CLIMATE ADAPTION: Hardy to about 0°F (−18°C); widely adaptable.
CULTURE: Needs good drainage. Minimal water requirement; blooms better with occasional irrigation in warmer areas. No fertilizer. Prune to groom. Propagate by seeds.
POSSIBLE PROBLEMS: Scraggly appearance when not blooming.

Oenothera stubbei, the Chihuahuan primrose, has yellow flowers that bloom in the evening; needs more supplemental water than most of the other species.

Olea europaea PLATE 157
PRONOUNCER: o-lee-ah yur-oh-*pay*-ah
FAMILY: Oleaceae
COMMON NAME: olive tree
Evergreen. Height: 30–40 ft. (9–12 m). Spread: 25–30 ft. (7.5–9 m). Rate of growth: Moderate. Light requirement: Sun to partial shade. Native to Mediterranean region.

A picturesque tree with gray-green foliage and gnarled trunk or trunks; lance-shaped leaves 1–2 in. (2.5–5 cm). The variety 'Swan Hill' is sold as a fruitless, low- to no-pollen producer. There also are dwarf-shrub cultivars.

FLOWER AND FRUIT: Tiny, white flowers in spring followed after several months by green olives which create an awful mess when they ripen, October–December, unless picked for very difficult processing. Fruit can be reduced by annual spraying.

LANDSCAPE USES: A desert standard for many centuries; blends well with other plants, good in containers, as a specimen or in groupings. Good wind tolerance. Banned in some areas due to its highly allergenic pollen.

CLIMATE ADAPTION: Hardy to about 18°F (−8°C); no heat problems; widely adaptable except for higher deserts.

CULTURE: Minimal soil requirement. Looks best in the summer with monthly, deep irrigation; needs little at other times. No fertilizer needed, but established trees respond to a cupful (225 g) of ammonium sulfate scattered under the canopy in spring. Prune regularly to keep within bounds and remove suckers. Propagation by hardwood cuttings in fall or winter; seeds.

POSSIBLE PROBLEMS: Fruit litter; pollen; ripe fruit attracts messy birds; suckering; verticillium wilt causes branch dieback.

Olneya tesota   PLATE 158

PRONOUNCER: *ole*-nee-ah te-*so*-tah
FAMILY: Leguminosae
COMMON NAME: desert ironwood

Evergreen. Height: 10–20 ft. (3–6 m). Spread: 15–20 ft. (4.5–6 m). Rate of growth: Slow. Light requirement: Sun. Native to southern Arizona, southeastern California and adjoining Mexico.

A picturesque, small tree that from a distance looks somewhat like the blue palo verde, *Cercidium floridum*; dense, gray-green foliage; gray trunk, often multitrunked; vicious, small thorns; rounded crown. The grayish bark provides a quick means of distinguishing it from the green-barked palo verde.

FLOWER AND FRUIT: Masses of sweetpealike, lavender flowers in clusters in the spring are followed by 2-in. (5-cm), brown pods with edible, peanut-flavored seeds.

LANDSCAPE USES: Specimen tree or in groups for screening. Fine choice in warmer-desert settings where it lends character to the landscape.

CLIMATE ADAPTION: Hardy to about 20°F (−6.5°C) but foliage damage occurs around 25°F (−4°C);

slow to recover. No problems with heat; best in low deserts and warmer locations of mid-elevation deserts.

CULTURE: Needs good drainage, likes deep soil. Minimal water requirement but does best with deep, ample, monthly irrigation in summer months. No fertilizer. Prune after flowering to shape or keep branches above head height. Propagate by seeds. Mature specimens are easily transplanted if boxed carefully.

POSSIBLE PROBLEMS: Thorns if planted in people traffic areas; litter; slow growth; bees like the flowers.

Osmanthus fragrans

PRONOUNCER: oz-*man*-thus *fray*-grans
FAMILY: Oleaceae
COMMON NAME: sweet olive

Evergreen. Height: 5–8 ft. (1.5–2.5 m). Spread: 6–9 ft. (2–2.75 m). Rate of growth: Moderate. Light requirement: Sun to part shade. Native to China.

A dense shrub with 2–4 in. (5–10 cm), oval, glossy, medium green leaves; sometimes seen as a small tree in old age.

FLOWER AND FRUIT White, very fragrant, tiny flowers in clusters, usually in spring but occasionally throughout the year, followed by 0.5-in. (1.3-cm) blue fruit.

LANDSCAPE USES: Handsome as a hedge, to fill a corner, by an entrance, or as a background screen. Excellent in large containers.

CLIMATE ADAPTION: Hardy to about 15°F (−9°C); widely adaptable; likes heat but needs some shade in youth and always needs afternoon shade in the low desert.

CULTURE: Needs good drainage; does not tolerate highly alkaline conditions. Minimal water requirement but accepts moderate to ample amounts. Minimal fertilizer. For a bushier plant, pinch growing tips; may be trained to upright growth or as a tree. Propagate by semihardwood cuttings.

POSSIBLE PROBLEMS: Iron-deficiency chlorosis in alkaline soils; foliage sunburns occasionally.

Parkinsonia aculeata   PLATE 159

PRONOUNCER: par-kin-*so*-nee-ah ah-kew-lee-*ah*-tah
FAMILY: Leguminosae
COMMON NAME: Mexican palo verde, Jerusalem thorn

Deciduous. Height: 20–30 ft. (6–9 m). Spread: 20–30 ft. (6–9 m). Rate of growth: Rapid. Light requirement: Sun. Native to Mexico.

A round-headed, small tree with yellow-green foliage and branches. Pairs of small, sharp thorns grow at the base of each compound leaf. Textured, gray bark develops on the lower trunk of mature trees. Thin leaf petioles and tiny leaflets provide an airy, fine-textured look on the 8–16 in. (20–40 cm) leaves.

FLOWER AND FRUIT: Giant display of yellow flowers in loose clusters in the late spring and from time to time during the summer; 5-in. (13-cm) pods with straw-colored midribs follow.

LANDSCAPE USES: Not for closely maintained areas but otherwise quite acceptable for filtered shade and color with other desert vegetation; may naturalize. Good wind tolerance.

CLIMATE ADAPTION: Hardy to about 20°F (−6.5°C); loves heat; best for deserts but often frost damaged in the higher desert.

CULTURE: Needs good drainage. Minimal water requirement but prefers deep, once-a-month irrigation in summer; not happy in lawn-sprinkler situations. To speed growth, apply in late winter 1 lb. (0.45 kg) ammonium sulfate per 100 sq. ft. (9 sq. m) under the leaf canopy. Prune to shape. To maintain the appearance of the canopy, head back the wildest branches or those that cross. Train young trees by raising the crown a foot or so a year by removing the lowest branches. Propagate by scarified seeds or semihardwood cuttings.

POSSIBLE PROBLEMS: Short lived; palo verde beetle can kill over several years; litter fall; reseeds heavily; thorns.

Pennisetum setaceum 'Cupreum'   PLATE 160

PRONOUNCER: pen-i-*see*-tum see-*tay*-see-um *coo*-pree-um

FAMILY: Gramineae

COMMON NAME: red fountain grass

Deciduous. Height: 3–4 ft. (about 1 m). Spread: 2–3 ft. (60–90 cm). Rate of growth: Fast. Light requirement: Sun. Native to South Africa.

A graceful, colorful, clumping, perennial grass with 1–2 ft. (30–60 cm) reddish, narrow leaf blades and dramatic seed plumes. There also is a rosy-purple cultivar, *P. setaceum* 'Rubrum'. Avoid the common "green" variety, which reseeds so prodigiously it becomes a weed.

FLOWER AND FRUIT: Narrow, bristly, reddish, 6-in. (15-cm) plumes on slender stalks in the warmest months.

LANDSCAPE USES: Makes a good contribution almost anywhere in the landscape; dramatic accent plant either individually or in groups; smog tolerant.

CLIMATE ADAPTION: No heat problems; widely adaptable; winter dormant. Root hardy to cold after a couple of years in the ground.

CULTURE: Minimal soil requirement. Drought resistant but likes monthly watering in the hottest areas in the warmest months. Apply a cup (225 g) of ammonium sulfate in early spring after the first year in the landscape. Cut close to the ground in winter after foliage dies. Propagate by divisions.

POSSIBLE PROBLEMS: Fire hazard if dead foliage is not removed.

Penstemon

PRONOUNCER: *pen*-ste-mun

FAMILY: Scrophulariaceae

There are so many beautiful penstemons that it is hard to recommend just a few. The several included here are fairly widely adaptable in the Southwest. Of the more than 200 known species, most are natives to western North America and are spectacular in bloom. The colors of their tubular flowers range from orange to red to purple to white, and just about everything in between. Hummingbirds love them.

Growth habits of these low-growing shrubs or perennials include ground covers with short, flowering spikes; small, woody plants covered at times with flowers; and basal rosettes that produce multiplying, tall, floral spikes.

In general, penstemons like full sun, but many do best in the low desert under partial shade. Most are widely adaptable to heat and cold.

Good drainage is essential. Some are quite drought resistant but many need some summer watering in hot areas. Be sure to allow growing space for each plant as they resent crowding. Most tend to die out after 3–4 years in the landscape.

Penstemon barbatus is a ground cover reaching about 6 in. (15 cm) tall with a 1-ft. (30-cm) spread; scarlet flowers in the spring.

Penstemon eatoni   PLATE 161

PRONOUNCER: *pen*-ste-mun *ee*-ton-eye

COMMON NAME: firecracker penstemon

Evergreen. Height: 1–2 ft. (30–60 cm). Spread: 1–3 ft. (30–90 cm). Rate of growth: Moderate. Light requirement: Sun to part shade. Native from southwest Colorado to California.

A low-growing shrub with broad, tapering, medium green leaves forming a compact mound.

FLOWER AND FRUIT: Many showy, red, tubular 1–2 in. (2.5–5 cm) flowers in the spring to early summer on stems ranging from 2–4 ft. (60 cm–1.2 m); usually among the first to bloom each spring in the low desert; many-seeded capsules.

LANDSCAPE USES: Provides a long-lasting spring color show; mass as a ground cover or group in borders or among boulders. Naturalizes.

CLIMATE ADAPTION: Widely adaptable; cold and heat tolerant in the Southwest.

CULTURE: Needs good drainage. Needs irrigation every two weeks in summer in the desert; less elsewhere and at other times of the year. Little to no fertilizer needed. Prune to remove any dead interior growth; allow seeds to set after bloom, then cut back to the leaves. Propagate by seeds, softwood cuttings or root division.

POSSIBLE PROBLEMS: Short lived.

Penstemon palmeri   PLATE 162

PRONOUNCER: *pen*-ste-mun *palm*-er-eye

COMMON NAME: Palmer beardtongue

Perennial. Height: 1.5–4 ft. (45 cm–1.2 m). Spread: 1–2 ft. (30–60 cm). Rate of growth: Moderate. Light requirement: Sun to partial shade. Native to Utah, Arizona and California.

A bluish gray plant with oblong to oval, basal leaves that are irregularly toothed and 1–3 in. (2.5–8 cm) long. Leaves on the upper stems are narrower.

FLOWER AND FRUIT: Pale pink to white, tubular flowers in late spring; seed capsules.

LANDSCAPE USES: Group in perennial borders for floral display.

CLIMATE ADAPTION: Widely adaptable in the Southwest.

CULTURE: Needs good drainage. Quite drought tolerant but needs twice-monthly irrigation in the low desert in the summer. Little to no fertilizer needed. Prune to groom. Propagate by seeds.

POSSIBLE PROBLEMS: Short lived.

Penstemon parryi   PLATE 163

PRONOUNCER: *pen*-ste-mun *pair*-ee-eye

COMMON NAME: Parry's penstemon

Perennial. Height: 1–1.5 ft. (30–45 cm). Spread: 1–2 ft. (30–60 cm). Rate of growth: Moderate. Light requirement: Sun to part shade. Native to the Sonoran Desert of Arizona and Mexico.

A low-growing plant forming a basal rosette of blue-green, tapering, 2–6 in. (5–15 cm) leaves with smooth margins.

FLOWER AND FRUIT: Very showy, tubular flowers in shades of pink on 2–3 ft. (60–90 cm) spikes in the early spring; seed capsules.

LANDSCAPE USES: Locate in front of desert shrubs to add to the flowering season or around trees such as mesquites and acacias. Very handsome massed in a rock garden.

CLIMATE ADAPTION: Widely adaptable; appreciates part shade in the low desert.

CULTURE: Needs excellent drainage. Minimal water requirement but likes supplemental watering every two weeks in the summer in hot areas. Little to no fertilizer. Groom by removing old flower stalks. Propagate by seeds or softwood cuttings.

POSSIBLE PROBLEMS: Dies quickly with too much water; becomes scraggly with too much shade.

Penstemon pseudospectabilis, the desert beardtongue, is a perennial reaching 3–4 ft. (about 1 m) high, with blue-green foliage and rose-purple flowers in the spring. Native from New Mexico to southern California.   PLATE 164

Penstemon spectabilis, from southern California and Baja California, has tall spikes of bluish flowers; grows 3–4 ft. (about 1 m) high.   PLATE 165

Penstemon thurberi, Thurber's beardtongue, is a slender, bushy perennial reaching a height of 1–3 ft. (30–90 cm); pink or blue tubular flowers in the spring and early summer. Native from New Mexico to southern California and Baja California.

Phoenix

PRONOUNCER: *fee*-nix

FAMILY: Palmae

Phoenix canariensis, the Canary Island date palm, is a somewhat smaller, thicker-trunked palm than *P. dactylifera*. Their cold tolerance is about the same.

Phoenix dactylifera   PLATE 166

PRONOUNCER: *fee*-nix dac-til-*if*-er-ah

COMMON NAME: date palm

Evergreen. Height: 50–65 ft. (15–20 m). Spread: 20–30 ft. (6–9 m). Rate of growth: Slow. Light requirement: Sun. Native to the Middle East.

A graceful, slender-trunked feather palm with a spreading canopy of gray-green leaves.

FLOWER AND FRUIT: This is the date producer of commerce. Trees are male or female. Flower clusters about 6 ft. (2 m) long dangle from the top fronds and require hand thinning. Hand pollination often is used to fertilize a single female, but the timing can be difficult. Otherwise, both a male and female tree are needed to produce fruit.

LANDSCAPE USES: Grow in groves or as a specimen in large landscapes around buildings or pools. Becomes too big for the typical home.

CLIMATE ADAPTION: Hardy to about 18°F (−8°C), loves heat and does best in the deserts but not at the higher elevations.

CULTURE: Needs good drainage. Enrich the existing soil at planting time by digging in one-third the volume of the total backfill with organic matter such as peat moss or forest mulch. Apply about 6 in. (15 cm) of supplemental water slowly twice a month in the warmest months and monthly in winter. Avoid lawn-sprinkler situations. An established palm with a 10-ft. (3-m) watering basin needs about 4 lbs. (2 kg) of ammonium sulfate scattered in the basin at watering time in the early spring. Bloodmeal is a good organic substitute. Adjust proportions sharply downward for younger trees and apply in 3–4 installments in warmer months. Remove old leaves and stalks each year; professional grooming may be needed to avoid a messy appearance. Propagate by offsets and seeds.

POSSIBLE PROBLEMS: Extremely sharp spikes; palm bud rot; palm-flower bud worm; pruning and fruit pollination needs; fruit attracts birds and the combination produces a mess under the tree without near-constant attention.

Phoenix reclinata, the Senegal date palm, is smaller than *P. dactylifera* and *P. canariensis* and much less hardy. It is killed around 25°F (−4°C). All three species will hybridize.

Pinus

PRONOUNCER: *pie*-nus
FAMILY: Pinaceae

Pines commonly grow in cool climates. Fortunately, some of these conifers adapt well to warm, dry conditions. They provide welcome shade and shelter and seem to radiate a feeling of coolness. They are easily recognized by their needlelike foliage, but looks differ from species to species. One species can provide a symmetrical while another an irregular, sculptural quality to the landscape. Some are broad crowned; others, such as *P. eldarica*, maintain a pyramidal, Christmas tree shape.

Under stress, pines, like most plants, become more susceptible to insect and disease attack.

Pinus brutia var. *eldarica*. *See* **P. eldarica**

Pinus canariensis, the Canary Island pine, is fast growing to about 60 ft. (18 m) with a slender habit; similar to *P. roxburghii*; much used and widely adaptable but not for the higher desert.

Pinus cembroides, the Mexican piñon, is closely related to *P. edulis* but is somewhat larger and with needles usually in clusters of three.

Pinus edulis

PRONOUNCER: *pie*-nus *ed*-ewe-lis
COMMON NAME: Colorado piñon

Evergreen. Height: 20–30 ft. (6–9 m). Spread: 15–25 ft. (4.5–7.5 m). Rate of growth: Very slow. Light requirement: Sun. Native to the semiarid, higher elevations of the Southwest.

A contorted, small tree with a rounded crown and horizontal branching; slender, slightly curved, yellowish green needles 1–2 in. (2.5–5 cm) long, usually in bundles of two.

FLOWER AND FRUIT: Broad, ovoid, resinous cones 1–3 in. (2.5–8 cm) ripen in the fall, producing a quite popular, edible nut.

LANDSCAPE USES: A picturesque specimen providing a sharp profile in small landscapes such as oriental or rock gardens; deep taproot. Among the most wind tolerant of the pines.

CLIMATE ADAPTION: Hardy to about −10°F (−23°C) but dislikes the heat of the low desert; best in mid- to higher-elevation deserts and coastal southern California.

CULTURE: Minimal soil requirement but must drain well. Best with monthly, deep irrigation in warmest periods. Minimal fertilizer. Prune to maintain its natural form. Propagate by seeds.

POSSIBLE PROBLEMS: Overwatering; aphids.

Pinus eldarica   PLATE 167

PRONOUNCER: *pie*-nus el-*dar*-i-cah
COMMON NAME: mondel pine, Afghan pine

Evergreen. Height: 50–80 ft. (15–24.5 m). Spread: 15–30 ft. (4.5–9 m). Rate of growth: Fast. Light requirement: Sun. Native to western Asia.

A dark green, pyramid-shaped pine with 3–6 in. (8–15 cm) needles in clusters of two or sometimes three; becomes quite dense with age. Also known as *P. brutia* var. *eldarica*.

FLOWER AND FRUIT: Insignificant flowers; cones 5–6 in. (13–15 cm).

LANDSCAPE USES: A fast-growing evergreen for difficult situations, good windbreak, tolerates lawn situations. May reach 6 ft. (2 m) from a 1-gal. (4-l) container within two years of planting.

CLIMATE ADAPTION: Hardy to about 0°F (−18°C); likes heat; widely adaptable, especially good in deserts.

CULTURE: Needs good drainage. Minimal water requirement; soil must dry between supplemental irrigations. Apply a cupful (225 g) of all-purpose fertilizer, such as 10–6–4, in early spring for a 6-ft. (2-m) tree with a 3-ft. (1-m) spread; adjust proportionally for those of different dimensions. Minimal pruning. Propagate by seeds.

POSSIBLE PROBLEMS: Root rot if overwatered.

Pinus halepensis

PRONOUNCER: *pie*-nus hal-ah-*pen*-sis

COMMON NAME: aleppo pine

Evergreen. Height: 30–50 ft. (9–15 m). Spread: 20–30 ft. (6–9 m). Rate of growth: Fast. Light requirement: Sun. Native to the Mediterranean region.

An open-branched, round-topped tree with slender, gray- to light green, 3–4 in. (8–10 cm) needles, usually in bundles of two but sometimes three.

FLOWER AND FRUIT: Insignificant flowers; rounded to oblong, brown cones 2–4 in. (5–10 cm) ripen in the fall.

LANDSCAPE USES: Probably the most-planted pine in the hottest desert areas; good windbreak and screen. Provides a pine-forest effect and excellent shade. Handsome as an individual specimen or as a lawn tree. Can reach 30 ft. (9 m) in 10 years from a 1-gal. (4-l) container size.

CLIMATE ADAPTION: Hardy to about 10°F (−12°C) after a year or two in the landscape; no heat problems; widely adaptable.

CULTURE: Needs good drainage. Does best in desert areas with deep, monthly irrigation in summer but survives in other areas with none. Apply a cupful (225 g) of all-purpose fertilizer, such as 10–6–4, in the early spring to a 6-ft. (2-m) tree with a 3-ft. (1-m) spread; adjust proportions for trees of different dimensions. Until plant has a 10-ft. (3-m) branch spread (insuring good root growth), thin periodically to prevent wind damage. Propagate by seeds.

POSSIBLE PROBLEMS: Aleppo pine blight sometimes causes browning of entire sections of the tree in the spring or fall. It is mainly a problem in the desert and is apparently physiological. Regular watering and nitrogen fertilizer may help. Mites.

Pinus pinea

PRONOUNCER: *pie*-nus pie-*nee*-ah

COMMON NAME: Italian stone pine

Evergreen. Height: 30–50 ft. (9–15 m). Spread: 30–40 ft. (9–12 m). Rate of growth: Moderate. Light requirement: Sun. Native to the

Mediterranean region.

A wide-crowned tree with a flat top, picturesque bark and stiff, bright green needles 3–7 in. (8–18 cm) long in bundles of two; older trees usually lack branches to a considerable height.

FLOWER AND FRUIT: Insignificant flowers; brown, oval cones, 4–6 in. (10–15 cm) long ripen in the fall and produce the edible, reddish brown pignolia nut favored in southern Europe.

LANDSCAPE USES: A massive tree best used in large open areas or along roads. Good wind tolerance. Becomes too large for the typical home landscape. Shows well at any age in groups or as an individual specimen.

CLIMATE ADAPTION: Hardy to about 10°F (−12°C); no heat problems; widely adaptable.

CULTURE: Needs good drainage. Water once or twice a month in hot areas in the summer; minimally elsewhere. Little to no fertilizer or pruning. Propagate by seeds.

POSSIBLE PROBLEMS: Eventual size.

Pinus roxburghii   PLATE 168

PRONOUNCER: *pie*-nus rox-*burj*-ee-eye

COMMON NAME: chir pine

Evergreen. Height: 60–80 ft. (18–24.5 m). Spread: 30–40 ft. (9–12 m). Rate of growth: Moderate. Light requirement: Sun. Native to the foothills of the Himalayas.

A large, graceful pine with long, drooping needles; narrow in youth but spreads with age. Similar in appearance to *P. canariensis*, the Canary Island pine, with which it sometimes hybridizes, but *P. roxburghii* has longer needles, is denser and looks more robust.

FLOWER AND FRUIT: Insignificant flowers followed by a 6–8 in. (15–20 cm) cone.

LANDSCAPE USES: A good choice for larger landscapes, parks and roadsides; branches and foliage present a handsome, tiered appearance.

CLIMATE ADAPTION: Widely adaptable; heat tolerant; more cold tolerant than *P. canariensis* and a better choice for the higher desert.

CULTURE: Minimal soil requirement; accepts alkaline conditions. Drought resistant and accepts little to moderate water; probably best with monthly, deep watering in the desert in warmest periods. Minimal fertilizer needed. Prune to remove lower branches, if desired. Propagate by seeds.

POSSIBLE PROBLEMS: Eventual size; drops needles more suddenly than other pines, giving it a brownish appearance for 1–2 weeks in the spring.

Pinus torreyana, the Torrey pine, is native to coastal

southern California, grows to 50–80 ft. (15–

24.5 m) with a broad, open crown and has 4–6 in. (10–15 cm) cones; widely adaptable except for the low desert.

Pistacia chinensis   PLATE 169

PRONOUNCER: pis-*tay*-see-ah chi-*nen*-sis
FAMILY: Anacardiaceae
COMMON NAME: Chinese pistache

Deciduous. Height: 40–50 ft. (12–15 m). Spread: 40–50 ft. (12–15 m). Rate of growth: Moderate. Light requirement: Sun. Native to China.

Erect trunk with pyramidal crown in youth and rounded crown in maturity; lustrous green foliage; short-petioled leaves about 1 ft. (30 cm) long in 10 or more leaflets; deep root system.

FLOWER AND FRUIT: Clusters of small, not showy flowers in spring, with male and female on separate plants; 0.5-in. (1.3-cm), inedible fruit turn red on females before foliage changes to oranges and reds on both sexes in late fall.

LANDSCAPE USES: If there is room, fall color alone provides enough reason to plant, but it is also very ornamental at other times. Provides excellent summer shade, allows winter sun, is well-suited to desert conditions and well-adapted to smog and high winds. Does not blend pleasingly with native Southwest vegetation.

CLIMATE ADAPTION: Hardy to at least 0°F (−18°C); no heat problems. While widely adaptable, avoid mild, coastal areas.

CULTURE: Needs good drainage. Minimal water requirement, but likes deep watering every 2–4 weeks in warmer months. Apply 8 oz. (225 g) ammonium sulfate in February after the first year. Prune young trees to eventually form a head-high canopy; may require staking. Propagate by seeds collected in the fall from the largest fruit.

POSSIBLE PROBLEMS: Verticillium wilt; not for areas known to harbor Texas root rot.

Pithecellobium flexicaule   PLATE 170

PRONOUNCER: pith-e-sell-*oh*-bee-um *flex*-e-call
FAMILY: Leguminosae
COMMON NAME: Texas ebony

Semideciduous. Height: 20–25 ft. (6–7.5 m). Spread: 10–15 ft. (3–4.5 m). Rate of growth: Slow. Light requirement: Sun to partial shade. Native to the southwestern United States.

Picturesque, small tree or large shrub with deep green, pinnately compound leaves, rounded crown, unusually dense branch structure, many thorns and a light gray trunk.

FLOWER AND FRUIT: Fragrant yellow or white flowers in clusters on short spikes in the spring and early summer, followed by brown, 4–6 in. (10–15 cm) seed pods containing reddish beans.

LANDSCAPE USES: A handsome specimen or a screen-barrier in groups. Provides dense shade and deep green color for desert landscapes. A low-spreading form without training.

CLIMATE ADAPTION: No heat problems; hardy to about 15°F (−9°C) but can lose its leaves in cold weather; best for low- and mid-elevation deserts.

CULTURE: Needs good drainage. Minimal water requirement, but a deep, monthly irrigation in summer speeds growth and improves appearance. Apply a half cup (115 g) of ammonium sulfate in early spring to promote growth. Prune to train, if desired, and to minimize thorns. Propagate by seeds, after filing or soaking; long taproot.

POSSIBLE PROBLEMS: Thorns, if planted in traffic areas; very slow starting; bees like flowers; litter from seed pods.

Pithecellobium undulatum, the Mexican ebony, is faster growing, somewhat larger, quite attractive, with creamy flowers in spring and less-dense foliage, but is not readily available.

Pittosporum phillyraeoides   PLATE 171

PRONOUNCER: pi-*tos*-per-um fil-lee-ray-*oy*-deez
FAMILY: Pittosporaceae
COMMON NAME: willow pittosporum

Evergreen. Height: 15–20 ft. (4.5–6 m). Spread: 10–15 ft. (3–4.5 m). Rate of growth: Slow to moderate. Light requirement: Full sun best. Native to Australian deserts.

A small, rugged tree with a slender growth habit. While main branches are erect, branchlets and foliage sweep down toward the ground, giving it a weeping appearance. The leaves are bright green, glossy, narrow and about 3 in. (8 cm) long.

FLOWER AND FRUIT: Fragrant, pale yellow, tiny, bell-shaped flowers line the branches in spring. Fruit is a colorful, yellow-orange, 0.5-in. (1.3-cm) capsule which contains fleshy, sticky, red seeds.

LANDSCAPE USES: Excellent choice as a specimen for small or narrow spaces, such as patios, walkways and entryways. The foliage mixes well with other arid-type plants.

CLIMATE ADAPTION: Hardy to about 15°F (−9°C); thrives in heat; widely adaptable but questionable for higher deserts.

CULTURE: Prefers good drainage; tolerates heavier soils if not overwatered. Minimal water requirement, but benefits from monthly, deep soakings during the hottest periods. To speed growth, apply 1 lb. (0.45 kg) ammonium sulfate per 200 sq. ft. (18 sq. m) under the leaf canopy in early spring. If desired, low-growing branches may be pruned to allow for traffic, visibility, and so on. Propagate by seeds or semihardwood cuttings.

POSSIBLE PROBLEMS: Young trees often look sparse; litter; root suckers.

Podranea ricasoliana　　　　　PLATE 172

PRONOUNCER: poh-*dray*-nee-ah ree-kah-soh-lee-*ah*-nah

FAMILY: Bignoniaceae

COMMON NAME: pink trumpet vine

Evergreen. Height: 8–10 ft. (2.5–3 m). Spread: 10–20 ft. (3–6 m). Rate of growth: Slow. Light requirement: Sun to partial shade. Native to Africa.

A twining, flowering vine with dark green, luxuriant leaves in pairs of oval, pointed, 2-in. (5-cm) leaflets.

FLOWER AND FRUIT: Spectacular, trumpet-shaped, 3-in. (8-cm) flowers that are pink with red veins, in spring and summer in terminal clusters; seed capsules.

LANDSCAPE USES: A lush vine providing interesting contrasts against cement block walls, where it needs support; climbs up posts or trellises.

CLIMATE ADAPTION: Foliage freezes back around 25°F (−4°C) but usually recovers from the roots in the spring; heat tolerant; best for low- and mid-elevation deserts and coastal and inland southern California.

CULTURE: Needs good drainage and planting soil improved with organic matter. Likes a deep, weekly irrigation in summer in the hottest areas, otherwise minimal. Little to no fertilizer. Prune to shape after bloom or to remove stems killed by frost. Propagate by seeds or softwood cuttings.

POSSIBLE PROBLEMS: Slow growth; wind may blow from supports.

Prosopis

PRONOUNCER: pro-*so*-pis

FAMILY: Leguminosae

For fast growth, winter sun and summer shade, it is hard to beat the mesquites in much of the arid Southwest, especially the deserts. They are well-adapted to heat and low humidity, accept minimal watering and care, and are cold hardy in most situations. In groups, mesquites make good privacy screens and windbreaks, but do equally well as specimen trees. All are deep rooted.

The velvet mesquite was regarded as the "tree of life" by many desert Indian tribes. They used the wood for fuel and lumber and the seeds for food. It forms extensive thickets along dry streambeds in the Southwest and provides shelter for many kinds of wildlife.

Prosopis glandulosa　　　　　PLATE 173

PRONOUNCER: pro-*so*-pis gland-ewe-*low*-sah

COMMON NAME: honey mesquite

Deciduous. Height: 25–30 ft. (7.5–9 m). Spread: 30–40 ft. (9–12 m). Rate of growth: Moderate. Light requirement: Sun. Native to Texas, New Mexico, Oklahoma, northern Mexico.

A medium-sized tree with a spreading crown of lacy, glossy, bright green foliage on a short, dark, rough trunk. Weeping form, thorny. Pinnately compound leaves in pairs with 10–20 open leaflets. Deep taproot.

FLOWER AND FRUIT: Dangling, greenish yellow, fragrant flower spikes in the spring; hanging clusters of 4–9 in. (10–23 cm), narrow, bright red seed pods in the late summer.

LANDSCAPE USES: A specimen or shade tree or effective barrier planting in groups; quite lush looking with supplemental water. Good wind tolerance. Seeds pods can be ground into flour.

CLIMATE ADAPTION: Hardy to about 5°F (−15°C); no problem with heat; best for the deserts and California's Central Valley.

CULTURE: Minimal soil requirement, but planting hole must drain well. Rainfall may be sufficient, but they adapt to regular watering with faster growth; appreciates monthly, deep watering in the growing season. To speed growth, spread 1 lb. (0.45 kg) ammonium sulfate for each 100 sq. ft. (9 sq. m) of branch canopy in the late winter. Prune to emphasize the natural form; may be trained to a single trunk, but is probably more attractive as a multitrunked plant. Propagate by fresh or scarified seeds.

POSSIBLE PROBLEMS: Thorns; invasive roots where moisture is available, such as around septic tanks; litter.

Prosopis hybrids　　　　　PLATE 174

COMMON NAME: South American hybrid mesquite

Semideciduous. Height: 20–30 ft. (6–9 m). Spread: 20–30 ft. (6–9 m). Rate of growth: Fast. Light requirement: Sun. Hybrids.

Upright to spreading trees with lush canopies of feathery foliage on rough, dark trunks; twigs are reddish brown. Often sold as Chilean mesquite, *P. chilensis*, or sometimes as

Argentine mesquite, *P. alba,* but such labeling is dubious. The South American species have hybridized with each other and with native Southwest species, producing varying forms. This mixing has led to much confusion in identifying the various forms. The thornless types are the most desirable; they also tend to be deciduous.

FLOWER AND FRUIT: Dangling, greenish yellow, 2–3 in. (5–8 cm) flower spikes in the spring; clusters of seed pods.

LANDSCAPE USES: To provide quick filtered shade, effective in lawns, around patios or along streets. Needs adequate space. Some of the best trees in the low desert because they can grow as much as 6 ft. (2 m) a year when young, providing quick effects.

CLIMATE ADAPTION: Hardy to about 15°F (−9°C); no problem with heat; best for low- and mid-elevation deserts and inland southern California.

CULTURE: Needs good drainage. Looks best with monthly irrigation; likes deep watering. Minimal fertilizer needed. Train to single- or multitrunked form. Propagate by scarified seeds.

POSSIBLE PROBLEMS: Rabbits nibble foliage of young trees; litter; invasive roots if moisture available.

Prosopis pubescens, the screwbean mesquite, is a Southwestern tree growing to 10–15 ft. (3–4.5 m); decorative clusters of seed pods have a tight, coiled appearance, often used in dried arrangements.

Prosopis velutina

PRONOUNCER: pro-*so*-pis vel-ewe-*tee*-nah
COMMON NAME: velvet or juliflora mesquite

Deciduous. Height: 15–40 ft. (4.5–12 m). Spread: 20–40 ft. (6–12 m). Rate of growth: Moderate. Light requirement: Sun. Native to streambeds in much of the Southwest.

A spreading large shrub or small tree with feathery, soft, gray-green foliage; the short, rugged, dark trunk can sometimes reach 3 ft. (1 m) in diameter; numerous branches, with stout, straight spines about 2 in. (5 cm) long. Quite common in nonpopulated areas, where it is more likely to be seen as a multitrunked shrub about 10 ft. (3 m) tall.

FLOWER AND FRUIT: Cream-colored flower spikes to 3 in. (8 cm) in mid-spring; clusters of tan seed pods ripen in the fall, can be ground into flour.

LANDSCAPE USES: A specimen tree for desert landscapes or informally as a tree or shrub in naturalized areas; provides filtered shade and tolerates lawn situations.

CLIMATE ADAPTION: Hardy to at least 0°F (−18°C); no problems with heat; does well in the deserts.

CULTURE: Needs good drainage. Survives on rainfall but likes monthly, deep watering in the summer. Apply 1 lb. (0.45 kg) ammonium sulfate for each 100 sq. ft. (9 sq. m) of canopy in late winter to speed growth. Train to single- or multitrunked form, as desired. Propagate by fresh or scarified seeds.

POSSIBLE PROBLEMS: Invasive roots, do not plant around septic tanks; litter; protect young plants from rabbits.

Prunus

PRONOUNCER: *proo*-nuss
FAMILY: Rosaceae

Prunus ilicifolia, the hollyleaf cherry, is somewhat similar to *P. lyonii* but with spiny leaves and is native to California's Coast Range; the two species often hybridize.

Prunus lyonii

PRONOUNCER: *proo*-nuss lie-*oh*-nee-eye
COMMON NAME: Catalina cherry

Evergreen. Height: 15–35 ft. (4.5–10.5 m). Spread: 10–40 ft. (3–12 m). Rate of growth: Fast. Light requirement: Sun to partial shade. Native to southern California's Channel Islands.

A spreading tree with slender branches forming a rounded crown or a dense, broad shrub; dark green, lustrous, oval-shaped leaves 2–4 in. (5–10 cm) long. Formerly known as *P. integrifolia.*

FLOWER AND FRUIT: Abundant, cream-colored, tiny flowers in clusters in the late spring; black, 0.5–1 in. (1.3–2.5 cm), shiny berries ripen in the fall.

LANDSCAPE USES: A patio or street tree, tall hedge, large, specimen shrub, or in naturalized groupings. Quite handsome and easily trained. Resistant to oak root fungus and wind damage.

CLIMATE ADAPTION: Best for coastal and inland southern California and California's Central Valley, but killed by prolonged freezing; does not like desert heat.

CULTURE: Needs good drainage. Quite drought tolerant but prefers infrequent, summer watering in the warmest areas. Minimal fertilizer needed. Prune to shape; accepts heavy pruning; needs training to form a tree. Propagate by seeds.

POSSIBLE PROBLEMS: Fruit stains and litter.

Punica granatum PLATE 175

PRONOUNCER: *pew*-ni-kah grah-*nah*-tum
FAMILY: Punicaceae
COMMON NAME: pomegranate

Deciduous. Height: 10–15 ft. (3–4.5 m). Spread: 8–15 ft. (2.5–4.5 m). Rate of growth: Moderate. Light requirement: Sun to part shade. Native to southern Asia.

Usually a large, bushy shrub or, with training, a small tree; slender, sometimes thorny branches; oblong, 1–3 in. (2.5–8 cm), glossy green leaves with red veins. The most commonly grown fruiting cultivar, 'Wonderful', is also one of the largest at about 12 ft. (3.5 m) high and 12 ft. (3.5 m) wide. Several other cultivars, including dwarf forms, are available.

FLOWER AND FRUIT: Orange-red, showy, 1-in. (2.5-cm), tubular flowers in summer, followed by juicy, many-seeded, 2–4 in. (5–10 cm), edible fruit ripening from September onwards. Does not require a pollinator; minimal chilling requirement.

LANDSCAPE USES: Natural hedge, fruit-specimen or espalier. Dwarfs are very ornamental in containers but usually do not produce edible fruit. Resistant to oak root fungus.

CLIMATE ADAPTION: Hardy to about 10–15°F (−12 to −9°C); likes heat; widely adaptable but not likely to fruit in coastal areas.

CULTURE: Needs good drainage; does well in extremely alkaline areas. For best fruiting, water deeply, twice monthly from spring through fall. Nonfruiting varieties need little water but tolerate a great deal. Minimal fertilizer. To train as a tree, remove lower branches as desired in winter. Propagate by hardwood cuttings or layering.

POSSIBLE PROBLEMS: Damage from late-spring frosts; fruit splits if soil alternates between wet and dry; ash whitefly; leaf-footed plant bug in hottest areas.

Quercus

PRONOUNCER: *kwair*-kus
FAMILY: Fagaceae

The long-lived oaks, with their thick trunks and heavy, spreading limbs, create strong silhouettes valuable in all kinds of landscapes. Numerous evergreen and deciduous species are native to the Southwest, and a number of non-natives are well-adapted.

The California natives found growing on hillsides and valley floors give a distinct regional flavor to the state. Unfortunately, many have fallen victim to urbanization. But efforts have begun in recent years to preserve specimens around construction and development sites.

Oaks are propagated from acorns, which can be planted directly in the ground. If container stock is purchased, make sure the plants are not rootbound. Soil of the planting site should drain well. Newly planted trees need regular, supplemental watering the first two years in the ground, mainly in the dry season. Avoid fertilizing the young plants during this period. In subsequent years, trees respond with faster growth to nitrogen applied in the early spring.

Special precautions should be taken when planting or building around large, established native oaks. They very much resent soil disturbances, including paving, grade changes and compaction in their vicinity.

Overwatering—such as from irrigation of nearby lawns or plants growing under oak trees—leads to disease problems with some regularity. Plant only species under oaks that require little to no supplemental watering and place them at least 6 ft. (2 m) away from the trunk.

Oaks are susceptible to a number of insect and disease problems. Crown rot is the most common disease of California oaks and results from excess moisture around the base of the trunk. Oak root fungus, also known as *Armillaria* root rot and shoestring root rot, is similarly caused by overly wet conditions. Many other genera are susceptible to oak root fungus; avoid planting them near oaks.

Quercus agrifolia PLATE 176

PRONOUNCER: *kwair*-kus ag-ri-*foh*-lee-ah
COMMON NAME: coast live oak

Evergreen. Height: 30–70 ft. (9–21.5 m). Spread: 40–80 ft. (12–24.5 m). Rate of growth: Moderate. Light requirement: Sun to partial shade. Native to California's coastal mountains.

A large, round-canopied tree with picturesque, thick, spreading branches; dark green, hollylike leaves 1–3 in. (2.5–8 cm) long and 1–2 in. (2.5–5 cm) wide; deep roots. Shape varies greatly as it adapts to winds. Deep gray bark.

FLOWER AND FRUIT: Inconspicuous flowers; brown, round acorns 1–1.5 in. (2.5–4 cm), August–October.

LANDSCAPE USES: A handsome shade tree but only where it has room to grow to its full size and the problems associated with it are not crucial. Becomes quite large within 10 years if conditions are right and freezing temperatures are not prolonged. Can be pruned into a large hedge.

CLIMATE ADAPTION: Hardy to about 20°F (−6.5°C),

but prolonged freezing is fatal; best for coastal and inland southern California; likes part shade in California's Central Valley; not for the deserts.

CULTURE: Minimal soil requirement, but growth rate slows in poor soils. Little to no supplemental watering, and avoid summer irrigation after the first two years in the landscape. Minimal fertilizer needed. Remove poorly formed branches in the fall and suckers at any time; accepts fairly heavy pruning. Propagate by fresh seeds.

POSSIBLE PROBLEMS: Suckers; crown rot due to too much moisture; caterpillars, mites and thrips; leaf and twig blight; drops old leaves within a short period of time in the spring.

Quercus chrysolepis, the canyon live oak, is a handsome, medium-sized, 30–60 ft. (9–18 m) evergreen tree native to canyons and slopes mainly in California.

Quercus engelmannii, the mesa oak, is a spreading, evergreen tree to about 60 ft. (18 m), native to the southern California foothills and Baja California.

Quercus ilex

PRONOUNCER: *kwair*-kus *eye*-lex
COMMON NAME: holly oak

Evergreen. Height: 30–60 ft. (9–18 m). Spread: 20–50 ft. (6–15 m). Rate of growth: Slow to moderate. Light requirement: Sun. Native to the Mediterranean region.

A dense tree, round-canopied and spreading; leaves are hollylike, variable in shape and size but usually 1.5–3 in. (4–8 cm) long and 0.5–1 in. (1.3–2.5 cm) wide, with either toothed or smooth edges; dark green on surface, yellowish or silvery underneath; deep roots.

FLOWER AND FRUIT: Insignificant flowers; brown, ovoid acorns about 1 in. (2.5 cm) with the top enclosing about half the nut.

LANDSCAPE USES: A specimen tree or space about 20 ft. (6 m) apart for a tall screen; uniformity of shape makes it a good choice in median strips along roadways. Fewer disease and pest problems than most oaks; good wind tolerance.

CLIMATE ADAPTION: Hardy to about 10°F (−12°C); tolerates heat; widely adaptable.

CULTURE: Needs good drainage. Minimal soil requirement; prefers deep loam. Minimal water requirement. Little to no fertilizer needed. Prune suckers and raise canopy in the fall as the tree develops; accepts clipping as a tall hedge. Propagate by seeds.

POSSIBLE PROBLEMS: Suckers.

Quercus lobata

PLATE 177

PRONOUNCER: *kwair*-kus loh-*bah*-tah
COMMON NAME: valley oak

Deciduous. Height: 40–100 ft. (12–30.5 m). Spread: 50–100 ft. (15–30.5 m). Rate of growth: Moderate. Light requirement: Sun. Native to California's Central Valley, inland valleys and slopes below 2,000 ft. (610 m).

A large, thick-trunked tree with heavy, spreading branches often sweeping to the ground; 2–4 in. (5–10 cm) leaves with 3–5 deeply cut lobes; deep roots. Said to be the largest of the North American oaks.

FLOWER AND FRUIT: Insignificant flowers; 2-in. (5-cm) acorns in the fall.

LANDSCAPE USES: A handsome specimen tree with much character for large properties, parks and naturalized areas.

CLIMATE ADAPTION: Hardy to about 15°F (−9°C); best for California's Central Valley and inland southern California.

CULTURE: Needs deep soil for best development. Little to no supplemental watering needed, but tolerates more summer irrigation than other California oaks. Responds to nitrogen fertilizers. Prune occasionally to thin interior and remove dead branches, as needed. Propagate by fresh seeds.

POSSIBLE PROBLEMS: Leaf galls caused by insects; size; aphids and scales.

Quercus suber

PRONOUNCER: *kwair*-kus *soo*-ber
COMMON NAME: cork oak

Evergreen. Height: 40–50 ft. (12–15 m). Spread: 40–50 ft. (12–15 m). Rate of growth: Slow to moderate. Light requirement: Sun. Native to the Mediterranean region.

A dense tree with a rounded crown; toothed leaves are alternate, about 3 in. (8 cm) long, dark green above, gray beneath; heavily fissured, soft bark; deep roots.

FLOWER AND FRUIT: Insignificant flowers; brown, rounded acorn about 1 in. (2.5 cm) long.

LANDSCAPE USES: This is the oak that produces the cork of commerce. An excellent specimen or shade tree but too messy for use around swimming pools.

CLIMATE ADAPTION: Hardy to about 10°F (−12°C); tolerates heat; widely adaptable.

CULTURE: Needs good drainage; avoid very alkaline soil and lawn situations. Needs supplemental watering every 3–4 weeks in the hottest areas in the summer. Little to no fertilizer. Prune suckers and weak branches in the fall. Propagate by seeds.

POSSIBLE PROBLEMS: Oak moth; oak root fungus; bark invites vandalism.

Quercus virginiana

PRONOUNCER: *kwair*-kus vir-gin-ee-*ah*-nah
COMMON NAME: southern live oak

Semideciduous. Height: 50–60 ft. (15–18 m). Spread: 60–70 ft. (18–21.5 m). Rate of growth: Moderate. Light requirement: Sun. Native from the southeastern United States into Texas.

A spreading tree with limbs occasionally arching gracefully to the ground; dark green leaves, 2–4 in. (5–10 cm) long and 0.5–2.5 in. (1.3–6 cm) wide; brown twigs and brown to gray, fissured bark.

FLOWER AND FRUIT: Hairy catkins 2–3 in. (5–8 cm) with yellow stamens; acorns follow in clusters of 3 to 5, brownish, about 0.5 in. (1.3 cm).

LANDSCAPE USES: This stately, moss-covered oak of the South also is the oak best adapted for desert conditions; give it room or minimize watering to restrain growth. Provides dense shade and creates the effect of a forest.

CLIMATE ADAPTION: Hardy to below 0°F (−18°C) but becomes deciduous around 10°F (−12°C); no problems with heat; widely adaptable.

CULTURE: Minimal soil requirement but prefers deep soil; stands considerable salinity. Drought tolerant but responds to monthly, summer watering and accepts lawn conditions. Minimal fertilizer needed. Prune to shape, as needed. Propagate by seeds.

POSSIBLE PROBLEMS: Heavy drop of leaves in spring; oak root fungus.

Quercus virginiana 'Heritage' is a faster-growing cultivar, to about 30 ft. (9 m), does well in the low desert and is resistant to Texas root rot.

PLATE 178

Rhamnus

PRONOUNCER: *ram*-nuss
FAMILY: Rhamnaceae

The clean foliage, decorative berries and hardiness of the evergreen shrubs in the genus *Rhamnus* make them very desirable landscape plants. They adapt to locations ranging from sunny, coastal areas to dry, shady places such as under oak trees. Coffeeberry makes a handsome, large background plant; the smaller, finely branched redberry is useful in borders or as a hedge. They tolerate a variety of soils. Watering in warmer areas should be adjusted according to soil type. They do not, however, like desert heat.

Rhamnus californica   PLATE 179

PRONOUNCER: *ram*-nuss cal-i-*for*-ni-cah
COMMON NAME: coffeeberry

Evergreen. Height: 3–20 ft. (1–6 m). Spread: 6–10 ft. (2–3 m). Rate of growth: Slow to moderate. Light requirement: Sun to partial shade. Native to California, Arizona, New Mexico, Oregon.

A shrub or small tree with oblong, shiny, olive green, 1–4 in. (2.5–10 cm) leaves. Tends to be low and spreading in coastal areas. There also are lower-growing, more compact cultivars, such as 'Eve Case', usually with broader leaves.

FLOWER AND FRUIT: Inconspicuous, tiny flowers in late spring and early summer followed by showy, 0.5-in. (1.3-cm) berries that change from red to black as they ripen and attract birds.

LANDSCAPE USES: Informal screening, clipped hedge, small tree or for stabilizing slopes. Excellent plant for semidry shade and native gardens. Good wind tolerance and generally pest free.

CLIMATE ADAPTION: Hardy to at least 10°F (−12°C); best for coastal and inland California; needs partial shade in California's Central Valley.

CULTURE: Minimal soil requirement. Looks best in warmest areas with monthly, deep irrigation in summer. Little to no fertilizer needed. Prune to shape or if training as a hedge. Propagate by fresh seeds or semihardwood cuttings.

POSSIBLE PROBLEMS: Poor appearance in summer without supplemental water in the warmest areas.

Rhamnus crocea

PRONOUNCER: *ram*-nuss *crow*-see-ah
COMMON NAME: redberry

Evergreen. Height: 3–6 ft. (1–2 m). Spread: 3–5 ft. (1–1.5 m). Rate of growth: Moderate. Light requirement: Sun to partial shade. Native to southern California's coastal mountains.

A multibranched, spreading shrub; 0.5-in. (1.3-cm) leaves are rounded, glossy green above and brownish underneath; margins with tiny teeth.

FLOWER AND FRUIT: Wintertime, inconspicuous, small flowers in clusters are followed in late summer to early fall by tiny, ornamental, bright red berries, which attract birds.

LANDSCAPE USES: Specimen, in groups or as a hedge. Good for semidry shade.

CLIMATE ADAPTION: Hardy to about 15°F (−9°C); best for coastal and inland southern California; likes afternoon shade in California's Central Valley.

CULTURE: Needs good drainage. Looks better in summer with monthly, deep irrigation in the warmest areas. No fertilizer. Minimal pruning needed, but can be clipped as a hedge. Propa-

gate by fresh seeds or semihardwood cuttings.
POSSIBLE PROBLEMS: Watering needs close attention in inland areas.

Rhamnus crocea ilicifolia, the hollyleaf redberry, tends to be larger and better adapted to drier areas.

Rhus

PRONOUNCER: roos
FAMILY: Anacardiaceae
Rhus is a diverse genus of evergreen and deciduous shrubs and trees. The southwestern sumacs extend from the coastal sage-scrub to the interior chaparral communities. The evergreen species maintain an attractive appearance year-round and make handsome screen and background plants. African sumac has proven to be a durable shade tree that tolerates desert heat well. All are related to the toxic poison oak (*R. diversiloba*) and poison ivy (*R. radicans*).

Rhus integrifolia   PLATE 180

PRONOUNCER: roos in-teg-ri-*foh*-lee-ah
COMMON NAME: lemonade berry
    Evergreen. Height: 3–12 ft. (1–3.5 m). Spread: 5–12 ft. (1.5–3.5 m). Rate of growth: Moderate. Light requirement: Sun to part shade. Native to coastal southern California and Baja California.
    A large, spreading shrub or, infrequently, a small tree; thick, rounded leaves, deep green, 1–3 in. (2.5–8 cm) long, with slightly toothed edges on red stems.
FLOWER AND FRUIT: Small clusters of pink to white flowers in early spring followed by 0.5-in. (1.3-cm), reddish berries which taste like lemon and can be used to flavor beverages.
LANDSCAPE USES: Windbreak screening, for naturalizing, as an espalier, as a small accent tree or compact hedge. A deep taproot makes it a good choice for slope stabilization. Fairly fire resistant if kept watered.
CLIMATE ADAPTION: Hardy to about 15°F (−9°C); best for coastal and inland areas of southern California; needs afternoon shade in California's Central Valley; not for the deserts.
CULTURE: Needs good drainage. Minimal water requirement in coastal areas but needs monthly deep watering inland. No fertilizer. Minimal pruning unless used as a close-cropped hedge or espalier. Can be kept about 1 ft. (30 cm) wide. Propagate by seeds.
POSSIBLE PROBLEMS: Suckers, verticillium wilt.

Rhus lancea   PLATE 181

PRONOUNCER: roos *lan*-see-ah
COMMON NAME: African sumac
    Evergreen. Height: 20–25 ft. (6–7.5 m). Spread: 20–30 ft. (6–9 m). Rate of growth: Slow. Light requirement: Sun. Native to South Africa but has naturalized in the Southwest.
    A graceful, broad-crowned, small tree with dark green foliage, three-lobed leaves about 3 in. (8 cm) long, reddish brown bark.
FLOWER AND FRUIT: Tiny, greenish flowers in winter are followed by clusters of tiny, red or yellow berries on females.
LANDSCAPE USES: Specimen tree for residential and public landscapes; provides dense shade in difficult conditions; unpruned plants make a good screen.
CLIMATE ADAPTION: Hardy to about 15°F (−9°C); relishes heat; borderline in the higher desert.
CULTURE: Prefers good drainage. Minimal water requirement; water every 3–4 weeks in summer. Apply a cup (225 g) of ammonium sulfate in early spring after the tree has been in the landscape a year. Trim scaffold branches of young trees as they grow to eventually permit headroom under them. Propagate by seeds.
POSSIBLE PROBLEMS: Reseeds; litter; overwatering; Texas root rot.

Rhus laurina

PRONOUNCER: roos lor-*eye*-nah
COMMON NAME: laurel sumac
    Evergreen. Height: 6–18 ft. (2–5.5 m). Spread: 8–15 ft. (2.5–4.5 m). Rate of growth: Fast. Light requirement: Sun. Native to southern California coastal foothills into Baja California.
    A large, rounded shrub with laurel-like, aromatic, narrow, 2–4 in. (5–10 cm) leaves, deep green on top and light green underneath with occasional red margins; red stems. Also known as *Malosma laurina*.
FLOWER AND FRUIT: Showy, 2–4 in. (5–10 cm) clusters of tiny, white flowers in summer months and sometimes around December; small, white berries follow.
LANDSCAPE USES: Very handsome in naturalized and background plantings, to control erosion, as an espalier or a spreading hedge. Regrows quickly even after heavy damage due to fires or frost.
CLIMATE ADAPTION: Cut to ground by temperatures under 30°F (−1°C) but recovers in the spring; leaves turn color at first frost; best in coastal and inland southern California.
CULTURE: Dies if soil remains soggy. Drought

resistant; looks best with monthly, deep irrigation in summer. No fertilizer. Shape from time to time to prevent a leggy form. Propagate by seeds.

POSSIBLE PROBLEMS: Cold sensitive; pruning requirements; suckers; a fire hazard in naturalized areas.

Rhus ovata
PRONOUNCER: roos o-*vah*-tah
COMMON NAME: sugar bush

Evergreen. Height: 6–15 ft. (2–4.5 m). Spread: 5–10 ft. (1.5–3 m). Rate of growth: Slow. Light requirement: Sun to part shade. Native to Arizona, California and Mexico.

A large, mounding shrub with glossy, bright to dark green foliage; 3-in. (8-cm), oval leaves on reddish stems; red buds in fall; grayish bark.

FLOWER AND FRUIT: Profusion of creamy to pink flowers on dense, 0.5-in. (1.3-cm) spikes in the spring followed by red, hairy, 0.3-in. (1-cm) fruit.

LANDSCAPE USES: Very decorative as a specimen, a wide screen or around a swimming pool. This is a better choice than *R. integrifolia* for the hottest areas. Refreshing, dark green foliage looks good in desert settings.

CLIMATE ADAPTION: Hardy to about 15°F (−9°C); no heat problems; widely adaptable.

CULTURE: Needs good drainage. Minimal water requirement but likes once-a-month, deep watering in the summer. Apply 4 oz. (115 g) ammonium sulfate in early spring after the plant has been in the landscape a year. Best without pruning. Propagate by fall-collected seeds.

POSSIBLE PROBLEMS: Excessive water kills quickly; sometimes has fungus problems in summer; difficult to establish; susceptible to oak root fungus.

Rhus trilobata　　　　　　PLATE 182
PRONOUNCER: roos try-lo-*bah*-tah
COMMON NAME: skunkbush, squawbush

Deciduous. Height: 3–5 ft. (1–1.5 m). Spread: 5–6 ft. (1.5–2 m). Rate of growth: Moderate. Light requirement: Sun to partial shade. Native from the Southwest to the northern Great Plains.

A densely branched, spreading shrub with deep green color through the hottest periods, frequently changing to red or purple in the fall; leaves divided into 1–2 in. (2.5–5 cm), oval leaflets, the terminal one of which is usually three-lobed.

FLOWER AND FRUIT: Greenish flowers in spikes before the leaves appear, followed by red, hairy,

0.3-in. (1-cm) fruit in clusters. Birds love the edible, acidic berries.

LANDSCAPE USES: A rugged performer for erosion control on slopes or nonirrigated areas; accepts extremes of heat, cold and wind; for fall color and as a low, natural hedge.

CLIMATE ADAPTION: Hardy to about −30°F (−34°C); best for mid-elevation and higher deserts; needs afternoon shade in California's Central Valley.

CULTURE: Needs good drainage. Minimal water requirement but looks best with deep watering once a month in the hottest periods. Responds to light nitrogen fertilizer. Needs no pruning; accepts shearing. Propagate by seeds or cuttings.

POSSIBLE PROBLEMS: Bruised leaves have odor similar to that released by a skunk, resulting in one of the common names; deer browse.

Rhus trilobata 'Autumn Amber' is a more prostrate cultivar.

Ribes
PRONOUNCER: *rye*-beez
FAMILY: Saxifragaceae

The genus *Ribes* is well represented in California with some 31 native species. Several do well in both coastal and interior landscapes. The often showy flowers and berries of these deciduous to evergreen shrubs are reason enough to plant them. Thorny species are known as gooseberries; the thornless forms are called currants.

Ribes speciosum　　　　PLATE 183
PRONOUNCER: *rye*-beez spee-see-*oh*-sum
COMMON NAME: fuchsia-flowered gooseberry

Semideciduous. Height: 3–6 ft. (1–2 m). Spread: 3–7 ft. (1–2.2 m). Rate of growth: Moderate. Light requirement: Sun to shade. Native to central California coast south to Baja California.

A spiny shrub with spreading, arching branches covered with bristles; shiny, bright green, rounded leaves to 1.5 in. (4 cm) across have toothed or lobed upper margins.

FLOWER AND FRUIT: Deep red, fuchsialike flowers with conspicuous stamens hang along the branches in winter and spring; hummingbirds love them. Round, 0.5-in. (1.3-cm), bristly berries are edible.

LANDSCAPE USES: A specimen shrub, for barriers, mixed plantings, or as an understory plant. Lush appearing, with handsome flowers.

CLIMATE ADAPTION: Hardy to about 15°F (−9°C);

best for coastal and inland southern California and California's Central Valley, where it needs afternoon shade.

CULTURE: Likes good drainage. Does best with infrequent, summer watering in the warmest areas; tends to drop its leaves with drought in late summer; irrigation helps to minimize leaf shed at this time. Minimal fertilizer needed. Prune after flowering to shape. Propagate by cuttings or cold-stratified seeds.

POSSIBLE PROBLEMS: Thorns; appearance during deciduous period.

Ribes viburnifolium

PRONOUNCER: *rye*-beez vy-burn-i-*foh*-lee-um
COMMON NAME: Catalina currant

Evergreen. Height: 3–5 ft. (1–1.5 m). Spread: 8–10 ft. (2.5–3 m). Rate of growth: Fast. Light requirement: Part to full shade. Native to the Channel Islands of California and Baja California.

Low, wide-spreading shrub with pleasantly fragrant foliage; leathery, oval, dark green, lobe-less leaves are lighter underneath, to 1.5 in. (4 cm) long; thornless.

FLOWER AND FRUIT: Small, pinkish flowers in axillary clusters in the spring; flowers not as showy as *R. speciosum*; small, red, edible berries.

LANDSCAPE USES: One of the best ground covers for dry, shady areas such as under oaks; good on slopes for erosion control.

CLIMATE ADAPTION: Hardy to about 15°F (−9°C); best for coastal and inland southern California and California's Central Valley; not for the deserts.

CULTURE: Prefers good drainage; coastal plantings require no extra water, but plants in warmer areas like a monthly, deep watering in summer. Little to no fertilizer. Prune to shape or control size as needed. Propagate by cuttings or cold-stratified seed.

POSSIBLE PROBLEMS: Needs room; spider mites.

Romneya coulteri   PLATE 184

PRONOUNCER: *rom*-nee-ah *cole*-ter-eye
FAMILY: Papaveraceae
COMMON NAME: matilija poppy

Perennial. Height: 5–8 ft. (1.5–2.5 m). Spread: 4–8 ft. (1.2–2.5 m). Rate of growth: Fast. Light requirement: Sun to part shade. Native to southern and Baja California.

A large, upright to spreading, woody-based perennial with gray-green stems and coarsely divided leaves; spreads by underground roots. Often hybridizes with the more compact *R. trichocalyx*.

FLOWER AND FRUIT: Fragrant, handsome, white flowers as much as 9 in. (23 cm) wide with yellow centers, 5 or 6 petals, May–July, or if watered, into fall; dry capsule. Blossoms remain open for many days.

LANDSCAPE USES: For spectacular floral displays in large areas such as parks, along roadsides or on slopes, where it also helps control erosion.

CLIMATE ADAPTION: Hardy to at least 15°F (−9°C); widely adaptable but needs part shade in the deserts and probably marginal in the low desert.

CULTURE: Minimal soil requirement. Withhold water if necessary to control invasive growth, but the plant will need some in summer to continue blooming. No fertilizer. Cut plants back to the crown in late fall. Propagate by rooted suckers from the spreading root system; be sure to maintain a firm ball of earth when transplanting.

POSSIBLE PROBLEMS: Can be very invasive; not for the typical home landscape.

Rosmarinus officinalis   PLATE 185

PRONOUNCER: roz-ma-*rye*-nus o-fish-i-*nal*-is
FAMILY: Labiatae
COMMON NAME: rosemary

Evergreen. Height: 1–2 ft. (30–60 cm). Spread: 3–5 ft. (1–1.5 m). Rate of growth: Fast. Light requirement: Sun to part shade. Native to Mediterranean coastal hills.

A perennial shrub with aromatic, dense, needlelike, dark green foliage. Low-growing cultivars, such as 'Lockwood de Forest' and 'Prostrata', are the forms usually planted. Larger-shrub types, such as 'Tuscan Blue', may reach 5 ft. (1.5 m). 'Collingwood Ingram', which grows to 2.5–4 ft. (75 cm–1 m), bears attractive blue-violet flowers.

FLOWER AND FRUIT: Numerous, tiny, blue flowers, mainly in the spring but sometimes in the fall; round nutlets. The cultivar 'Albus' has white flowers.

LANDSCAPE USES: Durable, low-growing ground cover or small hedge; for accent; in containers; cascading (some varieties) over raised planters or walls; for bonsai, and as a most useful culinary herb.

CLIMATE ADAPTION: Quite heat tolerant; sometimes damaged by a sudden freeze after a warm fall but otherwise cold hardy to about 15°F (−9°C); widely adaptable.

CULTURE: Needs good drainage. Drought resistant but prefers watering in summer every two weeks in the hottest areas. Apply 2 oz. (57 g) ammonium sulfate in early spring for plants in the landscape at least a year. Prune to groom;

pinch tips to encourage bushiness. Propagate by cuttings, divisions or layering.

POSSIBLE PROBLEMS: Spreads readily; flowers attract bees; easily tangled by Bermuda grass invasions.

Ruellia
PRONOUNCER: roo-*el*-ee-ah
FAMILY: Acanthaceae

Ruellia californica is similar to *R. peninsularis* under frost-free conditions.

Ruellia peninsularis   PLATE 186
PRONOUNCER: roo-*el*-ee-ah pen-in-suh-*lair*-is
COMMON NAME: desert ruellia
Evergreen. Height: 2–3 ft. (60–90 cm). Spread: 3–5 ft. (1–1.5 m). Rate of growth: Moderate. Light requirement: Sun. Native to Sonoran Desert of Mexico.
Open, rounded shrub with oval, bright green leaves about 1 in. (2.5 cm) long.
FLOWER AND FRUIT: Showy, tubular, 1-in. (2.5-cm), purple blooms are slightly fragrant; appear from spring to fall; small, four-seeded capsules.
LANDSCAPE USES: As a low hedge or in a setting with large rocks; combines well with other arid-adapted, flowering shrubs such as desert honeysuckle (*Justicia spicigera*).
CLIMATE ADAPTION: Hardy to about 20°F (−6.5°C) but incurs some foliage damage in even light frost; loves heat; best for low desert and inland southern California.
CULTURE: Needs good drainage. Drought resistant but looks best with twice-monthly watering in the hottest months. Apply 2 oz. (57 g) ammonium sulfate in the early spring for vigorous growth. Tip-prune lightly in the spring for more compact growth. Propagate by cuttings.
POSSIBLE PROBLEMS: Loses leaves in sudden frost.

Salvia
PRONOUNCER: *sal*-vee-ah
FAMILY: Labiatae
Many species of *Salvia* are native to the Southwest. Those selected for landscape use are notable for their colorful flowers and aromatic foliage. Their tubular, two-lipped flowers range from blue to purple to red and occur in loose to tight clusters held above the foliage.
Given good drainage, they are quite adaptable and bloom freely much of the year. Those grown in hotter locations need supplemental water to get through the summer.

Salvia chamaedryoides   PLATE 187
PRONOUNCER: *sal*-vee-ah kam-ay-dry-*oy*-deez
COMMON NAME: Mexican blue sage
Semideciduous. Height: 1–2 ft. (30–60 cm). Spread: 2–3 ft. (60–90 cm). Rate of growth: Moderate. Light requirement: Sun. Native to Mexico.
A low, gray shrub with a long bloom period; small, oval leaves with toothed margins.
FLOWER AND FRUIT: Deep blue flowers in loose clusters on spikes in the spring and summer; tiny nutlets.
LANDSCAPE USES: Fine border and contrast plant; beautiful with autumn sage (*S. greggii*).
CLIMATE ADAPTION: Hardy to about 10–12°F (−12 to −11°C); best for the deserts.
CULTURE: Needs good drainage. Water twice a month in the summer to improve appearance. Avoid fertilizer. Remove old flower stalks and any dieback. Propagate by cuttings and seeds.
POSSIBLE PROBLEMS: Can look poor when not in bloom.

Salvia clevelandii   PLATE 188
PRONOUNCER: *sal*-vee-ah kleev-*land*-ee-eye
COMMON NAME: chaparral salvia, Cleveland sage
Evergreen. Height: 4–5 ft. (1.2–1.5 m). Spread: 4–6 ft. (1.2–2 m). Rate of growth: Moderate. Light requirement: Sun to part shade. Native to the California chaparral of San Diego County south into Baja.
A rounded, gray-green shrub with aromatic foliage and flowers; soft, thick leaves are narrow, about 1 in. (2.5 cm) long.
FLOWER AND FRUIT: Blue-violet flowers clustered on spikes above plant, April–July, and sometimes into the fall; light yellow nutlets.
LANDSCAPE USES: Handsome mixed with other flowering shrubs such as autumn sage and ruellia and as a background shrub in perennial borders; plant on slopes for erosion control. Leaves can be used in cooking.
CLIMATE ADAPTION: Hardy to about 15°F (−9°C); heat tolerant; best for coastal and inland southern California; likes afternoon shade in California's Central Valley and the low- and mid-elevation deserts.
CULTURE: Needs good drainage. Give it occasional supplemental water in the summer in desert areas; minimal elsewhere. Little to no fertilizer while plants are becoming established; none thereafter. Trim back moderately after bloom to keep plants bushy and encourage bloom the following year. Propagate by cuttings or seeds.
POSSIBLE PROBLEMS: Hybridizes with some of the other salvias.

Salvia coccinea

PRONOUNCER: *sal*-vee-ah cok-*sin*-ee-ah
COMMON NAME: tropical sage

Evergreen to deciduous. Height: 2–3 ft. (60–90 cm). Spread: 2–3 ft. (60–90 cm). Rate of growth: Fast. Light requirement: Sun to partial shade. Native from the Southwest to Florida and the West Indies.

An evergreen perennial except in the coldest winters; continuous bloom with enough moisture and warmth; bright green, glossy, heart-shaped leaves on upright stems.

FLOWER AND FRUIT: Usually has bright red, showy, tubular flowers in spikes in the spring but may also be seen in white or bicolored versions; nutlets.

LANDSCAPE USES: A fast grower. Plant in mixed borders or in groups for a mass-flowering effect; nice in planters.

CLIMATE ADAPTION: Widely adaptable except in the higher deserts where it may freeze to the ground; appreciates afternoon shade in the low- and mid-elevation desert.

CULTURE: Needs good drainage. Looks and blooms best in the hottest areas with regular watering, up to once a week in the warmest months. Needs only occasional irrigation elsewhere. No fertilizer. Prune only to groom. Propagate by softwood cuttings or seeds.

POSSIBLE PROBLEMS: Becomes a weed in very favorable conditions.

Salvia farinacea   PLATE 189

PRONOUNCER: *sal*-vee-ah far-in-*ay*-see-ah
COMMON NAME: mealycup sage

Perennial. Height: 2–3 ft. (60–90 cm). Spread: 2–3 ft. (60–90 cm). Rate of growth: Fast. Light requirement: Full sun best. Native to Texas.

A mounding plant with 4-in. (10-cm), medium to gray-green, oblong leaves and herbaceous stems that die back in the coldest months. A number of cultivars have been selected.

FLOWER AND FRUIT: Clusters of blue, 0.5-in. (1.3-cm) flowers on spikes rising well above the leaves; cultivar 'Alba' has white flowers. Blooms on new growth from spring through fall. Nutlets.

LANDSCAPE USES: With other perennials or as an individual accent plant.

CLIMATE ADAPTION: Widely adaptable; likes heat; quite root hardy to cold but tops freeze back in mid-elevation and higher deserts and in California's Central Valley.

CULTURE: Minimal soil requirement. Needs ample water in the summer if grown in full sun in the hottest areas; cut irrigation sharply if grown in filtered light or elsewhere. Apply 1 oz. (30 g) ammonium sulfate in early spring on established plants. Remove spikes after flowering. Propagate by softwood cuttings.

POSSIBLE PROBLEMS: May die out following numerous frosts.

Salvia greggii   PLATE 190

PRONOUNCER: *sal*-vee-ah *greg*-ee-eye
COMMON NAME: autumn sage

Evergreen. Height: 2–3 ft. (60–90 cm). Spread: 2–3 ft. (60–90 cm). Rate of growth: Slow to moderate. Light requirement: Sun to partial shade. Native to Texas and Mexico.

A small, semidense shrub with 1-in. (2.5-cm), shiny, medium green leaves on upright branches.

FLOWER AND FRUIT: Loose clusters of tubular flowers on spikes are usually magenta, but those of various cultivars range from white to red. Often blooms from spring through fall. Nutlets.

LANDSCAPE USES: One of the very best plants for color in the low-water landscape; looks fine as an individual specimen, in groups or as a clipped hedge.

CLIMATE ADAPTION: Hardy to about 10°F (−12°C); no heat problems; widely adaptable.

CULTURE: Minimal soil requirement but likes organic matter such as forest mulch blended into the soil at planting time. Minimal water requirement except in the summer, when it does best with deep watering every two weeks. Caution: more frequent watering may lead to root fungus. Apply 2 oz. (57 g) ammonium sulfate in early spring after the plant's first year in the landscape. Looks best when pruned every now and then to keep it compact and dense; blooms on new growth, so pruning also maximizes flowering; remove old flower spikes. Propagate by softwood cuttings in spring or summer.

POSSIBLE PROBLEMS: Overwatering; sometimes difficult to establish; brittle branches.

Salvia leucantha   PLATE 191

PRONOUNCER: *sal*-vee-ah loo-*can*-thah
COMMON NAME: Mexican bush sage

Evergreen. Height: 3–4.5 ft. (1–1.4 m). Spread: 3–5 ft. (1–1.5 m). Rate of growth: Fast. Light requirement: Sun to part shade. Native to Mexico.

A medium-high shrub with very showy flower spikes rising above the foliage; leaves are medium to dark green, narrow, on white branches.

FLOWER AND FRUIT: Actual flowers are white, but they are held on woolly, reddish purple spikes;

128

Salvia leucophylla

blooms in spring, fall and winter; nutlets.
LANDSCAPE USES: Bold, flowering accent, or mix with other flowering shrubs; looks great with yellow cassias.
CLIMATE ADAPTION: Best for coastal and inland southern California; needs semishade in the low desert.
CULTURE: Minimal soil requirement; tolerates heavy soils. Needs once a week watering in the summer in low deserts; less in other recommended regions. Little to no fertilizer. Prune back in early spring. Propagate by divisions, cuttings or seeds.
POSSIBLE PROBLEMS: Looks unkempt if not pruned.

Salvia leucophylla
PRONOUNCER: *sal*-vee-ah loo-ko-*fil*-ah
COMMON NAME: purple sage
Evergreen. Height: 2–5 ft. (60 cm–1.5 m). Spread: 4–5 ft. (1.2–1.5 m). Rate of growth: Fast. Light requirement: Sun to part shade. Native to the Coast Range of southern California.
A colorful-blooming, small, mounding shrub with white stems, 1–3 in. (2.5–8 cm), crinkly leaves and a whitish appearance overall; winter growing.
FLOWER AND FRUIT: Purple, 0.5-in. (1.3-cm) flowers in clusters provide long-lasting color in the late spring and early summer; brownish-gray nutlets.
LANDSCAPE USES: Reliable, small accent shrub.
CLIMATE ADAPTION: Hardy to about 20°F (−6.5°C); best for coastal and inland southern California; likes afternoon shade in California's Central Valley.
CULTURE: Good drainage mandatory. Minimal water requirement, but summer irrigation every 4–6 weeks deflects normal summer dormancy. Apply 1 oz. (30 g) ammonium sulfate in the early spring to speed growth after first year in the landscape. Prune to shape in the early spring. Propagate by softwood cuttings or seeds.
POSSIBLE PROBLEMS: Root rot if soil does not drain perfectly.

Santolina chamaecyparissus   PLATE 192
PRONOUNCER: san-toh-*lee*-nah kam-ay-si-*pah*-ris-us
FAMILY: Compositae
COMMON NAME: lavender cotton
Evergreen. Height: 1–2 ft. (30–60 cm). Spread: 2–3 ft. (60–90 cm). Rate of growth: Moderate. Light requirement: Sun to partial shade. Native to the Mediterranean region.
A low-mounding, much-branching, gray-colored shrub with aromatic, finely divided foliage. The foliage is dense, somewhat like a cypress's.
FLOWER AND FRUIT: Tiny, yellow flowers on stalks in late spring or early summer; tiny, one-seeded fruit.
LANDSCAPE USES: A ground cover of easy culture for flower beds and borders; can be clipped into a low hedge. Nice, gray contrast.
CLIMATE ADAPTION: Hardy to about 5°F (−15°C); no heat problems; widely adaptable.
CULTURE: Needs good drainage. Needs twice-monthly watering in hottest areas during the summer for best appearance and growth. Apply 2 oz. (57 g) ammonium sulfate annually in the early spring after the plant has been in the ground for a year. To keep compact, shear before the new growth appears in the spring; for best appearance, remove seed heads. Propagate by softwood cuttings or seeds.
POSSIBLE PROBLEMS: After a few years, older plants look leggy even with the best of care; root rot if overwatered.

Santolina virens, green santolina, is similar to *S. chamaecyparissus* but has ferny, green foliage and is slightly taller. It is often combined with lavender cotton to create a pleasing contrast.

Sapindus drummondii
PRONOUNCER: *sap*-in-duss drum-*ond*-ee-eye
FAMILY: Sapindaceae
COMMON NAME: western soapberry
Deciduous. Height: 30–45 ft. (9–13.5 m). Spread: 30–45 ft. (9–13.5 m). Rate of growth: Moderate to fast. Light requirement: Sun. Native to the Southwest and Mexico.
A graceful tree with rounded crown; rough, gray bark; leaves 6–18 in. (15–45 cm) long with many narrow, light green, 2–4 in. (5–10 cm), lance-shaped leaflets.
FLOWER AND FRUIT: Creamy or yellow, cone-shaped flowers in showy clusters, March–June; round, 0.3-in. (1-cm), amber fruit in the fall. The fruit, which sometimes remains on the leafless trees over the winter, contains saponin, a toxic substance that produces lather in water and is sometimes used as a laundry soap.
LANDSCAPE USES: An attractive specimen tree, which in groups forms a graceful thicket. Foliage often turns bright yellow in the fall. Provides good shade.
CLIMATE ADAPTION: Hardy to at least 0°F (−18°C); no heat problems; best for the deserts and California's Central Valley.
CULTURE: Needs good drainage. Likes twice-

monthly, deep watering in summer in the hottest areas. Little to no fertilizer needed. Prune in the winter to shape or train; remove suckers at the base. Propagate by seeds or hardwood cuttings.

POSSIBLE PROBLEMS:. Tendency to sucker.

Simmondsia chinensis

PRONOUNCER: si-*mond*-see-ah chi-*nen*-sis
FAMILY: Buxaceae
COMMON NAME: jojoba, goat nut

Evergreen. Height: 3–6 ft. (1–2 m). Spread: 4–8 ft. (1.2–2.5 m). Rate of growth: Slow. Light requirement: Sun to partial shade. Native to Arizona, southern California, Mexico deserts.

A rounded, dense, medium-sized shrub with gray-green, oval, 2–2.5 in. (5–6 cm) leaves reaching to the ground.

FLOWER AND FRUIT: Tiny, yellow flowers, usually in the spring, followed on females by acornlike, brown seeds which are becoming commercially important in cosmetics and as a sperm whale oil substitute.

LANDSCAPE USES: A versatile accent plant for low-maintenance areas or as a hedge.

CLIMATE ADAPTION: Hardy to 15°F (−9°C), no heat problems; best in low- and mid-elevation deserts and southern California's inland valleys.

CULTURE: Needs good drainage. Minimal water requirement but grows faster with supplemental water every 3–4 weeks in the summer. Apply 2 oz. (57 g) ammonium sulfate in early spring after the plant is one year old. Prune to shape in spring; can be sheared for hedging. Propagate by seeds.

POSSIBLE PROBLEMS: Root rot; rabbits eat new plants; reseeds.

Sophora

PRONOUNCER: so-*for*-ah
FAMILY: Leguminosae

Sophora arizonica, the Arizona mountain laurel, is a rounded shrub with gray-green foliage. It grows very slowly to a height of 6–10 ft. (2–3 m).

Sophora gypsophila var. *guadalupensis,* the Guadalupe mountain laurel, reaches about 4 ft. (1.2 m) high with a spread of about 12 ft. (3.5 m); blooms at a much younger age than the other species.

Sophora secundiflora   PLATE 193

PRONOUNCER: so-*for*-ah se-kun-di-*flor*-ah
COMMON NAME: mescal bean, Texas mountain laurel

Evergreen. Height: 20–26 ft. (6–8 m). Spread: 8–12 ft. (2.5–3.5 m). Rate of growth: Slow. Light requirement: Sun to partial shade. Native to Texas, New Mexico and northern Mexico.

A large shrub or small tree with glossy, compound, dark green, 4–6 in. (7–15 cm) leaves divided into rounded leaflets; upright branches, velvet twigs, dark gray to black bark, multiple trunks and a dense crown.

FLOWER AND FRUIT: Fragrant, usually blue but sometimes white, wisterialike, 8 in. (20 cm) long flower clusters in the spring. Decorative, 4-in. (10-cm), gray seed pods split open in the late summer to reveal red beans known as *frijolitos,* another common name for the plant. The beans are poisonous, but children and pets usually find them too hard to chew.

LANDSCAPE USES: With training, a most decorative small tree around a patio. Also useful for massed shrubbery, hedge, informal screen or silhouette against buildings. Thrives under adverse conditions.

CLIMATE ADAPTION: Hardy to about 10°F (−12°C); no heat problems; best for the deserts and California's Central Valley.

CULTURE: Needs good drainage. Minimal water requirement but looks best with periodic, deep irrigation in the warmest months. Apply 2 oz. (57 g) ammonium sulfate in the early spring after the plant's first year in the landscape. No pruning needed unless training as a tree. Propagate by seeds; file to encourage germination.

POSSIBLE PROBLEMS: Poisonous seeds, flowers attract bees, slow growth, a caterpillar that feeds on the leaves.

Spartium junceum

PRONOUNCER: *spar*-tee-um *jun*-see-um
FAMILY: Leguminosae
COMMON NAME: Spanish broom

Evergreen. Height: 6–10 ft. (2–3 m). Spread: 4–8 ft. (1.2–2.5 m). Rate of growth: Fast. Light requirement: Sun. Native to the Mediterranean region but has naturalized in the western United States.

An upright shrub with many slender, green, nearly leafless branches; grown principally for its flowers. All parts are poisonous if eaten.

FLOWER AND FRUIT: Yellow, fragrant flowers about 1 in. (2.5 cm) long in clusters, March–August, in warm regions and later in colder regions; hairy seed pods follow.

LANDSCAPE USES: Flowering accent plant or as a bank cover for difficult sites, where it is likely to overtake native vegetation; ornamental flowers.

CLIMATE ADAPTION: Hardy to about 10°F (−12°C);

best for coastal and inland southern California and California's Central Valley.

CULTURE: Minimal soil requirement. Looks best with occasional summer watering in the warmest areas. Avoid fertilizer. Prune regularly for more compact growth. Propagate by softwood cuttings or seeds.

POSSIBLE PROBLEMS: Spreads easily; poisonous; caterpillars in southern California.

Tabebuia chrysotricha

PRONOUNCER: *tab*-e-bwee-ah cry-soh-*try*-kah
FAMILY: Bignoniaceae
COMMON NAME: golden trumpet tree

Deciduous. Height: 20–25 ft. (6–7.5 m). Spread: 20–25 ft. (6–7.5 m). Rate of growth: Fast. Light requirement: Sun. Native to South America.

A small, fast-growing tree with dazzling floral displays; dark green leaves in five-fingered, narrow leaflets, about 4 in. (10 cm) long; fuzz on twigs and underneath leaves; spreading, rounded growth.

FLOWER AND FRUIT: Clusters of yellow, trumpet-shaped flowers about 4 in. (10 cm) long in late spring after tree briefly loses leaves; hairy capsules up to 8 in. (20 cm) long.

LANDSCAPE USES: A luxurious-looking patio tree or flowering specimen.

CLIMATE ADAPTION: Hardy to about 25°F (−4°C); no heat problems; best for inland and coastal southern California and milder areas of the low desert.

CULTURE: Soil must drain well. Drought resistant but likes supplemental water every 1–2 weeks in the warmest areas. Minimal fertilizer needs but responds with a better floral display to an application of all-purpose fertilizer in early spring. Keep to single leader until head high; do any selective pruning after spring bloom. Propagate by cuttings, air-layering or seeds.

POSSIBLE PROBLEMS: Young trees need staking.

Tabebuia impetiginosa has pink to lavender flowers. PLATE 194

Tagetes lemmonii PLATE 195

PRONOUNCER: tah-*jee*-teez lem-*mow*-nee-eye
FAMILY: Compositae
COMMON NAME: shrubby marigold

Perennial. Height: 2–3 ft. (60–90 cm). Spread: 2–3 ft. (60–90 cm). Rate of growth: Fast. Light requirement: Sun to part shade. Native from southeast Arizona to Central America.

A shrublike, nearly evergreen plant with 4-in.

(10-cm), finely divided, medium green leaves; strongly aromatic. Related to the annual marigolds.

FLOWER AND FRUIT: Masses of 1-in. (2.5-cm), yellow-orange, daisylike flowers mainly in the late fall but often at other times of the year; one-seeded fruit.

LANDSCAPE USES: A showy, trouble-free, easy-to-grow plant. Good blooming displays. Combine with other flowering shrubs such as autumn sage.

CLIMATE ADAPTION: Freezes to the ground at around 25°F (−4°C) but usually recovers quickly in the spring; widely adaptable; no heat problems but does best with part shade in the low desert.

CULTURE: Minimal soil requirement. Looks best with supplemental water every 1–2 weeks in the summer in hottest areas. Minimal fertilizer. Prune to correct shape and size in the summer; prune close to the ground if damaged by frost. Propagate by seeds.

POSSIBLE PROBLEMS: Foliage odor disagreeable to some; frost damage.

Tagetes lucida is similar to *T. lemmonii* but somewhat smaller.

Tecoma stans PLATE 196

PRONOUNCER: te-*koh*-ma stanz
FAMILY: Bignoniaceae
COMMON NAME: yellow bells

Evergreen to deciduous. Height: 6–8 ft. (2–2.5 m). Spread: 6–8 ft. (2–2.5 m). Rate of growth: Moderate. Light requirement: Sun. Native from west Texas to Florida.

Large, upright shrub with delightful flowers and attractive, 4–8 in. (10–20 cm) leaves with 7–9, narrow, medium green leaflets. The more commonly available form can reach 20 ft. (6 m) over several years if not top-killed by frost. Better in desert areas is the smaller *T. stans* var. *angustata*, a Southwest native with smaller leaflets, less foliage.

FLOWER AND FRUIT: Clusters of 1–2 in. (2.5–5 cm), bell-shaped, slightly fragrant, yellow flowers show almost constantly in warm months but most heavily in spring and fall; followed by slender pods about 3 in. (8 cm) long.

LANDSCAPE USES: For tropical effect and flowers in a specimen plant or as a background screen; fine accent against evergreen background. Flowers attract hummingbirds.

CLIMATE ADAPTION: Roots are hardy but top growth may be cut to ground around 25°F (−4°C); recovers quickly in spring; grows larger in frost-free conditions. Loves heat. Widely adaptable.

CULTURE: Needs good drainage. Needs little water but looks best during blooming period with moderate amounts. Looks best with 2 oz. (57 g) ammonium sulfate in early spring. Prune dead matter when plant begins to leaf out; blossoms appear on new growth. Propagate by seeds or semihardwood cuttings.

POSSIBLE PROBLEMS: Late frost can cut back just as plant is starting to look great; seed pods; flowers attract bees.

Teucrium

PRONOUNCER: *too*-kree-um
FAMILY: Labiatae

Teucrium chamaedrys is low and spreading with showy purple flowers, well-suited as a ground cover or border plant.

Teucrium fruticans

PRONOUNCER: *too*-kree-um *froo*-ti-canz
COMMON NAME: bush germander

Evergreen. Height: 4–6 ft. (1.2–2 m). Spread: 4–6 ft. (1.2–2 m). Rate of growth: Moderate. Light requirement: Sun. Native to Europe.

Medium-sized shrub with oval to elliptic leaves, gray-green above and whitish below; stems white.

FLOWER AND FRUIT: Lavender, bell-shaped flowers in terminal spikes nearly year-round; small nutlets.

LANDSCAPE USES: Light-colored leaves and stems make it a good choice for contrast with darker greens, especially in California, where it does best.

CLIMATE ADAPTION: Cold and heat tolerant; widely adaptable.

CULTURE: Needs good drainage. Water about every 2–3 weeks in the summer in hot areas, but avoid overwatering. Apply 2 oz. (57 g) ammonium sulfate or balanced fertilizer in early spring to speed growth. Prune in early spring for more compact growth. Propagate by cuttings.

POSSIBLE PROBLEMS: Develops root rot with excess summer watering, especially in low-desert settings.

Teucrium fruticans var. *compactum* is lower growing and more compact.   PLATE 197

Trichostema lanatum   PLATE 198

PRONOUNCER: try-*kah*-stem-ah lah-*nah*-tum
FAMILY: Labiatae
COMMON NAME: woolly blue curls

Evergreen. Height: 3–5 ft. (1–1.5 m). Spread: 2–3 ft. (60–90 cm). Rate of growth: Fast. Light requirement: Sun to partial shade. Native to the coastal foothills of California.

A multibranched, erect to spreading shrub with narrow, 1–2 in. (2.5–5 cm) leaves, dark green on top, white underneath; leaf edges tend to roll under.

FLOWER AND FRUIT: Clusters of tubular, blue flowers with arching stamens on long stalks from April through much of the summer; their woolly appearance provides the common name; one-seeded nutlets.

LANDSCAPE USES: A handsome accent plant for a sunny hillside or for naturalizing in wildflower displays; long blooming period.

CLIMATE ADAPTION: Hardy to about 10°F (−12°C); best for coastal and inland southern California; needs afternoon shade in California's Central Valley; does not tolerate desert heat.

CULTURE: Needs near-perfect drainage. Minimal water requirement; likes infrequent, supplemental watering in the summer in warmer areas. Avoid fertilizer. Remove old flower stalks to prolong bloom. Propagate by seeds and cuttings.

POSSIBLE PROBLEMS: Overwatering; short lived.

Umbellularia californica

PRONOUNCER: um-bell-ewe-*lair*-ee-ah cal-i-*for*-ni-cah
FAMILY: Lauraceae
COMMON NAME: California bay, California laurel

Evergreen. Height: 20–50 ft. (6–15 m). Spread: 30–50 ft. (9–15 m). Rate of growth: Slow. Light requirement: Sun to shade. Native to California chapparal and mountains into Oregon.

Usually seen as a dense, rounded tree but sometimes as a large shrub; multitrunked with stiff, ascending branches; leaves 3–5 in. (8–13 cm) long and 0.7–1.5 in. (2–4 cm) wide, very aromatic, glossy green above, paler beneath.

FLOWER AND FRUIT: Small, yellow flowers in dense clusters in the early spring; plumlike, fleshy fruit about 1 in. (2.5 cm) from late summer into fall.

LANDSCAPE USES: Screening, multitrunked tree or large hedge. The dried leaves sometimes are used as a substitute for sweet bay, *Laurus nobilis*, as a culinary herb. In youth, makes a fine large container plant for many years.

CLIMATE ADAPTION: Hardy to about 10°F (−12°C); widely adaptable, but provide shade in the deserts.

CULTURE: Needs good drainage. Withstands some drought but best with ample water in the warmest months. Most commonly seen in moist places in the wild. After the plant's first year in the ground, apply an all-purpose fertilizer under the leaf canopy in the spring to promote growth; use 1 lb. (0.45 kg) 10–6–4 per inch (2.5 cm) of trunk diameter. Thin the crown regularly; withstands heavy pruning and may be trained to a single trunk; tolerates clipping to form a hedge. Propagate by seeds.

POSSIBLE PROBLEMS: Foliage odor unpleasant to some; tree may topple if the crown is not thinned.

Ungnadia speciosa PLATE 199
PRONOUNCER: ung-*nay*-dee-ah spee-see-*oh*-sah
FAMILY: Sapindaceae
COMMON NAME: Mexican buckeye

Deciduous. Height: 10–20 ft. (3–6 m). Spread: 8–15 ft. (2.5–4.5 m). Rate of growth: Slow. Light requirement: Sun. Native to southwest Texas, New Mexico and Mexico.

A large shrub or small tree, often multi-trunked; light gray bark; light green, 6–12 in. (15–30 cm) leaves with 5–7 leaflets; densely branched.

FLOWER AND FRUIT: Fragrant, small, pink flowers appear in clusters just before the leaves in the spring; about 1-in. (2.5-cm), woody capsules in the fall. Seeds are poisonous.

LANDSCAPE USES: Attractive as a small specimen tree or a tall background shrub. Resists Texas root rot.

CLIMATE ADAPTION: Hardy to about 0°F (−18°C); no heat problems; best for the deserts.

CULTURE: Needs good drainage. Minimal water requirement but appreciates once-a-month, deep watering in hottest periods. Minimal fertilizer needed but responds to nitrogen. Prune to shape; train to a single trunk, if desired. Propagate by seeds.

POSSIBLE PROBLEMS: Poisonous seeds; wood is brittle; suckers.

Vauquelinia
PRONOUNCER: vah-kwa-*lin*-ee-ah
FAMILY: Rosaceae

Vauquelinia angustifolia is similar to *V. californica*, but with much narrower leaves.

Vauquelinia californica PLATE 200
PRONOUNCER: vah-kwa-*lin*-ee-ah cal-i-*for*-ni-cah
COMMON NAME: Arizona rosewood

Evergreen. Height: 8–15 ft. (2.5–4.5 m). Spread: 5–7 ft. (1.5–2.2 m). Rate of growth: Slow. Light requirement: Sun to partial shade. Native to southern Arizona and northern Mexico.

A large shrub or small tree with dense, dark green foliage resembling oleander (*Nerium*); lance-shaped, leathery leaves about 3 in. (8 cm) long, 0.5 in. (1.3 cm) wide; gray to reddish bark; numerous, erect branches.

FLOWER AND FRUIT: Clusters of tiny, white flowers in summer followed by tiny, black capsules.

LANDSCAPE USES: Handsome as an unpruned hedge, a tall specimen shrub or for screening; may be trained into about a 15-ft. (4.5-m) tree with little effort. An alternate choice to oleanders. Space 4 ft. (1.2 m) apart for clipped hedge.

CLIMATE ADAPTION: Hardy to about 0°F (−18°C), no heat problem; best in the deserts.

CULTURE: Minimal soil requirement; likes good drainage. Minimal water requirement but does best with 2–4 in. (5–10 cm) monthly in the summer. Apply 2 oz. (57 g) ammonium sulfate in early spring after the plant begins growing well. Prune only for training or to control size. Propagate by fresh seeds or semihardwood cuttings.

POSSIBLE PROBLEMS: Spider mites or aphids; young plants are slow starting and need protection from rabbits.

Verbena
PRONOUNCER: ver-*bee*-nah
FAMILY: Verbenaceae

About 100 species of verbena are known, most of them native to the warmer parts of North and South America. Some perennials are valued as flowering ground covers. Flower colors range from red to pink to purple. Those included here provide some of the best purples for the garden. Other popular species include *V. peruviana* and *V. hybrida*.

Verbena gooddingii PLATE 201
PRONOUNCER: ver-*bee*-nah good-*ing*-ee-eye
COMMON NAME: Goodding verbena

Perennial. Height: 1–1.5 ft. (30–45 cm). Spread: 1–2 ft. (30–60 cm). Rate of growth: Fast. Light requirement: Sun. Native to the Southwest and northwestern Mexico.

A low grower with light green, deeply cut, oval leaves to 1 in. (2.5 cm) long accented for

133

Viguiera deltoidea var. *parishii*

long periods by bright flowers.

FLOWER AND FRUIT: Flat clusters of lavender-pink flowers on short spikes much of the year; small nutlets.

LANDSCAPE USES: Best as a short-lived ground cover. Plant 2 ft. (60 cm) apart for massing or combining in a bright, perennial border with other verbenas, blackfoot daisies and mealycup sage. Reseeds if moisture is adequate.

CLIMATE ADAPTION: Hardy to at least 15°F (−9°C); widely adaptable but better in the deserts.

CULTURE: Needs good drainage. Likes some supplemental watering while flowering, about once every 7–10 days in the hottest areas; cut back in the cooler months. Little to no fertilizer, but light nitrogen revitalizes plants in summer heat. Prune to groom. Propagate by softwood cuttings or seeds.

POSSIBLE PROBLEMS: Short lived.

Verbena rigida

PLATE 202

PRONOUNCER: ver-*bee*-nah *ri*-ji-dah

COMMON NAME: venosa

Perennial. Height: 8–18 in. (20–45 cm). Spread: 1.5–2 ft. (45–60 cm). Rate of growth: Fast. Light requirement: Sun. Native to Brazil, Argentina.

A low grower with rigid, oblong, dark green leaves, 2–4 in. (5–10 cm) long on a spreading plant; leaves are toothed, have a sandpapery feel; spreads by underground stems (rhizomes).

FLOWER AND FRUIT: Deep purple-blue flowers in round clusters on stiff stems rise above the plants in the spring and fall; tiny nutlets.

LANDSCAPE USES: Attractive when massed or used in borders, median plantings or other low-maintenance areas.

CLIMATE ADAPTION: Hardy to at least 15°F (−9°C); widely adaptable; may die back in colder areas but resprouts in the spring from the rhizomes.

CULTURE: Needs good drainage; vigorous in good soil but not as aggressive in less favorable conditions. Drought tolerant; needs watering every 1–2 weeks in summer in the hottest areas. No fertilizer needed unless grown as an annual, when ammonium phosphate may be applied sparingly. Prune to groom. Propagate by cuttings or seeds.

POSSIBLE PROBLEMS: Poor appearance when not flowering.

Verbena tenuisecta

PLATE 203

PRONOUNCER: ver-*bee*-nah ten-ewe-i-*sek*-tah

COMMON NAME: false sand verbena

Evergreen. Height: 3–6 in. (8–15 cm). Spread: 3–4 ft. (about 1 m). Rate of growth: Fast.

Light requirement: Sun to partial shade. Native to South America.

A low-growing, spreading ground cover with finely dissected, bright green foliage.

FLOWER AND FRUIT: Purple flower clusters in the spring and summer and often well into the fall; tiny nutlets.

LANDSCAPE USES: Excellent for massing on banks, slopes or in rock gardens; provides brilliant color for long periods; spreads naturally.

CLIMATE ADAPTION: Takes heat and cold from the higher deserts to coastal areas; widely adaptable.

CULTURE: Needs good drainage. Prefers weekly watering in the low desert in the summer; less elsewhere and at other times of the year; avoid overwatering. Apply light amounts of a balanced fertilizer in the early spring. Prune to contain, as necessary; can be mowed in the spring. Propagate from cuttings or seeds.

POSSIBLE PROBLEMS: Overwatering.

Viguiera deltoidea var. parishii

PRONOUNCER: vig-wee-*air*-ah del-*toy*-dee-ah pa-rish-ee-eye

FAMILY: Compositae

COMMON NAME: goldeneye, desert sunflower

Evergreen. Height: 2–3 ft. (60–90 cm). Spread: 2–5 ft. (60 cm–1.5 m). Rate of growth: Slow. Light requirement: Sun. Native to Arizona, Nevada, California and Baja California.

A multibranched shrub. Slender, hairy, tan-to-brown branches are erect with triangular to oval, hairy, toothed, 0.5–1.5 in. (1.3–4 cm), dull green leaves opposite or alternate on short petioles. There are about a dozen species of goldeneyes native to the Southwest, but this variety is probably the most widely adapted.

FLOWER AND FRUIT: Bright yellow, daisylike flowers in the spring, about 1 in. (2.5 cm) across on long stems; followed by small, oblong, one-seeded fruit.

LANDSCAPE USES: Looks attractive year-round, particularly when the flowers contrast with the leaves; good in borders or massed as a ground cover.

CLIMATE ADAPTION: Hardy to about 15°F (−9°C); no problems with heat; widely adaptable except for higher deserts.

CULTURE: Needs good drainage. Prefers infrequent summer watering in hot areas. Minimal fertilizer. Cut back from time to time to maintain a rounded form. Propagate by softwood cuttings or seeds.

POSSIBLE PROBLEMS: Overwatering.

Viguiera dentata, a hardy shrub from the Southwest and Mexico, reaches about 5 ft. (1.5 m).
PLATE 204

Viguiera laciniata, the San Diego sunflower, grows
to about 4 ft. (1.2 m); lacy, dissected foliage and
butter yellow flowers. PLATE 205

Viguiera stenoloba, the skeleton-leaf goldeneye, is
somewhat larger than *V. deltoidea* var. *parishii*
and has threadlike leaves.

Vitex agnus-castus PLATE 206
PRONOUNCER: *vy*-tex *ag*-nus *kas*-tus
FAMILY: Verbenaceae
COMMON NAME: chaste tree

Deciduous. Height: 15–25 ft. (4.5–7.5 m).
Spread: 20–25 ft. (6–7.5 m). Rate of growth:
Fast. Light requirement: Sun to partial shade.
Native to southern Europe; has naturalized in
Arizona.

Picturesque gray-green foliage and gray
bark; wide canopy; usually multitrunked; leaves
are fan-shaped, narrow, pointed leaflets 2–6 in.
(5–15 cm) long.

FLOWER AND FRUIT: Numerous, 7-in. (18-cm)
flower spikes in late spring; usually blue but
there are cultivars with rose and white flowers;
tiny, round "peppers" follow bloom.

LANDSCAPE USES: Specimen tree or large shrub
with irrigation; without it, remains about a 6-ft.
(2-m) shrub. Handsome branch structure after
leaves fall. In desert landscaping provides interesting foil to *Caesalpinia gilliesii* (yellow bird of
paradise). Good wind tolerance.

CLIMATE ADAPTION: Hardy to at least 0°F (−18°C)
but does best in heat; widely adaptable.

CULTURE: Minimal soil requirement. Moderate
water needs if grown as a tree; little or none if
growing as a shrub; better flowering with drier
conditions. Apply 8 oz. (225 g) ammonium
sulfate in late winter. Remove dead wood and
shape during dormant season. Propagate by
seeds or softwood cuttings.

POSSIBLE PROBLEMS: Sometimes develops wood
rot.

Washingtonia
PRONOUNCER: wash-ing-*toe*-nee-ah
FAMILY: Palmae

Palm-lined avenues are a common sight in
Southwest cities and the *Washingtonia* fan palms
are probably the most widely used. The tall,
thin-trunked Mexican fan palm and the stout
California fan palm offer distinctly different

forms. Due to their size, both are better suited to
public areas and large-scale landscapes. Intermediate forms may or may not be true hybrids.
Both species and hybrids are commonly available in the nursery trade.

The best time to plant palms is during the
warmer months from April to September. Roots
grow actively at this time, so plants recover
more easily from transplanting.

Washingtonia filifera PLATE 207
PRONOUNCER: wash-ing-*toe*-nee-ah fy-*lif*-ur-ah
COMMON NAME: California fan palm

Evergreen. Height: 20–45 ft. (6–13.5 m).
Spread: 10–15 ft. (3–4.5 m). Rate of growth:
Slow. Light requirement: Sun. Native to the
Mojave and Sonoran deserts in Arizona, Cali-
fornia and Nevada.

A heavy-trunked, erect fan palm with a
rounded crown formed by spreading leaves;
petioles about 3 ft. (1 m) long with stout,
hooked thorns. Dead leaves hang against the
trunk in a thick thatch.

FLOWER AND FRUIT: Long streamers emerge from
the crown in summer and develop small, white
flowers and black berries about 0.5 in. (1.3 cm)
long.

LANDSCAPE USES: Dramatic in large landscapes—
parks, commercial sites, along streets; too massive for the typical home landscape.

CLIMATE ADAPTION: Hardy to about 17°F (−8°C);
no heat problems; widely adaptable and one of
the best palms for the high desert.

CULTURE: Prefers rich soil but is quite tolerant.
Needs deep irrigation every 2–3 weeks in the
warmest months; taper off in winter. Apply 3–4
lbs. (1.5–2 kg) ammonium sulfate yearly to an
established plant with a 10-ft. (3-m) watering
basin, half in late winter and the other half in
early summer. Adjust the amount of fertilizer
for smaller trees. Remove thatch to keep the
form orderly. Propagate by seeds.

POSSIBLE PROBLEMS: Eventual size; palm bud rot;
thatch left on the tree is a fire hazard and haven
for rodents.

Washingtonia robusta PLATE 208
PRONOUNCER: wash-ing-*toe*-nee-ah row-*bus*-tah
COMMON NAME: Mexican fan palm

Evergreen. Height: 50–90 ft. (15–27 m).
Spread: 10–12 ft. (3–3.5 m). Rate of growth:
Fast. Light requirement: Sun. Native to Mexico.

A fast-growing, slender-trunked palm
producing a skyline silhouette very popular in
many southwestern cities.

FLOWER AND FRUIT: Long streamers in spring produce tiny, white flowers followed by small,

blackish berries.

LANDSCAPE USES: Looks best in groupings or rows, but use only in large landscapes; not for the average home landscape.

CLIMATE ADAPTION: Hardy to about 22°F (−5°C); no heat problems; widely adaptable except in the higher deserts.

CULTURE: Needs good drainage. Likes 6–8 in. (15–20 cm) of water every 2–3 weeks in the summer, applied slowly; taper off in the winter. For a large tree with a 10-ft. (3-m) watering basin, apply 2 lbs. (0.9 kg) ammonium sulfate in early spring and again in early summer. Water fertilizer in deeply. Adjust fertilizer proportionally for smaller trees. Prune to remove shag and old leaves. Propagate by seeds.

POSSIBLE PROBLEMS: Eventual size; will in time require professional grooming, which is expensive.

Xylosma congestum PLATE 209

PRONOUNCER: zy-*los*-mah con-*jess*-tum

FAMILY: Flacourtiaceae

COMMON NAME: shiny xylosma

Evergreen. Height: 6–20 ft. (2–6 m). Spread: 8–10 ft. (2.5–3 m). Rate of growth: Moderate. Light requirement: Sun to partial shade. Native to China.

Single- or multitrunked large shrub or small tree with shiny, light green foliage that has a bronze cast when new; leaves about 2 in. (5 cm) long, oval and pointed, with toothed margins. 'Compacta' is smaller, with tighter growth and branching; smaller leaves.

FLOWER AND FRUIT: Inconspicuous green flowers in the spring; tiny, round fruit.

LANDSCAPE USES: A first-rate plant in most situations; specimen shrub or small tree as well as a hedge. Easily trained and can be maintained at just about any size or form. Requires minimal maintenance.

CLIMATE ADAPTION: Hardy to about 15°F (−9°C); no heat problems; widely adaptable.

CULTURE: Needs good drainage. Tolerates some drought but likes twice-monthly, deep irrigation in the hottest areas in the summer. Minimal fertilizer needed. Clip it anytime but defer heavy pruning to the early spring. Propagate by leaf cuttings.

POSSIBLE PROBLEMS: Spider mites; scale; new growth sometimes damaged by late-spring frost; iron chlorosis in heavy alkaline soil; Texas root rot.

Yucca

PRONOUNCER: *yuk*-ah

FAMILY: Agavaceae

Like the agaves, yuccas are superb accent plants in the landscape. Yuccas, however, offer an added vertical dimension since many are treelike in habit. They blend well with other succulent and accent plants, such as palms, agaves and cactus. But they should not be confined to such uses for they make fine focal points when combined with soft-textured trees and shrubs such as acacias, Texas sage and cassias.

Yuccas are truly low-maintenance plants. They survive on minimal rainfall once established but should be watered occasionally to keep leaves fresh and plump. Pay heed to their sharp tips.

Yucca aloifolia

PRONOUNCER: *yuk*-ah al-oh-i-*foh*-lee-ah

COMMON NAME: Spanish bayonet

Evergreen. Height: 8–10 ft. (2.5–3 m). Spread: 4–6 ft. (1.2–2 m). Rate of growth: Slow. Light requirement: Sun to partial shade. Native to the West Indies, southern United States and Mexico.

Light green, narrow, 1–1.5 ft. (30–45 cm), stiff leaves are set close together along stalks that range from sprawling to leaning to erect; the tips are exceptionally sharp.

FLOWER AND FRUIT: Clusters of white flowers up to 4 in. (10 cm) wide on 2-ft. (60-cm) stalks in summer; green, oblong capsules, 2 × 1 in. (5 × 2.5 cm) long which become black at maturity follow.

LANDSCAPE USES: A striking foliage plant for arid landscapes in groupings, as a specimen or in containers. Leaves can be trimmed to provide a palmlike appearance in tropical gardens.

CLIMATE ADAPTION: Hardy to about 10°F (−12°C), no heat problems; widely adaptable.

CULTURE: Needs good drainage. Minimal water requirement but maintains greener look with moderate amounts monthly in the summer. Little to no fertilizer needed. Trim leaf stalks as needed to keep in bounds; remove old flower stalks. Propagate by seeds, offsets or cut leaf stalks dried in a protected location for a couple of weeks before planting.

POSSIBLE PROBLEMS: Extremely sharp-tipped leaves; agave snout weevil.

Yucca aloifolia 'Marginata' has yellow-margined leaves.

Yucca baccata
PRONOUNCER: *yuk*-ah bah-*kah*-tah
COMMON NAME: banana yucca

Evergreen. Height: 2–3 ft. (60–90 cm). Spread: 2–4 ft. (60 cm–1.2 m). Rate of growth: Slow. Light requirement: Sun. Native to Southwest deserts and Mexico.

A clumping yucca with thick, blue-green leaves about 2 ft. (60 cm) long and 2–3 in. (5–8 cm) wide with coarse, marginal threads.

FLOWER AND FRUIT: White flowers in 2–3 ft. (60–90 cm) clusters in the spring followed by fleshy fruit which can be eaten raw or dried; fruit varies from 4–9 in. (10–23 cm) long and 2–3 in. (5–8 cm) in diameter, with numerous seeds.

LANDSCAPE USES: For desert-plant groupings or as an individual specimen. Fibers of the leaves are much used in native crafts. A soap substitute known as *amole* is made from the roots.

CLIMATE ADAPTION: Hardy to at least 10°F (−12°C); best for deserts.

CULTURE: Requires good drainage. Minimal water requirement. No fertilizer. Prune to remove old leaves. Propagate by offsets or seeds.

POSSIBLE PROBLEMS: Sharp-pointed leaves.

Yucca brevifolia　　　　PLATE 210
PRONOUNCER: *yuk*-ah bre-vi-*foh*-lee-ah
COMMON NAME: Joshua tree

Evergreen. Height: 10–25 ft. (3–7.5 m). Spread: 5–10 ft. (1.5–3 m). Rate of growth: Slow. Light requirement: Sun. Native to Mojave Desert areas of Arizona, California, Nevada and Utah.

A picturesque, treelike plant with narrow, sharp, dull green leaves about 12 in. (30 cm) long at the top of a tall, wide trunk or at the ends of irregularly shaped branches.

FLOWER AND FRUIT: Clusters of 12-in. (30-cm), white, lilylike flowers in the late spring at the ends of the branches; 2.5–4 in. (6–10 cm) fruit.

LANDSCAPE USES: A dramatic accent plant in groupings with other desert plants such as agave, cactus, nolina and other yucca species. May be collected in the wild with a state tag. Difficult to establish.

CLIMATE ADAPTION: Hardy to about 10°F (−12°C); no heat problems; best for the deserts.

CULTURE: Needs good drainage. Best with some supplemental water in the warmest months but drought tolerant. No fertilizer. Remove old leaves. Propagate by offsets handled as cuttings.

POSSIBLE PROBLEMS: Staking until they reroot; small plants are slow to form a trunk.

Yucca elata　　　　PLATE 211
PRONOUNCER: *yuk*-ah e-*lah*-tah
COMMON NAME: soaptree

Evergreen. Height: 8–15 ft. (2.5–4.5 m). Spread: 4–12 ft. (1.2–3.5 m). Rate of growth: Slow. Light requirement: Sun to partial shade. Native from southwest Texas to Arizona and Mexico.

Light green, grasslike leaves, 0.5 in. (1.3 cm) wide, 2–3 ft. (60–90 cm) long; has the appearance of a short-trunked, small tree with brownish, fissured bark; thick thatch. Common name comes from the soapy liquid derived from the roots.

FLOWER AND FRUIT: Fragrant, white flower clusters on about 6-ft. (2-m) stalks in late spring; brown, oblong, 2-in. (5-cm) fruit capsules ripen in the early fall. The state flower of New Mexico.

LANDSCAPE USES: A large, erect specimen shrub for dramatic accent; probably the most widely planted desert yucca. Its leaf fibers are widely used for craft projects.

CLIMATE ADAPTION: Hardy to at least 10°F (−12°C); widely adaptable.

CULTURE: Needs good drainage. Minimal water requirement but looks best with monthly watering in the warmest areas in the summer. No fertilizer needed. Remove old flower stalks and dead leaves as desired. Propagate by offsets or seeds.

POSSIBLE PROBLEMS: May be difficult to transplant due to its long taproot.

Yucca recurvifolia　　　　PLATE 212
PRONOUNCER: *yuk*-ah re-cur-vi-*foh*-lee-ah
COMMON NAME: pendulous yucca

Evergreen. Height: 6–10 ft. (2–3 m). Spread: 4–6 ft. (1.2–2 m). Rate of growth: Moderate. Light requirement: Sun to partial shade. Native to the southeastern United States and Mexico.

Bold, dark green, 3-ft. (90-cm) leaves on one to several branches; leaves soft tipped, about 3 in. (8 cm) wide at the base. The leaves curve downward, hence the common name. Offsets will in time lead to the formation of large groups.

FLOWER AND FRUIT: 2-ft. (60-cm) clusters of small, white flowers on about 4-ft. (1.2-m) stalks in late spring; oblong capsules, 1–2 in. (2.5–5 cm) with numerous seeds.

LANDSCAPE USES: An accent plant for a tropical effect in low-maintenance areas; good near traffic areas. Useful in large containers. Of easy culture, very common.

CLIMATE ADAPTION: Hardy to about 20°F (−6.5°C); no heat problems; widely adaptable except for the higher deserts.

CULTURE: Needs good drainage. Prefers supplemental watering every 3–4 weeks in the summer in hot areas. Little to no fertilizer needed. Remove old flower stalks after bloom; cut back or remove foliage for shaping. Propagate by offsets or seeds.

POSSIBLE PROBLEMS: Agave snout weevil can kill; aphids as flowers begin to open; unpruned plants may become leggy.

Yucca rigida PLATE 213
PRONOUNCER: *yuk*-ah *ri*-ji-dah
COMMON NAME: blue yucca

Evergreen. Height: 12–15 ft. (3.5–4.5 m). Spread: 5–6 ft. (1.5–2 m). Rate of growth: Slow to moderate. Light requirement: Sun. Native to the Chihuahuan Desert of Mexico.

A branching yucca with narrow, blue-green leaves up to 3 ft. (90 cm) long.

FLOWER AND FRUIT: White flowers on stalks in the spring followed by capsules.

LANDSCAPE USES: An accent plant with handsome foliage that makes for excellent contrasts in desert landscapes.

CLIMATE ADAPTION: Cold and heat tolerant in the low to higher deserts, where it is best suited.

CULTURE: Needs good drainage. Little to no supplemental watering or fertilizer. Remove old, dried leaves and flower stalks. Propagate by seeds and offsets.

POSSIBLE PROBLEMS: Persistent thatch.

Yucca schidigera PLATE 214
PRONOUNCER: *yuk*-ah shy-*dij*-er-ah
COMMON NAME: Mojave yucca

Evergreen. Height: 3–15 ft. (1–4.5 m). Spread: 3–8 ft. (1–2.5 m). Rate of growth: Slow. Light requirement: Sun. Native to the Mojave Desert, where it is very common, the southern California chaparral and Baja California.

A branched or unbranched yucca with thick, stiff, medium to yellowish green leaves up to 3.5 ft. (about 1 m) long and about 1.5 in. (4 cm) wide. The leaf margins are conspicuously fibery.

FLOWER AND FRUIT: Cream-colored flowers in clusters on stalks in the late spring; cylindric capsules ripen later.

LANDSCAPE USES: One of the most dramatic yuccas; thick, rigid leaves add a strong sculptural look as an accent or focal point. Indians used the fiber to make rope.

CLIMATE ADAPTION: Frost and heat tolerant in the low- and mid-elevation deserts and inland southern California.

CULTURE: Prefers good drainage. Very drought tolerant; sensitive to too much water. Little to no fertilizer needed. Remove old flower stalks.

Propagate by seeds.

POSSIBLE PROBLEMS: Sharp-tipped leaves.

Yucca whipplei PLATE 215
PRONOUNCER: *yuk*-ah *whip*-lee-eye
COMMON NAME: Our Lord's candle

Evergreen. Height: 2–3 ft. (60–90 cm). Spread: 2–3 ft. (60–90 cm). Rate of growth: Slow. Light requirement: Sun. Native to southern California and northern Mexico.

A trunkless, clumping shrub that flowers only after several years and then dies. Very narrow, gray-green, sharp-tipped leaves about 2 ft. (60 cm) long.

FLOWER AND FRUIT: 5-ft. (1.5-m) clusters of white, lilylike flowers on the end of an 8-ft. (2.5-m), treelike stalk, followed by pods containing many seeds.

LANDSCAPE USES: Barrier groupings or as an accent plant.

CLIMATE ADAPTION: Hardy to at least 15°F (−9°C); no heat problems; widely adaptable.

CULTURE: Needs good drainage. Minimal water requirement. No fertilizer needed. Prune to groom. Propagate by seeds.

POSSIBLE PROBLEMS: Reseeding; dieback after bloom.

Zauschneria
PRONOUNCER: zosh-*neer*-ee-ah
FAMILY: Onagraceae

Zauschneria cana, from coastal California, grows to 2 ft. (60 cm), has threadlike, gray foliage and deep coral blossoms. Many additional cultivars are being tested. PLATE 216

Zauschneria latifolia PLATE 217
PRONOUNCER: zosh-*neer*-ee-ah lat-i-*foh*-lee-ah
COMMON NAME: hummingbird trumpet

Semideciduous. Height: 1–1.5 ft. (30–45 cm). Spread: 2–5 ft. (60 cm–1.5 m). Rate of growth: Fast. Light requirement: Sun to part shade. Native to Arizona, California and Mexico.

An herbaceous, low shrub with light green, oval to narrow leaves about 1 in. (2.5 cm) long; spreads by underground stems (rhizomes).

FLOWER AND FRUIT: Showy, bright red, trumpet-shaped flowers about 1.5–2 in. (4–5 cm) in the summer and fall; many-seeded capsules.

LANDSCAPE USES: Ground cover or in borders for difficult areas; a late-season bloomer when few other plants give color.

CLIMATE ADAPTION: Widely adaptable; dies to the ground most winters but resprouts in the spring; thrives in heat.

CULTURE: Minimal soil requirement. Minimal water requirement except in summer, when it needs some at least twice monthly. Little to no fertilizer. Cut back dead stems in the winter; pinch young shoots to develop a compact plant. Propagate by seeds and cuttings.

POSSIBLE PROBLEMS: Highly invasive; scraggly winter appearance.

Zinnia

PRONOUNCER: *zin*-ee-ah
FAMILY: Compositae

Zinnia acerosa, with white flowers and gray foliage, is more drought tolerant but not as showy as Z. *grandiflora*.

Zinnia grandiflora   PLATE 218

PRONOUNCER: *zin*-ee-ah grand-i-*flor*-ah
COMMON NAME: desert zinnia

Perennial. Height: 6–12 in. (15–30 cm). Spread: 1–1.5 ft. (30–45 cm). Rate of growth: Fast. Light requirement: Sun. Native to Southwest and Mexico.

A spreading, low-growing ground cover with narrow, light green leaves about 1 in. (2.5 cm) long; spreads horizontally by underground stems (rhizomes).

FLOWER AND FRUIT: Golden yellow flowers with orange centers about 1.5 in. (4 cm) across; blooms from spring to fall; one-seeded fruit.

LANDSCAPE USES: Ground cover, especially for control of soil erosion, and in borders, or mix with other low-growing perennials such as blackfoot daisy.

CLIMATE ADAPTION: Heat tolerant; best for the deserts.

CULTURE: Prefers good drainage. Minimal water requirement except in the low desert where it looks and blooms better with supplemental watering twice a month in the summer. No fertilizer. Prune to groom after flowering. Propagate by seeds or divisions.

POSSIBLE PROBLEMS: Plants in the ground are difficult to transplant.

Ziziphus

PRONOUNCER: *zi*-zi-fus
FAMILY: Rhamnaceae

The more commonly seen jujubes are a study in contrasts. One, the gray thorn, is a sprawling shrub from the North American deserts. The other, the Chinese date, is a fruit-bearing, medium-sized tree. But both do extremely well in warm, arid landscapes with little care.

Ziziphus jujuba

PRONOUNCER: *zi*-zi-fus *joo*-joo-bah
COMMON NAME: Chinese date

Deciduous. Height: 20–25 ft. (6–7.5 m). Spread: 15–20 ft. (4.5–6 m). Rate of growth: Slow. Light requirement: Sun. Native from China to southeastern Europe.

An upright tree with handsome foliage; brown, shaggy bark and gnarled, drooping, usually prickly branches; short trunk; leaves are 1–3 in. (2.5–8 cm) long, shiny, bright green and provide a yellow show in the fall. Deep and wide root system; suckers form extended groves unless controlled. The cultivar 'Inermis' is thornless.

FLOWER AND FRUIT: Small, yellow to white flowers in clusters, April–June; shiny, reddish brown, 2 in. (5 cm) long, edible fruits in the fall resemble dates and have an applelike flavor. They need a hot summer to ripen. The main fruiting cultivars are 'Li' and 'Lang', of which 'Lang' is the most popular. The first fruit appears a few years after planting.

LANDSCAPE USES: A specimen or shade tree for difficult locations with attractive foliage and fruit. Easy to grow with little care. The fruit is relished in many cultures around the world, particularly as a dessert. This tree has been cultivated for thousands of years.

CLIMATE ADAPTION: Hardy to about −20°F (−29°C); no heat problems; widely adaptable.

CULTURE: Needs good drainage; accepts alkaline and saline soils. Likes monthly, deep watering in all areas but adapts to desert conditions and, oddly, also thrives in lawn-sprinkler situations. Irrigation is needed for the best-quality fruit. Minimal to no fertilizer needed, but 4 oz. (115 g) ammonium sulfate applied in the late winter after the tree has been in the landscape a year speeds growth. Prune in the winter to shape. Propagate by seeds, softwood cuttings or grafting.

POSSIBLE PROBLEMS: Suckering; Texas root rot in the desert; birds relish the fruit; ants may become problem.

Ziziphus obtusifolia canescens   PLATE 219

PRONOUNCER: *zi*-zi-fus ob-toos-i-*foh*-lee-ah cah-*nes*-enz
COMMON NAME: gray thorn

Deciduous. Height: 4–12 ft. (1.2–3.5 m). Spread: 6–12 ft. (2–3.5 m). Rate of growth: Slow. Light requirement: Sun. Native to Arizona, California, Utah and northern Mexico.

A sprawling, spiny shrub with gray, smooth bark and oval, gray-green leaves about 0.5 in. (1.3 cm) on stiff branches; thorns are the same size or larger than the leaves.

FLOWER AND FRUIT: Insignificant, red flower clusters on twigs in the spring are followed by an edible, oval, blue to black fruit that is up to 0.3 in. (about 1 cm) long and is a favorite of quail.

LANDSCAPE USES: Screening, barrier or background shrub; with pruning, makes a good specimen; bird cover and shelter in naturalized areas.

CLIMATE ADAPTION: No heat or cold problems in the deserts, where it does best.

CULTURE: Needs good drainage. Likes monthly, deep irrigation in the summer. No fertilizer, but 2 oz. (57 g) ammonium sulfate in late winter speeds growth. Remove lower branches to form a canopy and expose the attractive bark. Propagate by seeds.

POSSIBLE PROBLEMS: Thorns; may not be readily available from commercial nurseries.

Recommended Reading

Benson, Lyman, and Robert Darrow. *Trees and Shrubs of the Southwestern Deserts.* 3rd ed. Tucson: University of Arizona Press, 1981.

Desert Plants. Frank S. Crosswhite, editor. Quarterly magazine published by the University of Arizona at the Boyce Thompson Southwestern Arboretum, Superior, Arizona, 1979–91.

Duffield, Mary Rose, and Warren D. Jones. *Plants for Dry Climates.* Tucson, Arizona: H. P. Books, 1981.

Emery, Dara E. *Seed Propagation of Native California Plants.* Santa Barbara, California: Santa Barbara Botanic Garden, 1988.

Gentry, Howard Scott. *Agaves of Continental North America.* Tucson: University of Arizona Press, 1982.

Harris, Richard W. *Arboriculture: Care of Trees, Shrubs and Vines in the Landscape.* Englewood Cliffs, New Jersey: Prentice-Hall, 1983.

Hartman, Hudson, and Dale Kester. *Plant Propagation: Principles and Practices.* 4th ed. Englewood Cliffs, New Jersey: Prentice-Hall, 1983.

Lenz, Lee W., and John Dourley. *California Native Trees and Shrubs.* Claremont, California: Rancho Santa Ana Botanic Garden, 1981.

McPherson, Gregory E., and Charles Sacamano. *Southwestern Landscaping That Saves Energy and Water.* Tucson: The Arizona Board of Regents, University of Arizona, 1989.

Nokes, Jill. *How to Grow Native Plants of Texas and the Southwest.* Austin: Texas Monthly Press, 1986.

Northington, David K., and J. R. Goodin. *The Botanical World.* St. Louis, Missouri: Times Mirror/Mosby College Publishing, 1984.

Perry, Bob. *Trees and Shrubs for Dry California Landscapes.* San Dimas, California: Land Design Publishing, 1987.

Phillips, Judith. *Southwestern Landscaping with Native Plants.* 2nd ed. Santa Fe: Museum of New Mexico Press, 1988.

Schmidt, Marjorie G. *Growing California Native Plants.* Berkeley: University of California Press, 1980.

Sunset Magazine editors. *Sunset Western Garden Book.* Menlo Park, California: Lane Magazine and Book Co., 1989.

U.S. Department of Agriculture. *Seeds of Woody Plants in the United States.* Agriculture Handbook No. 450. Washington, D.C.: U.S. Government Printing Office, 1974.

Vines, Robert A. *Trees, Shrubs and Woody Vines of the Southwest*. 6th ed. Austin: University of Texas Press, 1986.

Wasowski, Sally, and Andy Wasowski. *Native Texas Plants: Landscaping Region by Region*. Austin: Texas Monthly Press, 1988.

Western Fertilizer Handbook, published by the California Fertilizer Association, 2222 Watt Ave., Sacramento, California 95825.

Gardens
Worth Visiting
in the Southwest

The following gardens are well worth a visit for their arid-adapted plant collections. Also look for their occasional plant sales to locate unusual or hard-to-find species and upcoming introductions.

Arizona–Sonora Desert Museum, 2021 N. Kinney Rd., Tucson, Arizona 85743. Telephone: (602) 883-1380. Admission charge.

Boyce Thompson Southwestern Arboretum, three miles west of Superior, Arizona, on U.S. 60. Telephone: (602) 689-2723. Mailing address: P.O. Box AB, Superior, Arizona 85273. Admission charge.

Denver Botanic Gardens, 909 York St., Denver, Colorado 80206. Telephone: (303) 331-4000. Admission charge.

Desert Botanical Garden, 1201 N. Galvin Parkway, Phoenix, Arizona 85008. Telephone: (602) 941-1225. Admission charge.

Living Desert wildlife and botanical park, 47-900 Portola Ave., Palm Desert, California 92260. Telephone: (619) 346-5694. Admission charge.

Los Angeles State and County Arboretum, 301 N. Baldwin Ave., Arcadia, California 91006. Telephone: (818) 446-8251. Admission charge.

Rancho Santa Ana Botanic Garden, 1500 N. College Ave., Claremont, California 91711. Telephone: (714) 625-8767. Admission free.

Santa Barbara Botanic Garden, 1212 Mission Canyon Rd., Santa Barbara, California 93105. Telephone: (805) 682-4726. Admission free.

Tohono Chul Park, 7366 N. Paseo Del Norte, Tucson, Arizona 85704. Telephone: (602) 742-6455. Donation suggested.

Tucson Botanical Gardens, 2150 N. Alvernon Way, Tucson, Arizona 85712. Telephone: (602) 326-9255. Admission charge.

UC–Davis Arboretum, University of California at Davis, California 95616. Telephone: (916) 752-2498. Admission free.

Glossary

Acid soil: Soil with a pH below 7.0, not common in areas of low rainfall.

Alkaline soil: Soil with a pH above 7.0, quite common in the Southwest.

Annual: A plant that completes its life cycle in one year, as contrasted to a perennial or biennial.

Backfill: The planting-hole soil used in transplanting. Usually amendments such as organic matter are added.

Biennial: A plant with a two-year life cycle; flower and fruit production occur in the second year.

Bipinnate: Compound leaves that are twice divided (twice pinnate), often providing a feathery look.

Bulbil: A small bulb usually found on an above-ground part of a plant.

Caliche: An impervious layer of calcium carbonate commonly found in many Southwest soils. Also known as hardpan.

Chaparral: A type of plant community characterized by evergreen, dense-growing, low shrubs of twiggy, thorny habit.

Chelated iron: A formulation either by itself or included in fertilizers for combating iron-deficiency chlorosis. Usually expressed in terms such as Fe 138 or Fe 330.

Chlorosis: An abnormal yellowing of plants, usually caused by iron, nitrogen or other nutrient deficiencies.

Compaction: The compression of soil structure, quite common at construction sites because of the use of heavy equipment.

Compound leaf: A leaf with two or more leaflets.

Conifer: Cone-bearing, evergreen plants with needlelike foliage; evergreens also may be broad-leaved.

Cultivar: A variety of a plant that originated and has persisted under cultivation; a "cultivated variety."

Cuttings. *See* Hardwood cuttings, Semihardwood cuttings *and* Softwood cuttings

Deciduous: Not evergreen, said of a plant that sheds its leaves each year.

Deep watering: Applying water slowly over an extended period. In average soil, 6–8 hours of slow soaking will reach a depth of 4–5 ft. (1.2–1.5 m). Deep watering encourages the development of a deep root system, thus enhancing a plant's tolerance to drought.

Drainage: The movement of water through the soil surrounding a plant's root area.

Drip irrigation: An irrigation system for applying water in small amounts, using valves, emitters, pressure regulators, and other specified equipment.

Evergreen: A plant with foliage that remains green throughout the year. Foliage may be broad-leaved or narrow and needlelike. *See* Conifers

Exfoliate: To separate into strips and flake off, said of bark.

Family: A broad plant group. Members of a plant family include the individual genus or genera and share general characteristics.

Genus: A natural group of related species.

Gypsum: Calcium sulfate. Used to improve soils with a high sodium content.

Hardpan. *See* Caliche

Hardwood cuttings: Cuttings made during the dormant season from mature wood of the previous growing season.

Hybrid: A plant resulting from a seed cross of genetically dissimilar plants.

Iron: One of 16 elements essential to plant growth. Its deficiency causes a common condition known as iron-deficiency chlorosis in many non-native plants in the Southwest.

Iron-deficiency chlorosis. *See* Chlorosis

Leaching: The application of extra amounts of water to soil to flush out substances, such as soil salts, which accumulate at the root levels of plants.

Leader: The main growing point, usually referring to the highest, central point of a tree.

Leaflet: One part of a compound leaf.

Micronutrients: Iron, zinc, copper, manganese, molybdenum, boron and chlorine. While among the 16 elements essential to plant growth, they are needed in only small amounts and so are often referred to as trace elements. Carbon, hydrogen and oxygen are mainly taken from water and air.

Mulch: Loose material spread over the soil. Usually organic in origin, it serves various purposes, such as reducing evaporation.

Mulching: Applying mulch.

Naturalize: To grow randomly by spreading or reseeding; this may or may not be a desirable characteristic.

Nitrogen: One of 16 elements essential to plant growth. Nitrogen is the element most consistently missing from arid-region soils. By law, it is the first percentage listed on a fertilizer label, followed by percentages for phosphorus and potassium. *See* Phosphorus, Potassium

Offsets: Plantlets forming from the crown or roots of some plants, usually those which tend to clump. Remove with a sharp knife and transplant as desired.

Organic matter: Material such as forest mulch, compost, humus or manure added to soil to enrich it and improve drainage and tilth.

Palmate leaf: A leaf that is lobed or divided as in a human hand.

Perched water table: A condition of layered soil textures that creates extreme drainage problems.

Perennial: A plant that lives three or more years; can also refer to herbaceous, nonwoody plants that are short lived.

pH: A logarithmic scale of potential hydrogen. The pH scale ranges from 1 to 14, with 1 being the most acid, 14 the most alkaline and 7 neutral.

Phosphorus: One of 16 elements essential to plant growth. Phosphorus is the second percentage listed on fertilizer labels. In the formula 10–6–4, for example, 10 represents the percentage of nitrogen, 6 the percentage of phosphorus, and 4 the percentage of potassium.

Pinnate leaf: A compound leaf with leaflets on opposite sides of a central stem.

Plant classifications: Rankings of related plant groups. In descending order, these include family, genus, species, variety, subspecies. *See* individual listings.

Potassium: One of 16 elements essential to plant growth. Potassium is the third percentage listed on a fertilizer label, along with nitrogen and phosphorus.

Primary nutrients: Nitrogen, phosphorus, potassium.

Rhizome: An underground stem that roots at the nodes.

Rosette: A cluster of crowded, radiating leaves at a node or ground level.

Scarification: A treatment to speed propagation of seeds by breaking the seed coat.

Secondary nutrients: Sulfur, magnesium and calcium. They often are abundant in Southwest soils.

Semideciduous: A plant that may be evergreen all year under certain conditions, such as mild winters; will drop leaves with colder temperatures.

Semihardwood cuttings: Cuttings made from mature wood of the current season's growth.

Softwood cuttings: Cuttings made from the new, soft wood during the growing season.

Soil texture: The proportion of sand, silt and clay in a soil.

Species: A similar group of plants within a genus but with certain distinctive characteristics.

Specimen: A single, large plant that is a major focal point of a landscape.

Spike: A slender cluster of flowers without a stalk, or with barely any stalk.

Stratification: A treatment to promote rapid germination of seeds by breaking dormancy using cool, moist conditions.

Subspecies: Plants with genetic differences observable below the level of species.

Succulent: A plant with soft, fleshy foliage and/or stems.

Sucker: Usually a reference to an underground shoot of undesirable foliage arising below the bud union of a grafted plant. Sometimes used to describe a fast-growing stem on a branch or trunk.

Sulfur: One of the 16 elements essential to plant growth. Sulfur is used extensively in Southwest soils to lower alkalinity.

Taper: Gradual decrease in trunk diameter from base to top.

Taproot: The main root of a plant.

Trace elements. *See* Micronutrients

Variety: Plants with minor variations or differing characteristics that separate them from others in a species.

Xeriscape: A trademark-registered term for drought-resistant landscapes.

Appendix

A. Common Names Cross-Listed with the Botanical Names

COMMON NAME	BOTANICAL NAME
Abyssinian acacia	*Acacia abyssinica*
Afghan pine	*Pinus eldarica*
African aloe	*Aloe saponaria*
African sumac	*Rhus lancea*
Aleppo pine	*Pinus halepensis*
Aloe vera	*Aloe barbadensis*
Anacahuite	*Cordia boissieri*
Apache plume	*Fallugia paradoxa*
Arizona ash	*Fraxinus velutina*
Arizona cypress	*Cupressus arizonica*
Arizona mountain laurel	*Sophora arizonica*
Arizona rosewood	*Vauquelinia californica*
Australia pine	*Casuarina cunninghamiana*
Australian saltbush	*Atriplex semibaccata*
Australian tea tree	*Leptospermum laevigatum*
Australian willow	*Geijera parviflora*
Autumn sage	*Salvia greggii*
Bailey acacia	*Acacia baileyana*
Baja dalea	*Dalea bicolor* var. *orcuttiana*
Banana yucca	*Yucca baccata*
Bear grass	*Nolina microcarpa*
Big sagebrush	*Artemisia tridentata*
Big saltbush	*Atriplex lentiformis*
Bimble box	*Eucalyptus populnea*
Blackfoot daisy	*Melampodium leucanthum*
Bladderpod	*Isomeris arborea*
Blue jeans ceanothus	*Ceanothus* 'Blue Jeans'
Blue palo verde	*Cercidium floridum*
Blue yucca	*Yucca rigida*
Blue-leaf wattle	*Acacia saligna*

COMMON NAME	BOTANICAL NAME
Blueblossom	*Ceanothus thyrsiflorus*
Bottlebrush	*Callistemon phoeniceus*
Bottletree	*Brachychiton populneus*
Bougainvillea	*Bougainvillea*
Bright-bead cotoneaster	*Cotoneaster buxifolius*
Brittlebush	*Encelia farinosa*
Broadleaf mulga	*Acacia craspedocarpa*
Burrobush	*Ambrosia deltoidea*
Burrobush	*Ambrosia dumosa*
Bush dalea	*Dalea pulchra*
Bush germander	*Teucrium fruticans*
Bush lantana	*Lantana camara*
Bush morning glory	*Convolvulus cneorum*
Bush muhlenbergia	*Muhlenbergia dumosa*
Bush sunflower	*Encelia californica*
Cajeput tree	*Melaleuca quinquenervia*
California bay	*Umbellularia californica*
California buckwheat	*Eriogonum fasciculatum*
California fairy duster	*Calliandra californica*
California fan palm	*Washingtonia filifera*
California holly	*Heteromeles arbutifolia*
California laurel	*Umbellularia californica*
California sagebush	*Artemisia californica*
Canary Island date palm	*Phoenix canariensis*

149

COMMON NAME	BOTANICAL NAME	COMMON NAME	BOTANICAL NAME
Canary Island pine	*Pinus canariensis*	Desert bird of paradise	*Caesalpinia gilliesii*
Canyon live oak	*Quercus chrysolepis*	Desert broom	*Baccharis sarothroides*
Carmel ceanothus	*Ceanothus griseus*	Desert cassia	*Cassia nemophila*
Carmel creeper	*Ceanothus griseus* var. *horizontalis*	Desert chuparosa	*Anisacanthus thurberi*
		Desert hackberry	*Celtis pallida*
Carob tree	*Ceratonia siliqua*	Desert holly	*Atriplex hymenelytra*
Cat's claw	*Macfadyena unguis-cati*	Desert honeysuckle	*Anisacanthus thurberi*
Catalina ceanothus	*Ceanothus arboreus*	Desert honeysuckle	*Justicia spicigera*
Catalina cherry	*Prunus lyonii*	Desert ironwood	*Olneya tesota*
Catalina currant	*Ribes viburnifolium*	Desert mahonia	*Mahonia fremontii*
Catclaw	*Acacia greggii*	Desert olive	*Forestiera neomexicana*
Centennial baccharis	*Baccharis* 'Centennial'	Desert ruellia	*Ruellia peninsularis*
		Desert spoon	*Dasylirion wheeleri*
Century plant	*Agave americana*	Desert sunflower	*Viguiera deltoidea* var. *parishii*
Chaparral catclaw	*Mimosa biuncifera*		
Chaparral broom	*Baccharis pilularis* ssp. *consanguinea*	Desert willow	*Chilopsis linearis*
		Desert zinnia	*Zinnia grandiflora*
Chaparral salvia	*Salvia clevelandii*	Dwarf indigo bush	*Dalea greggii*
Chaste tree	*Vitex agnus-castus*	Emerald carpet manzanita	*Arctostaphylos* 'Emerald Carpet'
Chihuahuan desert sage	*Leucophyllum laevigatum*	English lavender	*Lavandula angustifolia*
Chihuahuan primrose	*Oenothera stubbei*	Fairy duster	*Calliandra eriophylla*
Chinese date	*Ziziphus jujuba*	False sand verbena	*Verbena tenuisecta*
Chinese pistache	*Pistacia chinensis*	Fan-tex ash	*Fraxinus velutina* 'Rio Grande'
Chir pine	*Pinus roxburghii*		
Chuparosa	*Justicia californica*	Feather bush	*Lysiloma watsonii*
Cleveland sage	*Salvia clevelandii*	Feathery cassia	*Cassia artemisioides*
Cliffrose	*Cowania mexicana*	Fern of the desert	*Lysiloma thornberi*
Coast live oak	*Quercus agrifolia*	Fiery bottlebrush	*Callistemon phoeniceus*
Coast silktassel	*Garrya elliptica*		
Coffeeberry	*Rhamnus californica*	Firecracker penstemon	*Penstemon eatoni*
Colorado piñon	*Pinus edulis*	Flame tree	*Brachychiton acerifolius*
Common manzanita	*Arctostaphylos manzanita*	Flannel bush	*Fremontodendron californica*
Concha ceanothus	*Ceanothus* 'Concha'		
Coolibah tree	*Eucalyptus microtheca*	Flooded gum	*Eucalyptus rudis*
Coquete	*Acacia pennatula*	Foothill palo verde	*Cercidium microphyllum*
Coral gum	*Eucalyptus torquata*		
Coral vine	*Antigonon leptopus*	Forman's mallee	*Eucalyptus formanii*
Cork oak	*Quercus suber*	Fortnight lily	*Dietes vegeta*
Coyote brush	*Baccharis pilularis*	Four-wing saltbush	*Atriplex canescens*
Creosote bush	*Larrea tridentata*	Fremont silktassel	*Garrya fremontii*
Dark star ceanothus	*Ceanothus* 'Dark Star'	Fremontia	*Fremontodendron californicum*
Date palm	*Phoenix dactylifera*		
Deer brush	*Ceanothus integerrimus*	French lavender	*Lavandula dentata*
Deer grass	*Muhlenbergia rigens*	Frosty blue ceanothus	*Ceanothus* 'Frosty Blue'
Desert agave	*Agave deserti*		
Desert beardtongue	*Penstemon pseudospectabilis*	Fuchsia-flowered gooseberry	*Ribes speciosum*

COMMON NAME	BOTANICAL NAME	COMMON NAME	BOTANICAL NAME
Germander	*Teucrium chamaedrys*	Juliflora mesquite	*Prosopis velutina*
Ghost gum	*Eucalyptus papuana*	Laurel sumac	*Rhus laurina*
Giant aloe	*Aloe arborescens*	Lavender cotton	*Santolina*
Goat nut	*Simmondsia chinensis*		*chamaecyparissus*
Golden lead ball	*Leucaena retusa*	Leatherleaf acacia	*Acacia craspedocarpa*
Golden trumpet		Lechuguilla	*Agave lechuguilla*
tree	*Tabebuia chrysotricha*	Lemon-flowered	*Eucalyptus*
Goldeneye	*Viguiera deltoidea* var.	gum	*woodwardii*
	parishii	Lemon-scented	
Goldwreath		gum	*Eucalyptus citriodora*
acacia	*Acacia saligna*	Lemonade berry	*Rhus integrifolia*
Goodding		Lilac orchid vine	*Mascagnia lilacina*
verbena	*Verbena gooddingii*	Lilac vine	*Hardenbergia violacea*
Gray thorn	*Ziziphus obtusifolia*	Little Sur	*Arctostaphylos*
	canescens	manzanita	*edmundsii*
Greasewood	*Larrea tridentata*	Little-leaf cordia	*Cordia parvifolia*
Green desert		Little-leaf palo	*Cercidium*
spoon	*Dasylirion acrotriche*	verde	*microphyllum*
Green santolina	*Santolina virens*	Lompoc	*Ceanothus ramulosus*
Green wattle	*Acacia decurrens*	ceanothus	var. *fascicularis*
Guadalupe fan		Maritime	
palm	*Brahea edulis*	ceanothus	*Ceanothus maritimus*
Guadalupe	*Sophora gypsophila*	Marri red gum	*Eucalyptus calophylla*
mountain	var. *guadalupensis*	Matilija poppy	*Romneya coulteri*
laurel		McMinn	*Arctostaphylos*
Guajillo	*Acacia berlandieri*	manzanita	*densiflora* 'Howard
Hearst's			McMinn'
ceanothus	*Ceanothus hearstiorum*	Mealycup sage	*Salvia farinacea*
Heavenly bamboo	*Nandina domestica*	Mediterranean	
Heritage oak	*Quercus virginiana*	fan palm	*Chamaerops humilis*
	'Heritage'	Mesa oak	*Quercus engelmannii*
Holly oak	*Quercus ilex*	Mescal bean	*Sophora secundiflora*
Hollyleaf	*Rhamnus crocea*	Mescat acacia	*Acacia constricta*
redberry	*ilicifolia*	Mexican bird of	
Hollyleaf cherry	*Prunus ilicifolia*	paradise	*Caesalpinia mexicana*
Honey mesquite	*Prosopis glandulosa*	Mexican blue	
Hopseed bush	*Dodonaea viscosa*	palm	*Brahea armata*
Horsetail tree	*Casuarina equisetifolia*	Mexican blue sage	*Salvia chamaedryoides*
Huachuca agave	*Agave parryi* var.	Mexican buckeye	*Ungnadia speciosa*
	huachucensis	Mexican bush	
Huajillo	*Calliandra eriophylla*	sage	*Salvia leucantha*
Huisache	*Acacia smallii*	Mexican bushbird	*Caesalpinia cacalocoa*
Hummingbird		Mexican ebony	*Pithecellobium*
trumpet	*Zauschneria latifolia*		*undulatum*
Incienso	*Encelia farinosa*	Mexican fan palm	*Washingtonia robusta*
Indigo bush	*Dalea versicolor*	Mexican palo	
Island bush poppy	*Dendromecon harfordii*	verde	*Parkinsonia aculeata*
Italian stone pine	*Pinus pinea*	Mexican piñon	*Pinus cembroides*
Jerusalem thorn	*Parkinsonia aculeata*	Mexican primrose	*Oenothera berlandieri*
Jojoba	*Simmondsia chinensis*	Missouri evening	*Oenothera*
Joshua tree	*Yucca brevifolia*	primrose	*missouriensis*
Joyce Coulter	*Ceanothus* 'Joyce	Mojave ceanothus	*Ceanothus greggii*
ceanothus	Coulter'	Mojave yucca	*Yucca schidigera*
Jujube	*Ziziphus jujuba*	Mondel pine	*Pinus eldarica*
Julia Phelps	*Ceanothus* 'Julia	Monterey	*Ceanothus rigidus*
ceanothus	Phelps'	ceanothus	'Snowball'

COMMON NAME	BOTANICAL NAME	COMMON NAME	BOTANICAL NAME
Mt. Aetna broom	*Genista aethnensis*	Purple sage	*Salvia leucophylla*
Mountain mahogany	*Cercocarpus montanus*	Quail bush	*Atriplex lentiformis*
Mulga	*Acacia aneura*	Queen's wreath	*Antigonon leptopus*
Murphey agave	*Agave murpheyi*	Raspberry jam wattle	*Acacia acuminata*
Myoporum	*Myoporum parvifolium*	Ray Hartman ceanothus	*Ceanothus 'Ray Hartman'*
Myrtle	*Myrtus communis*	Red barberry	*Mahonia haematocarpa*
Naked coral tree	*Erythrina coralloides*		
Nandina	*Nandina domestica*	Red bird of paradise	*Caesalpinia pulcherrima*
Narrow-leaved gimlet	*Eucalyptus spathulata*	Red clusterberry	*Cotoneaster lacteus*
Natal plum	*Carissa macrocarpa*	Red firecracker	*Justicia candicans*
Netleaf hackberry	*Celtis reticulata*	Red fountain grass	*Pennisetum setaceum 'Cupreum'*
Nevin's barberry	*Mahonia nevinii*		
New Mexico privet	*Forestiera neomexicana*	Red gum	*Eucalyptus camaldulensis*
New Zealand tea tree	*Leptospermum scoparium*	Red ironbark	*Eucalyptus sideroxylon*
Nichol's willow-leafed peppermint	*Eucalyptus nicholii*	Red wing hopbush	*Dodonaea microzyga*
		Red yucca	*Hesperaloe parviflora*
Ocotillo	*Fouquieria splendens*	Red-cap gum	*Eucalyptus erythrocorys*
Octopus agave	*Agave vilmoriniana*	Red-flowered mallee	*Eucalyptus erythronema*
Old man saltbush	*Atriplex nummularia*		
Oleander	*Nerium oleander*	Redberry	*Rhamnus crocea*
Olive tree	*Olea europaea*	River she oak	*Casuarina cunninghamiana*
Ongerup acacia	*Acacia redolens*		
Orchid rockrose	*Cistus purpureus*	Rosea ice plant	*Drosanthemum floribundum*
Oregon grape	*Mahonia aquifolium*		
Our Lord's candle	*Yucca whipplei*	Rosemary	*Rosmarinus officinalis*
Pajaro manzanita	*Arctostaphylos pajaroensis*	Round-seeded acacia	*Acacia cyclops*
Pale silktassel	*Garrya flavescens*	Russian olive	*Elaeagnus angustifolia*
Palmer beardtongue	*Penstemon palmeri*	Saffron buckwheat	*Eriogonum crocatum*
Palo blanco	*Acacia willardiana*	St. Catherine's lace	*Eriogonum giganteum*
Palo brea	*Cercidium praecox*		
Paper fruit vine	*Mascagnia macroptera*	San Diego sunflower	*Viguiera laciniata*
Parry's nolina	*Nolina parryi*	Salt river gum	*Eucalyptus sargentii*
Parry's penstemon	*Penstemon parryi*	Salt river mallet	*Eucalyptus sargentii*
Pearl acacia	*Acacia podalyriifolia*	Sandhill sage	*Artemisia pycnocephala*
Pendulous yucca	*Yucca recurvifolia*		
Pfitzer juniper	*Juniperus chinensis 'Pfitzeriana'*	Santa Barbara ceanothus	*Ceanothus impressus*
Pindo palm	*Butia capitata*	Santa Cruz Island buckwheat	*Eriogonum arborescens*
Pineapple guava	*Feijoa sellowiana*		
Pink ironbark	*Eucalyptus sideroxylon*	Screwbean mesquite	*Prosopis pubescens*
Pink melaleuca	*Melaleuca nesophila*	Senegal date palm	*Phoenix reclinata*
Pink trumpet vine	*Podranea ricasoliana*	Shagbark manzanita	*Arctostaphylos rudis*
Pomegranate	*Punica granatum*		
Popcorn cassia	*Cassia didymobotrya*	Shaw's century plant	*Agave shawii*
Poplar box	*Eucalyptus populnea*		
Prairie sage	*Artemisia ludoviciana*		

COMMON NAME	BOTANICAL NAME	COMMON NAME	BOTANICAL NAME
She oak	*Casuarina stricta*	Sydney golden wattle	*Acacia longifolia*
Shiny xylosma	*Xylosma congestum*	Tam juniper	*Juniperus sabina* 'Tamariscifolia'
Shinyleaf barberry	*Mahonia pinnata*	Texas ebony	*Pithecellobium flexicaule*
Shoestring acacia	*Acacia stenophylla*		
Shrubby marigold	*Tagetes lemmonii*	Texas lead ball tree	*Leucaena pulverulenta*
Shrubby senna	*Cassia wislizenii*		
Silk oak	*Grevillea robusta*	Texas mountain laurel	*Sophora secundiflora*
Silver bush lupine	*Lupinus albifrons*	Texas olive	*Cordia boissieri*
Silver dalea	*Dalea bicolor* var. *argyraea*	Texas persimmon	*Diospyros texana*
		Texas ranger	*Leucophyllum frutescens*
Silver dollar gum	*Eucalyptus polyanthemos*	Texas sage	*Leucophyllum frutescens*
Silver spreader	*Artemisia caucasica*		
Silverberry	*Elaeagnus pungens*	Thurber's beardtongue	*Penstemon thurberi*
Silverbush	*Convolvulus cneorum*	Torrey pine	*Pinus torreyana*
Silverleaf cassia	*Cassia phyllodinea*	Toyon	*Heteromeles arbutifolia*
Silverleaf cotoneaster	*Cotoneaster pannosus*	Trailing acacia	*Acacia redolens*
Sissoo tree	*Dalbergia sissoo*	Trailing indigo bush	*Dalea greggii*
Skeleton-leaf goldeneye	*Viguiera stenoloba*	Trailing lantana	*Lantana montevidensis*
Skunkbush	*Rhus trilobata*	Tree lupine	*Lupinus arboreus*
Smoke tree	*Dalea spinosa*	Triangle-leaf bursage	*Ambrosia deltoidea*
Soaptree	*Yucca elata*		
Sonoran palo verde	*Cercidium praecox*	Trinidad flame bush	*Calliandra tweedii*
Sotol	*Dasylirion wheeleri*	Tropical sage	*Salvia coccinea*
South American hybrid mesquite	*Prosopis* hybrids	Turpentine bush	*Ericameria laricifolia*
		Twisted acacia	*Acacia schaffneri*
		Valley oak	*Quercus lobata*
Southern bush monkey flower	*Diplacus longiflorus*	Velvet mesquite	*Prosopis velutina*
Southern flannel bush	*Fremontodendron mexicanum*	Velvetpod mimosa	*Mimosa dysocarpa*
Southern live oak	*Quercus virginiana*	Venosa	*Verbena rigida*
Spanish bayonet	*Yucca aloifolia*	Warminster broom	*Cytisus praecox*
Spanish broom	*Genista hispanica*		
Spanish broom	*Spartium junceum*	Weeping acacia	*Acacia pendula*
Spanish lavender	*Lavandula stoechas*	Weeping myall	*Acacia pendula*
Sprenger asparagus	*Asparagus densiflorus* 'Sprengeri'	Western coral bean	*Erythrina flabelliformis*
Squawbush	*Rhus trilobata*	Western hackberry	*Celtis reticulata*
Strawberry tree	*Arbutus unedo*		
Sturt's cassia	*Cassia sturtii*	Western mountain mahogany	*Cercocarpus betuloides*
Sugar bush	*Rhus ovata*	Western redbud	*Cercis occidentalis*
Sugar gum	*Eucalyptus cladocalyx*	Western soapberry	*Sapindus drummondii*
Sulfur buckwheat	*Eriogonum umbellatum*		
Summer holly	*Comarostaphylis diversifolia*	White bursage	*Ambrosia dumosa*
Swamp mallee	*Eucalyptus spathulata*	White evening primrose	*Oenothera caespitosa*
Sweet acacia	*Acacia smallii*	White ironbark	*Eucalyptus leucoxylon* 'Rosea'
Sweet hakea	*Hakea suaveolens*		
Sweet olive	*Osmanthus fragrans*		

COMMON NAME	BOTANICAL NAME	COMMON NAME	BOTANICAL NAME
White thorn acacia	*Acacia constricta*	Woolly grevillea	*Grevillea lanigera*
Willow acacia	*Acacia salicina*	Wright silktassel	*Garrya wrightii*
Willow peppermint	*Eucalyptus nicholii*	Yellow bells	*Tecoma stans*
Willow pittosporum	*Pittosporum phillyraeoides*	Yellow bird of paradise	*Caesalpinia gilliesii*
Winterfat	*Ceratoides lanata*	Yellow orchid vine	*Mascagnia macroptera*
Woolly blue curls	*Trichostema lanatum*	Yellow popinac	*Leucaena retusa*
Woolly butterfly bush	*Buddleia marrubiifolia*		

B. Shrubs with Showy Flowers

Acacia longifolia
Anisacanthus thurberi
Arctostaphylos edmundsii
Arctostaphylos pajaroensis
Buddleia marrubiifolia
Caesalpinia cacalocoa
Caesalpinia gilliesii
Caesalpinia mexicana
Caesalpinia pulcherrima
Calliandra californica
Calliandra eriophylla
Calliandra tweedii
Callistemon phoeniceus
Cassia artemisioides
Cassia didymobotrya
Cassia nemophila
Cassia phyllodinea
Cassia sturtii
Cassia wislizenii
Ceanothus arboreus
Ceanothus 'Blue Jeans'
Ceanothus 'Concha'
Ceanothus 'Dark Star'
Ceanothus 'Frosty Blue'
Ceanothus greggii
Ceanothus griseus
Ceanothus hearstiorum
Ceanothus impressus
Ceanothus 'Julia Phelps'
Ceanothus 'Joyce Coulter'
Ceanothus maritimus
Ceanothus ramulosus var. *fascicularis*
Ceanothus 'Ray Hartman'
Ceanothus rigidus 'Snowball'
Ceanothus thyrsiflorus
Cercis occidentalis
Cistus purpureus
Cordia boissieri
Cordia parvifolia

Cowania mexicana
Cytisus praecox
Dalea bicolor var. *argyraea*
Dalea pulchra
Dalea versicolor
Dendromecon harfordii
Encelia californica
Encelia farinosa
Eriogonum arborescens
Eriogonum giganteum
Eriogonum umbellatum
Erythrina coralloides
Erythrina flabelliformis
Eucalyptus formanii
Feijoa sellowiana
Fouquieria splendens
Fremontodendron californicum
Garrya elliptica
Garrya fremontii
Genista aethnensis
Grevillea lanigera
Hesperaloe parviflora
Heteromeles arbutifolia
Justicia californica
Justicia candicans
Justicia spicigera
Lantana camara
Lavandula angustifolia
Leptospermum laevigatum
Leptospermum scoparium
Leucophyllum laevigatum
Lupinus albifrons
Lupinus arboreus
Mahonia aquifolium
Mahonia fremontii
Mahonia 'Golden Abundance'
Mahonia haematocarpa
Mahonia nevinii
Mahonia pinnata
Melaleuca nesophila

Mimosa dysocarpa
Nerium oleander
Rhus integrifolia
Rhus laurina
Rhus ovata
Ribes speciosum
Romneya coulteri
Rosmarinus officinalis
Ruellia peninsularis
Salvia chamaedryoides
Salvia clevelandii
Salvia greggii
Salvia leucantha
Salvia leucophylla
Sophora secundiflora
Spartium junceum
Tagetes lemmonii
Tecoma stans
Trichostema lanatum
Viguiera deltoidea var. *parishii*
Vitex agnus-castus

C. Trees with Showy Flowers

Acacia aneura
Acacia baileyana
Acacia constricta
Acacia decurrens
Acacia podalyriifolia
Acacia saligna
Acacia smallii
Acacia willardiana
Arbutus unedo
Brachychiton acerifolius
Ceanothus arboreus
Ceanothus 'Ray Hartman'
Ceanothus thyrsiflorus
Cercidium floridum

Cercidium microphyllum
Cercidium praecox
Cercis occidentalis
Chilopsis linearis
Erythrina coralloides
Erythrina flabelliformis
Eucalyptus calophylla
Eucalyptus erythrocorys
Eucalyptus erythronema
Eucalyptus leucoxylon 'Rosea'
Eucalyptus sideroxylon
Eucalyptus torquata
Eucalyptus woodwardii
Genista aethnensis

Heteromeles arbutifolia
Leptospermum laevigatum
Leucaena retusa
Lysiloma thornberi
Melaleuca quinquenervia
Olneya tesota
Parkinsonia aculeata
Prunus lyonii
Punica granatum
Sophora secundiflora
Tabebuia chrysotricha
Vitex agnus-castus

D. Shade Trees

Acacia abyssinica
Acacia acuminata
Acacia baileyana
Acacia berlandieri
Acacia decurrens
Acacia greggii
Acacia salicina
Acacia saligna
Acacia schaffneri
Acacia smallii
Arbutus unedo
Brachychiton acerifolius
Brachychiton populneus
Casuarina cunninghamiana
Celtis reticulata
Ceratonia siliqua
Cercidium floridum
Cercidium microphyllum
Cercidium praecox
Dalbergia sissoo
Diospyros texana
Elaeagnus angustifolia

Eucalyptus calophylla
Eucalyptus camaldulensis
Eucalyptus citriodora
Eucalyptus cladocalyx
Eucalyptus erythrocorys
Eucalyptus erythronema
Eucalyptus formanii
Eucalyptus leucoxylon 'Rosea'
Eucalyptus microtheca
Eucalyptus nicholii
Eucalyptus papuana
Eucalyptus polyanthemos
Eucalyptus populnea
Eucalyptus rudis
Eucalyptus sargentii
Eucalyptus sideroxylon
Eucalyptus spathulata
Eucalyptus torquata
Fraxinus velutina
Fraxinus velutina 'Rio Grande'
Geijera parviflora
Grevillea robusta

Lysiloma thornberi
Olea europaea
Olneya tesota
Parkinsonia aculeata
Pinus halepensis
Pinus pinea
Pistacia chinensis
Pithecellobium flexicaule
Pittosporum phillyraeoides
Prosopis glandulosa
Prosopis hybrids
Prosopis velutina
Quercus agrifolia
Quercus ilex
Quercus lobata
Quercus suber
Quercus virginiana
Rhus lancea
Sapindus drummondii
Umbellularia californica
Ungnadia speciosa
Ziziphus jujuba

E. Small Trees

Acacia abyssinica
Acacia acuminata
Acacia aneura
Acacia baileyana
Acacia berlandieri
Acacia constricta
Acacia greggii
Acacia longifolia
Acacia pendula

Acacia pennatula
Acacia podalyriifolia
Acacia salicina
Acacia saligna
Acacia schaffneri
Acacia smallii
Acacia willardiana
Arbutus unedo
Arctostaphylos manzanita

Brahea armata
Butia capitata
Caesalpinia cacalocoa
Casuarina stricta
Ceanothus arboreus
Ceanothus 'Ray Hartman'
Ceanothus thyrsiflorus
Celtis pallida
Celtis reticulata

[E. Small Trees. Cont.]
Ceratonia siliqua
Cercidium floridum
Cercidium microphyllum
Cercidium praecox
Cercis occidentalis
Cercocarpus betuloides
Cercocarpus montanus
Chamaerops humilis
Chilopsis linearis
Comarostaphylis diversifolia
Cordia boissieri
Cupressus arizonica
Elaeagnus angustifolia
Erythrina coralloides
Erythrina flabelliformis
Eucalyptus erythrocorys
Eucalyptus erythronema
Eucalyptus formanii

Eucalyptus leucoxylon 'Rosea'
Eucalyptus populnea
Eucalyptus spathulata
Eucalyptus torquata
Eucalyptus woodwardii
Feijoa sellowiana
Forestiera neomexicana
Fremontodendron californicum
Fremontodendron mexicanum
Garrya elliptica
Garrya wrightii
Geijera parviflora
Genista aethnensis
Heteromeles arbutifolia
Leptospermum laevigatum
Leucaena retusa
Lysiloma thornberi
Nerium oleander
Olneya tesota

Parkinsonia aculeata
Pinus edulis
Pithecellobium flexicaule
Pittosporum phillyraeoides
Prosopis glandulosa
Prosopis hybrids
Prunus ilicifolia
Punica granatum
Rhamnus californica
Rhus integrifolia
Rhus lancea
Sophora secundiflora
Tabebuia chrysotricha
Ungnadia speciosa
Vauquelinia californica
Vitex agnus-castus
Ziziphus jujuba

F. Tall Screening and Background Plants, Reaching Average Heights of 6 ft. (2 m) or More

Acacia aneura
Acacia berlandieri
Acacia constricta
Acacia craspedocarpa
Acacia cyclops
Acacia longifolia
Acacia podalyriifolia
Acacia salicina
Acacia saligna
Acacia schaffneri
Acacia smallii
Acacia stenophylla
Arbutus unedo
Arctostaphylos manzanita
Arctostaphylos pajaroensis
Atriplex lentiformis
Baccharis sarothroides
Brachychiton populneus
Caesalpinia pulcherrima
Calliandra tweedii
Callistemon phoeniceus
Cassia nemophila
Ceanothus 'Blue Jeans'
Ceanothus 'Concha'
Ceanothus 'Frosty Blue'
Ceanothus 'Ray Hartman'
Ceanothus arboreus
Ceanothus integerrimus
Ceanothus thyrsiflorus
Celtis pallida

Cercocarpus betuloides
Comarostaphylis diversifolia
Cordia boissieri
Cupressus arizonica
Dodonaea viscosa
Elaeagnus angustifolia
Elaeagnus pungens
Eucalyptus formanii
Eucalyptus microtheca
Eucalyptus nicholii
Eucalyptus papuana
Eucalyptus polyanthemos
Eucalyptus populnea
Eucalyptus sargentii
Eucalyptus spathulata
Feijoa sellowiana
Forestiera neomexicana
Garrya elliptica
Garrya fremontii
Garrya wrightii
Geijera parviflora
Hakea suaveolens
Heteromeles arbutifolia
Juniperus chinensis 'Pfitzeriana'
Larrea tridentata
Leptospermum laevigatum
Leptospermum scoparium
Leucophyllum frutescens
Lysiloma thornberi
Mahonia fremontii

Mahonia haematocarpa
Mahonia nevinii
Mahonia pinnata
Nandina domestica
Nerium oleander
Olneya tesota
Osmanthus fragrans
Pinus halepensis
Pinus eldarica
Pithecellobium flexicaule
Pittosporum phillyraeoides
Prosopis glandulosa
Prosopis hybrids
Prosopis pubescens
Prosopis velutina
Prunus lyonii
Punica granatum
Quercus ilex
Rhamnus californica
Rhus integrifolia
Rhus lancea
Rhus laurina
Rhus ovata
Sophora secundiflora
Umbellularia californica
Ungnadia speciosa
Vauquelinia californica
Xylosma congestum
Ziziphus obtusifolia canescens

G. Plants for Low Screens, Hedges or Barriers, below 6 ft. (2 m)

Arctostaphylos densiflora
   'Howard McMinn'
Arctostaphylos rudis
Atriplex canescens
Atriplex hymenelytra
Atriplex nummularia
Baccharis sarothroides
Carissa macrocarpa

Cassia artemisioides
Cassia phyllodinea
Cassia sturtii
Ceanothus 'Dark Star'
Ceanothus 'Joyce Coulter'
Ceanothus rigidus 'Snowball'
Cowania mexicana
Isomeris arborea

Mahonia aquifolium
Mimosa dysocarpa
Myrtus communis
Rhamnus crocea
Rhus trilobata
Ruellia peninsularis
Salvia greggii
Simmondsia chinensis

H. Accent Plants

Aloe arborescens
Aloe barbadensis
Aloe saponaria
Agave americana
Agave deserti
Agave lechuguilla
Agave murpheyi
Agave parryi huachucensis
Agave shawii
Agave vilmoriniana

Brahea armata
Butia capitata
Chamaerops humilis
Dalea spinosa
Dasylirion wheeleri
Dietes vegeta
Fouquieria splendens
Muhlenbergia rigens
Nolina microcarpa
Nolina parryi

Pennisetum setaceum 'Cupreum'
Yucca aloifolia
Yucca baccata
Yucca brevifolia
Yucca elata
Yucca recurvifolia
Yucca rigida
Yucca schidigera
Yucca whipplei

I. Ground Covers

Acacia redolens
Agave lechuguilla
Arctostaphylos 'Emerald Carpet'
Ambrosia deltoidea
Ambrosia dumosa
Artemisia ludoviciana
Asparagus densiflorus 'Sprengeri'
Atriplex semibaccata
Baccharis 'Centennial'
Baccharis pilularis
Calliandra eriophylla
Carissa macrocarpa
Ceanothus griseus var.
   horizontalis
Ceanothus hearstiorum
Ceanothus maritimus
Cistus purpureus
Convolvulus cneorum
Dalea greggii
Drosanthemum floribundum
Eriogonum fasciculatum
Ericameria laricifolia
Genista hispanica
Juniperus sabina 'Tamariscifolia'
Lantana camara

Lantana montevidensis
Melampodium leucanthum
Myoporum parvifolium
Oenothera berlandieri
Oenothera calylophus var.
   hartwegii
Oenothera caespitosa
Oenothera stubbei
Penstemon eatoni
Ribes viburnifolium
Rosmarinus officinalis
Santolina chamaecyparissus
Santolina virens
Verbena gooddingii
Verbena rigida
Verbena tenuisecta
Viguiera deltoidea var. *parishii*
Zauschneria latifolia
Zauschneria cana
Zinnia grandiflora

J. Vines

Antigonon leptopus
Bougainvillea
Hardenbergia violacea
Macfadyena unguis-cati
Mascagnia lilacina
Mascagnia macroptera
Podranea ricasoliana

K. Perennials with Showy Flowers

Diplacus longiflorus
Lantana camara
Lantana montevidensis
Melampodium leucanthum
Oenothera berlandieri
Oenothera caespitosa
Oenothera missouriensis

Oenothera stubbei
Penstemon eatoni
Penstemon palmeri
Penstemon parryi
Penstemon pseudospectabilis
Romneya coulteri
Salvia coccinea

Salvia farinacea
Tagetes lemmonii
Verbena gooddingii
Verbena rigida
Verbena tenuisecta
Zinnia grandiflora

L. Desert Wildflowers

In nature, the blooming of desert wildflowers in the Southwest largely depends upon the timing and amount of the infrequent rains. So there will be few flowers in dry years but a profusion in the years when the rains are heavy. If wildflower seeds are planted in the home landscape, supplemental watering may augment this schedule somewhat.

The desert's spring wildflower show usually begins early in March and reaches its colorful peak around mid–April. Expect blooms then from:

Beadpod, *Lesquerella gordonii*, yellow
Blue-dicks, *Dichelostemma pulchellum*, pale blue
California buckwheat, *Eriogonum fasciculatum*, white and pink
Desertgold, *Geraea canescens*, yellow
Desert poppy, *Eschscholzia mexicana*, orange-yellow
Desert sage, *Salvia carnosa*, blue
Evening primrose, *Oenothera deltoides*, white
Fiddleneck, *Amsinckia intermedia*, yellow
Filaree, *Erodium cicutarium*, purple
Globe mallow, *Sphaeralcea ambigua*, apricot, white, red and purple
Goldfields, *Baeria chrysostoma*, yellow
Lupine, *Lupinus* spp., blue-purple
Mariposa lily, *Calochortus kennedyi*, orange-red
Monkeyflower, *Mimulus guttatus*, yellow with red spots
Owlcover, *Orthocarpus purpurascens*, reddish purple
Paintbrush, *Castilleja* spp., red
Paperflower, *Psilostrophe cooperi*, yellow
Penstemon, *Penstemon* spp., rose-purple

Prickly poppy, *Argemone platyceras*, white with yellow centers
Sand verbena, *Abronia villosa*, blue-violet
Scorpionweed, *Phacelia* spp., blue to violet
Sunray, *Enceliopsis argophylla*, yellow
Wild larkspur, *Delphinium scaposum*, blue

The desert's other main wildflower show follows the summer rains. Expect blooms from:

Arizona poppy, *Kallstroemia grandiflora*, yellow
Buffalo gourd, *Cucurbita* spp., yellow
Bullthistle, *Cirsium neomexicanum*, purple
Columbine, *Aquilegia chrysantha*, yellow
Desert aster, *Machaeranthera tephrodes*, blue
Desertgold, *Geraea canescens*, yellow
Desert marigold, *Baileya multiradiata*, yellow
Desert senna, *Cassia covesii*, yellow
Nightshade, *Solanum xanti*, purple
Prickle poppy, *Argemone platyceras*, white with yellow centers
Spreading fleabane, *Erigeron divergens*, violet with yellow centers
Telegraph plant, *Isocoma subaxillaris*, yellow
Thornapple, *Datura meteloides*, white
Windmills, *Allionia incarnata*, reddish-purple

A few of the natives also bloom from November through January, or the winter season:

Buckwheat, *Eriogonum* spp., white or pink
Desert marigold, *Baileya multiradiata*, yellow
Desert senna, *Cassia covesii*, yellow
Telegraph plant, *Isocoma subaxillaris*, yellow

Index

rooting hormone 36
scarification 35
seed-coat dormancy 35
seeds 35
stratification 36
Prosopis 118
  alba 119
  chilensis 118
  glandulosa 8, 118, Plate 173
  hybrids 8, 118, Plate 174
  pubescens 119
  velutina 119
Proteaceae 96, 97
Pruning 30, 31, 32, 33
  best time 31
  botched 30
  control plant size 30
  heading back 31, 33
  leader 32
  minimize problems 30
  rejuvenating 30
  restoring balance 30
  scaffold branches 32
  shrubs 33
  stimulating 30
  thinning 31, 33
  training 30, 32
  trimming 33
Prunus 119
  ilicifolia 119
  integrifolia. See P. lyonii
  lyonii 119
Punica granatum 120, Plate 175
  granatum 'Wonderful' 120
Punicaceae 120
Purple sage 11. 128
Purshia tridentata 78

Quail bush 57
Queen's wreath 51
Quercus 120
  agrifolia 120, Plate 176
  chrysolepis 121
  engelmannii 121
  ilex 121
  lobata 121, Plate 177
  suber 121
  virginiana 122
  virginiana 'Heritage' 122, Plate 178

Raspberry jam wattle 41
Ray Hartman ceanothus 70
Red barberry 106
Red bird of paradise 62
Red clusterberry 77
Red firecracker 99
Red fountain grass 113
Red gum 87
Red ironbark 91
Red wing hopbush 82
Red yucca 97
Redberry 122
Red-cap gum 88
Red-flowered mallee 88

Regional landscaping 2, 3
Rhamnaceae 67, 122, 138
Rhamnus 122
  californica 122, Plate 179
  californica 'Eve Case' 122
  crocea 122
  crocea ilicifolia 123
Rhus 11, 123
  integrifolia 123, Plate 180
  lancea 123, Plate 181
  laurina 123
  ovata 11, 124
  trilobata 124, Plate 182
  trilobata 'Autumn Amber' 124
Ribes 124
  speciosum 124, Plate 183
  viburnifolium 125
River she oak 66
Romneya coulteri 125, Plate 184
  trichocalyx 125
Rosaceae 74, 77, 92, 98, 119, 132
Rosea ice plant 82
Rosemary 125
Rosmarinus officinalis 125
  officinalis 'Albus' 125
  officinalis 'Collingwood Ingram' 125, Plate 185
  officinalis 'Lockwood de Forest' 125
  officinalis 'Prostrata' 125
  officinalis 'Tuscan Blue' 125
Round-seeded acacia 43
Ruellia 126
  californica 126
  peninsularis 126, Plate 186
Russian olive 82
Rutaceae 95

Saffron buckwheat 84
Sage-scrub community 4, 11
St. Catherine's lace 85
Salt river gum 91
Salt river mallet 91
Salvia 11, 126
  chamaedryoides 126, Plate 187
  clevelandii 126, Plate 188
  coccinea 11, 127
  farinacea 127, Plate 189
  farinacea 'Alba' 127
  greggii 127, Plate 190
  leucantha 127, Plate 191
  leucophylla 11, 128
San Diego sunflower 134
Sand 15, 17, 24. *See also* Soils
Sandhill sage 55
Santa Barbara ceanothus 69
Santa Cruz Island buckwheat 84
Santolina chamaecyparissus 128, Plate 192
  virens 128
Sapindaceae 82, 128, 132
Sapindus drummondii 128
SAWARA 3
  solar garden 3
Saxifragaceae 124

Scaffold branches 32. *See also* Pruning
Screwbean mesquite 119
Scrophulariaceae 81, 103, 113
Secondary nutrients 28. *See also* Fertilizing
Senegal date palm 115
Shagbark manzanita 54
Shaw's century plant 49
She oak 66
Shiny xylosma 135
Shinyleaf barberry 106
Shoestring acacia 46
Shoestring root rot. *See* Oak root fungus
Shrubby marigold 130
Shrubby senna 65
Silk oak 96
Silver bush lupine 104
Silver dalea 79
Silver dollar gum 90
Silver spreader 54
Silverberry 83
Silverbush 76
Silverleaf cassia 65
Silverleaf cotoneaster 77
Simmondsia chinensis 129
Sissoo tree 78
Skeleton-leaf goldeneye 134
Skunkbush 124
Smoke tree 79
Soaptree 136
Soils 15, 16, 17, 24, 26
  amendments 17
  calcerous 16
  classification 15
  conditions 15, 16, 24
  depth 15, 17
  gypsum 17
  properties 15
  salts 16, 26
  structure 15
  texture 15, 17
  water-logged 17
Sonoran Desert 4, 7, 8, 9, 10,
Sonoran palo verde 73
Sophora 129
  arizonica 129
  gypsophila var. *guadalupensis* 129
  secundiflora 129, Plate 193
Sotol 80
South American hybrid mesquite 118
Southern bush monkey flower 81
Southern flannel bush 94
Southern live oak 122
Spanish bayonet 135
Spanish broom 96, 129
Spanish lavender 102
Spartium junceum 129
Sprenger asparagus 55
Squawbush 124
Staking 34
Sterculiaceae 59